# Principles of Management

**T. RAMASAMY**

*M.Com., M.Phil., Ph.D., PGDHRD., PGDM., PGDMA.,*
*Department of Business Administration,*
*Government Arts College,*
*Paramakudi - 623 707.*

ISO 9001:2015 CERTIFIED

## PREFACE TO THE EIGHTH REVISED EDITION

It gives me great pleasure in revising this book. I have revised this book on the basis of encouragement given by the student community as well as the teaching faculty of various universities.

The revised edition of this book contains Approaches to Management, Policy, Procedure, Method and rule (Two new chapters), Planning Premises, Role and Functions of Manager, Responsibilities of a Manager, Entrepreneur and Manager, Management as Profession, Professional Management, Professionalisation of Management in India and the like.

I thank Shri.P.Periasamy, Srilakshmi Medicals, Srivilliputhur for his honest encouragement.

To my father Shri.T.Thangappan, mother Smt.T.Govinthammal, wife Sundari, our children Gohila and Thanga Saravanan, brothers Shri.T.Ramar, M.Sc.(Phy) and Shri.T.Lakshmanan, B.Com., I acknowledge a love debt. Their patience and assistances have much helped me to finish this project very successfully.

I do thank Mr. K. Sivadasan, Area Manager of Himalaya Publishing House for wide circulation of this book.

I thank Sri.Vijay Pandey and Sri.Niraj Kumar Pandey of M/s.Himalaya Publishing House for their honest co-operation and encouragements in bringing out this revised edition.

**Dr.T. RAMASAMY**

# CONTENTS

CHAPTER

1

# NATURE OF MANAGEMENT

INTRODUCTION
MEANING OF MANAGEMENT
DEFINITION OF MANAGEMENT
FEATURES OR CHARACTERISTICS OF MANAGEMENT
FUNCTIONS OF MANAGEMENT
IMPORTANCE OF MANAGEMENT
ADMINISTRATION AND MANAGEMENT
DIFFERENCE BETWEEN ADMINISTRATION AND MANAGEMENT
THE MANAGER
FUNCTIONS OF A MANAGER
ROLE OF A MANAGER
RESPONSIBILITIES OF A PROFESSIONAL MANAGER
ENTREPRENEUR AND MANAGER
MANAGEMENT AS PROFESSION,
MEANING OF PROFESSION,
DEFINITION OF PROFESSION,
CHARACTERISTICS OF PROFESSION,
OBSTACLES OF MANAGEMENT BEING A PROFESSION,
PROFESSIONAL MANAGEMENT,
NEED OF EFFICIENT PROFESSIONAL MANAGEMENT,
PROFESSIONALISATION OF MANAGEMENT IN INDIA,
YARDSTICKS OF PROFESSIONALISATION OF MANAGEMENT,
ARGUMENTS FOR PROFESSIONALISATION OF MANAGEMENT,
ARGUMENTS AGAINST PROFESSIONALISATION OF MANAGEMENT,
MODEL QUESTIONS

## INTRODUCTION

*A business develops* in course of time with complexities. With the increasing of complexities, managing the business concern becomes a difficult one. The need of existence of management has increased tremendously. Management is not only essential to business concerns but also essential to Banks, Schools, Colleges, Hospitals, Hotels, Religious bodies, Charitable trusts etc. Every business unit has objectives of its own. These objectives can be achieved with the co-operative efforts of several personnel. The work of a number of persons are properly co-ordinated to achieve the objectives through the process of management. According to E. Demock, "the management is not a matter of pressing a button, pulling a lever, issuing orders, scanning profit and loss statements, promulgating rules and regulations. Rather it is the power to determine what shall happen to the personalities and happiness of entire people, the power to shape the destiny of a nation and of all the nations which make up the world". Peter F. Drucker has stated in his famous book "The Practice of Management" that, "the emergence of management as an essential, a distinct and leading social institution is a pivotal event in social history. Rarely has a new basic institution, a new leading group, emerged as fast as management since the turn of this century. Rarely in human history has a new institution proved indispensable so quickly and even less often has a new institution arrived with so little opposition, so little disturbance and so little controversy".

## MEANING OF MANAGEMENT

Management is the art of getting things done by a group of people with the effective utilisation of available resources. An individual cannot be treated as a managing body running any organisation. A minimum of two persons are essential to form a management. These persons perform the functions in order to achieve the objectives of an organisation.

## DEFINITION OF MANAGEMENT

Peter F. Drucker defines, "Management is an organ; organs can be described and defined only through their functions."

According to Terry, "Management is not people; it is an activity like walking, reading, swimming or running. People who perform management can be designated as managers, members of management or executive leaders."

Ralph C. Davis has defined Management as, "Management is the function of executive leadership anywhere."

According to Mc Farland, "Management is defined for conceptual, theoretical and analytical purposes as that process by which managers create, direct, maintain and operate purposive organisation through systematic, co-ordinated co-operative human effort."

Louis Allan, "Management is what a manager does."

Henry Fayol, "To manage is to forecast and plan, to organise, to compound, to co-ordinate and to control."

Harold Koontz says, "Management is the art of getting things done through and with an informally organized group."

William Spriegal, "Management is that function of an enterprise which concerns itself with direction and control of the various activities to attain business objectives. Management is essentially an executive function; it deals with the active direction of the human effort."

Ross Moore states, "Management means decision-making."

Stanley Vance, "In essence, management is simply the process of decision making and control over the action of human beings for the express purpose of attaining pre-determined goals."

Donald J. Clough, "Management is the art and science of decision making and leadership."

Kimball and Kimball, "Management embraces all duties and functions that pertain to the initiation of an enterprise, its financing, the establishment of all major policies, the provision of all necessary equipment, the outlining of the general form of organisation under which the enterprise is to operate and the selection of the principal officers."

Sir Charles Reynold, "Management is the process of getting things done through the agency of a community. The functions of management are the handling of a community with a view to fulfilling the purposes for which it exists."

Joseph L. Massie, "Management is the process by which a co-operative group directs actions towards common goals."

Elmore Peterson and E.G. Plowman, "Management is a technique by means of which the purposes and objectives of a particular human group are determined, clarified and effectuated."

E.F.L. Brech, "Management is concerned with seeing that the job gets done, its tasks all centre on planning and guiding the operations that are going on in the enterprise."

Mary Cushing Niles, "Good management or scientific management, achieves a social objective with the best use of human and material energy and time and with satisfaction for the participants and the public."

S. George, "Management consists of getting things done through others. Manager is one who accomplishes the objectives by directing the efforts of others."

James D. Mooney and Alan C. Reiley, "Management is the art of directing and inspiring people."

F.W. Taylor, "Management is the art of knowing what you want to do and then seeing that it is done in the best and cheapest way."

Lawrence A. Appley, "Management is the art of getting things done through the efforts of other people. It concerns itself with guiding human and physical resources into a dynamic, hard-hitting organisation unit that attains its objectives to the satisfaction of those served and with a high degree of morale and sense of attainment on the part of those rendering the services".

R.M. Currie, "The organisation and control of human activity are directed towards specific ends."

John F. Mee, "Management is the art of securing maximum results with a minimum of efforts so as to secure maximum prosperity for the employer and employee and give the public the best possible service."

The American Management Association, "The art of getting things done through other people."

Knootz and O'Donnel, "Management is the creation and maintenance of an internal environment in an enterprise where individuals, working in groups, can perform efficiently and effec-tively towards the attainment of group goals. It is the art of getting the work done through and with people in formally organised groups."

Dr. James Lundy, "Management is principally a task of planning, co-ordinating," motivating and controlling the efforts of others towards a specific objective. It involves the combining of the traditional factors of production (land, labour and capital) in an optimum manner, paying due attention, of course, to the particular goals of the organisation."

Wheeler, "Management is centred in the administrators or managers of the firm who integrate men, material and money into an effective operating limit."

J.N. Schulze, "Management is the force which leads, guides and directs an organisation in the accomplishment of a pre-determined object."

Oliver Scheldon, "Management proper is the function in industry concerned in the execution of policy, within the limits set up by the administration and the employment of the organisation for the particular objectives set before it."

Keith and Gubellini, "Management is the force that integrates men and physical plant into an effective operating unit."

Newman, Summer and Warren, "The job of Management is to make co-operative endeavour to function properly. A manager is one who gets things done by working with people and other resources in order to reach an objective."

G.E. Milward, "Management is the process and the agency through which the execution of policy is planned and supervised."

Ordway Tead, "Management is the process and agency which directs and guides the operations of an organisation in the realising of established aims."

Management is the group of activities which drafts plans, prepares policies and arranges men, money, machine and materials required to achieve the objectives. The above definitions reveal that management is the activity of man who struggles for better living in the complex and competitive world. Besides, the management gives satisfaction to and rewards those who are engaged in the operation and ensuring an excellent performance. In other words, management is the process consisting of the functions of planning, organising, staffing, directing and controlling the operations to achieve specified objectives.

## FEATURES OR CHARACTERISTICS OF MANAGEMENT

From a critical analysis of the above definitions, the following features or characteristics of management evolve:

**1. Art as well as science:** Management is both an art and a science. It is an art in the sense of possessing of managing skill by a person. In another sense, management is the science because of developing certain principles or laws which are applicable in a place where a group of activities are co-ordinated.

**2. Management is an activity:** Management is the process of activity relating to the effective utilisation of available resources for production. The term 'resources' includes men, money, materials and machine in the organisation.

**3. Management is a continuous process:** The process of management mainly consists of planning, organising, directing and controlling the resources. The resources (men and money) of an organisation should be used to the best advantages of the organisation and the objectives to be achieved. The management function of any one alone cannot produce any results in the absence of any other basic functions of Management. So, management is a continuous process.

**4. Management achieving pre-determined objectives:** The objectives of an organisation are clearly laid down. Every managerial activity results in the achievement of objectives fixed well in advance.

**5. Organised activities:** Management is a group of organised activities. A group is formed not only in a public limited company but also in an ordinary club. All the organisations have their own objectives. These objectives will be achieved only by a group of persons. These persons' activities should be organised in a systematic way to achieve the objectives. The objectives cannot be achieved without any organised activities.

**6. Management is a factor of production:** The factors of production includes land, labour, capital and entrepreneurs. Here, land refers to a place where production is carried on. Labour refers to the paid employees of the organisation who are working in different levels as skilled, unskilled, semi-skilled, manager, supervisor and the like. Capital refers to the working capital as in the form of cash, raw materials and finished goods and fixed capital as in the form of plant facilities and production facilities. These land, labour and capital could not realise the organisation's goals. The organisation goals are achieved only when these are effectively co-ordinated by the entrepreneur. An individual can do such type of job as in the case of small businesses. In the case of big sized business units, co-ordination job is done by the management. So, management is also treated as one of the factors of production. According to Peter F. Drucker, "Whatever rapid economic and social development took place after World War II, it occured as a result of systematic and purposeful work of developing managers and management. Development is a matter of human energies rather than of economic wealth and the generation of human energies is the task of management. Management is the mover and development is a consequence".

**7. Management as a system of activity:** A *system* may be defined as a set of component parts working as a whole. *Authority* may be defined as a right to command others for getting a particular course of organisational work done.

Individuals are the foundation stones of the management. An individual has some goals as a member of the organisation. There may be a conflict between his own goals and the management's expectations from that individual. Such conflict is resolved by the management by ensuring balance between individual goals and organisational expectations.

Authority is vested with many persons to take decisions and influence the behaviour of the sub-ordinates. The very purpose of using the authority is to check and control the behaviour of the sub-ordinates. The sources of authority rest with superiors as given in the organisation chart and social norms. The utilisation of authority is based on the personality factors of the user and the behaviour of a person over whom it is used.

**8. Management is a discipline:** The boundaries of management are not exact as those of any other physical sciences. It may be increased by the continuous discovery of many more aspects of business enterprise. So, the management status as a discipline is also increased in the same manner.

**9. Management is a purposeful activity:** Management is concerned with achievement of objectives of an organisation. These objectives are achieved through the functions of planning, organising, staffing, directing, controlling and decision-making. The organisational objectives are clearly defined and explained to every employee.

**10. Management is a distinct entity:** Management is distinct from its functional activities. The functions have the nature of *"to do"* but the management has the nature of *"how to get things done"*. A manager requires some amount of skill and knowledge to get work done.

**11. Management aims at maximising profit:** The available resources are properly utilised to get desired results. The results should be the maximising profit or increasing profit by the economic function of a manager.

**12. Decision-making:** There are a number of decisions taken by the management everyday. Decision making arises only when there is availability of alternative courses of action. If there is only one course of action, need for decision-making does not arise. The quality of decision taken by the manager determines the organisations' performance. The success or failure of an organisation depends upon the degree of right decision taken by the manager.

**13. Management is a profession:** Management is a profession because it possesses the qualities of a profession. A fund of knowledge is imparted and transferred in this profession and the same is followed by management. The established principles of management are applied in practice.

**14. Universal application:** The principles and practices of management are applicable not to any particular industry alone but applicable to every type of industry. The practice of management is different from one organisation to another according to their nature.

**15. Managment is getting thing done:** A manager does not actually perform the work but he gets things done by others. According to Knootz and O'Donnel, "management is the art of getting things done through and with people in formally organised groups."

**16. Management as a class or a team:** A class may be defined as a group of people having homogenous characteristics to achieve common objectives. Engineers and doctors are grouped as a class in a society. Each and every doctor has the same objectives in life. Just like engineers and doctors, the management people have got similar aspirations to achieve corporate objectives.

**17. Management as a career:** Now-a-days, management is developed as a career focussed on certain specialisation. Financial Management, Cash Management, Portfolio Management, Marketing Management, Personnel Management, Industrial Management and Business Management are some of the specialisations of management. Specialists are appointed in the key posts of top management.

**18. Direction and control:** A manager can direct his sub-ordinates in the performance of a work and control them whenever necessary. If the available resources are not utilised properly by him, he fails to achieve the corporate objectives in the absence of direction and control. Generally, the direction and control deals with the activities of human effort.

**19. Dynamic:** The management is not static. In the fast developing business world, new techniques are developed and adopted by the manage-ment. Management is changed according to the social change. The social change is the result of the changing business world.

**20. Management is needed at all levels:** The functions of management are common to all levels of organisation. The top executives perform the functions of planning, organising, directing, controlling and decision making. The same functions are also performed by the lower level supervisor.

**21. Leadership quality:** Leadership quality is developed in the persons who are working in the top level management. According to R.C. Davis, "Management is the function of executive leadership everywhere."

## FUNCTIONS OF MANAGEMENT

Scholars in the field of management have their own classification of functions of management. Some scholars add few functions and delete some other functions. The important functions of management are briefly discussed below:

**1. Planning:** Planning is the primary function of management. Nothing can be performed without planning. Writing a book starts with plan-ning. In short, planning refers to deciding in advance that which will be done in the near future. In the business world, the organisation should achieve the objectives. In order to achieve objec-tives, the organisation plans what is to be done, when it is to be done, how it is to be done, and by whom it is to be done. Messie says, "Planning Pervades Management". George R. Terry has rightly said "Planning is a constructive reviewing of future needs so that present actions can be adjusted in view of the established goal. It is deli-berate conscious research used to formulate the design and orderly sequence of actions through which it is expected to reach objectives. Planning should take place before doing; most individual or group efforts are made by determining before any operative action takes place, what shall be done, where, how and who shall do it".

**2. Organising:** Organising is the distribution of work in groupwise or sectionwise for effective performance. Organisation provides all facilities which are necessary to perform the work. The business developed, the organisation takes responsibility to create some more departments under different managers. Hence, the organisation divides the total work and co-ordinates all the activities by authority relationship. Besides, organising defines the position of each person in the organisation and determines the paths through which communication should flow. The manager would determine who should report to whom and how.

According to Henry Fayol, "Organisation is of two kinds i.e., organisation of the human factor and organisation of the material factor. Organisation of the human factor covers the distribution of work to those who are best suitable along with authority and responsibility. Organisation of the material factor covers utilisation of raw materials, plant and machinery etc.." According to Knootz and O'Donnell, "Organising consists of conscious co-ordination of people towards a desired goal".

**3. Staffing:** Staffing function comprises the activities of selection and placement of competent personnel. In other words, staffing refers to placement of right persons in the right jobs. Staffing includes selection of right persons, training to those needy persons, promotion of best persons, retirement of old persons, performance appraisal of all the personnel, and adequate remuneration of personnel. The success of any enterprise depends upon the successful performance of staffing function.

According to Harold Knootz and Cyril O'Donnell, "the managerial function of staffing involves manning the organisational structure through proper and effective selection, appraisal and development of personnel to fill the roles designed into the structure".

**4. Directing:** The actual performance of a work starts with the function of Direction. Planning, organising and staffing functions are concerned with the preliminary work for the achievement of organisational objectives. But the direction deals with making the workers learn techniques to perform the jobs assigned to them. Direction includes guidance, supervision and motivation of employees. According to Joseph Massie, "Directing concerns the total manner in which a manager influences the action of his sub-ordinates. It is the final action of a manager in getting others to act after all preparations have been completed".

**5. Co-ordinating:** All the activities are divided groupwise or sectionwise under organising function. Now, such grouped activities are co-ordinated towards the accomplishment of objectives of an organisation. The difficulty of co-ordination depends upon the size of organisation. The difficulty of co-ordination is increased with the increasing of the size of the organisation. According to Knootz and O'Donnell, "the last co-ordination occurs when individuals see how their jobs contribute to the dominant goals of the enterprise. This implies knowledge and understanding of enterprise objectives".

**6. Motivating or actuating:** The goals are achieved with the help of motivation. Motivation includes increasing the speed of performance of a work and developing a willingness on the part of workers. This is done by an resourceful leader. The workers expect favourable climate conditions to work, fair treatment, monetary or non-monetary incentive, effective communication and gentleman approach. According to Earl P. Strong, "Motivating is the process of indoctrinating personnel with unity of purpose and the need to maintain a continuous, harmonious relationship".

**7. Controlling:** Controlling function ensures that the achieved objectives conform to pre-planned objectives. Necessary corrective action may be taken if there is any deviation. The control is very easy whenever the organisation has a fixed standard. A good system of control has the characteristics of economy, flexibility, understanding and adequacy to organisational needs.

Prof. Theo Haimann defines, "Control is the process of checking to determine whether or not, proper progress is being made towards the objectives and goals and acting, if necessary, to correct any deviation." According to Henry Fayol, "control consists in verifying whether everything occurs in conformity with the plan adopted, the instructions issued and principles issued".

**8. Innovation:** Innovation refers to the preparation of personnel and organisation to face the changes made in the business world. Continuous changes are being made in the business. Consumers are satisfied through innovation. Innovation includes developing new material, new products, new techniques in production, new package, new design of a product and cost reduction.

**9. Representation:** A manager has to act as a representative of a company. He has dealings with customers, suppliers, government officials, banks, financial institutions, trade unions and the like. It is the duty of every manager to have good relations with others.

**10. Decision-making:** Every employee of an organisation has to take a number of decisions every day. Decision-making helps in the smooth functioning of an organisation.

**11. Communication:** Communication is the transmission of human thoughts, views or opinions from one person to another person. Workers are informed about what should be done, where it is to be done, how it is to be done and when it is to be done. Communication helps the regulation of job and co-ordinate the activities.

Planning, organising, staffing, directing, co-ordinating, motivating or actuating and controlling are the main functions of management. Innovation, representation, decision-making and communication are the subsidiary functions of management.

Henry Fayol classifies the functions of management as forecasting, planning, organising, commanding, co-ordinating and controlling. Luther Gullik classifies the functions of management as:

POSDCORB, where —

P stands for Planning,

O for Organising,

S for Staffing,

D for Directing,

Co for co-ordinating,

R for Reporting and

B for Budgeting.

According to Harold Koontz and Cyrill O'Donnel, the functions of management include planning, organising, staffing, directing and controlling.

George Terry deals with the functions of management such as planning, organising, actuating and controlling.

Tennenbuam *et.al.,* classify functions of management as planning, organising and controlling.

Harold Smiddy of G.E. divides the functions of management into planning, organising, integrating and measuring, abbreviated as POIM.

E.F.L. Brech classifies functions of management as planning, motivation, co-ordination and control.

According to Lawrence A. Appley, functions of management include planning, executing and controlling.

L. Hall classifies the function of management as forecasting, planning, control, motivation and co-ordination.

Massic divides the functions of management into planning, organising, staffing, control, communication and direction.

According to Mary Cushing Nillas, the functions of management include organisation, co-ordination, administration and leadership.

## IMPORTANCE OF MANAGEMENT

Management is a must for every enterprise. The existence of management ensures proper functioning and running of an enterprise. Management can plan the activities to achieve the objectives and utilise the available resources at minimum cost.

Every business needs a direction. This direction is given by the management. The resources of production are converted into production. The resources will remain as resources in the absence of management. The conversion process is performed through the co-ordination of management.

The significance or importance of management is briefly explained below:

**1. Management meet the challenge of change:** In the modern business world, there are frequent changes. The changes place the business in a dangerous position. Only an efficient management can save the business from the dangers brought in by the challenges.

**2. Accomplishment of group goals:** The achievement of objectives of a business depends upon three factors. The proper planning of available resources, adjusting possibility of business unit with existing business environment and the quality of decision taken and control made by the business unit are the factors responsible for achieving objectives.

**3. Effective utilisation of business:** There are eight M's in the business. These are said to be man, money, materials, machines, methods, motivation, markets and management. Management is the topmost of all other 'M's. Management has control over other remaining 'M's.

**4. Effective functioning of business:** Ability, experience, mutual understanding, co-ordination, motivation and supervision are some of the factors responsible for the effective functioning of business. Management makes sure that the abilities of workers are properly used and co-operation is obtained with the help of mutual understanding. Besides, management can know the expectation of workers and the expectation is fulfilled through motivation techniques.

**5. Resource development:** Efficient management is the life boat of any developed business. The resources of the business may be identified and developed by the management. The term 'resources' includes men, money, material and machines.

**6. Sound organisation structure:** Management lays down the foundation for sound organisation structure. Sound organisation structure clearly defines the authority and responsibility relationship — who is responsible to whom, who will command whom and who is responsible for what. Care is taken in appointing qualified persons to the right job by the management.

**7. Management directs the organisation:** The human mind directs and controls the functioning of human body. Similarly, the management directs and controls the functioning of an organisation.

**8. Integrates various interests:** Each person has his own interests. These interests are different in nature. Management takes steps to integrate various interests to achieve the objectives of an organisation.

**9. Stability:** The fluctuations of business are stablised by the management. The fluctuations of business are caused by the changing policy of the government, pressures on the part of competitors and changing preferences of customers. The efficient management can run the business as per the policy framed by the government, face the competitors in the market and produce the articles as per the preferences of customers.

**10. Innovation:** New ideas are developed by the management and implemented in the organisation. Better performance is achieved through new ideas.

**11. Co-ordination and team-spirit:** All the activities of business are grouped department-wise. Management co-ordinates the activities of different departments and establishes team-spirit to achieve the objectives.

**12. Tackling problems:** Goog Management acts as a friend or a guide of workers while tackling problems. When workers get over confidence of solving the problems for effective performance of a job, they fail in tackling the problems efficiently.

**13. A tool for personality development:** Management gives direction to workers for effective performance of a job. Besides, new methods or techniques are taught to workers. The training facilities are arranged by the management. In this way, management is a tool to develop the personality of workers to raise their efficiency and productivity ability.

## ADMINISTRATION AND MANAGEMENT

The terms *administration* and *management* are used synonymously. Some writers argue that both these terms have same meanings and there is no difference between these two terms. Running of a business requires skill which is called *management* and functioning of government departments and non-profit institutions requiring skill is called *administration*.

Some writers argue that executive functions of a business unit are referred as Management and executive functions of other institutions are referred as administration. In this way, administration is distinguished as a top level function while management as a lower level function. Policy and objectives of a business are determined by the top level executives (Administration). At the same time, the lower level people (Managment) work to attain the objectives of the business unit and follow the policy framed by the administrators.

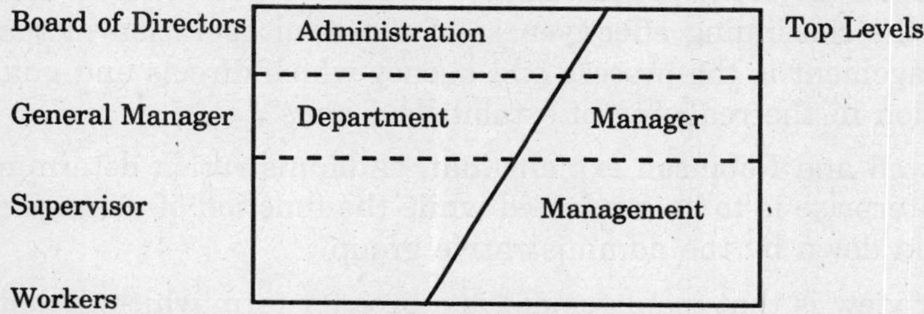


## DIFFERENCES BETWEEN ADMINISTRATION AND MANAGEMENT

### Oliver Sheldon

"Administration is the function in industry concerned with the determination of the corporate policy, the co-ordination of finance, production and distribution, the settlement of the compass (structure) of the organisation under the ultimate control of the executive."

"Management is the function in industry concerned with the execution of policy within the limits set up by the administration and the employment of the organisation for the particular objects set before it".

### William R. Spriegal

"Administration is that phase of business enterprise that concerns itself with the overall determination of institutional objectives and the policies necessary to be followed in achieving those objectives. Administration pre-determines the specific goals and lays down the broad areas within which those goals are to be attained. Administration is a determinative function, management on the other hand is an executive function which is primarily concerned with the carrying out of the broad policies laid down by the administration".

### G.E. Milward

"Administration is primarily the process and the agency used to establish the object or purpose which an undertaking and its staff are to achieve, secondarily, administration has to plan and stabilize the broad lines of principles which will govern action. These broad lines are in their turn usually called *policies*. Management is the process and the agency through which the execution of policy is planned and supervised".

Thus, administration is a thinking function and management is a doing function. According to this concept, owners of the business enterprise receive dividends in return for their capital contributed. Managers, i.e., the management people get salary for realising the objectives of administrators i.e., the owners. Besides, the managers direct and control the subordinates within the limits fixed by the administrators.

According to Professor Dalton E. Mc Farland, "In Government agencies, administration is preferred over management, although in recent years, the term management has become widely used in government agencies. Another possible distinction refers to the levels of organisation. In business, the term *administration* refers to the activities of the higher ups in the managerial ranks. Still another distinction related to organisational level is that administration refers to the determination of major aims and policies while management refers to the carrying out the operations designed to accomplish the aims and effecutate the policies. Here again, this distinction is not widely followed but it exists".

Ordway Tead describes, "Administration is the process and agency which is responsible for the determination of aims for which an organisation and its management are to strive, which establishes the broad policies under which they are to operate and which gives general oversight to the continuing effectiveness of the total operation in reaching the objectives sought. Management is the process and agency which directs and guides the operations of an organisation in the realizing of estabilished aims".

Leffingwell and Robinson explain that, "Administration determines the policies upon which the enterprise is to be conducted while the function of management to carry out the policies is laid down by the administrative group".

Another view is that management is a broader term which includes thinking function and executive function. Thus, administration is a part of management and carrying out the objectives laid down by the management. Eminent writers like E.F.L. Brech, Barry Pichman, Melwyn Copen, Henry Fayol, William Newman and Theo Haiman used the terms administration and management synonymously.

**E.F.L. Brech**

"Management is a social process entailing responsibilities for the effective and economical planning and the regulation of the operation of an enterprise, in the fulfillment of a given purpose or task. Administration is a part of management which is concerned with the installation and carrying out of the procedures by which it is laid down and communicated and the process of activities regulated and checked against plans".

**Henry Fayol**

"All undertakings require planning, organisation, command, co-ordination and control and in order to function properly, all must observe the same general principles. We are no longer confronted with several administrative sciences but with one which can be applied equally well to public and prive affairs."

**Theo Haimann**

"No two separate sets of personnel are required, however, to discharge administrative and managerial functions. Each manager performs both activities and spends part of his time administrating and part of his time managing".

Top management of the enterprise spends maximum time for policy framing and determination of objectives and spends few minutes for direction and controlling. Hence, administration is also one of the functions just like other functions as purchase, sales, production, finance, etc.

| *Sl. No.* | *Basis of Distinction* | *Administration* | *Management* |
|---|---|---|---|
| 1. | Policy and objectives | Determines policy to be followed and decide the objectives to be achieved. | Implements the policy and achieve the objectives. |
| 2. | Directing of human efforts | Not directly involves in the execution of plan and achievement of objectives. | Directly involves in the execution of plan and achieving objectives. |
| 3. | Main functions | Planning, organising and staffing. | Direction, motivation and control. |
| 4. | Levels of executive | Top level executives (Owners or Board of Directors). | Lower level executives (Manager, supervisor and workers). |
| 5. | Position | Acts as a Principal. | Acts as an agency. |
| 6. | Knowledge | Requires administra-tive ability more than technical ability. | Requires technical ability more than administrative ability. |

## THE MANAGER

Management is a creative process which integrates and uses various available resources effectively to accomplish certain goals. For which, an individual is responsible to develop ideas and get things done through others. The concerned individual is designated as manager. any person who perform the functions of planning, organisation, staffing, directing and controlling for the accomplishment of pre-determined organisation goals is called as manager.

Manager is not actually do the work but guide others to do things correctly. In other words, manager has not build factory uses or install machines and operate them or sell goods in the market.

A growing tendency in business requires professionally qualified persons. The reason is that manager should direct the efforts of others at lower levels of an organisation. The primary job of a manager is the management of people.

According to Peter F. Drueker, "Every job should be designed as an integrated set of operations which are varied enough to reduce boredom. The workers should be given a sufficient measure of freedom to organise and control their work environment. It is the duty of every manager to educate, train and develop people below him so that they may use their potentialities and abilities to perform the work allotted to them. He has also help them in satisfying their needs and aspirations through incentives and other things. For getting best contribution from the people working under him, he must provide them with proper environment. A manager must create a climate which brings in and maintain satisfaction and discipline among the people." Hence, the job of manage is very difficult one and requires some significant qualities to get the possible results. The manager should have the capacity and capabilities to meet the challenges of his job.

## FUNCTIONS OF A MANAGER

The somooth functioning of a business unit depends on the performance of the manager. If a manager has adequate skill, he can discharge his duties effectively. Generally, the following functions are performed by a manager.

**1. Planning the work:** Planning involves deciding the course of action well in advance. The manager can decide the procedure to be followed in order achieve the objectives of an organisation. Planning the work is a rational activity.

**2. Taking decisions:** Manager has to take a lot of decisions with regard to the assignment of work to every worker and delegation of authority to do a job. A wise decision can be taken by an efficient manager. Quality of decision is based on the intelligence of the manager.

**3. Delegating authority:** Manager should delegate authority whenever a project or work is assigned to others. Nobody can do anything without authority. So, the manager has to delegate authority on need basis.

**4. Solving the problems:** Sub-ordinates bring problems before the manager. The manager has to solve the problems instead of salving the problems quickly. Finding solution to a problem will prevent cropping up such problems in future.

**5. Co-ordination:** The tasks or activities of the sub-ordinates are co-ordinated for quick execution of a work. Increased productivity is to be achieved through effective co-ordination. Overall organisational objectives could be achieved only by the process of co-ordination of various individual efforts.

**6. Stimulating workers:** The workers have to be motivated to do their work. Workers will be idle in the absence of motivation. Motivation could be done by money or kind. The Manager has to choose between the two depending on the situation.

**7. Setting target:** Target is to be fixewd by the manager sectionwise. Setting of target indicates the workers the extent of contribution made by them in the overall performance. Target is fixed on the basis of the main objectives of an organisation.

**8. Guiding sub-ordinates:** Eventhough the manager is a boss to his sub-ordinates, he can guide the sub-ordinates in the performance of their work. The Manager is acting as a friend at this stage. The guidance of the manager is indispensible a tonic to sub-ordinates.

**9. Arranging the facilities:** Availing the facilities in the working place is imperative for effective performance of any work. So, the manager has to arrange the required facilities. Besides, the manager has to watch over the utilisation of the facilities.

**10. Control the deviations:** The Manager has to control the workers if there is any difference between standards of performance and actual performance. The control ensures the right performance. The exercise of control is in the hands of the manager.

## ROLE OF A MANAGER

Manager is responsible to integrates all the activities which are performed in an organisation. In otherwords, he has co-ordinate the talents of people working under him for the purpose of achieving the organisational goals. The role of a manager gets much importance than other executives in an organisation. Hence, a manager's job is very much complex and requires some special qualities to be a head.

**1. Director:** Manager gives direction to people working under him. Direction includes instructions. Manager has direct the executives towards achieving organisational goals.

**2. Motivator:** Manager understands likes and dislikes of executives and motivate them accordingly. Motivation stimulates the performance of job. Here, the manager stimulates the executives through motivation.

**3. Human being:** Manager treats all the people working under him equally and no personal bias. He has to mingle with others and understand the feeling of other executives.

**4. Guide:** Manager should be well aware of using the equipment, techniques and procedures involved in performing specific tasks. If so, he can guide others whenever a need arise.

**5. Friend:** Unnecessary misunderstanding may be arised among the executives. Now, the manager should come forward voluntarily and eliminate the misunderstanding at the earliest. Here, the manager is acting as a friend.

**6. Planner:** Day-to-day requirements of the organisation has to be identified and arranged by the manager. He has to plan the work and assign the same to the executives according to their position held.

**7. Supervisor:** Manager has to supervise and control, executives performance and maintain personal contacts with them. He has to perform this work alongwith the work to be performed by him.

**8. Reporter:** The feedback information is provided by the manager to the top management people. Sometimes, workers' problems have not been solved by the manager. If so, the same should be communicated to the top authorities.

## RESPONSIBILITIES OF A PROFESSIONAL MANAGER

Manager is getting things done through others. He prepares plan, build an organisation, help and motivate the employees according to plans for the purpose of achieving organisation goals. Even though, the manager is responsible for the non-performance of any work. He is answerable to every body.

**1. Planning of work:** Manager has to identify the work which are necessary to achieve the objectives. Every work should lead to the achievement of objectives. Manager is responsible for planning of work. The reason is that other than the manager has no idea and nobody approach and enquire other than the manager to know the work.

**2. Proper and Effective Communication:** There must be a freeflow of communication within the organisation. If there is any hurdle, the hurdle can be findout and removed only by the manager. Communication gap and misunderstanding are also traced out and ensure proper and effective communication.

**3. Co-ordination of Efforts:** The efforts of employees have more value than the finance. The finance can be earned through hardwork. But, if efforts are not properly co-ordinated, all the efforts are in vain. Once again, the efforts can not be generated and used. Therefore, the manager should prepare the system for proper channalisation of efforts.

**4. Getting co-operation of Employees:** Different nature of employees are working in an organisation. The absence of co-operation among employees leads to poor performance and non-achievement of objectives in time. Hence, the manager is responsible for getting co-operation from employees working under him.

**5. Encourages a team spirit:** The manager is not only guide the employees but also encourages a team spirit among them. Team spirit is created with the help of using polite words. The manager should know which type of approach creates a team spirit among the employees.

**6. Better utilisation of Resources:** Resources of any organisation is limited one. An organisation has more resources on certain items and limited resources on certain items. Here, the manager should measure the available resoruces and utilise the resources at the maximum. No resources will be wasted at any cost.

**7. Selecting the Procedure:** Top management executives frame the policy and goals of an organisation. But, the way of achieving the objectives cannot be decided by the top management people. There are many ways available to achieve the objectives. Even though, the manager is responsible to select a procedure which is more suitable and adoptable.

**8. Maintaining good human relations:** Employees are working in different temparaments. They approach the manager for different reasons. The manager is answerable on his own behalf and on behalf of top management people. He is responsible for maintaining good human relations with the employees and maintain good human relations among the employees also.

**9. Solve the problem:** Sometimes problem may be arised among the employees. When, the manager takes the initiative steps for solving such problems. Employees feel happy if the manager understand the problem and solve the problem immediately.

**10. Arranging training and development facilities:** Training and Development facilities should be arranged by the manager for the benefit the organisation and employees. Training and Development programme is not only benefit the employee but also gives benefit to the organisation. Hence, the manager has the responsibility of arranging training and development facilities.

## ENTREPRENEUR AND MANAGER

Both the entrepreneur and the manager are not one and the same. The entrepreneur and manager are used as interchangeable terms very often. Strictly speaking, an entrepreneur is different from a manager. An entrepreneur is a person who establishes business unit and utilises the other factors of production like land, labour and capital (adopts new techniques in the production) with a view to earn a profit. The manager is a person who utilises the factors of production like land, labour and capital under a specified system ie. Organisation on behalf of the entrepreneur. The main points of difference between the entrepreneur and manager are listed below:

| *Sl.No.* | *Basis of Difference* | *Entrepreneur* | *Manager* |
|---|---|---|---|
| 1 | Invention a job | He finds new ways to do status quo | He maintains the |
| 2 | Type of performance | Increases the productivity | Achieves the production target. |
| 3 | Utilisation of factors of production | He may find new combination in the factors of production. | He may effectively utilise the factors of production. |
| 4 | Policy | Frames the policy. | Implements the policy. |
| 5 | Risks | He avoids risks. | He minimises the risks. |
| 6 | Uncertainty | He converts uncertainty into certainty. | He encounters uncertainty. |
| 7 | Risk bearing | He assumes risks. | He does not share risks. |
| 8 | Reward | Increased profit. | Bonus. |
| 9 | Gains | Uncertain and irregular. | Certain and fixed. |
| 10 | Skills | Creative thinking. | Better human relations. |
| 11 | Status | Self-employed. | Salaried person. |
| 12 | Goals | Determines the goals. | Achieves the goals. |
| 13 | Nature of performance | He launches a new enterprise. | He operates the existing enterprise. |

## MANAGEMENT AS PROFESSION

Management is regarded as profession due to the development of business in size and nature. Besides, there is a difference between the ownership and management. Hence, there is a social recognition to the management as a profession.

## MEANING OF PROFESSION

Profession means an occupation by which apply the intelligence and efforts for the purpose of providing skilled service or advice to others for an agreed amount.

## DEFINITION

The dictionary defines profession as "calling in which on professes to have acquired a specialised knowledge which is used either in instructing, guiding or advising others." According to Carr Saunders "profession may perhaps be defined as an occupation based upon specialised intellectual study and training, the purpose of which is to supply skilled service or advice to others for a definite fee or salary."

Cogan defines profession as "a vocation whose practice is founded upon an understanding of a theoretical structure of some department of learning of science."

According to L.M.Prasad "profession is an occupation for which specialised knowledge, skills and training are required and use of these skills is not meant for self-satisfaction but these are used for larger interests of the society and the success of these skills is measured not in terms of money alone."

It is understood that all professions are occupation. The reason is that they provide means of livelihood. But at the same time, all occupations are not professions because some of them lack certain characteristics of a profession.

## CHARACTERISTICS OF PROFESSION

Houle has listed fourteen characteristics which are distributed associated with the dynamic process of organisation's improvement within the occupation. They are definition of the occupation's functions, mastery of theoretical knowledge, capacity to solve problems, use of knowledge, self-enhancement, public acceptance, ethical practice, penalties, relations to other vocations, relations to the users of the service.

Generally, the following characteristics are found in Management.

**1. Existence of knowledge:** Management has been developed as a distinct body of knowledge over the last seven-eight decades. The development of knowledge, in management is emerged due to the requirement for managing complex and large organisations in a better way. Thus management fulfills the requirement of profession i.e., existence of knowledge.

Eventhough new concepts and principles are being developed in management, this type of development does not affect its status as being a profession.

**2. Knowledge acquisition:** An individual can enter into a profession only after getting knowledge and skills through formal training. For example, medical graduates practice after undergoing formal training: A person who practices a profession as an expert, since he is the master of a particular branch. In this way, he is offering service to his patient. Here, the doctor gets the knowledge through some formal method. Likewise, the management can be regarded as profession since the management graduates are also getting inplant training and familiar with the various techniques of management.

**3. Professional Association:** An occupation should have an association. If not so, the occupation cannot be considered as profession. An association consisting of professionals needed to regulate and develop the professional activities. Besides, this association may also prescribe the criteria for individuals who want to enter into a profession. In the field of management, there are number of such association at various levels. All India Management Association (AIMA) has its chapters in most of the cities in India.

AIMA is developing professional activities and standardise the profession. In this way, management is termed as profession.

**4. Ethics:** There are some ethical standards for every profession. Every individual of the concerned profession is expected to maintain conformity with these standards. The reason is that a profession has high degree of power and this power can be used for the benefit of organisation. This has resulted many occupations issuing a code of ethics of professional practice so that the relevant individuals may know the standard and for adopt the same accordingly. In management also, code of conduct has been formulated to suggest the behavioural pattern for professional managers. Hence, management executives are supposed to be socially responsible and it is their duty to protect the interest of all parties associated with an organisation. The interested parties of an organisation are customers, suppliers, employees, financiers, creditors, government and the general public.

**5. Service motive:** Service motive insists the professionals keep social interest in their mind while charging fees for their professionals service. There is no market mechanism to measure the monetary value of professional service. But, the monetary value of professional service is measured out of competition prevailing among the professional themselves. At the same time, the success of any profession is not based on the money it earns but by the amount of social service it provides. Thus, management provides more social service and charge less fees from the organisation. The contribution of management cannot be measured, in terms of money alone because without integrating efforts of management, resources worth billions of rupees may be useless.

From the above discussion, it is concluded that the management has certain characteristics of profession. Reiss has classified profession into five categories and has suggested management as would be profession.

Caplow has the view of management is fast moving towards professional status. Peter F.Drucker observed that no greater damage could be done to our economy or to our society than to attempt to professionalise management by licensing managers or by limiting access to management to people with a special academic degree. Any serious attempt to make management scientific or a profession is bound to lead to the attempt to eliminate those disturbing nuisances, the unpredictability of business life-its risks, it ups and downs, its wasteful competition, the irrational choices of consumer-and in the process, the economy's freedom and its ability to grow.

## OBSTACLES TO MANAGEMENT BEING A PROFESSION

There are many obstacles in the way of management being recognised as a profession. Some of the obstacles are presented below:

1. There is no uniform and standard criteria for the evaluation of managerial performance.
2. Management executives have no uniform clients and do not perform uniform activities.

3. Persons without a degree or a diploma in management are also doing well like persons have a degree or diploma in management.
4. The theory of management is still changing and new principles are also being developed.

## PROFESSIONAL MANAGEMENT

The professional management is a 20th century practice. Upto 19th century, family management practice was followed. The professional management is getting importance only after increase in the complexity nature of business and no growth of business at one stage.

Businessmen are preferring to develop their business at high level and a need is arised to them for survival. Hence, management graduates are being preferred to fill managerial positions. In this way, professional management is developed in India.

Family management is the forerunner of professional management. The knowledge of family management is necessary to understand the professional management. The other name of family management is hereditary management. The features of family management are listed below:

A. Both ownership and control of the business are vested with the hands of family members.
B. The main aim of the family management is profit maximisation.
C. The family members may or may not have formal education and training in management.
D. The authority of decision making is vested with family members.
E. Outsiders are prohibited to move to the top posts of management and serve as yesman of the family members.

Only bloodties and costeties provide the passport to the top level management.

Family management was very effective during the initial period of industrialisation. There is an inability in the best utilisation of modern technology in the family management. Due to these types of nature are connected with the family management, professional management is emerged.

The authority of policy framing and decision making are vested with persons having professional education, training and experience in management. Today large number of management institutes and management consultancy firms have been established. These things are happening due to liberalisation, globalisation and privatisation and demand for professionally qualified managers. At present, top management positions are filled up with the help of persons having management education and training. In owner managed companies also, the same practice is followed. This shows that management is gradually getting professionalised.

The need for efficient managers is bound to increase in the years to come. Therefore, the professional management should be encouraged by everyone. The reason is that the system of political management is prevailing in the public sector. In the public sector, the decision making powers lies with the ruling party. Party affiliations and personalities are the determinants for entering into the decision-making circle. Even though, civil servant is the head of the public sector undertaking he/she has to toe the line decided by the politicians.

These civil servants are lacking management experience and autonomy. Their survival depends upon the will of their political god fathers.

Hence, they are working according to the instructions of ministers and office bearers of the party in power.

## NEED OF EFFICIENT PROFESSIONAL MANAGEMENT

The need for efficient professional management is necessary in India due to the following reasons:

1. Major portion of our economy is unorganised
2. Poor infrastructure
3. Less utilisation of modern technology
4. Low productive efficiency
5. Wide spread poverty and unemployment.

## PROFESSIONALISATION OF MANAGEMENT IN INDIA

The professionalisation of management is very popular in corporate management in India. The reason is that no one likes to be backward and inefficient. But the assessment of the extent of professionalisation of Indian management is a big question. The reason is that some top management positions are filled up with the help of family members if the owner of the business is few. In the case of diversed ownership organisation, management graduates are appointed as executives. Hence, it is very difficult to know the correct picture of Indian Management.

Somebody argue that the mere appointment of some persons with professional (management) degrees will not necessarily lead to professionalisation of management unless there is a change in management process. According to L.C.Gupta "professionalisation does not come automatically by employment of people with professional degrees, unless the professionals have the necessary authority and use their professionalism in decision-making. We may employ MBAs and other technocrafts in the purchase and sales departments but if buying and selling are to be done through family firms, where is the scope of professionalism? More than professional degrees what matters is professional ethics." In this context, P.L.Tandon observes that, "In a family business, you have professional engineers, accountants and marketers but all decision-making is centralised at the top, with the head of the family, who has no professionalism but perhaps only experience and intuition, the decisions are not likely to be as good as that of a modern professional board."

In Indian scenario, management is highly professionalised both in private sector as well as in public sector after 1980s. They have inducted management graduates at various levels of management.

## YARD STICKS OF PROFESSIONALISATION OF MANAGEMENT

The following conditions have been satisfied for the existence of professionalisation of management.

1. Introducing modern concepts of management.
2. Fraing organisational objectives by considering social needs.
3. Motivation for high level of performance.

4. Developing management concepts suitable for the country.
5. Attitudes towards management practices.

## ARGUMENTS FOR PROFESSIONALISATION OF MANAGEMENT

Professionalisation of management is desirable due to the following reasons:

1. Professionalisation leads the management executives to increase in their knowledge and skills. The reason is that businessmen expects persons having minimum educational qualification. Managerial environment of the future is going to be more challenging requiring a high degree of professionalisation from management executives. Trial and error method of managing practices cannot be a successful in the years to come.

2. Initially, the modern management concepts were applied by the subsidiaries and associates of multinational corporations operating in India. Many of these subsidiaries and associates were quite successful in terms of their growth and profitability. It was presumed that the success is the result of the application of modern management concepts. The increasing of size and complexity of business organisations necessitates the management executives for proper application of modern management concepts.

3. Professionalisation of management would improve the status and prestige of management career and of management executives. The impression of management executives interested only in maximising profits would be removed by giving importance to social needs.

4. There is a failure of many public sector undertakings and increasing the number of public sectors manifold during the plan period necessitates the government took a decision to induct professional managers with responsibility.

5. Increasing competition and fast development of technology paved the way for professionalisation of management. The competition is increased due to liberalisation, globalisation and privatisation. The technology has gone to a sea change within a short period.

6. An organisation grows beyond certain size demand that ownership and management should be divorced.

In this type of organisation, management positions should be placed by persons having professional skills and adequate training.

7. The statutory control over the management executives can be exercised through professionalisation of management. The statutory control minimise the malpractices like mismanagement, wrong payment unnecessary payment, speculation in stock market, frauds in management etc. If the management executives indulging in such practices, they will be debarred from practicing management.

8. Professionalisation will define the duties, powers, specialisation and responsibilities of management executives. The prescription of code of conduct ensures a healthy managerial environment within the business organisation.

9. Professionalisation would speed up management education, standard, criteria for entrants and training. It would also attract more talented people into management career.

## ARGUMENTS AGAINST PROFESSIONALISATION MANAGEMENT

Professionalisation of Management is opposed on the following grounds:

1. Minimum educational qualification is not enough to make effective managers. There are different types of organisations which require different set of management degree for getting success. Therefore, specialised degree in management cannot be used to license managers.

2. There is a popular belief and attitude among the businessman i.e., business is a matter of common sense and luck. This belief and attitude have paid good dividend in the past because of controlled economy and lack of competition. Hence, businessmen are in favour of professionalisation of management.

3. It is proved that businessmen have successfully created business empires on the basis of their family background (Heredity) and experience in India. They have not consider the management degree for getting success. Professionally qualified managers are not necessary for more efficient and effective performance.

4. In the private sector, both small scale organisations and joint stock company form of organisations, most of the organisations are functioning under one-man shows. Board is constituted in joint stock company to fulfill legal requirements but real control lies in a single person. Here, owner also performs the functions of a manager. The owner, who is an entrepreneur, performs managerial functions, his perspective is entirely differ from the professional manager. Owner-Manager's style of functioning is normally centralised and he believes in more direct control and often discourages professionalisation of management.

5. Management executives have no specified or definite clients just like lawyers and auditor. Hence, it is not practicable to define the obligations of management executives for the purpose of regulating their professional activities.

6. The management executives of many public sector enterprises are deputed civil servants from various departments. They have different academic qualifications. Hence, they could not develop right type of management culture. This has also worked against the professionalisation of management.

7. In India, there is no need of management degree to become the manager or management executives of any business organisation. Besides, there is no fully developed management education in India.

## MODEL QUESTIONS

1. Define the term, "Management".
2. Define the term, "Administration".
3. Explain the important functions of Management.
4. Why is Management?
5. What is mathematical or Management Science approach?
6. State and explain the meaning of Management?
7. What are the different levels of Management?
8. Distinguish between "Management" and "Administration"?
9. What is "Middle Management"?

10. What are the types of Management?
11. Explain the Imporatnce of "Management"
12. What are the important functions of Management?
13. What are the functions of "Management"?
14. Enumerate the various levels of importance of Management.
15. State the different Processes of management?
16. Define Managment. Describe the functions of a manager.
17. Discuss the importance of management in the present day.
18. What is management?
20. Enumerate the role and importance of management in the present society?
21. How would you define the term "Management"?
22. Discuss in brief the Nature of Management

# CHAPTER 2

# DEVELOPMENT OF MANAGEMENT THOUGHT

## INTRODUCTION

Management has developed since the time when the world came into existence. Whenever group efforts are necessary to achieve anything, there is a need for management. In ancient days, two or more persons collectively did the work which were common to all. These persons were directed and controlled by an individual. This individual had managerial efficiency. The inherent features of managerial efficiency were not known to our ancestors.

Kautilya's *Artha Sastra* and Saint Thiruvalluvar's *Thirukural* state the principles and concepts of management. These principles and concepts may be applied in our modern world and in the future also. An individual cannot achieve anything single-handed. Co-operation, group efforts, direction and control are necessary to achieve the objectives or goals of an individual. In our modern world, an individual cannot survive separately. He has to rely upon others. So, managerial efficiency is an essential requisite to human being.

## HENRY FAYOL (1841-1925)

Henry Fayol was a French industrialist. The observation of Henry Fayol on the Principles of Management were brought out in French language in 1916. Later, it was published in English language in 1949. The Principles of Management of Henry Fayol were known to the world only after 1949 leter the publication of his Management Thoughts in English.

He joined as an engineer in 1860 a mining company and became the Chief Managing Director of the same company because of his outstanding abilities. In the year 1918, he retired from the company. From1918 to 1926, Henry Fayol worked hard to popularise his priniciples of management. Besides, he delivered two lectures in 1900 and 1908 on management.

Henry Fayol concentrated on top management. It is known from his book 'General and Industrial Management'. Management plays a very important part in the government undertakings; of all undertakings, large or small, industrial, commercial, political, religious or any other. As such, in every concern, there is a management function to be performed. The management functions and organisational functions are different. The management functions include planning, organising, staffing, directing and controlling. But organisational functions include purchase, sales, production and accounting.

## CLASSIFICATION OF BUSINESS ACTIVITIES

Henry Fayol classified all the business activities into six functions. They are:

1. Technical activities relating to production.
2. Commercial activities relating to purchase of basic raw materials and other resources, selling of products and exchange.
3. Financial activities relating to identification and utilisation of available funds.
4. Security activities relating to the steps taken to protect the property of enterprise and persons.
5. Accounting activities relating to the recording and maintaining of accounts, stock taking and preparation of cost sheets, balance sheets and statistical data.
6. Managerial activities relating to planning, organising, commanding, co-ordinating and controlling.

Henry Fayol believed that the successful functioning of any business depends upon the performance of the above six functions.

## ELEMENTS OF MANAGEMENT

Henry Fayol made a difference between principles of management and elements of management. According to him, the following are the elements of management:

1. Planning.
2. Organising.
3. Commanding.
4. Co-ordination.
5. Control.

Commanding is nothing but direction. So, commanding means guiding and supervision of sub-ordinates in order to achieve specified objectives or goals. He also termed the elements of management as *functions* of management.

## QUALITIES OF A MANAGER

Henry Fayol identified the managerial qualities of a Manager. which are given below.

1. Physical (health, vigour and address)
2. Mental (ability to understand and learn, judgement, mental vigour and adaptability)
3. Moral (energy, firmness, willingness to accept responsibility, initiative, loyalty, tact and dignity)
4. General Education (general acquaintance with matters not belonging exclusively to the function performed)
5. Special knowledge (peculiar to the function, be it technical, commercial, financial, managerial etc.)
6. Experience (knowledge arising from work proper)

## PRINCIPLES OF MANAGEMENT

Henry Fayol has set forth the principles of management on the basis of his own experience in the mining company:

**1. Division of work:** Division of work makes a man a specialist. The reason is that division of work helps to specialise in an activity which increases the output with perfection. Besides, it avoids waste of time. According to Henry Fayol, division of work is applied to both technical and managerial kinds of work.

**2. Authority and responsibility:** Management is getting things done by others. A superior gives direction to his sub-ordinates to perform the job. Then the super-visor may exercise his authority. The post he holds invests him with this authority. Authority is closely connected with responsibility. Responsibility is shouldered whenever authority is exercised. Responsibility is essential to perform a job correctly.

**3. Discipline:** According to Koontz and O'Donnell, "Discipline is the respect for agreements which are directed at achieving obedience, application, energy and the outward marks of respect. According to Henry Fayol, discipline is essential in all levels of management people. Discipline is obtained through judicial application of penalties.

**4. Unity of command:** A subordinate has only one superior. If not so, the sub-ordinate does not perform any job perfectly. In other words, each subordinate is responsible to only one superior.

**5. Unity of direction:** The business activities are grouped on anyone of the bases, normally on functional basis. The activities of a group are assigned to a person who is said to be a manager. This manager is expected to look after all the activities of a particular group.

**6. Subordination of individual interest to group interest:** An individual has his own interest. At the same time, the organisation has its own interest. Here, the interest of an organi-sation is termed as *group interest*. Henry Fayol expected the reconcili ation of the individual interest with group interest. In no way, the individual interest should dominate the group interest.

**7. Remuneration of personnel:** According to Henry Fayol, employees should be given fair and reliable remuneration. The employees should get satisfaction out of their wages. The wages are determined on the basis of the work done by the employee and the wages payable are similar to those of other companies. Besides, the payment of wages should be made without any delay.

**8. Centralization:** Everything increases the importance of superior's role in centralization, while everything decreases the importance of superior's role in decentralization. In small firms, authority is centralized. In large firms, authority is decentralized. But, the centralization or decentralization of authority depends upon the personal character of the superior, his morality, reliability of resourcefulness and the like.

**9. Sclar chain:** According to Henry Fayol, "Scalar chain is the chain of superiors ranging from the ultimate authority to the lowest ranks." The communication flows from top to bottom. For example, A is the superior and has three subordinates in the order B, C and D. If A wants to communicate anything to D, it should be passed via B and C. Likewise, If D wants to communicate anything to A, it should be passed via C and B. This is called scalar chain.

**10. Order:** The principle of right place for everything and for everyone should be followed by the management. It is applied to both material and men. The material should be kept in order in the place where it is necessary. The personnel are selected scientifically and assigned duties according to their qualifications and ability.

**11. Equity:** Equity refers to a combination of fairness, kindness and justice. All the employees of the organisation are treated equally by the managers. The application of equity requires goodness and experience of managers. Besides, it requires loyalty and devotion from subordinates.

**12. Stability of tenure of personnel:** The security of job is an essential one. Insecurity of job results in the higher labour turnover. It increases the administration expenses. Unless and otherwise an employee has committed a mistake, no employee should be removed from service. The develop-ment of any organisation depends solely on the sincerity of labouerers.

**13. Initiative:** A manager should have the conceiving and executing initiative. It will have psychological effect over the subordinates. The subordinates are free to express their views or opinions in the execution of the work. Henry Fayol suggests that managers can take decisions after getting suggestions from the subordinates. Initiative is the keenest satisfaction of an intelligent man with experience.

**14. Esprit De Corps:** This means union is strength or team spirit. All the employees of the organisation are put together as a team in order to achieve the objectives of the organisation. If there is any misunderstanding or difference of opinions or distrust on other employees, the management should take corrective steps to remove them. The management should not follow the policy of divide and rule.

## FREDERICK WINSLOW TAYLOR (1856-1916)

F.W. Taylor was born in 1856. He started his career as an apprentice in Philadelphia in 1875. In 1878, Taylor joined Midvale Steel Company in U.S.A., as a machine shop labourer and became a supervisor. Finally, he became the Chief engineer in 1884 after gaining experience as time clerk, lathe gang boss, assistant foreman, master mechanic and chief draftsman. He had got M.E. degree (Master of Engineering) through evening course in 1883. Next, Taylor joined Bethlehem Steel Company, where he served from 1898 to 1901.

F.W. Taylor had observed the work performance of managers and workers. According to Taylor, they follow the traditional method of work and they do not have the concept of systematic performance of task. Besides, Taylor found that greater output was possible through systematization and standardization of methods of doing work. The techniques of managements are identified by Taylor through trial and error method. Nobody except F.W. Taylor devotes any attention to finding the exact nature of the work to be done or the best way of doing it.

F.W. Taylor reveals his findings through papers. He wrote many papers on the experiments he had done and the results of them. The major publications of F.W. Taylor include *A Piece Rate System (1895), Shop Management (1903), On The Art of Cutting Metals (1906) and The Principles of Scientific Management.* According to Professor T. Kempner, Taylor was an innovator of outstanding fruitfulness. Many of his ideas brought system, order and logic to areas where rule of thumb had previously prevailed in production planning, analysis of cost, systems of payment and many more. If he did not always invent such systems, he did carry them several stages further.

## SCIENTIFIC MANAGEMENT

In the 18th century, the production was affected by industrial revolution, when the management people wanted to increase their production. Their ambitions were fulfilled by the invention of the concept of Scientific Management by F.W Taylor in the 19th century. Taylor is the first person to find the concept of Scientific Management and develop it so, he is called as the father of Scientific Management.

According to F.W. Taylor, Scientific Management consists of a certain philosophy of scientific selection and training of right workers for the right job, providing adequate working conditions, providing a system of monetary incentives to efficient workers and assumption of responsibilities by managers and supervisors. The workers are selected scientifically and training is provided to both new and existing workers. The workers are placed according to their qualifications and experience. The effective doing of any work depends upon physical working conditions, lighting, ventilation, rest rooms, rest periods, drinking water, canteen, recreation, sanitation and the like are some of the physical working conditions. The system of monetary incentives should motivate the workers to work well. Managers and supervisors should accept responsibility for planning, scheduling, guiding and controlling. It means that planning and execution are different functions.

F.W. Taylor defined Scientific Management as the substitution of exact scientific investigations and knowledge for the old individual judgment or opinion; either of the workmen or the boss, in all matters relating to the work done in the establishment.

F.W. Taylor firmly believed that the objective of management should be the maximum prosperity for the employer and maximum prosperity to each employee. The prosperity for the employer means lower costs but higher returns. Maximum prosperity to the employee means fair as well as higher wages. These can be achieved through the adoption of Scientific Management.

## PRINCIPLES OF SCIENTIFIC MANAGEMENT

F.W. Taylor has given the principles of Scientific Management. They are briefly explained below:

**1. Science not rule of thumb:** It means the replacement of old method of doing work scientifically. The nature of work performed by each worker should be clearly determined. It includes the allotment of fair work to each worker, standardization in work, adoption of differential piece rate of payment system and the like.

**2. Harmony in group action:** F.W. Taylor has emphasized peace and friendship in group action. In other words, dissatisfaction of any worker is to be avoided in the group action. The dissatisfaction is eliminated through scientific selection, training and strategic placing of workers.

**3. Co-operation:** There should be a co-operation between management and workers and vice versa. Workers should help the management to get larger profits, better quality products and lower cost of production. Management should give fair wages to workers, recognize the performance of work and acknowledge the indispensability of workers in raising productivity. Then, better co-operation will be achieved. According to Taylor, substitution of war for peace, hearty and brotherly co-operation for discontentment and strife, replacement of suspicious watchfulness with mutual confidence of becoming friends instead of enemies result in co-operation. Mutual understanding and change in thinking are the factors necessary for co-operation.

**4. Maximum output:** Maximum output is achieved through division of work and assumption of responsibility by the management and workers jointly. Maximum output results in the increasing profit to the management and wages and bonus to the workers. Management should provide standard materials, tools and working conditions to perform the work economically and efficiently.

**5. Improvement of workers:** Under Scientific Management, all the workers should be given opportunity to improve to the fullest extent possible. It is necessary for the development of the company. Workers are scientifically selected and provided with the job training, so, the management should find out the physical, educational and psychological requirements of each job and find suitable persons to each job. Systematic training can shape the workers in relations to the job assigned to them.

## ELEMENTS OR FEATURES OF SCIENTIFIC MANAGEMENT

F.W. Taylor had conducted many experiments to find out how the workers could be made more efficient. These experiments help to improve the very essence of Scientific Management. Scientific Management has the following features:

**1. Separation of planning from executive function**: F.W. Taylor separated the planning function from the executive function. Before Taylor's period, both planning function and executive function were performed by one and the same worker. A worker himself plans the work and the instruments necessary to perform the work. The same workers do the job under the supervision of a supervisor. It results in disagreement on many issues between workers and supervisors. So, F.W. Taylor emphasized upon the separation of planning from execution. The planning function should be performed by the supervisors and executive function alone be assigned to the workers.

**2. Scientific task setting:** It means allotment of work to each worker on the basis of the capacity of an average worker functioning in normal working conditions. He should be able to complete the work in a working day. If there is no scientific task setting, the workers will work below their capacity. Taylor called it as 'a fair day's work'.

**3. Functional foremanship:** When there is a development of a supervision system, planning is separated from execution, as explained earlier. Taylor had found out the concept of functional foremanship. This is based on the specialisation of functions performed at supervision level. Under the functional foremanship system, there are eight persons. Out of eight persons, four persons are concerned with planning. They are Route clerk, Instruction card clerk, Time and cost clerk and Disciplinarian. The remaining four persons are concerned with the executive function. They are Speed boss, Inspector, Maintenance foreman and Gang boss.

**4. Work study:** Work study refers to the systematic critical assessment of efficiency required to do the job. It varies from one job to another job.

**5. Methods study:** The entire process of production is taken into account under this study. Efforts are made to reduce the distance passed by meterials and improvement in handling, transportation, inspection and storage of raw materials and finished goods. Best tools and machinery are provided to ensure best possible results.

**6. Motion duty:** A study relating to the movement of a machine operator and his machine while performing the job is called *motion study*. The very purpose of conducting this study is elimination of unnecessary movements of machine operator and machine. If these movements are eliminated, time required to perform the job is reduced to the optimum extent and the job is performed more efficiently.

**7. Time study:** Time study refers to the act of measuring the time required to perform a particular job. A standard time is fixed by conducting the time study. If the standard time is fixed, all the work is performed in the fixed time and control over it becomes easy.

**8. Fatigue study:** A study relating to the fixing of the working hours with rest periods to enable the workers to recoup the energy lost while performing the job is called *Fatigue study*. The fatigue may be mental or physical. In certain cases, both sap the energy of a worker. Health and efficiency of workers are well preserved by providing adequate rest to them. According to Taylor, Methods of Study, Motion Study, Time Study and Fatigue Study are parts of Work Study.

**9. Rate setting:** F.W. Taylor emphasized upon fair wages to workers, and had recommended differential piece rate wage system. The reason is that differential piece rate wage system may act as an incentive to lazy and less efficient workers.

**10. Standardisation:** Standarisation is made in respect of tools and instruments, working hours, volume of work, working conditions or atmosphere, cost of production etc. These are fixed on the basis of job analysis.

**11. Scientific selection and training:** The workers should be selected scientifically. Next, the appointment should be given to each worker according to the nature of the job requirement and his qualifications. Adequate training should be given to new as well as existing workers in order to update their knowledge. A job is assigned to a worker to suit his capacity best.

**12. Financial incentives:** Financial incentives can motivate the workers to show their efficiency. Provisions should be made in such a way that increase in efficiency should go with increase in wage structure. As per the differential piece rate wage system, the efficient workers get higher wages and vice versa. The differential piece rate wage system was charted out by F.W. Taylor.

**13. Mental revolution:** Mental revolution refers to change in thinking both on the part of the management and workers. If not, all the measures suggested in Scientific Management System would be useless. The success of implementation of Scientific Management depends on the mental revolution of Management and workers. According to Taylor, "The success of scientific management rests primarily on a fundamental change in the attitude of management and workers both as to their duty to co-operate in producing the largest possible surplus and to the necessity for substituting exact scientific knowledge for opinions or the old rule of thumb of individual knowledge."

**14. Economy:** The techniques of cost estimates and control should be considered in order to obtain economy. The available resources are used to the fullest possible maximum extent to eliminate wastage. Maximum profit is earned through this process. Various ways are given in Scientific Management to get economy in production and for maximizing profits.

## CONTRIBUTIONS OF F.W. TAYLOR

F.W. Taylor was the father of Scientific Mangement. He made some other contributions in the field of Management. They are listed below:

1. He has applied the principles of Scientific Management to solve the problems of Management.
2. According to him, it was the duty of the Management to tell the employees about the expectation of management from employees. Besides, the management should specify the way through which the job is to be completed.
3. He was the first person who supported mental revolution both on the part of the employer and the employee.
4. Time Study and Motion Study were first conducted by him.
5. Known as the first person to separate the planning function from executive function.
6. Functional foreman concept was first invented by him.

## CRITICISM OF SCIENTIFIC MANAGEMENT

F.W. Taylor's Scientific Management was treated as unique during the initial period of invention. The Scientific Mangement was criticised during the first quarter of the twentieth century. Some of the criticisms are summarized below:

1. The term *Scientific* refers to something new. People raised their voice against the use of the word Scienfitic before the management. The reason is that F.W. Taylor does not find anything new in management. Taylor had only made scientific approach to management.
2. According to Scientific Mangement, workers are forced to work hard to produce maximum output. At the same time, this concept of management fails to consider the physical and mental well-being of workers.

3. He laid much emphasis on production mangement. But, he does not give any weightage to financial management, sales management, management accounting and the like.
4. Tools and equipments, and materials are supplied to each worker. The foreman issues detailed instructions regarding the performance of the job and methods of performing them. Under such circumstances, the workers do not have any chance to show their ability and find new improved ways to perform the same job effectively.
5. According to him, maximum productivity is acheived only through employing first class workers. In practice, all the workers cannot be expected to be excellent.
6. Worker's efficiency was improved through adoption of standard techiniques and tools. Improving workers efficiency results in the increase of production. Increase in production per worker necessitate retrenchment of old workers or ban on new recruitment.
7. Increase in production is possible in Scientific Management. But, the wages of workers are not increased in direct proportion to increased production.
8. Conducive working conditions are provided to increase workers' efficiency. The standards regarding output, wages and working conditions are fixed. Increasing the efficiency of workers results in increasing the wages, whereas the importance and the role of the trade union is reduced to some extent.
9. It was argued that the time study, motion study, fatigue study, standardization of wage rates etc. were not scientifically measured.
10. The introduction of Scientific Management is an expensive one. Standardization of tools and equipments and working conditions involves heavy expenditure. The wages of workers have to be increased to reward efficient performance. Taylor has separated planning function from the executive function. Hence, it is necessary to appoint separate staff members for the planning function and executive function. This will increase the administrative expenditure of the management.
11. Wages are paid according to piece-rate system under Scientific Management. This system benefits the experienced and efficient workers. New workers and inefficient workers do not derive any benefits from this system. This creates a sense of insecurity of job in the minds of workers in general.
12. The introduction of Scientific Management disturbs the smooth functioning of the organisation. The Scientific Management cannot be introduced within a day. It requires lot of time, and introduced only after standardizing tools and equipments and altering the working conditions.
13. The principle of division of work is adopted in Scientific Management. Each worker is to do a portion of work of an entire process. The worker does not know how his work contributes to the manufacture of the final product.
14. Workers are treated as irresponsible and unambitious persons under Scientific Management. The workers are working under strict control and supervision, and so any slight change in the methods of production and working environment are opposed by the workers.

In spite of the above cited criticisms from various sections of people, Taylor's Scientific Management was supported by Henry L. Gentt, Carl B. Barth, Frank B. and Lillian M. Gilbreth.

## PETER F. DRUCKER

Peter F. Drucker was born in 1909 in Vienna. He was educated both in Austria and England. He started his career as a newspaper correspondent in 1929. He was also working as an economist for an international bank for some time. Peter F. Drucker became Professor of Management in the New York University in 1950.

Peter F. Drucker had written many books on Management. *'The Practice of Management'* (1954) is the best book of Drucker. His other publications are 'The End of Economic Man, 'The Future of Industrial Man,' 'Concept of the Corporation,' 'The New Society, Amercia's Next Twenty Years,' 'Landmarks of Tomorrow,' 'Managing for Results' (1964), 'The Effective Executive' (1967), 'The Age of Discontinuity' (1969) and 'Management Tasks, Responsibilities and Practices' (1974).

The concept of Management and its objectives were introduced by Peter F. Drucker. According to him, Management is not an exact science or profession. He also criticised Scientific Management and human relations approach.

## CONTRIBUTION OF PETER F. DRUCKER

The main contributions of Peter F. Drucker are summarised below:

**1. Nature of Management:** The basic objective of Management is innovation. The term *innovation* includes the development of new ideas, combination of the old idea with new idea and adoption of ideas from other fields. Management is treated as a discipline and a profession. As a profession, Management gives importance only to results in achievement rather than following the criteria of true profession. As a discipline, Management has separate tools, techniques, approaches and skills.

**2. Functions of management:** Management is the starting point of any institution. Management does not have any functions of its own and existence. The existence and functions of Management are concurrent with the existence and functions of a manager. A manager has to determine the objectives and activities, and is concerned with the direction and controlling of the activities.

**3. Organisation structure:** An effective organisation structure has the following three basic characteristics. They are:

(i) The structure is framed in such a way that it enables smooth performance;

(ii) Containing possible minimum number of managerial levels; and

(iii) Providing a chance to test the ability of young people who are accepting the responsibility.

**4. Centralised control with a structure of decentralisation:** It is similar to our Indian constitution. Central Government has more powers compared to State Governments. According to Drucker, Top management has more powers than various departments. But the decisions regarding the departments have to be taken by both of them. Departments are allowed to take decisions within the limits set up by the top management.

**5. Management by Objectives (MbO):** Drucker introduced the management by objective concept in 1954. Later, it was modified by Schleh and termed as management by results. Method of planning, setting standards, performance appraisal and motivation are the components of Management by Objectives (MbO). Which gives importance to self control rather than control made by others; so, it is necessary to change the organisation itself.

**6. Organisational changes:** Drucker has visualised rapid changes in society due to the rapid technological development. Besides, he realises the impact of such changes on human life. So, he stressed that human beings should develop an attitude to face the changes and consider them indispensable for making the society better. This is done by developing dynamic organisations. Dynamic Organisation is developed only by absorbing the rapid changes.

## FRANK BUNKER GILBRETH
### (1868-1924)

Gilbreth was born in Fairfield, Maine in 1868. He started his career as an apprentice in a brick laying company at the age of 17. He was promoted to the cadre of superintendent in the same company after 10 years. He was married to Lillian Moller. Mrs. Lillian Moller was having thorough knowledge of Management. Both worked as a team and devoted their time to findout the best way of doing a job.

Frank Bunker Gilbreth wrote several books which incorporate his research findings. His books are "Concrete System (1908)", "Bricklaying system", (1909). "Motion Study" (1911), "Primer of Scientific Management" (1912), "Fatigue Study" (1916) and "Motion Study for the Handicapped" (1920). He published research papers also with his wife. They are "What scientific management means to America's Industrial position" (1915), "Graphic control of the exception principle for Executives" (1916), "Process Charts (1921) and Symposium," "Stop-Watch Time Study," An indictment and a Defence (1921).

Frank B. Gilbreth gave importance to time study and motion study just like F.W. Taylor. Taylor was the first person to conduct time study and motion study. F.B. Gilbreth followed him. F.B. Gilbreth was not worried about the time required to do a job was concerned with finding out the best way to do it.

He stressed minimum motions and avoidance of unnecessary motions to discover the best way of doing a job. Gilbreth was of the view that unnecessary motions waste much of the efforts of the workers.

Gilbreth found out 18 basic elements in all work through the analysis of several methods of work. He identified these elements by using flow process charts. He called these elements as "therbligs." It is nothing but the name of Gilbreth spelled backwards with the exception of the last two letters.

These elements were 1. Search 2. Find 3. Select 4. Grasp 5. Position 6. Assemble 7. disassemble 8. Inspect 9. Transport loaded 10. Preposition 11. Release load 12. Rest 13. Wait-unavoidable 14. Avoidable delay 15. Use 16. Plan. These are all essential elements of an activity. Motion Study laid a foundation for job simplification, work standards and for framing incentive wage plans.

New machines and tools are developed in order to findout "one best way." Management tools such as flow process charts, diagrams and merit rating were developed by Gilbreth for employees. He proved that the productivity can be tripled by eliminating the unnecessary motions in bricklaying.

## MRS. LILLIAN MOLLER GILBRETH
### (1878-1972)

Lillian Moller was Gilbreth's wife. They got married in 1904. She was also one of the management experts. She preached the message of her husband after his death. She was a psychologist and had a thorough knowledge of human relations. She got doctorate degree for her work titled, "The psychology of management." Lillian Moller was awarded the degree of "The First Ambassador of Management" in 1960.

Dr. Lillian Moller Gilbreth Wrote many books to preach her management thoughts. They are The Psychology of Management, the Quest of the one Best way. The Home maker and Her job, Normal lives for the Disabled. The foreman and Manpower management and management in the Home. She wrote a number of articles on management and published papers also. She and her husband recognised the human factor which is very essential in management. According to Edwin H. Schell, " he greatest event of our time in the field of scientific management was the professional teaming up of the Gilbreths, in one of the strangest combination of complementary talents that we shall ever witness."

## MAX WEBER (1864-1920)

Max Weber was a German social scientist. He wanted to frame a rigid form of organisation. His proposed form of organisation is very similar to the form of organisation proposed by Henry Fayol. Max weber framed rigid rules to eliminate managerial inconsistencies which lead to ineffectiveness. An efficient form of organisation cannot be founded if managerial inconsistencies exist. So, he emphasised the strict adherence of rules and regulation in an organisation. These would make an efficient form of organisation. This type of organisation can be termed as "Bureaucracy." This is the oldest form of organisation. Bureaucracy is based on the principles of logic, order and legitimate authority.

## BUREAUCRACY

Max Weber analysed the various points before finalising an ideal form of organisation. Maximum benefits can be derived from a form of organisation. In this direction, Bureaucratic organisation offers a lot of benefits to the public.

## CHARACTERISTICS OR FEATURES

The basic characteristics or features of Bureaucratic organi-sation are discussed below:

**1. Functional Specialisation:** A work is to be divided into various parts by adopting the principle of division of labour. Each part of work is assigned to a separate person who is specialised in that type of work. Each person performs his work in a pre-determined manner. In this way a high degree of functional specialisation is obtained.

**2. Hierarchy of Authority:** A sub-ordinate is under the control and supervision of one of the superior authorities. A subordinate is responsible to his superior for his own decisions and actions. A clearly defined hierarchy of authority is needed to give commands for proper discharge of duties at various levels. Each superior has control over his subordinates with a right for making a report to higher authorities in a specified manner if needed.

**3. Rules and Regulations:** Well defined rules and regulations are laid down to govern the work behaviour of employees. The rules and regulations are framed to ensure consistency in the performance of work. A special training is provided to impart knowledge of rules and procedures.

**4. Rights and Duties:** Each and every employee can understand his rights and the duties to be performed. The procedure is to be taken into account while performing the work. Procedures are laid down for orderly performance of work.

**5. Technical Competence:** Qualification is prescribed for each and every job/position. Selection and promotion is followed on the basis of technical competence possessed by the candidates.

**6. Fixation of Procedure:** A procedure is fixed or framed by considering situations or work. Each procedure must be time-tested and adoptable by any person.

**7. Record-Keeping:** Every decision and action is taken only after writing in number of documents. Both draft form and original documents are preserved for future reference.

**8. Impersonal Relations:** Rewards should be given on the basis of efficiency. Family relationships or any other relationships should not influence presentation of awards. Personal preferences, emotions and prejudices should not influence the functioning of an organisation. This type of unbiased approach, certainly, will ensure maximum efficiency.

Max Weber said that bureaucracy is the best form of organisation and suitable for any nature of business because it crates scope for the proper channalisation of human energy and mechanical energy. Under bureaucracy, the organisation becomes the most perfect. The degree of bureaucratisation is higher in government departments and in army than in private business and social organisations (non-profit organisation i.e. voluntary organisation). Weber wants to improve the performance of the organisation gradually by following bureaucracy.

## ADVANTAGES OF BUREAUCRACY

Bureaucratic form of organisation gives certain benefits or advantages to the management. They are briefly discussed below.

**1. Specialisation:** Specialisation is achieved by assigning a specific task to each and very person

**2. Employee Behaviour:** Under bureaucracy, policies, rules and regulations are well framed and they could be applied to any type of company. It ensures consistent employee behaviour. The behaviour and reactions of employee are easily predictable. It facilitates the management to implement any project.

**3. Structure:** The structure or form of bureaucracy is created by fixing the duties and responsibilities. Besides, it specifies smooth relationships among employees. The fixed structure facilitates the easy functioning of the organisation.

**4. No Conflict:** Duties and responsibilities of each employee are clearly defined and explained. It avoids the overlapping or conflicting of job duties.

**5. Advance Decision:** A criteria is fixed to take a decision in routine matters. So, the decision maker can take a decision well in advance.

**6. Optimum Utilisation of Human Resources:** Hiring, selection and promotion are based on the technical competence possessed by the candidate i.e. purely on merit and expertise. This ensures the correct matching of the right worker with the right job. It helps the management to utilise the available human resources to the maximum.

**7. Democracy:** Under bureaucracy, no employee enjoys any privilege. All employees are treated equal. This makes the organisation more democratic.

**8. Perpectual Succession:** The job or position is emphasized rather than the person. No rules and regulations are relaxed for any employee. At the same time, no new rules and regulation are imposed on any employee. The organisation will continue evenafter the individual leaves the organisation.

## DISADVANTAGES OF BUREAUCRACY

A coin has two sides. So, bureaucracy has disadvantages or limitations also. The disadvantages or limitations of bureaucracy are given below.

**1. Rigidity:** Rules and regulations are very rigid and inflexible under bureaucracy. The initiative and creativity of employees are discouraged with rigid compliance of rules and regulations. There is a resistance to change on the part of employees also. The reason is that bureaucracy provides a scope to employees to shink responsibility for failures.

**2. Red Tapism:** There is too much red tapism and paper work. Every decision is taken after having detailed discussion with many persons. These discussions are recorded in a number of documents. These documents cannot be cancelled after having been taken. Bureaucracy has a lot of paperwork.

**3. Displacement of Goal:** An organisation has been divided into various units i.e. sub-units. The objective of sub-unit is also framed by the top management. A person who is incharge of a sub-unit may try to achieve its objective relecting the overall objectives of the organisation. In such a case, the management finds it very difficult to achieve the goals of the organisation.

**4. Impersonal Nature of Work:** Service with devotion is not expected from the employees. It does not faster in them a sense of belongingness. The employees do not care about the well being of the organisation. This is because of impersonal nature of work.

**5. Failure of Co-Operation and Co-Ordination:** Organisational rules and regulations are given priority over situation. Jobs are performed according to norms and procedures. It hampers the free flow of work. So, this restricts the management from getting the mutual co-operation and co-ordination.

**6. No Mutual Understanding:** Personal feelings, views, needs and opinions are not given any importance or consideration under bureaucracy. Contractual obligations are given much importance over human relations. This results non-existence of mutual understanding.

**7. Mechanical Treatment:** Initiative and creative thinking of an employee are not recognised. Employees are treated like machine and not like individuals.

**8. Empire Building:** Every superior tries to increase the number of his subordinates. The reason is that the maximum number of subordinates is considered a symbol of power and prestige. In other words, a person wants to have a number of followers while walking on a road. It is a symbol of prestige i.e. empire building.

## MARY PARKER FOLLETT
## (1868 - 1933)

Mary Parker Follett was born in 1868 in Boston, USA. She studied political Economy, Political Science, Law and Philosophy. She got degree from Cambridge College. She is considered to be a pioneer of management thought in the field of "Human Relations." She gave importance to the professional nature of management. She believed that psychology plays an important role in human activity. So, her writings mainly dealt with the application of psychology in management. She had no personal direct experience in managing a business. However, she could develop deep insights into the problems of managing a business. She had used pscyhology to solve the problems in managing a business. She considered the human character at various levels of management. Mary Parker Follett studied the character at worker's level, supervisory level and manager's level. She had no link with Hawthrone studies. But, the findings of Hawthorne Studies resembled the principles of Mary Parker Follett.

Mary Parker Follett wrote books to ventilate her views on management principles. Her major books are: The Speaker of the use of Representatives (1909), The New State (1920), Creative Experience (1924), Business Management as a profession (1927), Dynamic Administration and Freedom and Co-ordination. She published many papers on management. These papers have been collected, edited and published in book form by management experts. They are Metcass and Urwick. The collected papers of Mary Parker Follett express her views on Dynamic Administration and Freedom and Co-ordination.

Follett has expressed her views on different aspects of management. They are briefly explained below.

**1. Conflict:** According to Follett, a conflict may be removed through three ways (i.e.) domination, compromise and integration.

Follett has rejected domination and compromise ways of removing conflict. The reason is that domination creates a feeling of compulsion. Compromise leads to surrender of one person to another person. So, she was in favour of integration. Under integration, the wishes of both parties are integrated. In this way, both the parties would be satisfied without sacrificing their desires.

**2. Authority:** Authority is the root of all evils. Sub ordination of one person to another creates anger and increases human emotion. So, she viewed that authority should be depersonalised and introduced a concept i.e. "authority of function." Follett suggested that authority and responsibility should go equally with function. The employer and employee relationship is based on Co-operation rather than on status i.e. authority. A smooth employer and employee relationship is the foundation of good industrial organisation. It is possible through the substitution of power over the employees by power with the employees.

**3. Group:** A group is something more than a mere aggregation of individuals. The members of a group act towards each other and there is an overall impact of the group on individual members.

**4. Participation:** According to Follett, participation rests on understanding and co-ordination. She presented a paper titled, "The psychology of consent and participation" in 1927. She was of the view that the management should know the techniques of motivation of the individuals and the group. She lays importance on the clear understanding of human behaviour and the need of establishing co-ordination among human efforts and objectives of the organisation also.

**5. Integration:** According to Follett, the integration of interest is not only necessary within the organisation but also essential for the integration of the interests of the workers, investors and consumers.

**6. Leadership:** Follett was of the view that leaders are not only born but they could be made also through proper training in human behaviour. She did not believe in dominating leadership. Follett believed that, "the leader guides the group and at the same time is himself guided by the group, is always a part of the group. The power of leadership is the power of integrating. He stimulates what is best in men; he unifies and concentrates what we feel only groupingly and scateringly. He is a leader who gives form to inchoate energy in every man. The person who influences most is not he who does great deeds, but he who makes me feel that I can do great deeds."

**7. Co-Ordination:** Mary Parker Follett is well-known for her four principles of co-ordination. These principles of co-ordination provide a basis for good management. These principles are given below:

A. Co-ordination by direct contact by the responsible people concerned.

B. Co-ordination in the early stages of planning and policy making.

C. Co-ordination as a reciprocal relation of all factors in a situation and.

D. Co-ordination as a Continuous process.

The concepts and principles of Follett are well supported by the practical events. She believed that the principles of management can be taught in a simple way with illustration by practical events. So, her works are appreciated by many management experts. According to Urwick, "Mary Parker Follett not only evolved principles of human association and organisation especially in terms of industry, but also convinced large number of businessmen of the practically of these principles in dealing with their current problems."

## HENRY L. GANTT
## (1861-1919)

Henry L. Gantt was born in Calbert country Merrilane in the U.S.A. on 20th May 1861. He obtained Mechanical Engineering degree from Strevonce Institute of Technology in 1884 and joined as an engineer at Midvale Steel Company. Gantt was also one of the pioneers in the scientific management since he was an associate of F.W. Taylor. He experimented the principles of scientific management by purchasing and managing a big farm. Henry L. Gantt introduced "Gantt Task and Bonus Plan" and the Gantt Chart. Gantt wrote several books. They are Works, Wages and Profits (1910), Industrial Leadership (1916) and Organising for work (1919). He published several papers. They are A Bonus system of Rewarding Labour (1902), A Graphical Daily Balance of manufacture (1903), Training workmen in Habits of Industry and Co-operation (1908), The Relations between production and cost (1915) and Efficiency and Bureaucracy (1918).

Gantt understood the importance of trade union and introduced a new incentive wage plan i.e. Gantt Task and Bonus plan. Under this plan, proper reward is given to those who reach a high level of production.

Remuneration is calculated under this system as under

Output below standard — Time rate wages

Output at standard — Bonus of 20% on time rate

Output above standard — High piece rate on whole output

This system is an improvement of Taylor's Differential system of wage payment.

Gantt was the founder of a new movements known as "the new machine." It avoids the exercise of power and advocated harmonious relationship between the employers and the employees. Justice and human behaviour are the basis of this movement. Gantt believed that justice and human behaviour were important elements in industrial relations. Gantt distinguished between man and machine.

Gantt is popularly known by his chart i.e. Gantt chart. Gantt chart referred to the process of work. So, Gantt called this chart progress chart. Gantt's chart shows the fact of actual performance of a work against the time required to complete the job. Now, Gantt chart's is regarded as the best tool of production control. The U.S.A. used this chart in the factories manufacturing arms and in shipping industry during World War I. Undivided Soviet Union had also used Gantt chart in implementing its plan for development Gantt chart was a forerunner of PERT (Programme Evaluation and Review Technique). It facilitates the manager to compare the actual work with the planned one and carry on continuous preplanning of production. Gantt chart is also known as "Daily Balance Sheet Chart."

Gantt considered the psychological and social needs of workers. Gantt favoured the pursuance of service motive in a company. So, he had emphasised that individual, the firm, the industry and the government should work with service motive. Fred J. Miller was a friend of Gantt. Fred J. Miller was the manager of Remington Rand Typewriters Company where Gantt was appointed as adviser for eight years in 1910. According to Fred J. Miller, "Gantt gave major attention to man who was doing it... thus he perceived the weight of the human element in productivity and approached the concept of motivation as we understand it today."

## GEORGE ELTON MAYO
## (1880 - 1949)

The human civilization had entered the machine age after industrial revolution. Maximum output is emphasized during the machine age. Nobody considers human relations i.e. the relationship between employers and the employees to be significant. They lead to exploitation of workers and they do not care to fulfil the psychological needs of workers. The productivity is affected by the desires, attitudes and feelings of the workers. George Elton Mayo was the first person to look into the matter of human relations emphasizing the importance of desires, attitudes and feeling of the workers.

Hawthrone Experiments get credit for the change in the outlook of the management towards workers. Hawthorne Experiments were conducted by George Elton Mayo and his colleagues. Hawthrone Experiments are an important landmark in the history of the Human Relations Movement.

Elton Mayo was born in 1880 in Adelaide in Australia. He got his degree from Adelaide University. Elton Mayo worked as a teacher initially. Then, he was advised to study psychology. He had become a lecturer at the University of Queensland after studying psychology.

Elton Mayo went to the United States of America in 1922. In the U.S.A., he joined as a researcher the Wharton Business School in the University of Pennsylvania. Later, Elton Mayo was selected in the Graduate School of Business at Harvard University in 1926. He was a Professor of Industrial Research at Harvard University. He retired in 1947 and died in 1949.

Elton Mayo was regarded as the founder and father of modern sociological and psychological industrial research. He has published many books and papers. Democracy and Freedom (1919), The Human Problems of an Industrial Civilization (1933), The Social Problems of an Industrial Civilization (1945) and Management and the worker (1949) are the important books of Elton Mayo. What is monotony? (1929), Changing methods in Industry (1930), Frightened people (1939), The Descent into chaos (1941) and Supervision and what it means (1945) are the important papers of Elton Mayo.

## HAWTHORNE EXPERIMENTS

Hawthorne experiments were conducted at the Hawthrone Plant of the Western Electric Company in Chicago from 1924-1932. These experiments were conducted by Prof. Elton Mayo, F.J. Roethlisberger Whitehead, Dickson and their colleagues. The results of these experiments have been published into six volumes. They are the Human Problems of Industrial Civilization, The Social Problems of an Industrial Civilization, The Industrial worker, leadership in a Free Society, Management and worker and Management and morale.

The Hawthorne plant was a manufacturing telephone system bell. Nearly 30,000 employees worked during this experiment period. The objective of the experiment was to find out the behaviour and attitudes of employees under better working conditions. The benefits of pension and medical allowance were available to the employees. Besides, the management arranged recreational facilities. Even though, the employees derived job satisfaction. The productivity of the employees was not up to the expectations. So, in 1924, the management requested National Academy of Sciences to investigate the reasons for dissatisfaction of employees and decrease in productivity. On this basis, Prof. Elton Mayo and his team conducted researches in four phases.

They are

1. Illumination Experiments. (1924 — 27)
2. Relay Assembly Test Room Experiment. (1927 — 28)
3. Mass Interviewing Programme. (1928 — 30)
4. Bank Wiring Observation Room Experiments. (1931 — 32)

**1. Illumination Experiments:** This research was conducted to determine the effects of changes in lighting on productivity. The basic assumption of this research was that high lighting leads to productivity. This experiment was conducted for two and a half years.

Under this experiment, two groups were formed. The first group was termed as experimental group and the second group was termed as control group. In the case of experimental group, variations in lighting were made periodically and the results were observed and recorded. In the case of control group, there is no change in the lighting and the researchers were required to work under constant lighting system up to the end of the experiment. Interestingly, it was observed that the output of both groups increased steadily.

This experiment revealed that there is no relationship between lighting and productivity. The production decreased in two groups whenever the lighting fall below the normal level. The production is not affected in any way in the experimental group when the light is decreased upto the level of moon light. It means that the improved working conditions do not result in the increased productivity. As per this experiment, it is known that informal social relations among the group members is the reason for increased productivity.

**2. Relay Assembly Test Room Experiments:** Relay assembly test room experiments were conducted to determine the effect of changes in working conditions and productivity. These experiments had been conducted in three phases i.e. First Relay Assembly Test, Second Relay Assembly Group and The Mica Splitting Group.

Under this experiment, a group was formed. This group consisted of six girls. The girls were chosen on the basis of their past performance. The girls were placed in a separate test room. An observer was associated with the girls to supervise their work. The girls were told to work in natural way and allowed to comment freely about changes in the working conditions. The changes were made with durations ranging from four to twelve weeks. Whenever a change was introduced, the girls were allowed to express their views and opinions. At times, the girls were allowed to take decisions themselves. Periodical training was conducted for the girls.

Groups bonus incentive scheme was the first change made under this experiment. The productivity increased to some extent as compared to the previous one.

The changes in the variation of rests was the second one. There are two five minutes rests - one is in the morning and the another one is in the evening. Then, five minutes was increased to ten minutes. The productivity increased.

Free snacks and coffee or soup were provided in the rest time of two ten minutes duration. This was the third change. The productivity was increased at this stage.

Now, free snacks and coffee or soup were withdrawn but the number of rest period was increased into four each with five minutes duration. The productivity decreased slightly. It was found that the decreased productivity was due to frequent rest intervals and not because of withdrawing free snacks and coffee or soup. The group has complained that frequent rest intervals affect smooth flow of the work. So, the number of rests intervals was reduced to two of ten minutes duration each and provided coffee or soup in the morning and snacks in the evening. The productivity increased by as much as 30 per cent.

The introduction of changes in working hours and workday is the fourth stage. Saturday work will be eliminated and half an hour will be cut in the working hours. It was found that the productivity increased.

At this stage, the researcher decided to withdraw all benefits and facilities offered to the group girls, i.e., rest and other benefits. This is the fifth and last stage of Relay Assembly Test Room Experiments. It was found that, interestingly, productivity increased further instead of going down.

As and when the change was introduced, it was found that absenteeism decreased; the morale increased among the group girls and the needed supervision lessened. Since, the group girls were allowed to work freely, they developed a sense of responsibility and self-discipline. A close and friendly relationship prevailed between the supervisor and the group girls.

Thus five changes were introduced in the working conditions over a period of two years. But, the method of payment was not changed. Morale and productivity were maintained, even though the improvements or changes in working conditions were withdrawn. The research implied that productivity increased not because of improved working conditions, i.e., positive changes in physical factors but because of socio-psychological factors such as the feeling of being important, recognition, attention, complete communication, participation, small size of the informal cohesive work group and non-directive supervision. Therefore, Elton Mayo concluded that the work satisfaction depends to a large extent on the informal social pattern of the work group. Where norms of co-operativeness and high output are established the feeling of importance and physical conditions have little impact.

**3. Mass Interviewing Programme:** This interview programme was conducted to determine employees attitudes towards company, supervision, insurance plans, promotions and wages. Nearly 20,000 employees were interviewed, many of whom were interviewed more than once. This interview programme was started on September 1928 and ended on February 1929.

Initially, the interviews were more or less structured. Only direct questions were asked by the researchers. So, the researchers were not able to find the grass root of the problem. Hence, the interview method was changed into non-directive interview or unstructured interview. Under the non-directive interview method, the interviewer was asked to listen to instead of talking, arguing or advising. Besides, the employees were asked to discuss freely those issues which are relevant to the topics of their own choice. Here, the term employees includes supervisors also. So some interview were conducted for supervisors also.

The interview programme brought to the lime light many valuable insights about the employees attitudes to the company. Some of the major findings are given below:

1. Supervisors knew what was expected of them by the workers working under their control.
2. Male workers were more economically oriented than the female workers.
3. A complaint of a worker is a symptom of personal disturbance in the working place.
4. Many problems of worker management co-operation were the result of emotional attitudes of workers rather than of objective difficulties in the situations.
5. A satisfaction or dissatisfaction of an employee comes from his social status and expected social rewards.
6. The personal situation of the worker is arising out of mode of arrangement of his sentiments, desires and interests.
7. The position or status of a worker in a company gives a basis to the events, objects and features of his hours of work and his wages.
8. A morale booster for the workers has been developed by the process of paying attention to the views by the management.
9. A social demand for a worker is influenced by gaining experience both inside and outside the working place.
10. The individual behaviour was being influenced by group behaviour.

According to Mayo, "the workers were activated by a logic of sentiment but the Management is concerned with logic of cost and efficiency." Thus, a conflict between the workers and the management becomes inevitable.

**4. Bank Wiring Observation Room Experiments:** This experiment was conducted between 1931 and May 1932. A group has been formed to conduct this experiment. This group consisted of fourteen male workers. Out of these fourteen male workers, nine were wiremen, three were soldier men and two were inspectors.

The main aim of this experiment was to analyse how a group could influence a worker to restrict his output even in the face of attractive incentive schemes for larger output. Hourly rate of wages was fixed on the basis of average output of each worker and a group bonus scheme was announced. Group Bonus was to be determined on the basis of average group output. It was assumed that workers would produce more and more in order to get maximum group bonus. Besides, the workers could help each other to produce more.

The company had not improved the working conditions for this experiment and the company was not ready to analyse cause - effect relationships. But, a general observation was made to know about an individual behaviour and the impact of group behaviour on the individual behaviour.

Under this experiment, workers have decided their target by themselves. The company target was more than the target fixed by the workers. However, the workers have failed to achieve the target due to the following reasons.

**1. Unemployment Problem:** Workers feel that if they produce more, a few workers among them would be put out of employment.

**2. Unduly High Standard:** Most of the workers were of the view that if they had reached the standard level of production, the management would raise the standard level of production still more unscrupulously.

**3. Protection of Slow Workers:** The workers were friendly on the job as well as off the job. They told that the fellow workers have responsibility which required them to remain in the job. So, the fast workers protected the slow workers by slowing down their production. If they did not do so, slow workers were likely to be retrenched.

**4. Satisfaction of Management:** Workers were confident of the management accepting lower production. In otherwords, management seemed to accept the lower production rate and no one was being punished for lower production.

Bank wiring observation room experiments helped to arrive at the following conclusions.

1. An informal relationship is responsible for deciding the human behaviour.
2. The counselling was helpful in resolving management-employee conflicts.
3. The existence of informal organisation is quite common in all organisations.
4. The group had fixed standard output of their own only because of social pressure.
5. The output could not increase despite group incentive scheme as a result of existence of social pressure.

## FINDINGS OF HAWTHORNE EXPERIMENTS

Hawthrone experiments have opened new vistas in human behaviour. Human relations are very important to motivate workers in order to develop teamspirit in an organisation. Teamspirit is essential to achieve organisational goals. Hawthorne experiments have identified the factors which are responsible for motivating workers at the work place.

The following are the major findings and conclusions of the Hawthrone experiments.

**1. Social Factors:** Hawthorne experiments proved that social factors are responsible for deciding the level of output. A business organisation is a social group basically. According to Elton Mayo, "A business organisation is a social system, a system rituals and a mixture of logical, non-logical and illogical behaviour." The socio-psychological characteristics of the workers determine the output levels and efficiency. Financial incentives may play a limited role in motivating the workers. But, non-financial incentives may affect the behaviour or workers significantly and their productivity.

**2. Group Influence:** Workers create groups which are different from official group. These groups are formed to overcome the shortcomings of formal relationships. Such created group determines the norms of members behaviour. If a worker is not ready to accept a particular norm of group behaviour, he tries to change his group. The reason is that any deviation from the group norm will make him unacceptable to the group. So, the management cannot deal with the worker independently. The reason is that group behaviour can influence the individual behaviour.

**3. Production Level:** The production level is determined by social norms but not by physiological capacities. In other words, there is no direct relationship between production level and working conditions. For example, during experiments, the production was not affected when lighting was decreased upto moonlight. Production level was decreased only when the workers could not see things properly.

**4. Motivation:** Workers are not merely motivated by money. For example, during experiments, workers did not improve their production eventhough the management announced group bonus scheme.

**5. Conflicts:** There may be conflicts between management and workers' group. Here, workers group refers to the group created by workers informally. The conflict arises since the objective of management differ from the objectives of workers' group. Conflict may also arise because of maladjustment of workers with management.

**6. Leadership:** Leadership is important for directing group behaviour. A superior is accepted as a leader if his style is in accordance with human relations approach. It was concluded from the bank wiring experiments that the inspectors i.e. superiors could not exert pressure on the work group about the production. The reason is that the superior was under considerable pressure to accept the group. The superior is accepted as a leader only because of his identification with group of objectives.

**7. Cordial Relationship:** The workers preferred to maintain amicable relations with their co-workers rather than earn more money. It was ascertained that the efficient workers were not ready to increase the group output to get more group bonus. The efficient workers fear that increased output would lead to loss of employment to the inefficient workers. No worker wishes to be divested of the sympathy of his co-workers. So, they fixed low level of production.

**8. Behaviour of Workers:** Workers are not as individuals but as members of a group. The informal groups have their own norms and beliefs. A leader of a group has an over influence on the attitudes behaviour and performance of individual workers.

**9. Supervision:** The supervisory climate is also one of the factor which determines the rate of output. The friendliness and genuineness of the supervisor affects the productivity. Productivity was not affected in Hawthrone Experiments only because of the existence of friendly relationship between the supervisor and the workers.

**10. Communication:** The experiments show that communication is an important aspect of an organisation. Workers can explain their views and feelings relating to a particular action. Participation of workers is possible in decision-making process. The problems faced by the workers can be easily identified and they can be easily solved. These things are possible only through proper communication. Communication helps the management and workers to have better mutual understanding.

**11. Reaction of Workers:** Complaints and criticism by workers are symptoms of deeper satisfaction.

## CRITICISM OF HAWTHRONE EXPERIMENTS

The findings of the Hawthrone experiments have been criticised in many ways. Some of the criticisms are listed below:

**1. Derecognization:** The Hawthrone researchers did not give recognization to the forces which are responsible for productivity in work place. The forces of class consciousness were not recognized by the researchers.

**2. Pro-management Bias:** Elton Mayo has concluded that management is always logical whereas workers are largely driven by emotions. This is not true always. There are number of workers available to work whole heartly in practice without giving any place to sentiments.

**3. No Scientific Enquiry:** Hawthorne experiments were not conducted scientifically. There is no strong reason for selecting a work for experiment. The workers were not selected scientifically. The Western Electric Company has all facilities to work efficiently. But, the company requested the researchers to conduct only elementary researches.

**4. Clinical Bias:** Howthorne experiments were conducted in such a way that a research is carried on in a clinic. So, the findings did not have practical value.

**5. Lack of Universal Application:** The research was conducted in The Western Electric Company which is not the representation of an industry. It is also said that the workers selected for the research did not constitute a representative sample of the industrial workers of America. As such, the findings are not applicable universally.

**6. Overlooking Social Factors:** Elton Mayo omitted detailed study of the impact of social factors on workers' behaviour and total work situation within an organisation.

**7. Limited Scope of Research:** Hawthorne experiments have not taken into account the labour laws and trade union activities. Both labour laws and trade union activities could play a vital role in shaping the attitudes of the workers.

**8. Treatment of Workers:** Hawthorne experiments look upon the worker as a means to an end and not an end in himself. Workers should accept the goals of management. If not, the workers are convinced to accept the goals of management.

**9. Undue Importance to Observation:** Elton Mayo gave undue importance to observation and collection of facts. Valid results have not been arrived at out of observation. Empirical research alone gives valid results.

**10. Doubtful Validity:** Nearly 30,000 workers were employed during Hawthorne Experiments' period. But, only six girls were selected for Relay Assembly Test Room Experiments. The reactions of small groups can hardly be taken as valid. So, the conclusions cannot be generalised.

**11. Undue Importance to Worker Satisfaction:** Elton Mayo has assumed that a satisfied worker would be productive in the same manner as a contented cow would yield more milk. During experiments, researchers gave much importance to workers satisfaction by providing first class working conditions. But the findings were different. There is no link between working conditions and productivity.

**12. Highlighting only Known Facts:** The findings of Hawthorne experiments were not new but were all know long ago. Elton Mayo did not discover any new point regarding the importance of groups in social life.

### Evaluation

In spite of these criticisms, Hawthorne experiment proved to be a landmark in the evolution of human relations. The research made a significant contribution towards human interest and the need of management to consider human interest. In other words, no management can succeed without considering human interest. Several new concepts of industrial psychology, individual sociology. Social psychology and group dynamics were developed with the help of Hawthrone experiments.

## MODEL QUESTIONS

1. What is the contribution of Peter F. Drucker to Management?.
2. Enumerate the contributions of Henry Fayol for Management Thought.
3. Write short notes on Peter F. Drucker.
4. Write short notes on F.W. Taylor.
5. What are the contributions of Henry Fayol towards Management?
6. Distinguish between Scientific Management and Human Relations Schools.
7. Discuss Principles, Nature and Role of Scientific Management.
8. Enumerate Fayol's Principles of Management.
9. Describe the factors responsible for slow development of Management Thought.
10. Briefly examine the contributions of F.W. Taylor.
11. Explain the Management Thought of Peter F. Drucker.
12. Briefly discuss the main elements of Taylor's Scientific Management.
13. Give a brief account of the evolution of Management Thought from the early times to modern.
14. Discuss the contribution made by Henry Fayol to Management Thought.
15. How is Henry L. Gantt responsible for many contributions to management thought?
16. Discuss how Follet is responsible for many contributions to management thought.
17. Explain the contributions made by Elton Mayo to Managment Thought.

# CHAPTER 3

# APPROACHES OF MANAGEMENT

## APPROACHES OF MANAGEMENT

### INTRODUCTION

Management thought was developed due to the contributions of many intellectuals who have different background. These contributions have not been suitably and adequately integrated to give a unified theory of management. Hence, various approaches for management analysis have been developed over the passage of time. The management techniques were developed from the stage of human beings started living and working together in groups. The wonders of the world (Pyramids of Egypt, the Chinese wall etc) could not be possible without the application of management techniques.

There are many approaches in management thought. Each approach tries to explain the nature and content of management separately and has different beliefs and views. Some of the approaches are closely related with others and others have only little relationship among them.

No one can clearly count the number of approaches in management practices. The reason is that new approaches are developed due to changes in the business environment. In 1961, only six approaches was developed and followed in management thought.

In 1966, Stogdill had classified the approaches into eighteen. But Koonty O'Donnel and Weihrich have identified eleven approaches for studying management. They are empirical or case approach, operational theory approach, interpersonal behaviour approach, managerial role approach, group behaviour approach, contingency or situational approach, co-operative social systems approach, mathematical or management science approach, socio-technical systems approach,

systems approach and decision theory approach. Thus, there is neither uniformity over the number of approaches nor clarity regarding the suggestion of a particular approach. Hence, Koontz describe this situation as "Management theory jungle". Therefore, approaches are selected for brief discussion.

## SYSTEMS APPROACH

Systems approach was developed only after 1950's and has attracted the attention of many management thinkers at present. This approach is based on the empirical data. Initially, Weiner had create a seed for the development of systems approach. Later, Ludwig Von Bertalanffy and Kenneth Boulding evolved the General System Theory (GST). Besides, Lawrence J.Henderson, A.K.Rice, W.G.Scott. E.L.Trist, Deniel Katz, D. S. Pough, Robert, L.Khan, W. Buckley and J.D.Thompson have made significant contributions to the development of the systems approach. They viewed an organisation (main system) as an organ which is composed of interacting and interdependent parts called subsystems.

## MEANING OF A SYSTEM

A system is a set of inter-connected and inter-related elements or components parts which are arranged in order and operate together to achieve certain goals.

One of the most important characteristic of an system is that it is composed of hierarchy of sub-systems. For example, the major system of national economy has various industries as sub-systems.

## DEFINITION OF A SYSTEM

Richard A.Johnson defined, "a system is an organised or complex whole, an assemblage or combination of things or parts forming a complex unitary whole".

Manmohan Prasad defined, "a system is an established arrangement of components which leads to the accomplishment of particular objectives as per plan".

The systems approach is to identify the parts of the organisation and to discover how these parts operate interdependently.

## PARTS OF A SYSTEM

A system has three parts. They are input, process, and output. These parts are briefly explained below.

**1. Input:** A system is operated to achieve the specified objectives. The nature of input is based on the objectives to be achieved. Hence, the inputs may be rawmaterials or informations.

**2. Process:** A mechanical process is carried on to convert the shape or form of raw materials. An information is to be interpreted and analysed in a systematic way to get clear cut idea or conclusion.

**3. Output:** The input of raw materials is available as finished goods in output. The input of information is available as alternatives or conclusions in output.

## KINDS OF SYSTEMS

There are four types of systems. They are discussed below.

**1. A Closed System:** A system is operated without any interaction from the outside environment. The closed system does not require any element from outside to operate. The closed systems approach was represented by principles such as unity of command, span of control and equal authority and responsibility and concentrated on internal relationship and consistency. The closed systems approach ignores the effect of he external environment

**2. An Open System:** The operation of a system is dependent on the outside environment for survival. All organisational systems are depend upon the outside environment for feed back and resources and for disposal of the finished product. The management must analyse the external factors of resource availability, current technological trends, market trends and social changes.

**3. General Systems:** The general systems approach to management has a relation with formal organisation and technical socio-psychological and philosophical concepts.

**4. Specialised System:** The speciliased system includes the areas of organisation structure, job design, computerised information and the like. The systems analysts are required not only by traditional organisations but also by modern organisations due to their actual occupational position.

The basic of system theory is that a manager can not give more importance to any one aspect of the organisation and ignore other aspects of organisation.

## ELEMENTS OF SYSTEMS APPROACH

The main elements of systems approach are as follows.

1. An organisation is a unified and purposeful system. An organisation as a system is consisting of several interconnected, interacting and interdependent parts.

2. The parts and sub-parts of a system have mutual relationship with each other. The nature of mutual relationship may be more, less, direct or indirect. Therefore a change in one part has an impact on other parts according to the nature of relationship.

3. An organisational system has a boundary that determines which parts are internal and which are external.

4. The parts and sub-parts of a system are arranged in an orderly manner. The reason is that systems approach is oriented towards the accomplishment of objectives.

5. A sub-system gets its strength by its association and interaction with other sub-systems. As a result, the contribution of whole organisation is greater than the aggregate of individual contribution of its sub-systems.

6. System transforms inputs into outputs. This transformation has three process. They are inputs, mediator and outputs. This process is essential for the survival of the system. The reason is that there is a restoring the in inputs in this process. Here, the restoring refers to earning profit.

7. The reaction of the outputs environment is known as feedback. Feedback is useful in evaluating and improving the functioning of the system.

The attention is paid towards the overall performance of the system rather than the performance of the sub-systems. The interdependence of the sub-systems is taken into account. According to Fred Luthana, " A system may provide the impetus to unify management theory and the systems approach may succeed where the process approach has failed to lead management out of the theory of jungle". Chester I Barnard was the first person to utilise the systems approach in the field of management.

## FEATURES OF MANAGEMENT AS SYSTEM

Management is regarded as a system, under the systems approach, on account of the possession of the following features.

**1. Social System:** Management is a social system since the management has all the characteristics of social system. To be a social system, the management has many divisions (many sub-systems) which are integrated to constitute an entity.

**2. Open System:** Management has the interaction with the environment. Management takes various resources, allocates and combines these resources to produce desirable outputs which are exported to the environment. Therefore, it is understood that management has no freedom to decide the things on its own. But, at the same time, due weightage has to be given to the environmental factors affecting the management of an organisation.

**3. Adaptive:** Adaptive means continuous adjustment to changing environment for survival. The management has made internal modification of organisational functioning to meet the needs of the changing world. The internal modification is made on the basis of feedback mechanism.

**4. Multidisciplinary:** Management draws and integrates knowledge from various disciplines and schools of thought like economics, psychology, sociology, anthropology, mathematics, statistics and so on. It takes only the relevant aspects from these disciplines and the integration of relevant knowledge from these disciplines.

**5. Dynamic:** Always, management moves towards growth and expansion. For which, there is a need of effectiveness of management. Both, internal processing process and interaction with external environment are determining the effectiveness of management.

**6. Integrated Approach:** Happening of an event is due to many factors. Management tries to identify such factors and reasons. At the end, management tries to integrate the various factors to find out the reasons behind an event.

**7. Probability:** Management has the character of probability. The reason is that the outcome of an action can be predicted accurately to some extent in management. For example, There is a pay cut for an unauthorised absent. If so, nobody absent without prior permission. Hence, the management can make forecast very clearly to a certain degree.

**8. Multivariable:** There is no simple and single cause - effect phenomenon. Generally, an event may be the result of so many variables. These variables themselves are interrelated and interdependent.

**9. Multidimentional:** Management has both macro and micro approach. At macro level, the whole business organisation is taken into consideration for approach. At micro level, part of a business organisation is taken into consideration for approach. Thus, both parts and whole are equally important in managing.

## EVALUATION OF SYSTEMS APPROACH

Systems approach helps in studying the functions of complex organisation and bring out the inter-relationship prevailing among the various functions like planning, organizing, directing and controlling. It highlights inter-dependence between different elements of an organisation as well as between an organisation and its environment. Under this approach, a problem is analysed in relation with other problems. Likewise, no problem is analysed in isolation. Systems approach provides clues to the complex behaviour of people in an organisation.

This approach cannot be easily applied to large and complex organisations. At the same time, there is no tools and techniques provided to the managers. It cannot directly and easily be applied to practical problems. Systems approach is not suitable for small organisations. Looking into these short comings of systems approach, researchers and management experts have tried to modify the systems approach. Hence, situational or contingency approach is emerged.

## CONTINGENCY OR SITUATIONAL APPROACH

Management is facing numerical problems everyday under different situations. Hence, there is a need of solving such problems on the basis of the situations prevailing. If a manager wants to change the behaviour of any part of the organisation, he must try to change the situation influencing it.

The basic theme of the contingency is that there is no single best solution to the problems arised in all situations. So, the situational approach is regarded as latest approach to the existing management executives. During the 1970's contingency theory was developed by J.W. Lorsch and P.R. Lawrence. They say that "contingency approach is an approach where behaviour of one sub-unit is dependent on its environment and relationship to other units or sub-units that have some control over the sequences desired by the sub-unit". According to Tosi and Hammer, "when a sub-system in an organisation behaves in response to another system or subsystem, the response is contingent on environment". Kast and Rosenzweig say that the contingency approach seeks to understand the inter-relationships within and among sub-systems as well as between the organisation and its environment and to define patterns of relationships or configurations of variables. Contingency views are ultimately directed toward suggesting organisation designs and managerial actions most appropriate for specific situations.

In one way, contingency approach is treated as the extention of systems approach. Contingency approach spell out the relationship between the organisation and its environment which is absent in systems approach. It is the responsibility of management to analyse the contingencies or conditions peculiar to each situation and then choose the right approach to deal with it.

Contingency approach requires common sense for application and requires the ability to analyse and diagnose a managerial situation correctly. Besides, the contingency approach requires knowledge and understanding of different principles, techniques and styles of management.

Torn Burns, G.W. Stalker, Joan Wood Ward, James Thampson, Paul Lawrence, Joy Lorsch and Jay Galbraith have made significant contributions to contingency approach.

### Features of Contingency Approach

In the light of the above discussion, the contingency approach has the following features.

1. There is no one best way of doing things. Hence, the managers should prepare strategies, policies and plans according to the situation prevailing.

2. Management action is situational to outside the system or sub - system as the case may be.

3. Managerial policies and practices to be effective, if they adjust to changes in environment.

4. No action can be universal because of specific relationship between organisation and environment. The action varies situation to situation.

5. Contingency approach improves diagnostic skills so as to anticipate and ready for environmental changes.

6. Human relations skill is necessary to managers for accommodate and stabilise change.

7. Contingency approach gives contingency model in designing organisation structure. The contingency model is developing effective information and communication system.

## EVALUATION OF CONTINGENCY APPROACH

The contingency approach discloses the role and performance of manager in an organisation, it exhorts managerial choices to be made in the light of environmental factors. Hence, it alert the managers according to changing situational needs and can stimulate managers to innovate new and better approaches for application.

Contingency approach recognises that managerial functions and principles are useful but should be used with discretion and care to suit the specific situation. This approach has no theoretical base. A manager is expected to know all the alternative course of action before taking an action.

## SYSTEMS APPROACH VS CONTINGENCY APPROACH

| Systems Approach | Contingency Approach |
|---|---|
| 1. It treats all organizations as same and has no unique nature. | It treats each organization as unique |
| 2. The contributors of systems approach are social psychologists | The contributors of contingency approach are sociologists |
| 3. Systems approach is the pioneer to the contingency approach. | Contingency approach has been built ever systems approach. |
| 4. Systems approach may spec-ify situations under which a particular type of organization can function well. | Management action is situational and no situational is predicted accurately. |
| 5. It provides a global theoretical model for understanding organizations. | It provides operational tools and techniques for analyzing and solving problems. |
| 6. Systems approach is vague and unspecific. | Contingency approach is pragmatic, specific and action oriented. |
| 7. The main concepts are input, output process, open system, system boundary, synergy, dynamic equilibrium, entropy and equifinality. | There is no specific concepts. |
| 8. Systems approach emphasizes interactions and inter relationships among systems and subsystems. | Contingency approach emphasizes interrelationships and interdepencies and their influence on organizational design and managerial style. |
| 9. It appears to be neutral and non-committal on the universality of classical principles. | It rejects the universality of principles, no one best way of managing. |
| 10. Systems Approach suggest definite solutions of problems to a specified organization. | Contingency approach suggests probable and flexible approach to problems. |
| 11. It focus the internal environment of an organization. | It focus the external environment of an organization. |

Contingency approach has emerged out of the systems approach. Contingency theorists have accepted the basic tenets of systems approach. Managers should not ignore the importance of taking actions according to the needs of the situations. Hence, the managers should use their highest skills for analysing the situations.

## MODEL QUESTIONS

1. What do you understand by a system? Discuss management as a system bringing out its basic features as such.
2. What is the contingency theory of management? What are its implications and relevance?
3. What is systems approach to management? Explain the salient features of this approach.
4. "Contingency approach to management is a common sense approach" Comment.

# CHAPTER 4

# POLICY, PROCEDURE, METHOD AND RULE

## INTRODUCTION

Each management is taking a number of decisions. These decisions may be for long term purpose or short term purpose. Sometimes, a decision may be taken within the purview of an earlier decision. Likewise, a decision gives guidelines to implement a plan in the days to come. Here, policy, a part of planning, is important in providing guidelines to take a valuable decision.

The term policy is derived from Latin word "Politis" which means polished. A clear cut information is given to take a decision. The decision maker may be self-regulated with the help of policy. In other words, norms are provided by the policy.

## MEANING OF POLICY

Policy is a norm or guideline which is used to take a decision for achieving objectives in consideration of the organizational climate.

According to New Webster Dictionary, policy means the art or manner of governing a nation, the line of conduct which rulers of a nation adopt on a particular question specially with regard to foreign countries, the principle on which any measure or course of action is based.

Policy is a type of standing plan. Policy can guide sub-ordinates in order to execute the work assigned to them. Sub-ordinates can take decisions within the framework of the policy without reference to higher authorities. In this way, a policy is a predetermined course of action established to guide the performance of work towards the realization of accepted objectives.

## DEFINITION OF POLICY

Eduin B. Flippo, "A policy is a man - made rule or predetermined course of action that is established to guide the performance of work towards the organization. It is a type of standing plan that serves to guide subordinates in the execution of their task".

George A. Steiner, John B. Miner and Edmund R. Gray, "Policy is a management's expressed or implied intent to govern action in the achievement of company's aims".

James B. Bom, "Policies are statements of the organization's overall purposes and its objectives in the various areas with which its operations are concerned personnel, finance, production, marketing and so on".

L.M. Prasad, "A Policy is the statement or general understanding which provides guidelines in decision - making to members of an organization in respect to any course of action".

Dale Yoder, "A Policy is a pre-determined and accepted course of thought and action that is defined and established as a guide towards accepted goals and objectives".

According to Newman, Sumner and Warren, a policy may:

(i) Be specific or broad in nature

(ii) Deal with one or many aspects of a problem or situation

(iii) Place wider or narrow limits within which action is to be taken

(iv) Specify the steps to be taken when a decision is to be made.

Therefore, a policy can be defined as follows:

"A policy is a predetermined course of action and thought that are defined and established as a guide to achieve accepted goals and objectives".

## FEATURES OF POLICY

On the basis of the above definitions, the following features are identified.

1. A policy gives guidelines to the employees of the organization for taking a decision
2. A policy restricts the freedom of the employees in an organization. An employee has to take a decision within the purview of the policy.
3. A policy provides and explains an employee as how and what he should do rather than what he is doing.
4. A policy provides some discretion to employees. So, an employee can take a decision by considering the prevailing situation. If not so, policy will become a rule.
5. A policy is framed on the basis of the objectives of the organization.
6. A policy permits the top executives to delegate authority and still retain control of action.
7. A policy is a predetermined course of action.
8. Policies are generally expressed in qualitative, conditional or general way.
9. Policy is framed by all managers in an organization in their respective areas.
10. Policies are the recognized intention of the top management.

## NEED AND IMPORTANCE OF A POLICY

The very purpose of framing a policy is to achieve the overall objectives of an organization. Policy stimulates an employee to take a decision at operating level. A fair treatment of an employee is available. The spontaneous co-operation of employees can be achieved through a policy formulation.

**1. Achieving the objectives:** Policies are used as guidelines to do a work and achieve the overall objectives of an organization. So, policy enables the employees to concentrate and increase their efforts to achieve the objectives.

**2. Clear thinking:** The top executives may be well aware of gaps, contradictions and vagueness in the existing policies. The identified gaps, contradictions and vagueness are to be set right with clear thinking.

**3. Uniformity:** Decisions are taken uniformly by following the guidelines i.e. policy. Line managers are taking a decision keeping in view the personnel policies uniformly in their respective departments. If a person is transfered and another person takes charge of the office, the decisions to be taken by the new staff member are very similar to those of the previous staff due to the predetermined policies of the organization.

**4. No Exploitation:** There is no personal bias while taking a decision. So, there is no possibility of exploitation of employees. Policy minimizes favouritism.

**5. Continuity:** Written policy transmits the heritage of the company from one generation to another. There is continuity in following a policy by more than one generation. The top executives of an organization may retire, die or resign but, the policy adopted by these persons is to be continued to be adopted by their successors.

**6. Delegation of authority:** Policy enables the executives to delegate the authority. Delegation of authority is to be done without consulting the superiors every time.

**7. Stability:** Continuity of a policy promotes stability in the organization. The succeeding employees can understand the bitter experiences and achievements of their predecessors. In this way, stability is to be maintained.

**8. Better control:** Policies specify the relationship between the management and employees and employees inter se. So, there is no possibility of conflict in the implementation of policy of both management and employees. Policies are served as standards or yardsticks. Thus, policies provide better control.

**9. Orientation:** Orientation is given to new employees of an organisation. The policy helps the new entrants to understand the ways of functioning of an organisation.

**10. Efficiency evaluation:** The efficiency of the employees is evaluated in the light of the policies followed by them. Actual performance of the employees is assessed on the basis of the results achieved. The existing policy may be amended or a new policy is to be framed by considering the extent of efficiency shown by the employees.

**11. Training:** Training is needed to both new employees as well as existing employees. Training is classified into two i.e. on the job training and off the job training. Training schedules are framed separately to new employees and existing employees and even separately for on the job training and off the job training.

**12. Self Confidence:** Policy is standard and provides security if a person acts according to it. Policy creates a self-confidence in the minds of the employees who may know where they stand in the organization.

**13. Team Work:** Well structured policies enable the employees to know the overall picture of the organisation and know how their contributions are responsible for the achievement of the organisations's goals. In this way, team work spirit is developed among the employees.

**14. Motivation:** Policy of the organisation guides the workers in achieving the objectives. Policy gives a kind of motivation to workers. If the workers are motivated, the predetermined objectives can be achieved without much

**15. Loyalty:** Participation of employees in policy formulation increases mutual understanding between management and employees. Mutual understanding stimulates the employees to work with loyalty to achieve objectives.

**16. Morale:** A well defined policy helps the employees to have an overall picture of the organisation. Fair treatment and justice are available to employees. These are responsible to build up morale among employees.

**17. Guide to Management:** Policy guides the management about the treatment of employees. This method of treatment avoids personnel problems at the maximum. Management can clearly understand and decide how to get the work done.

**18. Quick Decision:** Carefully defined policy enables the management to take valuable and quick decisions. This system avoids wastage of time and energy.

## SOUND POLICY

A policy is an ornament of an organisation. The prestige of an organisation is based on the policy. Besides, policy provides clearcut directions or proper guidelines for taking managerial decision. Therefore, policies should be developed on a sound basis. If not, the management people will not be able to take quality decisions. A policy can be a sound one on some occasion and unsound on another occasion. Circumstances or situations evaluate a policy as sound or unsound. A sound policy reflects the overall practices of the management and behaviour. A sound policy avoids misninter-pretation and helps the organisation to get early success. A due weightage is given to practical difficulties in the implementation of a policy. The strength of an organisation is taken into account while formulating a policy.

## CHARACTERISTICS OF SOUND POLICY

The major characteristics of a sound policy are briefly explained below:

**1. Relationship with objectives:** There is a close relationship between objectives of an organisation and its policy. Therefore, the policy helps an organisation to achieve the objectives within a short span of time. A sound policy eliminates unnecessary activities and attaches much importance to necessary activities to the achievement of objectives.

**2. Definite and simple:** A policy should be definite and easily understood by any person. Only a clear policy serves as a guide to the management to take a decision.

**3. Realistic approach:** A policy is to be formulated only after careful planning. Since policies are relatively permanent in nature, such formulated policy should solve any problem which will arise in the future. Reality is to be taken into account before formulating a policy.

**4. Evidence:** A policy should be had in written form as far as possible. The reason is that written form will be a basis for future evidence.

**5. Ensure Understanding and Uniformity:** Policy can prevent loss. There is the possibility of ensuring clearcut understanding of a policy. This will ensure the uniformity in the application of policy.

**6. Broad outlines:** A policy can fix the area within which the manager could take a decision. If the policy gives full details it dilutes the initiative and style of the executives. Besides, the full details may be given different interpretation in certain cases.

**7. Consistency:** The same policy is to be followed in every operation of the organisational functions. The reason is that each function is related to other functions of the organisation. If the policy in one function is inconsistent with that of another function, there may be conflict between different function and if may result in inefficiency.

**8. Changes:** Once a policy is formulated, it can be used for long period. At the same time, the policy should be changed at fairly long intervals if there is any need.

**9. Balance:** A sound policy maintains balance between stability and flexibility. On the one hand, a policy is to be followed for long period. It helps the executives to attend to the important matters. On the other hand, the policy can be changed. If not so, policy becomes obsolete. The policy is to be changed according to the situation.

**10. Adequate policies:** There should be an adequate number of policies in an organisation. There must be a specified policy with regard to production, sales, purchase, finance, personnel and the like separately. At the same time, there should not be any duplication of policy.

**11. Communication:** Whenever a policy is formulated, such formulated policy should be communicated properly to the persons concerned. If not so, there is no meaning of formulating such a policy. Therefore, a system should be developed to communicate the policies in an organisation.

**12. Recognition of interest:** A sound policy recognises the interest of all the parties the employer, employees and the general public. In other words, a policy should reflect the interests of all parties.

**13. Practicable:** An organisation is known by the policies it follows. Policy is the image builder in the business world. So, the formulated policy should be logical in every aspect. Only then, the management executives can rely on the policy.

**14. Compromise:** A sound policy compromises with overall policies of the organisation. In this way, the organisational goal is to be achieved.

**15. Flexible:** A formulated policy may have to be changed at regular intervals. The framed policy must be flexible while it is being implemented. The policy should be flexible enough to be adjusted to the circumstances for the time being.

**16. Participation:** A sound policy is formulated only with the active participation of the executives, supervisors and workers at all levels of the trade unions.

**17. Acceptable:** Whatever the policy formulated by the organisation, it should be accepted by everyone. It means the formulated policy has to be welcomed and accepted by all the employees of an organisation.

## FACTORS INFLUENCING POLICY MAKING

There are several factors influencing policy making. Some factors are visible and some factors are invisible. Among those factors, important factors are presented below.

1. Psychology of the owner or businessman.
2. Willingness of the owner or businessman
3. Experience of the owner or businessman
4. Beliefs on the policy.
5. Perception of the owner and top management people.
6. Financial resources.
7. Reaction of employees.
8. Policy of the competitors.
9. Achievements of the competitors.
10. Government regulation and control
11. Business environment.
12. Objectives of the organisation
13. Price
14. Public attitudes and behaviour.
15. Customer and Consumer behaviour

## FORMULATION OF A POLICY

The process of policy formulation involves the following steps.

**1. Identification of area:** Management has to identify the areas of the policy. In other words, areas have to be find out for which the policy is to be formulated. Even the existing policy may be changed in this manner. A management could have clear cut idea only after selecting the area for policy formulation.

**2. Objectives:** Organisational objectives play a vital role in the formulation of a policy. Objectives are foundation for policy formulation. Objectives give clear cut directions to formulate a policy. The reason is that the policy is formulated in order to achieve the objectives.

**3. Analysis of Environment:** A policy reflects the circumstances under which such a policy is formulated. A policy is formulated according to situation. Management tries to achieve objectives under any situation. So, the management should analyze the environment before policy formulation.

**4. Corporate Analysis:** Analysis of environment refers to the analysis of external factors. Corporate analysis refers to the analysis of internal factors. The strength, weaknesses, opportunities and threats of an organisation are taken into account while formulating a policy. This type of analysis gives a clear picture of the functioning of the organisation.

**5. Collection of information:** The next step in the formulation of a policy is the collection of information. An intelligent person may be appointed to collect the information in the case of small organisation. In the case of big organisation or multinational organisation, a committee may be formed and assigned the duty of collecting the information. Information can be collected not only from within the organisation but also from outside the organisation.

**6. Analysing the Information:** Collected information may be analysed to assess the value of information. Proper attention should be paid to the attitudes, aspirations and customs of the employees and the philosophy of top management people should also be considered. Widespread consultation and discussions are held with experts for analysing the information.

**7. Identification of Alternatives:** On the basis of collected information, different alternative policies are developed to achieve the objectives of an organisation. Here the alternative policies are formed with the help of active participation of employees. Active participation of the employees helps the easy implementation of the policy.

**8. Appraisal of Policies:** Appraisal of policies is very important. Feasibility, financial implication, pros and cons of each policy are taken into consideration while appraising a policy. Value of a policy could be correctly assessed only through the process of appraisal of policies.

**9. Selection of a Policy:** Management can select anyone of the policies among the appraised policies which is most suitable to a particular situation. The appraisal process of policies facilitates the management to select or formulate the best policy.

**10. Approval of Policy:** The policy draft should be sent to the top management at the right time for its approval. The top management has to approve the policy only after considering whether a policy represents the objectives of the organisation or not.

**11. Communicating the Policy:** The approved policy should be communicated to the concerned persons. Policy manual has to be prepared or meetings have to be conducted for communicating the policy. Besides, an educational programmer may be conducted to educate the employees as how to apply the new policy.

## TYPES OF POLICIES

An organisation has different kinds of policies. They are briefly discussed below.

**1. Internal Policy:** It is otherwise known originated policy. This type of policy is formulated by the management executives at different levels-top, middle and lower. Internal policy is prepared on the basis of nature of business and scope of the management. If a policy is prepared by top management people, it is applicable to the whole organisation. Likewise, if a policy is prepared by the department manager, it is applicable to the concerned department only.

**2. Appealed Policy:** This type of policy is formulated only on the requests of the subordinates. This policy helps the sub ordinates to handle some situations. If the existing policies do not give any scope to handle extraordinary situations; appealed policy is to be formulated.

**3. External Policy:** It is otherwise known as imposed policy. An outsider of an organisation may be instrumental to the formulation of a policy. For example, if the Government places an order regarding the working conditions of the employees, the organisation is bound to formulate a policy to provide such type of working conditions. In this way, external policy is formulated.

**4. General Policy:** A policy which does not create an impact on the performance of the employees. The policy may represent the philosophy of the top management executives. For example, motivating the employees to do a job in a better way. It is a general policy.

**5. Specific Policy:** A policy is formulated with regard to any specific issue i.e. transfer, promotion, compensation etc. A specific policy must conform to the broad outlines mentioned in the general policies.

**6. Written Policy:** A policy is formulated and intimated in written form. It is a written policy. Here, there is no possibility of any degree of deviation. Everyone should adhere to the written policy.

**7. Implicit Policy:** A policy is inferred from the behavior of the superior. It is an implicit policy. Such policies are more flexible than other policies.

## MERITS OF POLICY

A well formulated policy helps an organisation to be attributed with the following merits. Such merits are briefly discussed below.

**1. Guide to Thinking:** Policy helps the manager to take valid decisions. Thus a policy serves as a guide to think and take a decision.

**2. Uniformity:** Policy ensures uniformity in the treatment of employees throughout the organisation. Policy avoids favoritism and minimises discrimination.

**3. Consistency:** Policy provides a basis to the management executives to take a decision. If a policy is followed for 5 years continuously, there is a similarity between a decision taken in the first year and a decision taken in the fifth year. So, there is a consistency.

**4. Applicability:** A policy is to be formulated only after considering the pros and cons and evaluation. Practical problems regarding the implementation of a policy is also taken into account before formulation of a policy. Such formulated policies are practically applicable.

**5. Continuity:** Well formulated written policies are used by the organisation for more than one generation. Such succeeding generations can derive good experience from implementing the policy. This type of policy which could be followed for long enables to maintain stability in an organisation.

**6. Builds Confidence:** Readymade answers are available in the well formulated policy. So, the management executives can meet the challenges with confidence. Besides, if the management executives strictly adhere to the polices, they need not worry about the results. Such striking fast creates a self confidence in the minds of the management executives.

**7. Security:** Management executives have a sense of security by adhering to the policy. Nobody gets any punishment if an organisation incurs a loss due to the implementation of inadequate or improper policy. As a result, management executives feel a sense of security.

**8. Quick decision:** Manager can take a decision for routine and repetitive issues. Policy prevents the wastage of golden time of top management people. So, the problem can be easily solved by taking a decision very quickly.

**9. Delegation of Authority:** Policy helps the manager regarding the delegation of authority. Subordinates are ready to accept responsibility and assume authority. The reason is that the policy indicates the expectation of sub ordinates.

**10. Control:** Policy is used as standards or yardstick to measure performance of activities. Controlling the functions is very easy to top management. The reason is that the deviation is clearly identified and it enable to exercise the control function.

**11. Orientation and Training:** Policy can be used as orientation and training to new employees. New employees can understand the outlook of the top management through policies. So, policy relieves the top management executives from providing orientation and training to new employees.

**12. Team Work:** A well designed policy gives a clear picture of an organisation. It stimulates the employees to extend their co-operation and it promotes mutual understanding. In this way, team work is easily built up in the organisation.

**13. Loyalty:** There is no possibility of favoritism. Management could maintain fair treatment of all employees at any cost by implementing the policy. This creates loyalty in employees for the organisation.

## DEMERITS OF POLICY

There are some demerits in policy. Those are briefly presented below:

**1. Not applicable to every problem:** A policy can solve anyone of the problems. But, all the problems can not be solved with the help of a single policy. Eventhough, the company has many policies, they may be outdated. The reason is that circumstances are likely to change in the days to come.

**2. No Instant Solution:** Policy is a guideline but not a solution. A solution is to be found out by the management executives. Policy puts constraints on the decision maker. So the decision-maker will be frustrated in finding a solution to every problem.

**3. No value for Human beings :** Human beings are not taken into consideration while formulating a policy. Besides, human beings are not considered important while implementing a policy. So, there is no value for human beings. It minimises the interest of the employees.

**4. Reduce Initiative:** Management executives are expected to tackle the problem within the limits prescribed in the policy. It gives no scope for the innovative thinking of the employee's. So, policy reduces the initiative of the employees automatically.

**5. No substitute for Human Judgment:** The decision of the management executive depends upon his own sense of judgment. There is no parameter to evaluate the sense of judgment. So, the management executives are not in a position to find a substitute for human judgment.

## PROCEDURE

The actual performance of assigned work is completed with the help of procedure. A policy is acting as a guideline. Policy does not offer any way or means by which the objectives of an organisation could be achieved. A well formulated policy is properly implemented with the help of procedure. There is a lacunae between formulation of a policy and its implementation. This lacunae is filled up by procedure. The procedure decides the task to be performed specifically and the persons who will perform the work within a specified time. Procedure lays down the process to be followed and sequences of activities for the work to be done. According to Ernest C.Miller," Policies are general instructions-procedures are specific applications."

A time table can be fixed for starting of a work and completion of a work under procedure. The procedure is designed to achieve the objectives of an organisation and for effective utilisation of available resources economically. Different phases of the work are identified under procedure. These are used to find proper ways or means for completion of a work.

## DEFINITION OF PROCEDURE

George R. Terry has defined a procedure as "a series of related tasks that make up the chronological sequence and the established way of performing the work to be accomplished."

Procedure can be defined as establishing sequence of activities by identifying different phases of the work and completing the work successfully with the help of available resources in order to achieve the objectives of an organisation.

## IMPORTANCE OF PROCEDURE

Procedure is very important in the effective functioning of an organisation. The extent of importance is presented below:

1. Procedure relieves the manager from directing the sub-ordinates. A sub-ordinate can be well-directed by procedure. Procedure specifies the steps to be taken, time and order of performance of a work.

2. Procedure facilitates the management to exercise control function. Management by exception principle is followed here.

3. Procedure gives a readymade solution to solve repetitive problems. It saves time and energy of the management executives.

4. Procedure can be used as a parameter to judge whether a work is done perfectly or not. Procedure serves as a basis for control.

5. Procedure helps the employees to improve their efficiency adhering to the standard.

6. Procedure facilitates orientation of new employees and training of existing and new employees .

7. Procedure can be used to boost/increase the morale of the employees.

8. Procedure ensures consistency and uniformity of action.

9. Procedure speeds up not only clerical work but also any type of work and increases the speed of flow of information.

10. A well designed procedure facilitates proper delegation of authority and fixation of responsibility.

11. Procedure facilitates the co-ordination of function of the top management people.

## ESSENTIALS OF SOUND PROCEDURE

A procedure should be a sound one. If not so, it results in various confusion and involves heavy expenditure with delay in the completion of any work. The following should be taken into account while framing a sound procedure.

1. A procedure is framed on adequate information for a particular situation. No procedure is framed on guesses or wishes of any employee.

2. Procedure must ensure the achievement of objectives through implementing policies of an organisation.

3. Procedure fixes the responsibility of an employee who has been favored with delegation of adequate authority.

4. Procedure is stable for a specified period.

5. Procedure is reviewed at regular intervals to bring in it changes for changed business conditions.

## MERITS OF PROCEDURE

**1. Standard:** Procedure lays down the sequence of activities required in the performance of a work. It specifies the systematic performance of work. In this way, a standard is fixed for better performance.

**2. Better Communication:** A specified procedure is followed for free flow of communication within the organisation. So, all the employees could get every piece of information without any hindrances.

**3. Best Control:** Control function is very easy. A standard is fixed for any work through a proper procedure. So, procedure ensures the best control of the employees.

**4. Co-ordination:** Co-ordination function is performed by top management people. Procedure facilitates top management people to co-ordinate various activities of employees. There is a link between one procedure with another. So, the procedure helps co-ordination of function.

**5. Saves Time and Energy:** Procedure eliminates unnecessary movements of employees and canalizes the flow of work. In this way, procedure saves time and energy of the employees.

**6. Better Utilisation of Resources:** Unnecessary wastages are avoided through a well drafted procedure. The resources of an organisation are properly utilised by the employees.

**7. Consistency:** Today, a procedure is followed in the completion of work in an organisation. The same procedure is followed for completing the same type of work the next day. So, there is a consistency in the adoption of procedure.

## LIMITATIONS OF PROCEDURE

There are some limitations also. The limitations of procedure are presented below:

**1. Avoids Initiative:** Once a procedure is framed it can be retained for many more years. As a result, age old procedures are not useful for current business conditions. The employees are also prohibited to find a new procedure.

**2. Rigidity:** Procedure does not permit the employees even for one degree of variation in the performance of a work. Rigidity has to be adopted if a procedure is framed.

**3. Outdated:** Procedures need to be constantly reviewed and evaluated. The existing procedure can be suitably modified or altered according to the changed business conditions. This type of practices can not be followed in many organisation.

## DIFFERENCES BETWEEN POLICY AND PROCEDURE

The differences between policy and procedure are indicated in the following table.

| *SI.No* | *Policy* | *Procedure* |
|---|---|---|
| 1 | It guides the thinking and decision-making process | It guides the action process |
| 2 | It is derived from the objectives of an organisation | It is derived from the policies of an organisation |
| 3 | It discloses the attitude of management towards certain specific issues | It discloses the ways to be used for handling events systematically |
| 4 | It is formulated by top management people | It is framed by middle level and lower level management people |
| 5 | It gives more discretion | It gives less discretion |
| 6 | It is not based on procedure | It is based on policy |
| 7 | It lays down broad area | It lays down little area |
| 8 | It acts as a bridge between purpose and performance | It acts as a bridge between activities and results |
| 9 | It is a part of strategy | It is a tool of tactics |

## METHODS

A method is a standing plan which is more specific and detailed than a procedure. Method specifies the way in which the specified work is to be performed. A method is the manual or mechanical means by which each work or operation is performed. Therefore, it is helpful in the use of a procedure with minimum expenditure of time, money and efforts.

A method is more limited scope than procedure. Method is the performance of a single operation of a procedure. Methods are formalised and standardised ways of performing repetitive and routine jobs. Standard methods prescribe one best way of doing a given task. In this way, method is facilitating the work of planning and also keep operations running on the planned lines. Besides, methods prevent confusion, ensure economy and efficient performance and keep the communication line clear. Methods are used as uniform norms to guide and control operations and performance. In nutshell, method explains the operation in more detailed than procedure.

## ADVANTAGES OF METHOD

1. Methods are parts of enterprise structure just like the nails, nuts and bolts of a product

2. One best way of doing a job prevents subjective handling of the matters.

3. It helps in the smooth functioning of the departments.

4. Communication line is cleared.

## METHODS VS PROCEDURES

Methods are differ from the procedure in the following ways.

1. Method is concerned with a particular step but procedure is concerned with series of steps.

2. Methods are specific but procedure is not specific.

3. Methods are standardized but procedure is not standardized.

4. Method involves one department but procedure involves many departments.

5. Methods lay down the best way of doing a specific step of a procedure.

## RULE

A rule is a guide to employees who are working in an organization like a procedure. But, the rule has no sequence of action as in the case of a procedure. A rule specifies what is to be done and what may not be done

in a given situation. Rule do not give any scope for decision - making. For example "No Admission without permission". This is a rule. These rules do not give any scope for discretion on the part of entrant. Rule is to be enforced rigidly, and a fine or penalty may be imposed for ignoring the rule.

Rule is a standing plan. A rule is a part of procedure. It is more rigid than a policy. Rules generally pertain to the administrative area of a procedure. Rule indicates the limits of acceptable behaviour of the employees of an organization. Rule helps the manager to improve the efficiency and predict the behaviour of subordinates in the given situation. Rules channel the behaviour of employees towards the accomplishment of objectives. The comparison of behaviour of people and groups is done with the help of rule.

Rules are helpful in maintaining discipline. Problems arise not due to rules themselves but because of the way of exercising rules on the employees. Hence, the purpose of every rule should be explained to the employees by the management. Rules should be so planned that they do not curtail initiative and creativity and at the same time help in smooth flow of work.

## FEATURES OF A RULE

The following are the features of rules.

1. It is a simplest type of a plan.
2. Rules are very rigid.
3. A fine is imposed if the rule is not followed
4. There is no scope of any decision-making.

## DIFFERENCE BETWEEN RULE AND POLICY

The important difference between rule and policy are as follows.

| *Rule* | *Policy* |
|---|---|
| 1. Rule is a specific statement telling the employees what should or should not be done. | Policy is a general statement of a management decision |
| 2. Rule is a guide of behaviour | Policy is a guide to decision making |
| 3. Rule constitutes the most specific type of standing plan | Policy is a less specific type of standing plan |
| 4. Rule is rigid, no exceptions or deviations. | Policy is flexible and has some exceptions |
| 5. Rule does not give any scope of discretion and its implementation. | Policy gives some discretion to the executives concerned with its implementation. |

## DIFFERENCE BETWEEN RULE AND METHODS

The difference between rules and methods are given below.

| *Rule* | *Methods* |
|---|---|
| 1. Rule gives norms for performance | Methods are standard ways of doing things. |
| 2. Rule wants to ensure discipline | Methods are helping to increase efficiency of operation. |
| 3. No standardization is required | Standardization is required |
| 4. Rule is based on common sense and objectives | Methods are based on research and analysis. |
| 5. Penalty is specified for rules violation | There is no penalty for violation of method. |
| 6. Rule is regarded as official and authoritative | Methods are regarded as logical or rational |
| 7. Rule is associated with control. | Methods are not directly associ-ated with control. |
| 8. Rule is related to the behavior of individuals and groups. | Methods are related to physical and other tasks. |

## DIFFERENCES BETWEEN RULE AND PROCEDURE

The difference between rule and procedure are listed below.

| *Rule* | *Procedure* |
|---|---|
| 1. Rule is a specific statement to do or not to do something Example: No Admission | Procedure specifies series of steps to be taken. |
| 2. No time sequence is specified in rule | A chronological order (in which steps are to be taken) is laid down in the procedure. |
| 3. Rule is rigid in nature There is no discretion allowed. | Procedure may allow discretion. |
| 4. Rule can be positive and negative. | Procedure is always positive in nature. |
| 5. Rule may be a part of procedure. | Procedure is not a part of rule. |

## MODEL QUESTIONS

1. "Policies are guides for managerial action", Discuss ?
2. Should policies be permanent or subject to ready change? Explain.
3. Differentiate policy from procedure ?
4. What are the differences between rule and method ?

# CHAPTER 5

# PLANNING

- INTRODUCTION
- MEANING
- DEFINITION
- CHARACTERISTICS OF PLANNING
- OBJECTIVES OF PLANNING
- NATURE OF PLANNING
- FORECASTING
- IMPORTANCE OF PLANNING
- ADVANTAGES OF PLANNING
- STEPS IN PLANNING PROCESS
- METHODS OF PLANNING
- LIMITATIONS OF PLANNING
- OBSTACLES IN PLANNING
- MODEL QUESTIONS

## INTRODUCTION

Planning is essential in every walk of life. Each and every person has to frame a plan to proceed in his schemes. A person whether he is engaged in business or not, has framed a number of plans during his life. The plan period may be short or long. According to Arnold Toynbee, "One of the characteristics of being human is that he makes plan."

Planning is the first and foremost function of management. All eminent writers have said that the planning function preceeds all other managerial functions. Effective planning facilitates early achievement of objectives, which depends upon the efficiency of the planner. A planner is a person who frames a plan to put his schemes into practice.

The planner can develop his efficiency by preparing himself to face the future developments.

## MEANING

Planning is an intellectual process of thinking resorted to decide a course of action which helps achieve the pre-determined objectives of the organisation in future.

F.W. Taylor had pointed out in his report on Scientific Management, that planning is separated from execution. Separate plans are prepared for various departments; then, the top executive of the organisation takes steps to co-ordinate the various departmental plans.

## DEFINITION

Let us now study the definitions of various eminent writers in the field of management.

Koontz and O'Donnel, "Planning is deciding in advance what to do, how to do it, when to do it and who is to do it. It bridges the gap from where we are to where we want to go."

According to Terry, "Planning is the selecting and relating of facts and the making and using of assumptions regarding the future in the visualization and formulation of proposed activities believed necessary to achieve desired results."

M.S. Hurley, "Planning is deciding in advance what is to be done. It involves the selection of objectives, policies, procedures and programmes from among alternatives."

Allen, "A plan is a trap laid to capture the future."

Haynes and Massie, "Planning is that function of the manager in which he decides in advance what he will do, It is a decision-making process of a special kind. It is an intellectual process in which creative thinking and imagination are essential."

Kast and Rosenzweig, "A plan is a determined course of action."

H.Fayol, "Planning is deciding the best alternatives among others to perform different managerial operations in order to achieve the pre-determined goals."

J.P. Barger, "Planning is an ability to visualize a future process and its results."

W.H. Newman, "Generally speaking, planning is deciding in advance what is to be done, that is, a plan is a projected course of action."

L. Urwick, "Planning is fundamentally a mental pre-disposition to do things in an orderly way, to think before acting and to get in the light of facts rather than of guesses."

Theo Haimann, "Planning is deciding in advance what is to be done." Peter F. Drucker, "Planning is the continuous process of making present entrepreneurial (risk taking) decisions systematically and with best possible knowledge of their futurity, organizing, systematically the efforts needed to carry out these decisions and measuring the results of these decisions against the expectations through organized, systematic feedback."

Cyril L. Hudson, "To plan is to produce a scheme for future action; to bring about specified results, at specified cost, in a specified period of time. It is a deliberate attempt to influence, exploit, bring about and control the nature, direction, extent, speed and effects of change. It may even attempt deliberately to create change, remembering always that change (like decision) in anyone sector will in some way affect other sectors. Planning takes place at each managerial and supervisory level. Therefore, the overall plan must be made at the top and subsidiary plan making must be relevant to and consonant with the major plan. In short, planning must be a carefully controlled and co-ordinated activity."

Hamilton Church, "Planning is, in essence, the exercise of foresight."

Hodge and Johnson, "Planning is an attempt to anticipate the future in order to achieve better performance."

Hart, "Planning is the determination in advance of a line of action by which certain results are to be achieved."

Dalton E. Mc. Farland defines planning as, "Planning may be broadly defined as a concept of executive action that embodies the skills of anticipating, influencing and controlling the nature and direction of change.

Billy E. Goetz, "Planning is fundamentally choosing and a planning that arises only when an alternative course of action is discovered."

Alford and Beatty, "Planning is the thinking process, the organised foresight, the vision based on fact and experience that is required for intelligent action."

## CHARACTERISTICS OF PLANNING

The following are the characteristics of planning:

1. Planning is looking into the future.
2. Planning involves pre determined line of action.
3. Planning discovers the best alternative out of available many alternatives.
4. Planning requires considerable time for implementation.
5. Planning is a continuous process.
6. Planning's object is to achieve pre determined objectives in a better way.
7. Planning integrates various activities of organisation.
8. Planning is done for a specific period.
9. Planning not only selects the objectives but also develops policies, programmes and procedures to achieve the objectives.
10. Planning is required at all levels of management.
11. Planning is an inter-dependent process which co-ordinates the various business activities.
12. Planning directs the members of the organisation.
13. Growth and prosperity of any organisation depends upon planning.

## OBJECTIVES OF PLANNING

Planning in any organisation serves to realise the following objectives:

**1. Reduces uncertainty:** Future is an uncertainty. Planning may convert the uncertainty into certainty. This is possible to some extent by, planning which is necessary to reduce uncertainty.

**2. Brings co-operation and co-ordination:** Planning can bring co-operation and co-ordination among various sections of the organisation. The rivalries and conflicts among departments could be avoided through planning. Besides, planning avoids duplication of work.

**3. Economy in operation:** As already pointed out, planning selects best alternatives among various available alternatives. This will lead to the best utilisation of resources. The objectives of the organisation are achieved easily.

**4. Anticipates unpredictable contingencies:** Some events could not be predicted. These events are termed as contingencies. These events may affect the smooth functioning of an enterprise. The planning provides a provision to meet such contingencies and tackle them successfully.

**5. Achieving the pre determined goals:** Planning activities are aimed at achieving the objectives of the enterprise. The timely achievement of objectives are possible only through effective planning.

**6. Reduce competition:** The existence of competition enables the enterprise to get a chance for growth. At the same time, stiff competition should be avoided. It is possible, toreduce competition through planning.

## NATURE OF PLANNING

There are number of ways available to complete a certain job. Planning chooses any one of the best alternatives out of the available ones. Economy and certainty are considered while selecting the best alternative. Thus, the nature of planning is briefly discussed below:

**1. Primary of planning:** The functions of management include planning, organising, staffing, directing and controlling. Eminent writers may add other new ones to these functions or those which have not been included in these functions. Anyway, writers unanimously accept that planning is the primary function of all the other functions. The reason is that the manager wants to achieve the pre determined objectives in a better way.

**2. Planning contributes to objectives:** There is a close connection between objectives and planning. Planning is based on the objectives. If there is no link between planning and objectives, the former will only be a mental exercise and of no use. Planning contributes to the attainment of objectives.

**3. Planning an intellectual activity:** Planning includes the selection of the best alternative available and thinking before selection of the best alter native. It involves the ability to foresee mishaps in future which might affect the smooth func tioning of an organisation. So, planning is an intellectual activity.

**4. Planning results in higher efficiency:** Planning efficiency is measured in terms of input and output ratios. Planning leads to maximum output with minimum expenditure. This input and output relationship is not only determined by money, labour hours and production units but also by the degree of satisfaction available to the individual as well as the group. The high degree of human satisfaction motivates the workers to produce more within the specified time.

**5. Planning is a continuous process:** Planning does not come to an end with the establishment of a business concern. Planning in other functions is also required. After the establishment of a business concern, certain decisions are taken. Planning is necessary to implement the decisions. A number of decisions are taken during the life time of the business concern. So, planning is necessary throughout the running of the business concern as a continuous process.

**6. Planning is flexible:** As already pointed out, while planning, any one of the available alternatives is selected. Planning selects the best alternative based on certain assumptions. If the assumptions are proved wrong, the selected alternative tends to be an incorrect one. There is a possibility of a dead log in the functions of the management. Planning has one more alternative to suit future situations.

**7. Unity and consistency:** Every department manager resorts to planning at different times. The planning is related to the achievement of objectives. In other words, managerial actions of different managers are unified in order to achieve the objectives. Policies and procedures of the organisation provide a basis for the consistency of executive behaviour and action in matters of planning.

**8. Planning is common to all:** Planning work is done by every person who is working in a business unit. He may be a managing director or a foreman.

Being of a higher place, the planning for a managing director is to frame the policies and procedures to be adopted. Being at a lower place, planning for a foreman is to allocate the work to his subordinates. So, planning is common to all.

**9. Basis for all managerial functions:** Planning is found at all levels of management. Top management looks after strategic planning. Middle management looks after administrative planning and the lower level management looks after operational planning.

**10. Getting co-ordination:** Planning co-ordinates various business activities. Without planning, nothing can be co-ordinated.

**11. Considering limiting factors:** Every plan is formulated after considering the limiting factors. The limiting factors may be money, skilled labour, quality materials, plant and machinery.

## FORECASTING

Many of us confuse planning with forecasting. Planning is entirely different from forecasting. Forecasting is nothing but the guessing of the future course of events correctly. It is basically a technique of anticipating events related to future. Planning is a wider term which includes forecasting. Forecasting is a part of planning and is based on the past experience. According to Haimann, "In fact, the success of a business depends in large measure upon the skill of management in forecasting and preparing for future events."

According to Mc Farland, "Forecasts are predictions or estimates of the changes, if any, in characteristic economic phenomena which may affect one's business plans." Louis A. Allen, "Forecasting is a systematic attempt to probe the future by inference from known facts."

## IMPORTANCE OF PLANNING

Planning is an important and basic function of management. Orderly procedure is possible through planning. Planning states the way through which the objectives are achieved and anticipates the activities well in advance *i.e.*, planning should take place before doing.

According to George R. Terry, "Planning is basic to the other fundamental management functions, that is organizing, actuating and controlling. Without the activities determined by planning, there would be nothing to organize, no one to actuate, and no need to control. This viewpoint stresses the importance of planning in the management process."

Defective planning and inadequate planning leads to failure of the organisation. Everybody knows that no activity could be performed in an organisation without planning. Proper planning coordinates the activities of different sections of people working in an organisation. According to Earnest C. Miller, "Managerial planning attempts to achieve a consistent, co-ordinated structure of operation focused on desired ends. Without plans, action must become merely random activity, producing nothing but chaos."

The business unit has to work in uncertain and ever changing conditions. It is very difficult to continue the business under such situations. Effective planning can anticipate the uncertain events and help prepare the workforce to meet the situation to survive. George R. Terry has rightly said that, "Planning is the foundation of most successful actions of any enterprise."

Planning helps the businessman get early success. Success without planning is almost impossible in business. So, the planning function is very important due to the following reasons:

**1. To manage by objectives:** All the activities of an organisation are designed to achieve the framed objectives. However, planning makes the organisation focus on the objectives for early achievement.

**2. Convert uncertainty into certainty:** Future is full of uncertainties. These uncertainties may be predicted through forecasting. Then, the planning provides necessary provision to face the uncertainties. Besides, planning evaluates the alternative course of action for the continuous growth and prosperity of the organisation.

**3. Economy in operation:** Planning selects any one of the available alternatives which will help produce the best results at minimum costs.

**4. Help in co-ordination:** The co-ordination is obtained by the management through planning, well-published policies, programmes and procedures. So, planning also helps the management get co-ordination. According to Koontz and O'Donnell, "Plans are selected courses along which the management desires to co-ordinate group action."

**5. Tackling increasing complexities of business:** At present, there is need for many people with different qualifications to run a business. This makes it necessary for the management to plan the business activities clearly as to who is to do, what is to be done, where is to be done, when it is to be and how it is to be done.

**6. Effective Control:** Control is necessary only when there is a deviation in the actual performance from the planned performance. In the absence of a plan, there are no standards to compare. In simple words, planning without control are useless and control without planning is impossible. H.G. Hicks has said that, "Planning is clearly a prerequisite for effective controlling. It is utterly foolish to think that controlling could be accomplished without planning; without planning there is no predetermined understanding of the desired performance."

**7. Effective utilisation of resources:** Planning involves deciding in advance of the business activities. Then, the business activities are completed without any delay. It leads to effective utilisation of resources at the cheapest and in the best manner.

**8. Avoiding business failures:** Planning includes the selection of best objectivities, conversion of uncertainty into certainty, economy in operation, co-ordination, facing the complexities, effective control and effective utilisation of resources and avoiding business failures.

## ADVANTAGES OF PLANNING

Planning helps the organisation achieve its objectives early. In this way, planning helps the organisation in many ways. Some of the advantages of planning are briefly explained below:

**1. Better utilisation of resources:** Planning decides what to produce and how to produce. Then, there is the possibility of utilising the resources effectively.

**2. Helps in achieving objectives:** Planning sets goals or objectives of an organisation. This gives effective direction to the control of employees of the organisation. In this way, planning helps the organisation accomplish the pre-determined goals or objectives.

**3. Economy in operation:** Unnecessary production, ineffective utilisation of resources and unnecessary activities of an organisation are eliminated through planning. This results in the economy of operations.

**4. Minimises future uncertainties:** The uncertain future increases the importance of planning. Planning foresees the changes and uncertainties taking shape in future and devices methods to face them. Some future uncertainties are thus, minimised through planning.

**5. Improves competitive strength:** Competitive strength is improved by adding new line of products, changes in quality and size of the product, expansion of plant capacity and changes in methods of work. These are achieved through planning.

**6. Effective control:** Control without planning is an impossible one. Control is used only when there is a well-chalked out plan. So, planning provides a basis for controlling.

**7. Motivation:** A well-prepared plan encourages the employees of an organisation and gives them a sense of effective participation. Planning motivates the employees as to what the organisation wants to achieve and defines it to the employees.

**8. Co-operation:** Planning helps the management pull the individual to achieve common objectives or goals. Planning provides well-defined objectives, unity of direction, well-published policies, procedures and programmes. All these facilitate to get co-ordination, which consequently avoids duplication of work and interdepartmental conflicts.

**9. Promote growth and improvement:** Planning sets a standard to control purpose. So, useless and aimless activities are avoided. It leads to the growth and improvement of an individual and the organisation.

**10. Develops rationality among management executives:** Disciplined thinking of management executives is geared up through formal planning. Management executives take action only after putting their thoughts in blueprint. In this way, planning brings rational thinking and approach among management executives.

**11. Prevents hasty judgment:** We can analyse a problem through a plan and consider the alternatives before taking a sound decision. It is possible to plan in advance as to what will be done and how it will be done. This process avoids hasty judgment.

**12. Reduces red-tapism:** Junior most executive can act according to pre-planned decisions. There is no need for him to get any fresh permission for his action. It saves time, energy and cost and reduces red-tapism.

**13. Encourages innovative thought:** A good plan should provide a basis for new thinking in any individual. It seeks a way to encourage people to co-ordinate and to achieve common objectives. According to D.E.Hussey "A good planning process will provide avenues for individual participation, will throw up more ideas about the company and its environment, will encourage an atmosphere of frankness and corporate self-criticism and will stimulate managers to achieve more.

**14. Improves ability to cope with change:** Planning helps managers improve their ability to cope with changes but it cannot prevent changes from happening. This creates an awareness among the managers regarding the incidence of change.

**15. Creates forward looking attitude in management:** Managers may lose their prosperity facing day to day problems. Planning helps a manager to become more prosperous and creates a forward looking attitude in him, thus such a planning ensures stability to management.

**16. Development of efficient methods:** Planning helps the management develop efficient methods and procedures of action.

**17. Delegation of authority facilitated:** A well-prepared plan will always facilitate the delegation of authority.

**18. Anticipation of crisis:** Careful planning will avoid the crisis which is likely to occur. In this way, management can reduce the internal organisational disturbances.

## STEPS IN PLANNING PROCESS

The planning process is different from one plan to another and one organisation to another. Given below is a planning process which may be treated as commonly acceptable.

**1. Analysis of External Environment:** It is necessary to consider the external environment of an organisation. The term *external environment* includes socio-economic conditions and political conditions prevailing in a country. Socio-economic condition refers to classification of society on the basis of income, age, class, living conditions, aspirations, expectations and the like. These factors are not controllable ones. But, every organisation has to prepare the plan according to the changing trends in the external environment.

**2. Analysis of internal environment:** It can be otherwise called as *Resource audit*. Resource audit means an analysis of the strength and weaknesses of an organisation. Due consideration is made on the availability of resources, profitability, plant capacity, available manpower, communication effectiveness and the like.

**3. Determination of objectives:** The objectives of an organisation are pre- planned. Objectives specify the results expected. Once the organisation's objectives are determined, the section-wise or department-wise objectives are planned at the lower level. Defining the objectives of every department is a very essential one; then only clear-cut direction is available to the departments. Control process is very easy if the objectives are clearly defined.

**4. Determining planning premises and constraints:** Planning is forward looking. Therefore, planning is based on forecasting. Forecasting means the assumption of and the anticipation of certain events. It implies a calculation of how certain factors will behave in future. The planning must consider the likely behaviour of these factors. In this sense, these constitute the planning premises.

Generally, forecasting is made in the following ways:

(i) What will be the market force? Market force refers to demand, supply, buying capacity and the like.

(ii) The expectation of volume of sales.

(iii) What kind of products are to be sold and in what price?

(iv) What would be their manufacturing costs?

(v) What would be the tax policy and economic policy of the Government?

(vi) The expectation of technology change in production

(vii) How is the finance raised for expansion and/or modernisation of the business?

**5. Examination of alternative courses of action:** An action may be performed in many ways but a particular way is most suitable to the organisation. Hence, the management should find alternative ways and examine them in the light of planning premises.

According to Koontz and O'Donnell, "There is seldom a plan made for which reasonable alternatives do not exist. Moreover, before weighing alternatives and reaching a decision, one is wise to search for alternatives that may not be immediately apparent. Quite often an alternative does not immediately prove to be the most profitable way of undertaking a plan."

**6. Weighing alternative course of action:** All the alternatives are not suitable to an organisation. Each alternative has its own strong and weak points. So, there is a need for weighing all the alternatives to determine the best alternative.

**7. Selection of the best alternative course of action:** The selection of the best alternative is based on the weighing of various alternatives. A course of action is determined according to the circumstances prevailing. No partiality is shown while selecting the best alternative.

**8. Establishing the sequence of activities:** The determined course of action is adopted for each section or department, product, for a quarter, month, week, etc. Finally, the manager should draft a final plan in definite terms.

**9. Formulation of action programmes:** The term *action programme* includes fixing time limit for performance, allocation of work to individuals and work schedule. These are necessary to achieve the objectives within the specified period.

**10. Determining secondary plans:** Secondary plans flow from the primary or basic plan. The preparation of a secondary plan is necessary to expedite the achievement of the basic plan. For example, Once a basic plan of sales is decided upon, a number of secondary plans could be prepared. Here, the secondary plan includes production schedule, purchase of plant and machinery, purchase of raw materials, consumable stores, selection, training and placement of personnel and the like.

**11. Securing participation of employees:** The successful execution of any plan depends upon the extent of participation of employees. So, the management should involve employees in planning through communication, consultation and participation.

**12. Follow-up and evaluation:** There should be a system of follow-up. The management should watch how the planning is being done. The shortcomings of planning can be identified through a follow-up action and rectified then and there. The continuous evaluation of planning is also necessary. It means that the actual performance is compared with the planning and then corrective action is taken if there is any deviation.

## METHODS OF PLANNING

(Types of planning, components of planning or elements of planning).

According to the usage and nature of planning, the methods of planning are divided into the following categories:

**1. Objective plans:** Objectives are treated as basic plans. These basic plans are necessary for all types of planning operation. The entire management activity is geared upon only through the formulation of objective plans. Objectives not only dominate the planning activity but also play an important role in the managerial work of organising, directing and controlling.

**2. Standing Plans:** Standing plans include policies and procedures and they are liable to repetitive action. An action may be divided into two categories i.e. repetitive and non-repetitive actions.

Standing plans provide a ready guideline for solving recurring problems. Standing plans will be of no use if the problems do not recur in an organisation. Special problems are not solved with the help of standing plans but solved in a different way. Standing plans limit the freedom of manager for ensuring integrated and co-operative action. The reason is that the manager should adopt policies and procedures in action.

**3. Master Plans:** Master Plan covers the complete course of action along with consideration of time and strategy. Small plans are added together in an orderly way to speed up the course of action. In terms of scope, plans may be either broad or detailed in character. If the plans are prepared function-wise, plans may be concerned with production, sales, purchase and similar activities.

## LIMITATIONS OF PLANNING

Though planning function is a primary function of management and it facilitates other functions of management, it suffers from certain limitations.

**1. Inflexibility:** The more detailed and widespread the plans are, the greater inflexibility they are. This inflexibility arises an account of the philosophy of management. If the management has the philosophy of production of high quality goods at high cost, it may be difficult for them to plan for a cheaper quality product.

**2. Limitation of forecasts:** Planning is fully based on forecasts. If there is any defect in forecasts, the planning will lose its value.

**3. Unsuitability:** In planning, objectives, policies, procedures etc. are set after careful investigation of all the relevant factors. But in practice, business is facing new opportunities and challenges by nature. So, there is a need for modernisation of alteration of such framed objectives and policies in the light of new opportunities and challenges. Hence, planning is unsuitable.

**4. Time consuming:** The management cannot prepare any plan simply. It has to collect various information and hold discussions with others. So, planning is a time-consuming process.

**5. Costly:** Planning is preceded with collection of necessary information, careful analysis and interpretation of various courses of action, selection of the best one among them. This work cannot be completed without incurring any expenses. At the same time, there is no guarantee of getting any benefits from such planning. So, planning process is a costly one.

**6. Mental ability:** Planning is a mental exercise. The most careful planning is made only by an able and skilful manager. If the executives or managers do not have such ability, there will be no effective planning. According to George A.Steiner, "Planning is hard work. It requires a high level of imagination, analytical ability, creativity and fortitude to choose and become committed. Management must exert pressure to demand the best efforts in managers and the staff. Both the talents required are limited and the maintenance of high quality planning is difficult to achieve.

**7. False sense of security:** Future is uncertainty. Planning is concerned with future. The management people think that there is security, if planning is properly adhered to. But, this is not true in practice. So, the course of action is limited and planning becomes precise. This difficulty makes the management have a false sense of security.

**8. Delay during emergency period:** Planning does not give any benefits to an organisation during the emergency period. Spot decision dominates the planning. If planning is followed during the emergency period, there will be a possibility of delay in performing the work.

**9. Capital investment:** If sizeable amounts are invested in fixed assets, the ability to change future course of action will be limited and planning will become precise. This difficulty continues upto the liquidation of investments or it creates a necessity to write off the investment.

**10. Political climate:** Government can change its attitudes according to the changes of the political climate. Taxation policy, regulation of business and finances through financial institutions are generating constraints on the organisational planning process.

**11. Trade Unions:** The freedom of planning is restricted through the organisation of trade unions at national level. Trade unions can interfere in the management activities on work rule, fixation of wages, productivity and associated benefits. Hence, managers are not free to take decisions in this area to some extent.

**12. Technological changes:** When there is a change in technology, the management has to face number of problems. The problems may be high cost of production, competition in the market etc. The management is not in a position to change its policies according to technology changes. It will affect the planning.

## OBSTACLES IN PLANNING

Planning may face certain difficulties or obstacles in the planning process. These obstacles are summarised below:

**1. Unreliability of Forecasts:** Future has uncertainty. Therefore, the probable events cannot be ascertained accurately. So, the degree of unreliability is increased correspondingly with the long-term planning. In other words, planning is an ineffective one.

**2. Recurrence of same type of problems:** The form and shape of problems are changed with the passage of time. Some problems may be postponed and appear after the lapse of time. So, there is a need for maintaining standing plans. It increases the work load of the managerial personnel.

**3. Expensive:** Planning involves some expenses. The expenses may be borne by the small business unit. The available planning benefits should be more than the expenses incurred. But this is not possible for a small business unit and expensive to a big business unit if the business unit fails to adhere to the planning after preparing it.

**4. Loss of initiative:** Every person has some idea of his own. These ideas cannot be materialised and suppressed due to pre-planned programmes. Some firms have suggestion boxes, but the weightage is not available to the suggestions offered because planning sets standards and the work should be carried accordingly.

## PLANNING PREMISES

Planning is prepared for the future. But, the future has more uncertainty. Therefore, the management executives are making certain assumptions about the future while preparing a plan. These assumptions should not be based upon intuition or guesswork. The assumptions should be developed through scientific forecasting of future events since the planning is prepared on the basis of such planning known as planning premises.

According to Koontz and O'Donnell, "Planning premises are the anticipated environment in which plans are expected to operate. They include assumptions or forecasts of the future and known conditions that will affect the course of plans, such as prevailing policies and existing company plans that control the basic nature of supporting plans." Effective planning is largely depend upon the well developed planning premises. If planning premises are changed, planning will have to be modified accordingly. Likewise, if there is any error in assessment of planning premises. It leads to managerial plans unreliable. Therefore, correct assessment of planning premises is the most significant step in managerial planning.

The environment of business is affected by innumerable forces and factors. The management executives should consider these forces and factors while formulating planning premises. The factors and forces which have material impact on business environment are to be concentrated in much and ignore the forces and factors which have affect the business environment to a lesser extent. The recognition of affecting forces and factors guides the management executives to select the proper and perfect planning premises upon which they may raise the super structure of planning. The main purpose of planning premises is to facilitate the planning process by guiding, directing, simplifying and reducing the degree of uncertainties in it. If a planning is done by any person without considering planning premises, planning may become wastage of time and money. Hence, developing sound premises is very important for successful planning.

## CLASSIFICATION OF PLANNING PREMISES

Planning premises may be classified as under:

**1. External Premises:** External premises are lying outside the firm. Economic, technological, political, social conditions and market conditions are some of the kinds of external premises. Economic premise refers to purchasing power of the customers, technological premise refers to application of latest technology, political premise refers to policy of the governments, social condition refers to culture and market condition refers to demand and supply forces for the product or service.

**2. Internal Premises:** Internal premises are existing within a business enterprise. Human resources, material resources, machine resources, financial resources and methods are some of the kinds of internal premises. The most import5ant internal premises are competence of managerial personnel and skill of labour force.

**3. Tangible Premises:** Quantified factors can be termed as tangible premises. Money, time and units of production are some of the kinds of tangible premises. Money can be quantified as rupees, time can be quantified as seconds, minutes and/or hours and units of production can be quantified as Kilogram, Liter, Horse Power and the like.

**4. Intangible Premises:** Qualitative factors can be termed as intangible premises. Goodwill of the company, loyal of the employees, public relations, employee morale and motivation are some of the kinds of intangible premises. Both tangible and intangible planning premises must be taken into account in planning.

**5. Controllable Premises:** Premises which are entirely within the control and realm of management are known as controllable premises. Policies, methods, procedures, systems, programmers, rules and regulations are some of the kinds of controllable premises.

**6. Uncontrollable Premises:** Premises which can not be controllable by the realm of management are known as uncontrollable premises. Besides, these types of premises cannot be unpredictable. Even though, uncontrollable premises should be taken into account while framing a plan. War, natural calamities, new discoveries and inventions and human behaviour are some of the kinds of uncontrollable premises.

**7. Semi-controllable Premises:** Some premises can be predicted and controllable to some extent are known as semi-controllable premises. In other words, the management has partial control on some premises which are known as semi-controllable premises. Trade union and management relations, employer and employee relations, superior and subordinate relations, inter-department relations, supply position in market are some of the kinds of semi-controllable premises.

**8. Fixed or Constant Premises:** Some pre3mises have not changed irrespective of action taken by the management. They are definite, known and well understood. Hence, the management need not consider these type of premises. While framing a plan, men, machine and money are some of the kinds of fixed or constant premises.

**9. Variable Premises:** Some premises may be changed in relation to the course of action taken by the management. These premises have a significant bearing on the success of the plan. Hence, the management should consider these premises with due importance while formulating plans. Sales volume and production expenses are some of the kinds of variable premises.

**10. Foreseeable Premises:** Some premises are definite and well known and can be foreseen with certainty. All fixed or constant premises can be treated as foreseeable premises.

**11. Unforeseeable Premises:** Some premises cannot be controllable. Hence, these types of premises cannot be unpredictable also. War, strike, natural calamities, consumer preferences and consumer taste are some of the kinds of unforeseeable premises.

## MODEL QUESTIONS

1. Discuss the steps in Managerial Planning.
2. What is the importance of planning?.
3. How external factors affect planning?.
4. What is the definition of 'Planning'?
5. What are the steps in planning?
6. What are the different types of planning?
7. What is planning?
8. What are the various objectives of planning?
9. What are the different methods of planning?
10. Explain the different steps of planning?
11. Explain the obstacles of effective planning?
12. Planning is the essence of management — Elucidate.
13. Procedures are a guide to action — Comment.
14. Explain the importance of forecasting.
15. "Forecasting is the essence of planning." In the light of this statement, discuss the relationship between forecasting and planning.
16. What are the different types of plans? Describe various steps in the planning process.
17. Define planning. Enumerate the various components of planning?
18. Describe the essentials of a sound plan and the different stages in the process of planning?
19. Define planning. Explain its features. Point out the various aspects that are necessary for effective managerial policy?
20. What do you mean by single use plans and standing plans?
22. Why is flexibility a characteristic of a good plan?
23. What is meant by capacity planning?
24. What do you understand by "Planning"?
25. Discuss the steps involved in planning process?
26. What is meant by planning premises?
27. Enumerate the steps in the process of planning?

# CHAPTER 6

# FORECASTING

- INTRODUCTION
- MEANING
- DEFINITION
- FEATURES OR CHARACTERISTICS
- FORECASTING PROCESS
- IMPORTANCE OF FORECASTING
- AREAS OF FORECASTING
- FORECASTING TECHNIQUES OR TYPES OR METHODS
- ADVANTAGES OF FORECASTING
- LIMITATIONS OF FORECASTING
- DIFFERENCE BETWEEN FORECASTING AND PLANNING
- MODEL QUESTIONS

## INTRODUCTION

Forecasting is the technique of estimating the relevant future events and problems on the basis of past and present behaviour or happenings. The future cannot be guessed without knowing the events which have occurred in the past and are occurring presently. Thus, forecasting involves detailed analysis of the past and present events to get a clear cut idea about probable events in the future. So, forecasting may require the use of various statistical techniques. At the same time, all the forecast does not require the same type of statistical analysis or techniques. Thus, forecasting depends upon an analysis of past events and current conditions with a view to draw conclusions about future events.

## MEANING

Forecasting is a systematic guessing of the future course of events with the help of analysis of past and present events.

Forecasting provides a basis for a planning. Planning cannot be done without forecasting. According to Fayol, forecasting includes both assessing the future and making provision for it.

## DEFINITION

Neter and Wasserman state that, "Business forecasting refers to the statistical analysis of the past and current movement in the given time series so as to obtain clues about the future pattern of those movements."

Webster's New Collegiate Dictionary defines that "A forecast is a prediction and its purpose is to calculate and predict some future event or condition."

## FEATURES OR CHARACTERISTICS

On the basis of the above definitions of forecasting, the following features or characteristics of forecasting can be identified.

1. Forecasting is concerned with future events.
2. Forecasting is necessary for planning process. Planning is not possible without forecasting.
3. The impact of future events has to be considered in the planning process.
4. Forecasting is a guessing of future events. Therefore, the future events that might happen could be guessed only to some extent.
5. Inferences or conclusions are drawn from past and present relevant events under scientific forecasting.
6. Forecasting considers all the factors which affect organisational functions.
7. The analysis of various factors may require the use of scientific, mathematical and statistical techniques.
8. Personal observation also helps forecasting.
9. The application of scientific, mathematical and statistical techniques is much more reliable than the use of ordinary tools for obtaining conclusions.

## FORECASTING PROCESS

Forecasting period may be a short-term or long-term. In either of the cases certain stages or steps have to be passed through while making the forecast. These stages or steps have been briefly discussed below.

**1. Thorough Preparation of Foundation:** Detailed investigation and complete analysis of the company are necessary for forecasting. Forecasting is based on the organisational structure of the company and its past performance. The growth of a company or a business is assessed over a period of time and the factors responsible for such are identified. Besides this, the extend of the dependence of one factor on other factors which ensure the growth of a company has to be studied. The very purpose of thorough preparation of a foundation is that the forecasting is based on the foundation.

**2. Estimation of Future:** The prosperity of the future can be estimated with the help of past experience and performance as well as the talents possessed by top management executives. The brightness of future period can be estimated in consultation with the key personnel and it may be communicated to all the employees of the business unit. This type of communication will help the management to fix the responsibility of each employee fulfilling the promises of these forecast and accountability for any deviations from this forecast.

**3. Collection of Results:** All the information can be collected. Relevant records are prepared and maintained to collect the results. Nothing can be omitted and irrelevant information can be avoided while collecting the results.

**4. Comparison of Results:** The actual results are compared with estimated results to know deviations. If there are significant deviations between the estimation and actual results, the reasons for such deviations can be investigated. This will help the management to estimate the future (forecasting).

**5. Refining the Forecast:** The forecast can be refined in the light of deviations which seem to be more realistic. If any factors or conditions have changed during the period understudy, then those factors or conditions have to be taken in consideration for the future estimation. In this way, the forecast can be refined and improved.

## IMPORTANCE OF FORECASTING

The need and importance of forecasting can be found out with the help of key role played for forecasting in the management process especially in planning process. Whatever planning is done by the management executives, their planning has to be based on the forecasting. Forecasting helps the management in the following ways.

**1. Pivotal Role in an Organisation:** Planning is the backbone of effective functioning of an organisation. Many organisations have failed because of lack of forecasting or faulty forecasting. The reason is that planning is based on accurate forecasting. According to Louis A.Allen,

"A systematic attempt to probe the future by inference from known facts helps integrate all management planning so that unified overall plans can be developed into which divisional and departmental plans can be meshed."

**2. Development of a Business:** Business is established in order to achieve specified objectives. The specified objectives can be achieved by performing certain activities. The performance of these activities depends upon the proper forecasting. So, the development of a business or an organisation is fully based on the forecasting.

**3. Implementation of Project:** Many entrepreneurs implement a project on the basis of their experience. Forecasting helps an entrepreneur to gain experience and ensures him success. In this way, forecasting is an important factor which enable the entrepreneur to get success.

**4. Primacy to Planning:** Planning decides the future course of action. Planning cannot be done without forecasting. The information required for planning is supplied by forecasting. So, forecasting is the primacy to the planning.

**5. Co-ordination:** Forecasting helps the management executives in effective co-ordination indirectly. Forecasting helps to collect the information about internal and external factors. Thus, collected information provides a basis for co-ordination.

**6. Effective Control:** Management executive can ascertain the strength and weaknesses of sub-ordinates or employees through forecasting. Then the executive can take appropriate action to the sub-ordinates. So, forecasting can provide adequate information for exercising effective control.

**7. Key to Success:** All business organisations are facing risks. Success is the reward for facing risks and functioning under uncertainties. Risks and uncertainties could be reduced with the help of forecasting. Forecasting provides clues about risks and uncertainties. The management executives can save the business and get success by taking appropriate action. So, forecasting is a key to success.

## AREAS OF FORECASTING

The decision of today affects the business environment of tomorrow. So, the decision should be a sound one. A sound decision can be taken with the help of systematic and rational forecasting. Then, forecasting is an integral part of efficient management. Accurate forecasts is necessary for efficient management. So, making accurate forecasts is of utmost necessity in the following areas.

**1. Competition:** It is necessary to predict the strategies followed by the competitors. The strategy may be of low cost, granting credit facility, allowing discount, long guarantee period, free articles and the like. A new business unit may enter an industry. The market share of each competitors has to be taken into consideration for forecasting. Forecasting helps the management to enhance the market share of the company.

**2. Supply of Labour:** The supply of labour is changing in its structure. The labour can be divided into three categories (i.e.) skilled workers, semi-skilled workers and unskilled workers. There is high demand for skilled workers. Work demanding skill is being allotted to skilled workers. The management can forecast the availability of labour force. In the present fast developing internet world, there is a need for specialised worker. It means that specialists (skilled workers) are required for effective performance of a job. If the management has a plan for expansion or modernisation, the prime forecast of management will pertain to the supply of labour. No industry can be expanded or modernized without adequate labour force.

**3. Economic condition:** The economic condition of a business unit can be assessed by the management. The strength of any business unit depends on its economic condition. Here, the term economic condition includes cash position, working capital requirement, repaying capacity and the like. The operating efficiency of any unit could be improved by the sound economic condition. In other words, good economic condition assists in the growth of the company.

**4. Growth Trend:** A detailed analysis of growth trend of business is also necessary. A forecast on growth trend helps the management to decide the operating level. The upward growth trend is preferred by any entrepreneur. This could be achieved through forecasting. Failure to make an accurate forecasting on growth trend may put the company out of business.

**5. Social Change:** The consumer tastes, demands and attitudes may change. The change can be identified with the help of proper forecasting. Convenience and comforts are responsible for changes. Here forecasting could predict the convenience and comforts that would be enjoyed by the consumers in future.

**6. Political Change:** Forecasting in the field of politics is also very important one. The reason is that any political change will surely affect the smooth running of any business unit. Frequent changes in politics bring about changes in the policy of Government towards business.

**7. Technology:** The invention of new technology may change the operations of an organization. So, forecasts predict the new technological developments. An active organisation keeps almost of new technological developments and adopts new technology to make the performance of any job more effective. Failure to forecast on technology may ruin the company. It will find it very difficult to survive in the business world.

**8. New Laws and Regulations:** A meticulous adoption of new laws and regulations is necessary for effective functioning of an organisation. Laws relating to consumer protection assume much importance now-a-days. Consumer is a king to any business. The operational style of any business is affected by new laws and regulations.

## FORECASTING TECHNIQUES OR TYPES OR METHODS

Various techniques of forecasting are used in the field of business because the future of any business can never be predicted with certainty. An accurate forecasting may reduce the degree of uncertainty. However, no technique can be considered as a correct one which universally applicable. In practice, more than one technique can be combined for making the forecasting effective. So, some of the techniques are discussed below.

**1. Similarity Events Method:** It is otherwise called Historical analogy method. In this method, forecast is made on the basis of events happened in the past which are most similar to current events. For example, in analysing the changes in the attitude of employee regarding in equality, the management can find out prudential attitude of employee in the days to come by considering past attitude. The similarity of events of past and present is properly analysed in order to make an effective forecast.

**2. Jury of Executive Option:** The opinion of experts is sought under this method and the meritorious one is accepted. For example, an opinion on profitability of starting a new unit is received from various experts and decision is made on the basis of experts opinion. The opinion may be on the area of sales, finance, purchase and the like. Some ideas are generated which can be evaluated for their feasibility and profitability. Experts may requested comment on the opinion of the others in order to arrive at a consensus of opinion. The reason for favouring a particular opinion by an expert is known to the management.

**3. Survey Method:** Field survey can be conducted to collect information regarding the attitude of people. For example, information may be collected through surveys about the savings habits of the public. Both quantitative and qualitative information may be collected.

Such information is useful for proper forecasting. The demand for both new and existing products can be forecast through survey method.

**4. Sales Person's Opinion:** The sales force of the existing product can be forecast with the help of opinions of sales persons. Sales persons are very closer to the consumers and/ or customers. So, the opinions expressed by the sales persons are of great value. A reasonable sales trend can be predicted based on the opinions of sales persons.

**5. Business Barometers:** Index Numbers are used to measure the state of condition of business between two or more periods. Business trend, seasonal fluctuations of a business and cyclical movements are studied with the help of index numbers. Index numbers indicate the direction in which the business is going on. Besides these index numbers give some advance signals for likely changes in the future. For example, a pay rise to the government employees, industrial and agricultural employees may reflect higher sales volume and higher income after some time. Thus, it is very easy to forecast the future trend of a business with the help of business activity index number. However, index numbers do not give an assurance for success. The reason is that all types of business do not follow the general trend.

**6. Expectation of Consumer:** Under this method, a survey is conducted in order to know the future needs of consumers. An overall forecast can be made on the basis of the expectations of consumers. An organisation can find out the consumer preferences, impact of advertisement on buying behaviour and the lacuna prevailing in the existing product. This is also known as "Marketing research Method."

**7. Time Series Analysis:** In time series analysis, the future is forecast on the assumption that past activities are good indicators of future activities. In other words, future activities are the extension of the past. This method is quite accurate where future is expected to be similar to the past. Time series analysis can be applied. Only when the data are available for a long period of time. In a nutshell, forecasts are based on the assumption that the business conditions affecting its steady growth or decline are reasonably expected to remain unchanged in the future.

**8. Delphi Method:** Rand corporation has developed the Delphi method initially in 1969 to forecast the military events. Then, it has been applied in other areas also. A panel of experts is prepared. These experts are requested to give their opinions in writing for a prescribed questionnaire. Their opinions are analysed, summarized and submitted once again to the same experts for future considerations and evaluations. The authors of these opinions are not disclosed, so that no expert is influenced by other's opinions. This process is continued up to the stage at which a consensus opinion is obtained. Delphi method is useful when past data are not available and where the past data do not give an indication for the future events. Delphi method is highly useful in problems like future petroleum and diesel needs, likely or probable after effects of a price expected social changes and the like.

**9. Extrapolation:** Extrapolation means estimation of future behaviour from the known data (i.e.) past behaviour. Some of the factors are responsible for the behaviour change. Here, the effects of such various factors are taken into consideration. The reason is that it assumes that the effect of these factors is of a constant and stable pattern and would continue as such in future. It is necessary that the future behaviour is to be decided only after a very careful study of past behaviour.

**10. Regression Analysis:** Regression analysis is used to find out the effect of changes of the relative movements of two or more inter-related variables. In other words, a change in one variable has an effect on the other inter-related variables. In the modern business conditions and situations, number of factors are responsible for the changes made in the variables. Here, Regression analysis helps in isolating the effects of such factors to a great extent.

For example, if we take two inter-related variables viz cost of production and profit, there will be a direct relationship prevailing between these two variables. It is possible to have an estimate of profit on the basis of cost of production, provided other things remain the same. In this way, forecasting can be made.

**11. Input and Output Analysis:** Under this method, a forecast can be made if the relationship between input and output is known. At the same time, the input requirements can be forecast on the basis of output. In other words, input can be determined on the basis of need of output. For example, power requirement of the country can be forecast on the basis of its present usage rate in various sectors viz. industry, transport, household etc. and on the basis of how the power requirements of these various sectors will increase in future. This is possible. The reason is that various sectors of economy are interrelated. Besides this, the prevailing inter relationship among the various sectors of the economy can be well established.

**12. Econometric Models:** It is otherwise called causal models. The complex relationship of various variables is responsible for the future behaviour of one variable. For example, sales is affected by many variables, say, time, changes in personal disposable income, changes in preferences, availability of substitute products in the market, credit availability, changes in life style and the like. All these variables have produced some effects on present sales in addition to past sales. This forecasting technique is applied in projecting Gross National Product. Here, the past data have been used to know the degree of relationship prevailing among these variables.

These are some of the forecasting techniques. These techniques, broadly, can be divided into two categories viz. Qualitative techniques and Quantitative techniques. Qualitative techniques are based on human judgement. The reason is that there is no availability of sufficient information and data. If sufficient information and data are available, quantitative technique can be applied to forecasting. Qualitative and Quantitative may help in forecasting the unexpected future events or happenings or opportunities or threats. But, quantitative techniques does not make any provision for finding out the unexpected occurrences.

## ADVANTAGES OF FORECASTING

Forecasting helps a business man in a number of ways. The anticipation of future problems and events will make it imperative to accelerate an early achievement of objectives. Some of the advantages or merits of the forecasting are briefly discussed below:

**1. Facilitates Planning:** Forecasting facilitates the planning function of management. Forecasting provides a basis for preparing a possible plan. Planning will be impossible in the absence of forecasting. Planning requires the estimation of probable changes likely to take place in the future. Forecasting helps the management to be cautious against trade cycle and points out the weaknesses of the management. This will minimise the business risk. In this way, the forecasting facilitates planning.

**2. Ensures — Co-ordination:** Forecasting of an organisation cannot be done by an individual. It involves group effort. This group consists of all department members of the organisation. This creates team spirit and ensures co-ordination. According to Henry Fayol,

"The act of forecasting is a great benefit to all who take part in the process and is the best means of ensuring adaptability to changing circumstances, The collaboration of all concerned leads to a unified front, an understanding of the reasons and a broadened outlook."

**3. Easy Controlling:** Forecasting helps the management to exercise control. Control is necessary if there is any deviation, the actual from the predicted result. The result can be predicted on the basis of forecasting. Control is not possible in the absence of forecasting. So, control will be an easy function in the presence of forecasting.

## LIMITATIONS OF FORECASTING

1. Forecasting is to be made on the basis of certain assumptions and human judgements. Faulty assumptions and human judgements, will yield wrong results.
2. Forecasting cannot be considered as a scientific method for guessing future events, since it does not specify any concrete relationship between past and future events.
3. Too much is expected of forecasting. This will cause disappointment and impair the initiative of the executives.
4. Forecasting requires high degree of skill and the process of forecasting must be undertaken by specialists. But in practice, no such experts are available for forecasting.
5. Proper forecasting needs adequate reliable information. It is very difficult to collect reliable information. Hence, it is not possible to forecast correctly.
6. Forecasting is the prediction of future events. But, there is no certainty of occurrence of such events.
7. The more number of days constituting the period of forecasting, higher will be the degree of error. Forecasting cannot be applied to a long period.
8. Heavy cost and time is involved in forecasting but the benefits derived from them will not be worthy. The collection of information and conversion of qualitative data into quantitative one involves a lot of time and money. So, smaller organisations, cannot afford the cost and time required for forecasting.

## DIFFERENCE BETWEEN FORECASTING AND PLANNING

Both forecasting and planning deal with future events. Is spite of the differences between them, they are briefly explained below:

Forecasting is an integral part of the planning process. So, each and every person plan his future course of action on the basis of forecasting. Forecasting provides scope for guessing of future happenings. According to Henry Albers. "A successful forecast is something of a miracle and often occurs for the wrong reasons. A part of the problem is that too much is expected from forecasting people want more precise answers than are possible in an environment characterized by uncertainty. So, forecast serves as a guidelines to the executives for proper planning."

| NO. | FORECASTING | PLANNING |
|---|---|---|
| 1. | Forecasting is basis for planning | Planning is basis for future course of action. |
| 2. | No decision can be taken without the help of forecasting. | Planning helps to arrive at certain decisions. They are regarding what is to be done, how is to be done and when is to be done. |
| 3. | Forecasting is done at the middle or lower level of management. | Planning is done at the top level of management. |
| 4. | A few members are involved in forecasting process | A large number of persons are involved in planning process. |
| 5. | Forecasting does not stimulates activity among employees. | Planning stimulates some activity to achieve the objective of the organisation |
| 6. | Forecasting is a tool of planning. | Planning is not a tool of forecasting. |
| 7. | Forecasting is done by experts. | Planning can be done any person. |

## MODEL QUESTIONS

1. What is Business Forecasting? Explain its need and limitations?
2. What do you understand by forecasting? How is it related with planning?
3. Discuss the various techniques of forecasting.
4. What are the differences between forecasting and planning?

# CHAPTER 7

# OBJECTIVES AND MBO

## INTRODUCTION

Every institution or organisation is established for the purpose of achieving some objectives. An individual who starts a business, has the objective of earning profits. A charitable institution, which starts schools and colleges, has the objective of rendering service to the public in the field of education. So, the objective may differ from one organisation to another organisation. But anyhow, each organisation has its own objectives.

## DEFINITION

Mc Farland has defined, "Objectives are the goals, aims or purposes that organisations wish to achieve over varying periods of time."

Terry has defined that, "A managerial objective is the intended goal which prescribes definite scope and suggests direction to the efforts of a manager."

In the words of Knootz and O'Donnel, "Objective is a term commonly used to indicate the endpoint of a management programme."

Simply, objectives may be defined as the expectation of end results for which an organisation is established and which it tries to achieve.

## FEATURES OF OBJECTIVES

The following are the features of objectives:

1. Each individual has objectives of his own. If the individuals collectively form into a group, the group has more than one objective. The created group tries to achieve these objectives.
2. The objectives of any organisation are specially mentioned. The objectives may be short-term or long-term and broad objective or specific objective. Broad objective refers to the one which ensures earnings of profit. Specific objective refers to that objective which tells how such profits are earned for a particular period.
3. The objectives of an organisation should be clearly defined. The clearly defined objectives are interpreted by the executives preferably at the top level. The clearly defined objectives are very much useful to the top executives for the right direction of personnel.
4. At top level, the organisation has broad objectives *i.e.,* to earn certain rate of return on investments. The whole organisation is divided into several sections. Each section has specific objectives. The production section has the specific objectives regarding accomplishing certain level of production. The sales section has the objective regarding achieving certain level of sales and the like. All the sections try to achieve the broad objectives of the organisation. In this way, a hierarchy of objectives is created.
5. The objectives of the organisation must conform to the general needs of the public. The objectives of all the existing organisations have conformity to the requirements of the society. Some restrictions are put through social norms, rules and customs while framing the objectives of the organisation.
6. All the organisations have several objectives at a time. The reason is that the objectives are necessary in the various areas of business. According to Peter F. Drucker, the objectives of business may be relating to marketing, innovation,

profitability, productivity, physical and financial resources and the development of social responsibilities.

7. The objectives of the organisation may be changed in due course. The old objectives are replaced by new ones. The objectives are changed in order to survive in the business world. The policy of govt. and social changes are the main factors responsible for the changes in objectives.
8. The objectives are expressed in numerical terms, say Rs.1,000 to 10,000 units. The profit or sales may be expressed in rupees. The production may be expressed both in rupees and physical units. This helps in measuring the actual performance done to realise the objectives.
9. The framed objectives should be achievable. In other words, whatever may be the objectives, they should be achievable and reasonable ones.

## ADVANTAGES OF OBJECTIVES

The following are some of the advantages of objectives which are briefly explained below:

**1. Unified planning:** Various plans are prepared by several people in an organisation. These plans are consistent to the objectives of an organisation. Then, these objectives encourage unified planning.

**2. Individual motivation:** The objectives of an organisation specifie the purpose of each job and fix the individual goals along with the overall organisations goals. Then, automatically, the individual accepts the organisation's objectives as desirable and attempts to achieve them.

**3. Co-ordination:** Whenever the individual accepts the organisation's objectives as desirable, the possibility of getting co-ordination is very easy.

**4. Control:** Objectives provide the yardstick for performance. The actual performance is compared with standard performance. This will facilitate the control process.

**5. Basis for Decentralisation:** Department-wise or section-wise objectives are fixed in order to achieve common objectives of an organisation. Thus, objectives provide a basis for decentralisation.

## MANAGEMENT BY OBJECTIVES (MBO)

MBO is a management system in which each member of the organisation effectively participates and involves himself. This system gives full scope to the individual strength and responsibility. MBO harmonises the goal of an individual with the organisation's goal. It creates self-control and motivates the manager into action before somebody tells him to do something.

MBO is popularised in the USA by George Odiorne. According to him, MBO is a system wherein the superior and the sub-ordinate managers of an organisation jointly identify its common goals, define each individual's major area of responsibility in terms of the result expected of him and use these measures guides for operating the unit and assessing the contribution of each of its members.

Prof. Reddin defines MBO as, "the establishment of effective standards for managerial positions and the periodic conversion of those into measurable time bound objectives linked vertically and horizontally and with future planning."

## FEATURES OF MBO

1. An attempt is made by the management to integrate the goals of an organisation and individuals. This will lead to effective management.
2. MBO tries to combine the long range goals of organisation with short range goals.
3. Management tries to relate the organisatioon goals with society goals.
4. MBO's emphasis is not only on goals but also on effective performance.
5. It pays constant attention to refining, modifying and improving the goals and changing the approaches to achieve the goals on the basis of experience.
6. It increases the organistional capability of achieving goals at all levels.
7. A high degree of motivation and satisfaction is available to employees through MBO.
8. Recognises the participation of employees in goal setting process.
9. Aims at replacing the exercise of authority with consultations.
10. Encourages a climate of trust, goodwill and a will to perform.

## PROCESS OF MBO

The MBO process is characterised by the balance of objectives of the organisation and individual. The process of MBO is explained below:

**1. Defining organisational objectives:** Initially, organisational objectives are framed by the top level employees of an organisation. Then, it moves downwards. The definition of organisational objectives states why the business is started and exists. First, long-term objectives are framed. Short-term objectives are framed taking into account the feasibility of achieving the long-term objectives.

**2. Goals of each section:** Objectives for each section, department or division are framed on the basis of overall objectives of the organisation. Period within which these objectives should be achieved is also fixed. Goals or objectives are expressed in a meaningful manner.

**3. Fixing key result areas:** Key result areas are fixed on the basis of organisational objectives premises. Key Results Areas (KRA) are arranged on a priority basis. KRA indicates the strength of an organisation. The examples of KRA are profitability, market standing, innovation etc.

**4. Setting subordinate objectives or targets:** The objectives of each subordinate or individual are fixed. It is preferable to fix the objectives at lower level in quantitative units. There should be a free and frank discussion between the superior and his subordinates. Subordinates are induced to set standards themselves by giving an opportunity. If subordinates are allowed to do so, they may set high standards and the chances of their accomplishment are higher. In this way, the objectives or targets of the subordinates are fixed.

**5. Matching resources with objective:** The objectives are framed on the basis of availability of resources. If certain resources (technical personnel or scarce raw material) are not adequately available, the objectives of an organisation are changed accordingly. So, there is a need for matching resources with objectives. Next, the available resources should be properly allocated and utilized.

**6. Periodical review meetings:** The superior and subordinates should hold meetings periodically in which they discuss the progress in the accomplishment of objectives. The fixed standards may be changed in the light of progress. But the basic conditions do not change. The periodical review meeting is held during the period set for achieving the objectives.

**7. Appraisal of activities:** At the end of the fixed period for achieving the objectives, there should be a discussion between the superior and subordinates. The discussion is related with subordinates' performance against the specified standards. The superior should take corrective action. According to Earl P. Strong, "Only by bringing company objectives down from long range to short range, from company level to individual position level, from pre-performance to post-performance and by penalizing for failure and rewarding for success can the effective programme of managing by objectives be accomplished."

The superior should identify the reasons for failure of achieving objectives. The problems faced by the subordinates should be identified and steps should be taken to tackle such problems.

**8. Reappraisal of objectives:** An organisation is living in a dynamic world. There are a lot of changes within short period. The survival and growth of a modern business organisation largely depends upon putting up with the changing conditions. So, the top management executive should review the organisation's objectives to frame the objectives according to the changing situation. According to Newman, Summer and Wanen, "Every manager must frequently reappraise the emphasis he gives to his various objectives. The job is like that of a captain of a large ship who is continually changing his speed and direction in relation to his present position, tides, winds and other conditions."

## BENEFITS OF MBO

The benefits of MBO are explained below:

1. Managers are involved in objectives setting at various levels of management under MBO and this commitment ensures hard work to achieve them.
2. MBO process helps the managers to understand their role in the total organisation.
3. Manager recognises the need for planning and appreciates the planning.
4. MBO provides a foundation for participative management. Sub-ordinates are also involved in goal setting.
5. A department does not work at cross purpose with another department. In other words, each department's objectives are consistent with the objectives of the whole organisation.
6. Systematic evaluation of performance is made with the help of MBO.
7. MBO gives the criteria of performance. It helps to take corrective action.
8. Delegation of authority is easily done with the help of MBO.
9. The practice of MBO helps the manager attend to job enrichment.
10. MBO motivates the workers by job enrichment and makes the jobs meaningful.
11. The responsibility of a worker is fixed through MBO.
12. Decision is taken by the management very quickly. The reason is that each worker knows the purpose of taking a decision and does not oppose the decision.

## PROBLEMS AND LIMITATIONS OF MBO

The problems and limitations of MBO arise due to the application of the MBO. These are discussed below:

1. MBO fails to explain the philosophy; most of the executives do not know how MBO works, what is MBO and why is MBO necessary and how participants can benefit by MBO.
2. MBO is a time consuming process. Much time is needed by senior people for framing the MBO. Next, it leads to heavy expenditure. Sometimes, managers are frustrated over MBO. MBO requires heavy paper work.
3. MBO emphasises only on short-term objectives and does not consider the long-term objectives.
4. The status of subordinates is necessary for proper objec- tives setting. But, this is not possible in the process of MBO.
5. MBO is rigid one. Objectives should be changed according to the changed circumstances, external or internal. If it is not done, the planned results cannot be obtained.
6. The objectives are set without considering the available resources.

## GUIDELINES FOR SETTING EFFECTIVE OBJECTIVES

The limitations of MBO can be reduced to some extent if the organisation follows certain guidelines. These guidelines are offered by Prof. Terry. These guidelines should be followed while setting objectives:

1. Objectives are framed only by the participants who are responsible for implementing them.
2. All the objectives should support the overall objectives of the organisation.
3. Objectives should be attainable ones.
4. Objectives should result in the motivation of workers.
5. A periodical review of objectives is necessary for proper implementation.
6. Objectives should have the characteristics of innovation.
7. The number of objectives for each management member should be a reasonable one. Four or five objectives is a reasonable number.
8. Objectives should be ranked on the basis of their importance.
9. Objectives should be in balance within a given organisation or enterprise.
10. Objectives should be simple and clearly defined.
11. Objectives should be specific and time bound.

## MODEL QUESTIONS

1. What do you understand by "Management by Objectives?.
2. How are Objectives determined?
3. What are the advantages and disadvantages of Management by Objectives?
4. Explain the various principles of Management by Objectives.
5. Describe the various principles of Management by Objectives.

6. Explain the Benefits and Weakeness of MBO.
7. What do you mean by "Management of Objectives"? What are the steps involved in it?
8. What is the concept of hierarchy of objectives? Discuss top-down and bottom-up approaches to objectives-setting.

# CHAPTER 8

# DECISION-MAKING

## INTRODUCTION

Decision-making is also one of the functions of the management. The management executive takes a number of decisions every day. They are not able to discharge their duties without taking any decisions. A decision may be a direction to others to do or not to do. Thus, a decision may be rational or irrational. There are a number of alternatives available to the management. The best one is selected out of the available alternatives.

Best decision-making is necessary for effective functioning of management. The success of management depends upon the quality of decision. If the manager fails to take correct decision, he may not extract any work from his sub-ordinates and may not find a way to finish his work also. Some of the decisions are taken emotionally. This should be avoided with great care. Emotional decision leads to a lot of confusion. So, the decision-making is an important work of the superiors.

## DEFINITION

Manely H. Jones, "It is a solution selected after examining several alternatives chosen because the decider foresees that the course of action he elects will be more than the others to further his goals and will be accompanied by the fewest possible objectionable consequences."

Andrew Smilagyi, "Decision-making is a process involving information, choice of alternative actions, implementations, and evaluation that is directed to the achievement of certain stated goals."

George R. Terry, "Decision-making is the selection based on some criteria from two or more possible alternatives."

John MacDonald, "The business executive is by profession a decision-maker. Uncertainty is his opponent, overcoming it is his mission. Whether the outcome is a consequence of luck or wisdom, the moment of decision-making is without doubt the most creative event in the life of the executive."

D.E. Mc Farland, "A decision is an act of choice wherein an executive forms a conclusion about what must be done in a given situation. A decision represents a behaviour chosen from a number of possible alternatives."

Henry Sisk and Clifston Williams, "A decision is the selection of a course of action from two or more alternatives; the decision-making process is a sequence of steps leading to that selection."

Shull-et-al, "Decision-making is a conscious and human process, involving both individual and social phenomenon based upon factual and value premises, which concludes with a choice of one behavioural activity from among one or more alternatives with the intention of moving towards some desired state of affairs."

Mary Cushing Nites, "Decision-making takes place in adopting the objectives and choosing the means and again when a change in the situation creates a necessity for adjustments."

R.S. Davar, "Decision-making may be defined as the selection based on some criteria of one behaviour alternative from two or more possible alternatives."

## CHARACTERISTICS OF DECISION-MAKING

The following are the characteristics of decision-making:

1. Decision-making is a selection process. The best alternative is selected out of many available alternatives. If there is only one alternative, there is no decision-making.
2. Decision-making is the end process. Decision-making is preceded by detailed discussion and selection of alternatives.
3. Decision-making is the application of intellectual abilities to a great extent. An intelligent man alone can take a good decision.
4. Decision gives happiness to an endeavour who takes various steps to collect all the information which is likely to affect a decision.
5. Decision-making is a dynamic process. An individual takes a number of decisions each day.
6. Decision-making is situational. An individual takes decision according to the situations prevailing. Different decisions may be taken to solve the same problem. The reason is that the situation is changed from time to time.
7. Decision is taken to achieve the objectives of an organisation.
8. Decision-maker has the freedom to take a decision which involves the using of resources in specified ways.
9. Decision-making involves the evaluation of available alternatives through critical appraisal methods.
10. A decision may be both negative or positive. A decision may direct others to do or not to do.

## ELEMENTS OF DECISION-MAKING

1. A problem is fully analysed and the available alternatives are considered before taking a decision.
2. The best decision-making requires intelligence, experience and insight into a problem.
3. A decision is taken according to the environment of business.
4. Centralisation and decentralisation of authority affect the decision indirectly. If authority is centralised, all important decisions are taken by the chief executive. If it is decentralised, key decisions are taken by the top executive and routine decisions are taken by the lower level management people.
5. The psychology of an individual is involved in decision-making.
6. A decision discloses the preferences, intellectual maturity, experience, educational standard, social and religious attitudes, optimism or pessimism, designation and status of a decision maker.
7. Decisions are taken when they are needed.
8. As soon as the decisions are taken, they must be communicated to the concerned persons. Decisions are communicated without ambiguity.
9. Employees are also involved in a decision-making process.

10. Political and social environment of business affect the decision-making. If the management takes a decision after consulting the employees, the following advantages may accrue:
    1. Better relations with employees.
    2. Loyalty to the management.
    3. There is no hindrance in the implementation of a decision.
    4. Efficiency of the employees is increased.
    5. Issuing directions to employes is very easy.

## DECISION-MAKING PROCESS

Decision-making is not an easy job. It requires a lot of skill. A decision-making is affected by a number of factors. So, the manager can take good decisions by adopting a procedure.

A manager may not be able to take good decisions if he fails to follow a sequential set of steps. The decisions-making process depends upon the nature of problem and the nature of organisation. The following is the simple process followed in taking a decision in normal situations:

**1. Identification of a problem:** Identification of a problem means recognition of a problem. Problem arises due to difference between what is and what should be. The changes of business environment form the main reason for creating of a problem. So, the manager should define what the problem is. A well defined problem is half solved. Then, the manager should find the causes of a problem. This is not an easy job. Finding of causes of a problem is used to take quality decision. The manager should continuously watch the decision-making environment and understand the real problem and its causes.

The manager may look into the management reports, find deviations from budget if any, compare the company's results with the competitor's results and efficiency of employees etc. These are used to identify the problem correctly. Here, the manager has to use his experience, imagination and judgement in order to find out the real nature of the problem.

**2. Diagnosing the problem:** There is a slight difference between problem identification and diagnosing the problem. A doctor can diagnosé the disease of a patient. A patient cannot find out what is the real disease. But, a doctor can do so with the information given by a patient. Information is very useful to the doctor. In management, the manager is acting as a doctor while diagnosing the problem.

**3. Collect and analyse the relevant information:** The next step is that required at various levels information should be collected by the manager. Then, the manager has to study the information with great care. It is very useful to analyse the problem from different angles. If the problem is analysed from different angles, a quality and quick decision may be taken by the manager. The manager should see that only relevant information alone is collected and analysed.

**4. Discovery of alternative course of action:** Creative thinking is necessary to develop or discover many alternative courses of action. If there is no alternative, there is no need of taking a decision. If there are more and more of alternatives, the manager will have more freedom to take a decision. A problem can be solved in many ways. At the same time, a solved problem should not arise again in the future.

It is advisable to the manager that he should discover a number of alternatives. The problem of limiting factors is also considered by the manager. Some alternatives cannot be selected due to limiting factors. Time and cost are the probable limiting factors of an organisation.

**5. Analysing the alternatives:** Next, the pros and cons of available alternatives are analysed. Some alternatives offer maximum benefits than others. An alternative is compared with other alternatives. The decision maker can prepare a list of limits for each alternative.

**6. Screening of alternatives:** The available alternatives are screened in the order of maximum benefits derived from them. Each alternative is evaluated in terms of risks involved in implementing them. Both tangible and intangible factors are considered while evaluating or screening each alternative.

Tangible factors include profits earned, time taken, money invested, rate of returns on investment, rate of depreciation etc. Intangible factors include public relations, goodwill of the company, loyalty of employees etc. Sometimes, two or more alternatives are equally suitable by nature. The decision-maker should find the actual difference of alternatives which will be the deciding factor to select an alternative.

Peter F. Drucker has suggested the following criteria to evaluate the available alternative course of action:

(a) Risk — Degree of risks involved in each alternative.

(b) Economy of efforts — Cost, time and efforts involved in each alternative.

(c) Timing or situation — Whether the problem is urgent.

(d) Limitations of resources — Physical, financial and human resources available with the organisation.

**7. Selection of best alternative:** Now, the decision maker can select the best alternative after careful evaluation. An alternative which gives maximum benefits to the organisation is selected. At the same time, the selected alternative should fit with the organisational objectives. The following approaches may be adopted while selecting an alternative.

**A. Experience:** A manager can select an alternative on the basis of his past experience. The past prevailed situation cannot be the same as the present prevailing situation. Situation changes from time to time. Past decisions may be rationally amended to suit the present situation. So, the past experience helps a lot to the manager in taking a decision.

**B. Experimentation:** Each alternative is put into practice and the results are observed under this approach. An alternative which gives best results will be selected. For example, before an organisation selects a production technique, it goes to trial production. The organisation finally selects production techniques which result in a quality production with minimum loss and expenses. This approach, being expensive and time consuming, should be used only on limited scale.

**C. Research and analysis:** This approach is also rarely adopted. In case of critical situation, a decision is taken under this approach. If a lot of calculations are required, they are completed with the help of computers.

**8. Conversion of decision into action:** The future course of action is scheduled on the basis of selected alternative or decision. Here, the manager has to consider the policy of the management. The selected alternative decision is comm-unicated to concerned persons.

This communication facilitates easy implementation of decision. The language of decision should be simple and easily understandable.

**9. Implementation:** Next, the manager has to implement the decision to achieve desired goals. Decision-making process comes to an end with the actual implementation of decision. Implementation is equally important to the selection of alternatives. Implementation plan should provide for time and procedure sequence. Necessary resources should also be allocated and responsibility for specific tasks should be assigned to individuals.

**10. Verifying the decision:** It is the duty of every manager to see whether the decision is properly implemented or not. Verification of implementation of decision ensures the achievement of objectives. The selected alternative may be a ill-chosen one and might cause loss to the organisation. This can be measured with the help of verifying the decision if the manager feels that the selected alternative is not the best one; an amendment may be made to achieve desired goals. This is the simple process of decision-making.

## PRINCIPLES OF DECISION-MAKING

A quality decision may be taken by the manager if he adopts certain principles. These principles are discussed below:

**1. Marginal theory of decision-making:** Many economists have suggested marginal theory of decision-making. They believe that a business is started to earn profits. A manager must take a decision which results in maximising the profits. Therefore, economists argue that the very purpose of an organisation is aimed at maximising profits.

Decision-making should be based on marginal analysis. Here, the manager adopts the Principle of Law of Diminishing Returns. If the management appoints additional labour and uses additional capital, the production may be increased proportionately at reduced rates. A time comes when there is no increase in production with the appointment of additional labour and using additional capital. Then, the appointment of additional labour and using of additional capital will be stopped. In this way, the production of the last unit is marginal. Thus, this marginal principle is applied while taking decisions relating to sales, advertisement, promotion, training and the like.

**2. Mathematical theory:** Venture analysis, game theory, probability theory and waiting theory are some of the mathematical theories. A manager takes a decision on the basis of mathematical theory. Mathematical theory gives scientific approach to the manager while taking a decision.

**3. Psychological theory:** A manager takes a decision on the basis of his aspiration, technological skill, personality, social status and organisation status. Though the manager is expected to take a decision confined to the scope of his responsibility and authority, there is an impact of psychology over the decision. The reason is that decision-making is a mental process.

**4. Principle of alternatives:** If there is only one alternative to solve a problem, there is no need of taking a decision. Decision is a selection process (Please refer to Decision-making Process). All the alternatives are evaluated and screened in the order of their usefulness. Finally, the best alter-native is selected according to the circumstances and purpose.

**5. Principle of limiting factors:** The fundamentals of a problem are studied. An inference or a conclusion is drawn on the basis of study. The manager takes a decision with the help of conclusion or inference. The decision may be based on a limiting factor. The limiting factor may be time, cost or resources. Decisions are supposed to be good and the limiting factor is considered while taking a decision. The reason is that this decision can be implemented in a particular situation.

**6. Principle of participation:** This principle is based on human behaviour and human relationship. Each and every person wants to be treated as an important person. So, the management may allow the employees to have a say in the process of decision-making.

Subordinates should be consulted and due weightage should be given to the opinion expressed by the subordinates, even though they are not concerned with the matter. This will honour the presence of subordinates and result in winning their confidence. The management can ascertain the reaction of the employees to the proposed decision.

## CHARACTERISTICS OF GOOD DECISION OR EFFECTIVE DECISION

A decision is taken after passing various stages. The basic objective of passing through all the stages is to solve the problem. The solution of the problem depends on how effectively the decision has been made or implemented. Thus, a good decision has the following characteristics:

**1. Action orientation:** Various steps are necessary in implementing the decision. For implementation, decisions should have utility. There is no use of taking a decision if the management does not find it necessary to implement the decision. Thus, a good decision has the character of various stages.

**2. Goal direction:** An organisation is functioning to achieve certain goals. Each and every day, the manager takes a number of decisions. These decisions are taken and action is directed to achieve the goals. The value of decision depends upon the quantum of goals achieved. A decision which helps in achieving the goal is a good decision.

**3. Efficiency in implementation:** An effective decision alone will have scope for implementation. The reason is that a good decision is taken only after cosidering all possible internal and external factors. Studying these factors is necessary to implement the decision effctively. A decision is implemented with full co-operation of employees, which in turn will produce good results.

## ADMINISTRATIVE PROBLEMS IN DECISION-MAKING

**1. Accuracy:** The decision-maker should analyse the situation. The reason is that if the decision is taken by analysing the situation, the problem can be easily solved. The correctness of information for analysis will help taking accurate decision.

**2. Environment for decision:** Organisational and physical environments are responsible for effective decision. Mutual co-operation and proper understanding among employees are necessary for creating a satisfactory environment. Such a congenial good environment will lead to taking effective decisions.

**3. Timely decision:** Time plays an important role in decision-making. If any decision is taken without considering time, that will not be considered a business decision. Besides, the decision will be a waste if the decision-maker fails to take timely decision.

**4. Communication of decision:** The decision-maker should communicate the decisions to needy persons. The language selected by the decision-maker should be known to the persons to whom the decisions are communicated. Simple and unambiguous words are used while communicating the decisions.

**5. Participative decision-making:** The extent of participation of workers in decision-making depends upon the willingness of the top management.

The top management people think that they have monopoly in decision-making and the dignity of top management is affected if the workers participate in decision-making. Even suggestions are not invited from the workers while taking a decision. But it is necessary to allow workers to play their role while taking a decision.

**6. Implementation:** The decision-maker has responsibility to implement a decision. If not, there is no use of taking a decision. The decision-maker should get the co-operation of his subordinates to implement a decision. The decision-maker explains the importance of imple-mentation of a decision. He should convince the subordinates. He may lose many of his so-called friends while implementing a decision. But, he should be firm in the implementation. He should consider only the welfare of his organisation.

## TYPES OF DECISIONS

Some of the decisions are discussed below:

**1. Programmed decisions:** They are otherwise called *routine decisions* or *structured decisions*. The reason is that these types of decisions are taken frequently and they are repetitive in nature. This decision is taken within the purview of the policy of the organisation. Only lower level management takes programmed decision and has short-term impact. Granting over time work, placing purchase order (for materials) etc., are some of the examples of programmed decisions. There is a clear cut procedure to take programmed decisions. The decision-maker need not ask anything from the Personnel Manager or Board of Directors while taking programmed decisions.

**2. Non-programmed decision:** They are otherwise called *strategic decisions* or *basic decisions* or policy decisions or unstructured decisions. This decision is taken by top management people whenever the need arises. A careful analysis is made by the management before taking a policy decision. The management may publish its policy in small book which is known as policy manual. Policy decision involves heavy expenditure to management. Starting a new business, whether to export or not, acquisition of a business etc. are some of the examples of non-programmed decisions. This decision has a long-term impact on business. A slight mistake in the policy decision is bound to injure the entire organisation.

**3. Major decision:** Major decision relates to the purchase of fixed assets with more value. The purchase of land and building is an example of major decision. This decision is taken by the top management.

**4. Minor decision:** Minor decision relates to the purchase of current assets with less value. Purchase of pencil, pen, ink, etc., are some of the examples of minor decision. This decision is taken by lower level management people.

**5. Operative decision:** A decision which relates to day-to-day operation of an organisation is known as operative decision. This type of decision is taken by middle level management people normally. The reason is that they are working at supervisory level and have a good knowledge of the operations. The time of payment of overtime wages is fixed by middle level management people. It is an example of operative decision.

**6. Organisational decision:** The decision-maker takes a decision and implements it for effective functioning of organisation and it is called organisational decision. He takes this decision on his authority and capacity.

**7. Personal decision:** The decision-maker takes a decision for his personal life which is known as personal decision. He implements this decision in his home and sets right his personal life. This decision does not reflect the functioning of an organisation. The decision-maker is not a member of an organisation while taking a personal decision.

**8. Individual decision:** Confusion exists regarding the difference between individual decision and personal decision. They are not one and the same. The decision-maker is a member of an organisation while taking an individual decision. He can implement it in the organisation. He is delegated with authority to take individual decision. He considers the policy and situation prevailing in an organisation while taking individual decision.

**9. Group decision:** A committee is formed by the top management for specific purposes. Here, the top management feels that no individual can take effective decision to solve a problem. The top management fixes the time within which the committee is expected to submit its report with concrete decisions.

**10. Departmental decision:** Here, the decision-maker is department head or department manager. He takes a decision to run the department. Department decision has no impact on other departments. This decision is implemented within the concerned department itself.

**11. Non-economic decision:** Non-economic decision refers to a decision which does not incur any expenses. These types of decisions are taken at all levels of management. A decision which relates to setting right the morale behaviour of workers is termed as *non-economic* decision.

**12. Crisis decision:** A decision is taken to meet unexpected situations. There is no possibility and time for the decision-maker for getting through investigation while taking a crisis decision. It may be otherwise called spot decision. The reason is that whenever a need arises, the decision maker has to take a decision without wasting a second.

**13. Research decision:** A decision is taken after analysing the pros and cons of a particular matter. There is no pressure on the decision-maker to take such a decision. Research decision requires a lot of information. The quality of research decision is fully depending upon the availability of reliable information.

**14. Problem decision:** A decision is taken to solve a problem. The problem may be an expected one or unexpected one. Besides, the arrived decision does not create any more problem to the organisation.

**15. Opportunity decision:** This pertains to a decision taken to make use of the advantages available to the company or organisation. The advantages may be increasing the turnover, introducing a new product, building of another similar unit to avoid competition etc.

**16. Certainty decision:** Here, the term certainty refers to accurate knowledge of the outcome from each choice. For example, ascertaining how much profits will be maximised by introducing a new product or increasing the selling price and the like. There is only one outcome for each choice. The decision-maker himself knows the outcome and consequences of choice.

**17. Uncertainity decision:** The outcome is not accurate or several outcomes are possible whenever a decision is taken. The reason is that the decision-maker has incomplete knowledge and he does not know the consequences. For example, while marketing a new product, the decision (amount of profits) depends upon the prosperity period of that product. If the prosperity period is long, the amount of profit is high and vice versa.

Management people take a number of decisions everyday. These decisions are aimed at solving the existing problems. No decision creates any new problem to the management. There should be justice in taking a decision.

## PERSONAL PHASE OF DECISION-MAKING

Decision-maker may not take the best decision in all cases. Next, there is no method available to him to test his decision to find out whether it is the best or right one. There is a need of definite policies and criteria in an organisation to test a decision as to its goodness or to its rightness. A structured organisation has definite policies and criteria.

Generally, the manager is a decision-maker in an organisation. Two managers do not take same decision even though the same data are supplied to them. So, there are some differences in decision-making. These are due to personal characteristics and qualities of managers. The existence of different characteristics and qualities in managers is due to the following:

**1. Intelligence:** Here, intelligence is the ability of using common sense in decision-making. So, the intelligence is not concerned with formal education. Highly educated persons do not take best decisions in all cases. There is a need of perception of quality managers to take the best decisions.

**2. Education:** Education develops the broad outlook of the decision-maker. Higher education is different from good education. A good education helps the decision-maker to take best decision even in complex situations rather than higher education. Higher education is nothing but getting master degree from a recognised educational institution. In other words, good education is acquiring thorough knowledge in a particular area of subject-matter. At the same time, the level of knowledge may not increase correspondingly to the long years of education. If a person has inner urge to learn more and more, he will become an expert in taking decisions.

**3. Experience:** The experience of an individual can improve the decision-making ability. Decision-maker can survive only when he has skill for original thinking. Decision-maker should use his personal experience in taking a decision.

**4. Courage:** The decision-maker should have courage to take and implement a decision. The very success of decision depends upon the courage of the decision-maker.

**5. Motivation:** Everybody wants recognition for their action. Likewise, a person who takes a decision wants to have it by his colleagues. If it is not so, he will not take even a simple decision in future. Recognition of a decision is a motivation tonic to the decision-maker. Next, the decision-maker does not expect both criticism and suggestions.

**6. Forecasting ability:** The quality of a decision depends upon the forecasting ability of the decision-maker. If the decision-maker has the forecasting ability, even decisions made in a hurried manner may produce good results at times. Besides, he may use the available opportunities and avoid problematic situations. In this way, the need for taking additional decisions is also avoided.

**7. Self-confidence:** First, the decision-maker has correctness of his decision. Then, he will place the decision before others to be accepted. The self-confident decision-maker can take decision as and when required. On the other hand, if the decision-maker has no self-confidence, he will make delay in the decision-making process and it will make the situation go from bad to worse. So, there is a need of self-confidence on the part of a decision-maker.

## MODEL QUESTIONS

1. Explain various steps of decision-making.
2. What are the different steps in decision-making?
3. What are the features of decision-making?
4. What are the various level of importance of decision-making?
5. Describe any four quantitative techniques used for management decision-making?
6. What is the difference between choice making and decision-making?
7. Define decision-making. Explain the need for and the factors involved in decision-making.

# CHAPTER 9

# ORGANISATION

- INTRODUCTION
- MEANING
- DEFINITION
- FUNCTIONS OF ORGANISATION
- PRINCIPLES OF ORGANISATION
- NATURE OR CHARACTERISTICS OF ORGANISATION
- IMPORTANCE OF ORGANISATION OR ADVANTAGES OF ORGANISATION
- CLASSIFICATION OF ORGANISATION
- FORMAL ORGANISATION
- CHARACTERISTICS OF FORMAL ORGANISATION
- ADVANTAGES OF FORMAL ORGANISATION
- ARGUMENTS AGAINST FORMAL ORGANISATION
- INFORMAL ORGANISATION
- CHARACTERISTICS OF INFORMAL ORGANISATION
- ADVANTAGES OF INFORMAL ORGANISATION
- DISADVANTAGES OF INFORMAL ORGANISATION
- DIFFERENCE BETWEEN FORMAL AND INFORMAL ORGANISATION
- THEORIES OF ORGANISATION
- CLASSICAL THEORY
- CHARACTERISTICS OF CLASSICAL THEORY
- CRITICISM OF CLASSICAL THEORY
- NEO-CLASSICAL THEORY
- CONTRIBUTIIONS OF NEO-CLASSICAL THEORY
- CRITICISM OF NEO-CLASSICAL THEORY
- MODERN THEORY
- ESSENTIALS OF MODERN THEORY
- CRITICISM OF MODERN THEORY
- MOTIVATION THEORY
- DECISION THEORY
- MODEL QUESTIONS

## INTRODUCTION

Organisation is a mechanism or structure which helps the activities to be performed effectively. The organisation is established for the purpose of achieving the business objectives. The business objectives may differ from one business to another. Whatever may be the business objectives, there is a need of an organisation.

The word 'Organisation' is derived from the word 'Organism' which means an organised body with connected interdependent parts sharing common life. When a group of persons working together to achieve a common goal, the problems such as who decides what issues, who does what work and what action should be taken on the basis of certain conditions may arise.

## MEANING

Organisation is the detailed arrangement of work and working conditions in order to perform the assigned activities in an effective manner.

Organisation can be compared to a human body. The human body consists of hands, feet, eyes, ears, nose, fingers, mouth, etc. These parts are performing their work independently and at the same time, one part cannot be a substitute to another. The same principles can be identified in the organisation also. The organisation consists of different departments. Each department performs its work independently and cannot be a substitute to another.

## DEFINITION

Haney, "Organisation is a harmonious adjustment of specialised parts for the accomplishment of some common purpose or purposes."

Mc Farland, "An identified group of people contributing their efforts towards the attainment of goals is called an organisation."

Allen, "The process of identifying and grouping the work is to be performed, defining and delegating responsibility and authority and establishing relationships for the purpose of enabling people to work most effectively together in accomplishing objectives."

Mooney and Reily, "Organisation is the form of every human association for the attainment of a common purpose."

Chester Bernard, "A system of co-operative activities of two or more persons is called organisation."

R.C. Davis, "Any group of people, large or small, which has been implemented adequately and is co-operating willingly under the direction of competent executive leadership in an effective, economical accomplishment of certain common objective."

G.R. Terry, "Organising is the establishing of effective beha-vioural relationships among persons so that they may work together effectively and gain personal satisfaction in doing selected tasks under given environmental conditions for the purpose of achieving some goal or objective."

Koontz O'Donnel, "Organising involves the establishment of an international structure of roles through determination and enumeration of the activities required to achieve the goals of an enterprise and each part of it; the grouping of these activities, the assignment of such groups of activities to the manager, the delegation of authority to carry them out and provision for co-ordination of authority and informational relationship, horizontally and vertically, in the organisation structure."

Louis Al Allen, "Organisation is that process of identifying and grouping the work to be performed, defining and delegating responsibility and authority and establishing relationships for the purpose of enabling people to work most effectively together in accomplishing objectives."

Oliver Sheldon, "Organisation is the process of so combining the work which the individual or groups have to perform with the facilities necessary for its creation that the duties so performed provide the best channels for the efficient, systematic, positive and co-ordinated application of the available efforts."

Spriegel, "In its broadest sense, organisation refers to the relationship between the various factors present in a given endeavour.... Factory organisation concerns itself primarily with the internal relationships within the factory such as responsibilities of personnel arrangement and grouping of machines and material control. From the stand-point of the enterprise as a whole, organisation is the structural relationship between the various factors in an enterprise."

Wheeler, "Internal organisation is the structural framework of duties and responsibilities required to personnel in performing various functions within the company.... It is essentially a blue print for action resulting in a mechanism for carrying out the function to achieve the goals set up by the company management."

## FUNCTIONS OF ORGANISATION

From the above definitions, it is understood that the functions of organisation includes determination of activities, grouping of activities, allotment of duties to specified persons, delegation of authority, defining relationships and the co-ordination of various activities.

**1. Determination of activities:** It includes the deciding and division of various activities required to achieve the objectives of the organisation. The entire work is divided into various parts and again each part is sub-divided into various sub-parts. For example, the purchase work may be divided into requisition of items, placing of an order, storage and so on.

**2. Grouping of activities:** The next function of organisation is that the identical activities are grouped under one individual or a department. The activities of sales such as canvassing, advertisements and debt collection activities are grouped under one department *i.e.,* sales department.

**3. Allotment of duties to specified persons:** In order to ensure effective performance, the grouped activities are allotted to specified persons. In other words, the purchasing activities are assigned to the Purchase Manager; the production activities are assigned to Production Manager; the sales activities are assigned to Sales Manager and the like. Besides, adequate staff members are appointed under the specified persons. The specified persons are specialised in their respective fields. If there is any need, appropriate training would be provided to such persons.

**4. Delegation of authority:** Assignment of duties or allotment of duties to specified persons is followed by delegation of authority. It will be very difficult for a person to perform the duties effectively, if there is no authority to do it. While delegating a authority, responsibilities are also fixed. Thus, the Production Manager may be delegated with the authoriy to produce the goods and fixed with the responsibility of producing quality goods.

**5. Defining relationship:** When a group of persons is working together for a common goal, it becomes necessary to define the relationship among them in clear terms. If it is done, each person will know who is his boss, from whom he has to receive orders and to whom he is answerable. In another sense, each boss should know what authority he has and over which person.

**6. Co-ordination of various activities:** The delegated authority and responsibility should be co-ordinated by the Chief Managerial Staff. The reason is that there must be a separate and responsible person to see whether all the activities are going on to accomplish the objectives of the organisation or not.

## PRINCIPLES OF ORGANISATION

The work can be completed in time whenever a technique or a principle is adopted. So, the success or failure of an organisation depends upon the principles to be followed in the organisation. The principles of organisation may be termed as a tool used by the organisation. Some experts like Taylor, Fayol and Urwick have given the principles of organisation. They are briefly discussed below:

**1. Principle of definition:** It is necessary to define and fix the duties, responsibilities and authority of each worker. In addition to that the organisational relationship of each worker with others should be clearly defined in the organisational set up.

**2. Principle of objective:** The activities at all levels of organisation structure should be geared to achieve the main objectives of the organisation. The activities of the different departments or sections may be different in nature and in approach, but these should be concentrated only for achieving the main objectives.

**3. Principle of specialisation or division of work:** Division of work means that the entire activities of the organi-sation are suitably grouped into departments or sections. The departments or sections may be further divided into several such units so as to ensure maximum efficiency. This will help to fix up the right man to the right job and reduce waste of time and resources.

The work is assigned to each person according to his educational qualification, experience, skill and interests. He should be mentally and physically fit for performing the work assigned to him. The required training may be provided to the needy persons. It will result in attaining specialisation in a particular work or area.

**4. Principle of co-ordination:** The objectives of the organisation may be achieved quickly whenever co-ordination exists among the workers. At the same time each work can be done effectively by having co-ordination. The final objective of all organisations is to get smooth and effective co-ordination.

**5. Principle of authority:** When many persons are working together in one place, there will be a difference of power and authority. Of these persons, some will rule and others will be ruled. Normally, maximum powers are vested with the top executives of the organisation. These senior members should delegate their authorities to their subordinates on the basis of their ability. In certain cases, the subordinates are motivated through the delegation of authority and they perform the work efficiently with responsibility.

**6. Principle of responsibility:** Each person is responsible for the work completed by him. Authority is delegated from the top level to the bottom level of the organisation. But the responsibility can be delegated to some extent. While delegating the authority, there is no need of delegation of responsibility. So, the responsibility of the junior staff members should be clearly defined.

**7. Principle of explanation:** While allocating duties to the persons, the extent of liabilities of the person would be clearly explained to the concerned person. It will enable the person to accept the authority and discharge his duties.

**8. Principle of efficiency:** Each work can be completed efficiently wherever the climate or the organisational structure facilitates the completion of work. The work should be completed with minimum members, in less time, with minimum resources and within the right time.

**9. Principle of uniformity:** The organisation should make the work distribution in such a manner that there should be an equal status and equal authority and powers among the same line officers. It will avoid the problems of dual subordination or conflicts in the organisational set up. Besides, it increases co-ordination among the officers.

**10. Principle of correspondence:** Authority and responsibility should be in parity with each other. If it is not so, the work cannot be effectively discharged by any officers, whatever his ability may be. At the same time, if authority alone is delegated without responsibility, the authority may be misused. In another sense, if responsibility is delegated without the authority, it is a dangerous one.

**11. Principle of unity of command:** This is also sometimes called the *principle of responsibility*. The organisational set up should be arranged in such a way that a subordinate should receive the instruction or direction from one authority or boss. If there is no unity of command in any organisational set up, the subordinate may neglect his duties. It will result in the non completion of any work. In the absence of unity of command, there is no guidance available to the subordinates and there is no controlling power for the top executives of the organisation. Further, some subordinates will have to do more work and some others will not do any work at all.

**12. Principle of balance:** There are several units functioning separately under one organisational set up. The work of one unit might have been commenced after the completion of the work by another unit. So, it is essential that the sequence of work should be arranged scientifically.

**13. Principle of equilibirum balance:** The expansion of business activities require some changes in the organisation. In certain periods, some sections or departments are overloaded and some departments are under loaded. During this period, due weightage should be given on the basis of the new work load. The overloaded sections or departments can be further divided into sub sections or sub-departments. It would entail in the effective control over all the organisational activities.

**14. Principle of continuity:** It is essential that there should be a re-operation of objectives, re-adjustment of plants and provision of opportunities for the development of future management. This process is taken over by every organisation periodically.

**15. Principle of span of control:** This is also called *span of management* or *span of supervision* or *levels* of organisation. This principle is based on the principle of relationship.

Span of control refers to the maximum number of members effectively supervised by a single individual. The number of members may be increased or decreased according to the nature of work done by the subordinate or the ability of the supervisor. In the administration area, under one executive, nearly four or five subordinates may work. In the lower level or the factory level, under one supervision, the twenty or twenty five number of workers may work. The span of control enables the smooth functioning of the organisation.

**16. Principle of leadership facilitation:** The organisational set up may be arranged in such a way that the persons with leadership qualities are appointed in key positions. The leadership qualities are honesty, devotion, enthusiasm and inspiration.

**17. Principle of exception:** The junior officers are disturbed by the seniors only when the work is not done according to the plans laid down. It automatically reduces the work of middle level officers and top level officers. So, the top level officers may use the time gained by reduction in workload for framing the policies and chalking out the plans of organisation.

**18. Principle of flexibility:** The organisational set up should be flexible to adjust to the changing environment of business. The organisation should avoid the complicated procedures and permit an expansion or contraction of business activities.

**19. The scalar principle:** This is also called *chain of command* or *line of authority*. Normally, the line of authority flows from the top level to bottom level. It also establishes the line of communication. Each and every person should know who is his superior and to whom he is answerable.

**20. Principle of simplicity and homogeneity:** The organisation structure should be simple. It is necessary to understand a person who is working in the same organisation. If the organisation structure becomes a complex one, junior officers do not undestand the level and the extent of responsibility for a particular activity. The simplicity of the organisational structure enables the staff members to maintain equality and homogeneity. If equality and homogeneity are maintained in one organisation, it is possible to determine whether the staff members discharge their duties to realise the objective of the organisation.

**21. Principle of Unitty of Direction:** This is also called the *principle of co-ordination*. The major plan is divided into sub-plans in a good organisational set up. Each sub-plan is taken up by a particular group or department. All the groups or departments are requested to co-operate to attain the main objectives or in implementing major plan of the organisation.

**22. Principle of joint decisions:** In the business organisation, there are number of decisions taken by the officers to run the business. If a complicated problem arises more than one member examines the problems and takes the decisions. Whenever the decision is taken jointly, the decision gives the benefit for a long period and the decision is based on various aspects of the organisational set up.

## NATURE OR CHARACTERISTICS OF ORGANISATION

Organisation is the pioneering step of the management. The functions of management are sitting over the strong organisational set up. A palace may be constructed only when a very strong foundation is laid. The same principle is followed here. Organisation is the foundation of management. Without organisation, the functions of management such as planning, organising, staffing, directing, co-ordinating and controlling cannot succeed.

Organisation supplies the human and material resources and helps to achieve the objectives of business. The organisation provides the means or techniques with strong efforts for more production and effective completion of the work. Organisation increases the certainity and promptness in the completion of work by assigning fixed duties to every person. Whenever the duties are fixed, it automatically develops team spirit towards the realisation of common goals. Initially, the total work of the enterprise can be divided into various parts and then linked with all the parts as and when the need arises to achieve main objectives. The connection of various parts of the organisation is given by the authority relationship of organisational structure. The relationship may operate upward, downward, and sidewise of the organisation.

**1. Division of labour:** The total work can be divided into many parts for effective performance of the work. Each part of work may be completed by one person or a group of persons. But, all the parts of the work are done with the aim to achieve the main objective of the organisation. The work is assigned to a person who is specialised in that particular work.

If there is a proper division of labour, no person will be allowed to do anything according to his own way unless and otherwise he is not well equipped. The division of labour results in the creation of specialised persons because a person does the same work again and again. No waste of time, energy and resources are some of the advantages of division of labour. In addition to this, the division of labour results in the increase of quality output and quantity of product without any additional capital.

**2. Co-ordination:** Different persons are assigned different works in one organisation. But, all the works are performed to achieve the objectives. It implies that there is a need of co-ordination among the workers in an organisation. Each and every department or section of the organisation should have relationship with each other, to get mutual co-operation.

**3. Objectives:** The objectives of the organisation should be defined clearly. The objectives cannot be achieved without the existence of a good organisational structure. In turn, the organisation cannot exist without objectives for a long period.

**4. Authority-responsibility structure:** An organisation means an arrangement of position of executives by adopting a rank system. In other words, a subordinate has one boss and a superior has control over the subordinate specifically. The position of each of the executives is defined with regard to the extent of authority and responsibility vested in him to discharge the duties.

**5. Communication:** Every organisation has its own communication system and the methods. The success of management depends upon the effective system of communication. The reason is that each and every person working in an organisation should know the techniques of communication and the importance of communication. The channels of communication may be divided into formal, informal, downward and upward or horizontal.

## IMPORTANCE OF ORGANISATION OR ADVANTAGES OF ORGANISATION

Organisation creates the relationship between top level executives and lower level staff members. The top level executives perform the functions, like planning, organising, staffing, directing, controlling the lower level people. The actual work is completed at lower level of the organisation. In this way, the organisation maintains the relationship with each other in an enterprise.

**1. Facilatate administration:** Administration aims at earning the highest profit by utilising the available resources properly. There is a planning, policy making, direction and co-ordination in the administration level to achieve the objectives. Besides, the administration classifies the activities of the business department-wise and appoints the officers, assistants, supervisors, executives to facilitate the achievement of objectives.

There should be an effective administration to achieve the objectives of the business. Duplication of work, wrong planning, inefficient personal, lack of motivation, improper allocation of duties and responsibilities, absence of co-ordination, communication gap, improper instructions are the ingredients of ineffective administration. This ineffective administration can be removed by having a sound organisation. Allen observes that *"A properly designed and balanced organisation facilitates both management and operation of the enterprise. Inadequate organisation may not only discourage but also actually preclude effective administration"*.

**2. Increases the efficiency of management:** Under good organisation, there is a chance of exhausting the worker's ability in full and utilisation of resources effectively. Confusion, delay and duplication of work are avoided in good organisation. It automatically motivates the employees who are working in an organisation and increases the efficiency of management.

**3. Facilitates growth and diversification:** The structure of the company depends upon the structure of the organisation. The structure of the company can be changed whenever the growth and expansion activities are carried out. The growth of business means an increase in the scale of operation and diversification means starting of production of a new type of products. Changes in the organisation may result in the appointment of additional staff members, de-centralisation of authority and responsibility, raising of additional capital, identification of the consumer's satisfaction and preferences, expansion of sales promotion activities and the like.

**4. Ensures optimum utilisation of material resources and human efforts:** Division of work and specialisation are the tools used to achieve the objective of optimum utilisation of material, resources and human efforts. Right man, right time and the right job can also be applied to them. Good organisation increases the efforts of the employees and the working facilities.

**5. Adoption of new technology:** The effectiveness of an enterprise is measured by the reaction of staff members to the adopting of a new technology. In the scientific world, there is a lot of innovations and inventions identified in the area of production, distribution and personnel management. If the new technology is adopted by the enterprise, the maximum benefits can be obtained in any field or activity. A flexible organisational structure is needed to adopt a new technology.

**6. Places proportionate importance to the various activities of the enterprise:** Organisation classifies the entire business activities into departments. Each department is receiving attention according to its importance it has in the achievement of business objectives. Money and efforts are spent in proportion to the contribution made by each and every department. It does not mean that less important department activities are neglected. It means that due importance is given to each department according to its contribution towards the achievement of the objectives.

**7. Encourages creativity and initiative:** A sound organisational structure will give an opportunity for the staff to show their hidden talents which will help the enterprise to achieve the business goals and earn higher profits. Clear distribution of authority and responsibility, incentives offered for specialised work and freedom given to personal work, increases the spirit of constructive and creative approach in management.

**8. Facilitates co-ordination:** The activities of different departments are grouped together to achieve the business objectives. Each department performs its own function in a closely related manner and not as competitors.

**9. Facilitates training and development of managerial personnel:** A sound organisational provides training to new staff members before placement and give refresher training to the existing staff members to improve their efficiency. The training may be given within the company or outside the company according to the training facilitates available. Now-a-days training institutes give training to the needy persons with the help of the different experts from various fields. These training institutes are collecting data directly from the field used in the training.

**10. Prevents the growth of secret, influence and corruption:** Sound organisation develops the morale, honesty, devotion to duty and loyalty of business organisations. Normally, these help remove corruption, secret and influence. Only an unsound organisation develops secret, influence and corruption.

## CLASSIFICATION OF ORGANISATION

The organisation can be classified on the basis of authority and responsibility assigned to the personnel and the relationship with each other. In this way, an organisation can be either *formal or informal*.

## FORMAL ORGANISATION

The formal organisation represents the classification of activities within the enterprise, indicates who reports to whom and explains the vertical journal of communication which connects the chief executive to the ordinary workers. In other words, an organisational structure clearly defines the duties, responsibilities, authority and relationships as prescribed by the top management.

In an organisation, each and every person is assigned the duties and given the required amount of authority and responsibility to carry out this job. It creates the co-ordination of activities of every person to achieve the common objectives. It indirectly induces the worker to work most efficiently. The inter-relationship of staff members can be shown in the organisation chart and manuals under formal organisation.

## CHARACTERISTICS OF FORMAL ORGANISATION

The important characteristics of a formal organisation are given below:

1. It is properly planned.
2. It is based on delegated authority.
3. It is deliberately impersonal.
4. The responsibility and accountability at all levels of organisation should be clearly defined.
5. Organisational charts are usually drawn.
6. Unity of command is normally maintained.
7. It provides for division of labour.

## ADVANTAGES OF FORMAL ORGANISATION

1. The definite boundaries of each worker is clearly fixed. It automatically reduces conflict among the workers. The entire building is kept under control.

2. Overlapping of responsibility is easily avoided. The gaps between the responsibilities of the employees are filled up.

3. Buck passing is very difficult under the formal organisation. Normally exact standards of performance are established under formal organisation. It results in the motivating of employees.

4. A sense of security arises from classification of the task.

5. There is no chance for favouritism in evaluation and placement of the employee.

6. It makes the organisation less dependent on one man.

Keith Davis observes that formal organisation is and should be our paramount organisation type as a general rule. It is the pinnacle of man's achievement in a disorganised society. It is man's orderly, conscious and intelligent creation for human benefit.

## ARGUMENTS AGAINST FORMAL ORGANISATION

1. In certain cases, the formal organisation may reduce the spirit of initiative.

2. Sometimes authority is used for the sake of convenience of the employee without considering the need for using the authority.

3. It does not consider the sentiments and values of the employees in the social organisation.

4. The formal organisation may reduce the speed of informal communication.

5. It creates the problems of coordination.

## INFORMAL ORGANISATION

Informal organisation is an organisational structure which establishes the relationship on the basis of the likes and dislikes of officers without considering the rules, regulations and procedures. These types of relationships are not recognised by officers but only felt. The friendship, mutual understanding and confidence are some of the reasons for existing informal organisation. For example, a salesman receives orders or instructions directly from the sales manager instead of his supervisors.

The informal organisation relationship exists under the formal organisation also. The informal organisation relationship or informal relations give a greater job satisfaction and result in maximum production.

According to C.J. Bernard, "Informal organisation brings cohesiveness to formal organisation. It brings to the members of a formal organisation a feeling of belonging, status of self respect and gregarious satisfaction. Informal organisations are important means of maintaining the personality of the individual against certain effects of formal organisation which tend to disintegrate personality."

## CHARACTERISTICS OF INFORMAL ORGANISATION

1. Informal organisation arises without any external cause i.e., voluntarily.
2. It is a social structure formed to meet personal needs.

3. Informal organisation has no place in the organisation chart.
4. It acts as an agency of social control.
5. Informal organisation can be found on all levels of organisation within the managerial hierarchy.
6. The rules and traditions of informal organisation are not written but are commonly followed.
7. Informal organisation develops from habits, conduct, customs and behaviour of social groups.
8. Informal organisation is one of the parts of total organisation.
9. There is no structure and definiteness to the informal organisation.

## ADVANTAGES OF INFORMAL ORGANISATION

The advantages of informal organisations are briefly explained below:

1. It fills up the gaps and deficiency of the formal organisation.
2. Informal organisation gives satisfaction to the workers and maintains the stability of the work.
3. It is a useful channel of communication.
4. The presence of informal organisation encourages the executives to plan the work correctly and act accordingly.
5. The informal organisation also fills up the gaps among the abilities of the managers.

## DISADVANTAGES OF INFORMAL ORGANISATION

The disadvantages of Informal Organisation are summarised below:

1. It has the nature of upsetting the morality of the workers.
2. It acts according to mob psychology.
3. Informal organisation indirectly reduces the efforts of management to promote greater productivity.
4. It spreads rumour among the workers regarding the functioning of the organisation unnecessarily.

## DIFFERENCE BETWEEN FORMAL AND INFORMAL ORGANISATION

Some of the differences between Formal Organisation and Informal Orgainsation are discussed below:

## THEORIES OF ORGANISATION

Organisation theory means the study of the structure, functioning and performance of organisation and the behaviour of individual and groups within it.

The various theories of organisation are given below:

1. Classical theory.
2. Neo-classical theory.
3. Modern theory.
4. Motivation theory.
5. Decision theory.

| *Formal Organisation* | *Informal Organisation* |
|---|---|
| 1. It arises due to delegation of authoriy. | It arises due to social interaction of people. |
| 2. It gives importance to terms of authority and functions. | It gives importance to people and their relationships. |
| 3. It is created deliberately. | It is spontaneous and natural. |
| 4. The formal authority is attached to a position. | The informal authority is attached to a person. |
| 5. Rules, duties and responsi-bilities of workers are given in writing. | No such written rules and duties followed in informal organisation. |
| 6. Formal organisation comes from outsiders who are superior in the line of organisation. | Informal organisation comes from those persons who are objects of its control. |
| 7. Formal authority flows from upwards to downwards. | Informal authority flows upwards to downwards from or horizontally. |
| 8. Formal organisation may grow to maximum size. | Informal organisation tends to remain smaller. |
| 9. It is created for technological purposes. | It arises from man's quest for social satisfaction. |
| 10. Formal organisation is per-manent and stable. | There is no such permanent nature and stability. |

The explanation of the above theories are given below:

## 1. CLASSICAL THEORY

The classical theory mainly deals with each and every part of a formal organisation. The classical theory was found by the father of scientific management, Frederick W.Taylor. Next, a systematic approach to the organisation was made by Monney and Reicey.

The classical theory is based on the following four principles:

A. Division of labour;

B. Scalar and functional processes;

C. Structure; and

D. Span of control.

**A. Division of labour:** This theory fully depends upon the principle of division of labour. Under the division of labour, the production of a commodity is divided into the maximum number of different divisions. The work of each division is looked after by different persons. Each person is specialised in a particular work. In other words, the work is assigned to a person according to his specialisation and the interest he has in the work . The division of labour results in the maximum production or output with minimum expenses incurred and minimum capital employed.

**B. Scalar and functional processes:** The Scalar process deals with the growth of organisation vertically. The functional process deals with the growth of organisation horizontally. The scalar principles refer to the existence of relationship between superior and subordinate. In this way, the superior gives instructions or orders to the subordinates (various levels of management) and gets back the information from the subordinate regarding the operations carried down at different levels or stages. This information is used for the purpose of taking decision or remedial action to achieve the main objectives of the business.

The Scalar chain means the success of domination by the superior on the subordinate from the top to the bottom of organisation. The line of authority is based on the principle of unity of command which means that each subordinate does work under one superior only.

**C. Structure:** The organisational structure may be defined as the prescribed patterns of work related behaviour of workers which result in the accomplishment of organisational objectives. The organisational structure is used as a tool for creating a relationship among the various functions which make up the organisation.

Specialisation and co-ordination are the main issues in the design of an organisational structure. The term specialisation includes the division of labour and the usage of special machines, tools and equipments. Specialisation is obtained when a person is requested to do a single work and it results in the increase in productivity. The facilities or advantages of suitable training, easy allocation of work, job scheduling and effective control are also obtained from specialisation.

Co-ordination means an orderly performance in operations to achieve organisational objectives. Normally, the business units are organised on a functional basis. The functions are performed by different persons of different nature. It is also necessary to co-ordinate the various functions to achieve the main objectives and at the same time a function does not conflict with any other function.

**D. Span of control:** Span of control means an effective supervision of maximum number of persons by a supervisor. According to Brech, "Span refers to the number of persons, themselves carrying managerial and supervisory responsibilities, for whom the senior manager retains his over-embracing responsibility of direction and planning, co-ordination, motivation and control."

From the above discussion, we can know that the classical theory emphasised unity of command and principle of co-ordination. Most of the managers' time is wasted in the co-ordination and control of the subordinates. In many organisations, a single supervisor supervises the work of 15-20 workers and does not follow the principle of span of control. Some of the experts hold that a manager can supervise 4-8 members at higher levels and between 8-20 members at the lower levels of the organisation. But according to Lyndall Urwick, a maximum of 4 members at higher levels and between 8-12 members at lower levels can be supervised by the superior to constitute an ideal span of control.

## CHARACTERISTICS OF CLASSICAL THEORY

1. It is based on division of labour.
2. It is based on objectives and tasks of organisation.
3. It is concerned with formal organisation.
4. It believes in human behaviour of the employees.
5. It is based on co-ordination of efforts.
6. Division of labour has to be balanced by unity of command.
7. It fixes a responsibility and accountability for work completion.
8. It is centralised.

## CRITICISM OF CLASSICAL THEORY

1. This theory is based on authoritarian approach.
2. It does not care about the human element in an organisation.
3. It does not give two way communication.
4. It underestimates the influence of outside factors on individual behaviour.

5. This theory neglected the importance of informal groups.
6. The individual is getting importance at the expense of the group.
7. It also ignores the influence of outside factors on individual behaviour.
8. The generalisations of the classical theories have not been tested by strict scientific methods.
9. The motivational assumptions underlying the theories are incomplete and consequently inaccurate.

## 2. NEO-CLASSICAL THEORY

This theory is developed to fill up the gaps and deficiencies in the classical theory. It is concerned with human relations movement. In this way, the study of organisation is based on human behaviour such as how people behave and why they do so in a particular situation. The neo-classical scholars used classical theory as the basis for their study and modified some of the principles for the study. The neo-classicals have only given new insights rather than new techniques.

The scholars also pointed out the practical difficulties of the working of scalar and functional processes. The main contribution of this theory highlights the importance of the committee management and better communication. Besides, this theory emphasised that the workers should be encouraged and motivated to evince active participation in the production process. The feelings and sentiments of the workers should be taken into account and respected before any change is introduced in the organisation.

The classical theory was production-oriented while neo-classical theory was people-oriented.

### CONTRIBUTIONS OF NEO-CLASSICAL THEORY

1. Person should be the basis of an organisation.
2. Organisation should be viewed as a total unity.
3. Individual goals and organisation goals should be integrated.
4. Communication should be moved from bottom to top and from top to bottom.
5. People should be allowed to participate in fixing work standards and decision-making.
6. The employee should be given more power, responsibility, authority and control.
7. Members usually belong to formal and informal groups and interact with others within each group or sub-group.
8. The management should recognise the existence of informal organisation.
9. The members of sub-groups are attached with common objectives.

### CRITICISM OF NEO-CLASSICAL THEORY

A survey conducted by American Management Association (AMA) indicates that most of the companies reported found little or nothing useful in behavioural theory. According to Ernest Dale, "neither classical theory nor neo-classical theory provides clear guidelines for the actual structuring of jobs and provision for co-ordination."

### 3. MODERN THEORY

The other name of Modern Theory is Modern Organisation Theory. According to one authority, it was organised in the early 1950s. This theory composed of the ideas of different approaches to management development. The approach is fully based on empirical research data and has an integrating nature. The approach reflects the formal and informal structures of the organisation and due weightage is given to the status and roles of peronnel in an organisation.

Like the general system theory, modern organisation theory studies:

1. The parts (individual) in aggregates and the movement of individuals and out of the system.
2. The interaction of individual with the environment found in the system.
3. The interaction among individual in the system.

#### ESSENTIALS OF MODERN THEORY

The followings are the some of the essentials of Modern Theory:

1. It views the organisations as a whole.
2. It is based on systems analysis.
3. The findings of this theory are based on empirical research.
4. It is integrating in nature.
5. It gives importance to inter-disciplinary approach to organisational analysis.
6. It concentrates on both quantitatives and behavioural sciences.
7. It is not a unified body of knowledge.

#### CRITICISM OF MODERN THEORY

The Modern Theory has the following criticisms:

1. This theory puts old wine into a new pot.
2. It does not represent a unified body of knowledge. There is nothing new in this theory bacause it is based on past empirical studies.
3. This theory forms only the questions and not the answers.
4. It is based on behavioural, social and mathematical theories. These are management theories in themselves.

### 4. MOTIVATION THEORY

It is concerned with the study or work motivation of employees of the organisation. The works are performed effectively if proper motivation is given to the employees. The motivation may be in monetary and non-monetary terms. The inner talents of any person can be identified after giving adequate motivation to employees. Maslow's hierarchy of needs theory and Honberg's two factor theory are some of the examples of motivation theory.

### 5. DECISION THEORY

The other name of decision theory is decision making theory. This theory was given by Herbert. A. Simon. He was awarded Nobel Prize in the year of 1978 for this theory. He regarded organisation as a structure of decision makers. The decisions were taken at all levels of the organisation and important decisions (policy decisions) are taken at the higher levels of organisation. Simon suggested that the organisational structure be designed through an examination of the points at which decisions must be made and the persons from whom information is required if decisions should be satisfactory.

## MODEL QUESTIONS

1. What is meant by division of work?
2. What is meant by Unity of Command?
3. Explain "The scalar principle".
4. What is "formal organisation"?
5. What is "Informal organisation"?
6. Explain the term "Formal organisation".
7. Describe the principles and steps that constitute the organising process.
8. Explain the branches of organisation.
9. What is meant by Unity of Command?
10. Explain the principles of organisation.

# CHAPTER 10

# DELEGATION OF AUTHORITY AND DECENTRALISATION

## INTRODUCTION

Authority is the power to make decisions which guide the action of others. Delegation of authority contributes to the creation of an organisation. No single person is in a position to discharge all the duties in an organisation. In order to finish the work in time, there is a need to delegate authority and follow the principles of division of labour. Delegation permits a person to extend his influence beyond the limits of his own personal time, energy and knowledge.

## DEFINITION OF AUTHORITY

Henri Fayol, "Authority is the right to give orders and the power to exact obedience."

Kootnz and O'Donnell, "Authority is the power to command others to act or not to act in a manner deemed by the possessor of the authority to further enterprises or departmental purposes."

Terry, "Authority is the power to exact others to take actions considered appropriate for the achievement of a predetermined objective."

According to Barnard, "Authority is the character of a communication (order) in a formal organisation by virtue of which it is accepted by a contributor to or member of the organisation as governing the action he contributes; that is, as governing or determining what he does or is not to do so far as the organisation is concerned."

Daris defines authority as the "right of decision and command."

Louis Allen, "The sum of the powers and rights entrusted to make possible the performance of the work delegated."

Simon, "The power to make decisions which guide the actions of another. It is a relationship between the individuals — one superior, the other subordinate. The superior frames and transmits decisions with the expectation that they will be accepted by the subordinates. The subordinate expects such decisions and his conduct is determined by them."

Dr. Paterson defines, "The right to command and expect and enforce obedience."

Strong says, "Authority is the right to command."

Massie defines, "The formal right to exercise control."

Tannenbaum defines, "The concept authority describes an interpersonal relationship in which one individual, the subordinate, accepts a decision made by another individual, the superior, permitting that decision directly to affect his behaviour."

## CHARACTERISTICS OF AUTHORITY

The characteristics of authority are briefly explained below:

**1. Basis of getting things done:** Authority gives a right to do things in an organisation and affect the behaviour of other workers of the organisation. It leads to the performance of certain activities for the accomplishment of the defined objectives automatically.

**2. Legitimacy:** Authority implies a legal right (within the organisation itself) available to superiors. This type of right arises due to the tradition followed in an organisation, custom or accepted standards of authenticity.

The right of a manager to affect the behaviour of his sub-ordinates is given to him on the basis of an organisational hierarchy.

**3. Decision-making:** Decision-making is a pre-requisite of an authority. The manager can command his subordinates to act or not to act. This type of decision is taken by the manager regarding the functioning of an office.

**4. Implementation:** Implementation influences the personality factors of the manager, who is empowered to use authority. The subordinates or group of subordinates should follow the instructions of the manager regarding the implementation of decisions. The personality factor of one manager may differ from another manager.

## SOURCES OF AUTHORITY

There are broadly three theories regarding the sources from which authority originates. They are:

1. The formal authority theory.
2. The acceptance of authority theory.
3. The competence theory.

Brief explanations of the above three theories are given below:

**1. The Formal Authority Theory:** According to this theory, the authority flows from top to bottom through the structure of an organisation. In other words, the authority flows from the General Manager to his departmental manager and in turn, from the departmental manager to his superintendent and the like. This is explained in the following diagram.

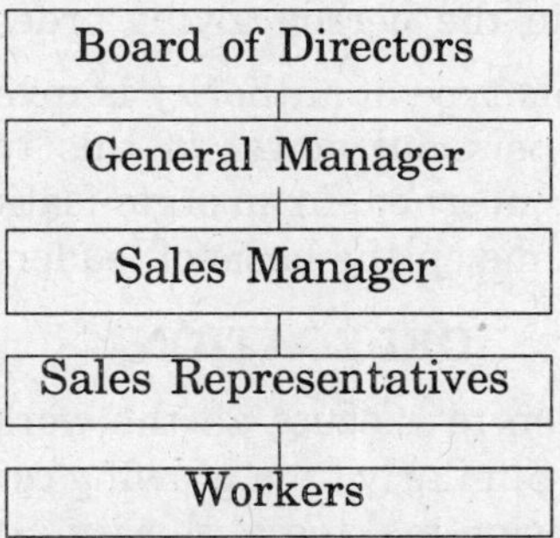


The Formal Authority Theory is otherwise called *Traditional Authority Theory and Top Down Authority Theory.*

In the case of a public limited company, the authority is in the hands of shareholders and they delegate their authority to top management and in turn, a part of this authority is delegated to the middle management.

**2. The Acceptance of Authority Theory:** Chester Bannard gave this theory. According to this theory, the authority flows from the superior to the subordinates whenever there is an acceptance on the part of the subordinates. The subordinates should accept the authority but there is no compulsion made by the superior. If the sub-ordinates do not accept the command of their superior, then the superior cannot be said to have any authority over them.

According to Bannard, "An individual will accept the exercise of authority if the advantages accruing to him from accepting plus the disadvantages accruing to him from not accepting exceed the advantages accruing to him from not accepting plus the disadvantages accruing to him for accepting and conversely, he will not accept the exercise of authority if the latter factors exceed the former".

The authority of a superior will be effective only when there is willingness on the part of the subordinate to accept authority and ineffective when there is lack of readiness to accept the authority on the part of the subordinate. The subordinate will not analyse each and every order of the superior to accept it or not. In fact, certain orders of the superior are accepted by the subordinate without a second thought. If an order of the superior is accepted by the subordinate without any hesitation, it is known as zone of acceptance.

Zone of acceptance will be determined by a number of factors:

1. The subordinate believes that rewards will be given to him in appreciation of his efforts and skills.
2. Sincere services of subordinate to the orgainsation will be rewarded.
3. A subordinate thinks that he has to accept the authority in a particular situation.
4. The non-acceptance of authority will result in dismissal of the subordinate from organisation.
5. It is also accepted on account of special knowledge that a man may possess.
6. It is accepted because a subordinate is aware of his status in the organisation.
7. There is no other way available than to accept authority.
8. It is the duty of the subordinate or it may be the policy of the organisation to impose the authority.
9. People have confidence in the person giving orders.

**3. Competence Theory:** This type of authority is invested with the persons by virtue of the office held by them. The personal power of this type of persons is based on the leadership qualities of the person concerned. In an organisation, only one person gets a higher position than others in course of time on the basis of leadership qualities possessed by him.

## DELEGATION

It is impossible for any person to execute all the work in an organisation, to achieve the objectives of the organisation. Similarly, in a growing concern also, a single person could not be vested with the entire decision-making authority. So, the superior assigns duties or responsibilities to his subordinates and also delegates necessary authority to them.

## MEANING

Delegation is a process which enables a person to assign a work to others and delegate them with adequate authority to do it.

## DEFINITION

Louis A. Allen, "Delegation is the dynamic of management, it is the process a manager follows is dividing the work assigned to him so that he perform that part which only he, because of his unique organisational placement, can perform effectively and so that he can get other to help them with what remains".

Mc Farland, "Delegation is the primary formal mechanism by which the net work of authority relationship is established".

E.F.L. Brech, "Delegation means, in brief, the passing to others to share in the four elements of the management process that is to say, in the command of the activities of other people and in the responsibility for the decision that will determine the planning, co-ordination and control of the activities of such other people".

Terry, "Conferring authority from the executive or organisational unit to another in order to accomplish particular assignments".

Hodge and Johnson, "A process whereby a superior divides his total work assignment between himself and subordinate managers or operative personal in order to achieve other operative and management specialisation.

Dougcas C. Basil, "Delegation consists of granting authority or the right to decision-making in certain defined areas and charging the subordinate with responsibility for carrying through an assigned task".

## IMPORTANCE OF DELEGATION

Delegation is considered to be one of the most important methods of training subordinates and building morals. The delegation of authority helps the manager to concentrate on the important work of planning, organising and controlling.

Delegation is a universal process, wherever human beings work in groups, one or the other form of delegation is practised by them. In our democratic India, the people delegate their authority to the members of the legislatures. The members of legislatures delegate their authority to any of the elected leaders who in turn delegates some of his authority to the cabinet ministers chosen by him.

An individual can accomplish several simple and complex works. Delegation enables a person not only to discharge his responsibility but also to discharge it effectively and economically. To a business unit which has different branches situated at different places, there is no alternative except delegation. It is acknowledged that delegation of authority is one of the surest and the best methods of getting better results. A very good superior can use the delegation of authority as a tool for motivating and eliminating cumbersome information systems.

## ELEMENTS OF DELEGATION

The following are the three elements of delegation :

**1. Assignment of duties or responsibilities:** This work is being done only at the time, when a superior has no time to accomplish all the work. The superior automatically assigns the work of responsibility to his immediate subordinate.

**2. Delegation of authority:** If the work is assigned to any subordinate, there will be a need for authority to accomplish it.

After the delegation of authority, the subordinate can get powers to accomplish the tasks in a specified time and in order.

**3. Accountability:** Accountability means that the subordinate is answerable to his immediate senior. If there is any mistake or fault committed by the subordinate, the subordinate should accept responsibility for it. In certain cases, the assignment may be made to the subordinate if the work is not accomplished as per the instructions issued by the superior. The superior (one who delegates authority) is answerable to the management but not the subordinate (to whom authority is delegated).

## PRINCIPLES OF DELEGATION

**1. Delegation to go by results expected:** The nature of duty has equal rank with the extent of delegation of authority. It should be noted that the objectives of the organisation are to be accomplished in time. The superior should clearly know what he expects from the subordinate before the delegation of authority.

**2. Non-delegation of responsibility:** A superior can delegate authority but not responsibility. Assigning duties does not mean delegation of responsibility. The superior should be in touch with the subordinates to know whether duties are performed and the authority is exercised properly. The ultimate responsibility for the performance of duties remains with the superior.

**3. Authority and responsibility should commensurate with each other:** A subordinate can discharge his duties effectively and efficiently if there is proper delegation of authority, otherwise a subordinate cannot succeed in accomplishing the assigned tasks.

Authority without responsibility will make the subordinate a careless person. Likewise, responsibility without authority will make the subordinate an inefficient person. So there should be a proper balance between authority and responsibility.

**4. Unity of command:** The principle of unity of command insists that a subordinate should get instruction from only one superior. In other words, a subordinate should be assigned duties and responsibilities by only one superior and he is accountable only to the concerned superior.

If a subordinate gets orders, instructions and directions from more than one superior, it will create uncertainty and confusion in the organisation. In such a situation, the subordinate will find it very difficult to determine whose instructions, orders or directions he should carry out first.

**5. Definition of limitations of authority:** A person knows well that an authority alone can delegate the authority properly. There should be written manuals which help a person to understand the authority in right direction. This will avoid confusion regarding the delegation of authority and enable effective functioning of the concerned person.

## TYPES OF DELEGATION

A brief explanation of the different types of delegation is given below:

1. General.
2. Specific.
3. Written.
4. Unwritten.
5. Formal.
6. Informal.
7. Downward.
8. Accrued.
9. Sideward.

**1. General delegation:** *General delegation* means granting authority to the subordinate to perform various managerial functions and exercise control over his subordinates. At the same time, the same persons are regulated and supervised by the top management.

**2. Specific delegation:** Under specific delegation, the orders, instructions or directions are delegated to a particular person specifically. For example, the Personnel manager may be delegated authority for selection of personnel, training of personnel, placement of personnel and the like.

**3. Written delegation:** This type of delegation is made by written orders, instructions etc. The proper usage of words is essential to this type of delegation.

**4. Unwritten delegation:** *Unwritten delegation* means the authority is delegated on the basis of custom, conversion or usage. Here, there is no evidence available for future reference.

**5. Formal delegation:** The duties and authority are shown in the organisational structure of the enterprise. For example, the production manager is assigned the responsibility and accompanying authority to maintain and increase production.

**6. Informal delegation:** In certain cases, a person has to use the authority without getting it from the top management. The reason is that he can perform his assigned duties effectively in time.

**7. Downward delegation:** *Downward delegation* states when a superior could delegate duties and authority to his immediate subordinate. This type of delegation is followed in most of the organisations.

**8. Accrued delegation:** Under this type of delegation, a subordinate can delegate his authority to his immediate superiors. It occurs seldom in an organisation.

**9. Sideward delegation:** A person delegates authority to another person who is also in the same rank as he is in the organisation.

## ADVANTAGES OF DELEGATION

The delegation of authority gives several advantages to the organisation. The important advantages of delegation of authority are given below:

**1. Basis of effective functioning:** Delegation lays the basis for effective functioning of an organisation. It creates the relationship with others and achieves various objectives of the organisation. It creates the relationship with others and achieves various objectives of the organisation.

**2. Saving of time:** Delegation of authority enables the superior to allot more time to important matters like planning, organising, staffing, directing, co-ordinating, controlling and decision-making.

**3. Reduction of work:** Delegation relieves the superior from attending to the routine matters. Normally, the routine matters are allocated to subordinates. It helps the superior to carry out more responsible work alone.

**4. Opportunity for development:** Delegation of authority gives a very good opportunity to the subordinate to grow. It helps in identifying the best person among the various subordinates for development.

**5. Benefit of specialised service:** Delegation helps the superior to get the benefit of specialised knowledge of various persons at lower levels. For example, production is delegated to the production manager, sales to the sales manager, legal matters to the lawyer and the like.

**6. Delegation of authority enables effective managerial supervision**

**7. Efficient running of branches:** If the business has any branch, the branch affairs or activities are looked after by a separate person. He is supposed to be incharge of this branch. When he can get adequate authority with responsibility he could work for the smooth and effective functioning of the particular branch.

**8. Interest and initiative:** Whenever the delegation of authority takes place, the subordinate may do the work with interest. In certain cases, the subordinate by himself takes initiative do the work properly.

**9. Satisfaction to subordinates:** Delegation of authority will satisfy the self-actualization needs of the individuals.

**10. Expansion and diversification of business activity:** The subordinates are fully trained in decision making in various fields of the business by using the delegation of authority. This type of talents of subordinates can be used by the top management in the expansion and diversification of the business activities.

## PROBLEMS OF DELEGATION

Every superior is expected to delegate part of his duties and responsibility to his subordinates. A single person cannot perform all the work. So, delegation is a very important characteristic of the organisation.

The proper delegation of authority is made only at the time of a proper balance between feelings of the superior and subordinates.

### I. HESITATION ON THE PART OF SUPERIOR

The following are the reasons for the lack of willingness on the part of the superior to delegate authority:

**1. Perfectionism:** Many superiors think that he is better than others. This is true to some extent. The reason is that the superior may have had experience in doing and developed a degree of skill. If such a practice is followed by a superior, he is not a loyal employee of the organisation. He should open the door to the subordinate to develop his abilities by delegating authority.

**2. Autocratic attitude:** Some superiors prefer retain powers in their hands. These persons don't have belief in the delegation of authority and they interfere with the limited authority of their subordinates.

**3. Directions:** Many superiors lack of the ability to direct the subordinates. Subordinates may misinterpret the instructions which the superior gives. Then, the superiors cannot get the expected efficiency from the subordinate.

**4. Confidence:** Superiors also tend to show lack confidence in subordinates. In the society life can not he lived without reposing in the ability of other so, each superior is expected delegate his powers to his sub-ordinates. If the delegation is not made, the superior has no chance to gain experience from delegation of authority. Confidence is developed gradually on the basis of success of the delegation of authority.

**5. Control:** The superior has control over his subordinates. He wants to retain the control over his subordinates and keep up the importance of his role. Hence he hesitates to delegate his authority. Besides, the superior feels that he might be dominated if he delegates his authority.

**6. Avoidance of risk:** Risk may arise through the delegation of authority to a subordinate. Whatever maybe the risk, the superior will have to take the responsibility for it. But only few managers are ready to run the risk.

**7. Competition:** Subordinates learn much than the superior by taking advantage of delegation of authority. This results in the emergence of more talented persons than the superior. This is not liked by the superior and he avoids competition in future.

**8. Inability of the subordinate:** The subordinate does not have any ability to accept any new work. The superior, who knows this fact, hesitates to delegate powers.

**9. Inability of the superior:** If the superior is an inefficient person, the work method and procedures designed by him are likely to be faulty. So, the superior wants to keep all the authority with himself.

## II. HESITATION ON THE PART OF SUBORDINATES

Sometimes, the subordinates are not willing to accept delegation even though the superiors are very much interested in delegation. The reasons for not accepting the authority by the subordinates are given below:

**1. Love of spoon-feeding:** If a subordinate has been given a chance to take a decision, he may not like to decide things himself.

**2. Easier to ask:** Subordinates often find it easy to ask their superiors for an answer than to find it out for themselves. Some superiors will accept only one solution to a problem and allow the subordinates to find out other solutions by themselves. In such a situation, a subordinate does the work effectively and approaches his superior for an answer.

**3. Fear of criticism:** Sometimes, a subordinate may fear that even for a silly mistake in a decision, his superior may criticize him. This suppresses the initiatives of the subordinate and proves drastic to his self-confidence.

**4. Lack of information (or) resource:** A subordinate may hesitate to accept new work due to lack of information or resources to do the work effectively.

**5. Lack of self-confidence:** Lack of self-confidence in a subordinate is also one of the reasons for not accepting any authority.

**6. Other work:** Subordinate may feel that they will not be able to finish any additional work along with the existing work. Subordinates think that if they accept authority, they may be forced to accept more work in the future.

**7. Inadequate incentives:** A subordinate may not come forward to accept any authority if there is not personal gain in doing so.

**8. Fear of failure:** Some subordinates feel that they may fail and so they do not want to accept additional responsibilities.

## EFFECTIVE DELEGATION

The superior has the aim to practice and encourage delegation for the efficient accomplishment of the organisational objectives. Hence, it is necessary that the nature and content of each job should be scientifically analysed to pinpoint the job that can he entrusted to subordinates.

Normally, minor and routine types of jobs are entrusted to the subordinates. The superior is not ready to perform even the ordinary routine jobs but at the same time, there are certain jobs which cannot be entrusted; for example, the preparation of budget, formulation of policies and framing rules and regulations.

## STEPS INVOLVED IN SUCCESSFUL DELEGATION

The following steps will aid more successful delegations of authority:

**1. Establishment of definite goals:** The purpose of delegation is to enable efficient accomplishment of organisational objectives. But delegations will be meaningless if the objectives are not properly defined. Subordinates may hesitate to accept the authority, if they do not know exactly what is expected of them.

**2. Developing personal discipline for supervision:** Superior should have faith in the ability of his subordinates and tolerate the mistakes committed by them. Then, every subordinate will be ready to accept the authority for efficient performance.

**3. Establishment of definite responsibility:** The authority and responsibility of each subordinate should be in clear terms. This will avoid the duplication of delegation.

**4. Motivation:** Subordinates are ready to accept the responsibility if proper motivation is available to them. Motivation may be by means of increased wages and the like.

**5. Determining what to delegate:** This will necessitate the appraisal of the capacity of the people and needs of the jobs. Only authority appropriate to be delegated will be considered.

**6. Training:** Subordinates should be properly trained in handling delegated work. Technical and non-technical training should be given to the subordinates. The non-technical training includes the development of the morale self-confidence and leadership qualities of the subordinates.

**7. Report:** After delegation of any authority, the subordinate is expected to submit a report on them. Only in this way, the superior will be freed from authority jobs to concentrate on other important functions.

**8. Control:** The superior is held responsible to the top management even after the delegation of authority. So, it is necessary to establish a suitable control system to keep a careful watch over the performance of subordinates. If the superior finds a deviation from the predetermined procedures, he should take corrective action in time.

## PRE-REQUISITES FOR EFFECTIVE DELEGATION OF AUTHORITY

A supervisor can delegate his authority after acquiring knowledge of the following pre-requisites of effective delegation:

1. The supervisor must understand the authority and res-ponsibility of their own.
2. The supervisors must decide the portion of his authority that he wants to delegate to subordinates.
3. The supervisor should have thorough knowledge of the abilities and inabilities of subordinates.
4. The supervisor must ensure that the subordinates have understood the delegated work in the right direction.
5. The supervisor should delegate only the routine functions to subordinates.
6. The supervisor must understand thee need, importance and value of delegation.
7. The supervisor should delegate the work which can be performed independently.
8. The supervisor must dissuade the subordinate from being tempted to take decision by themselves.

9. The supervisor must release the decision making powers to his subordinates.
10. There should be adequate communication network within the organisation.
11. There should be a clear definition of standard of accountability.
12. Delegation must be done in accordance with the overall plan for the completion of the work.
13. The delegation of authority should be confined to the organisational structure.

## COMMON FAULTS IN DELEGATION

**1. Close supervision:** The supervisor has to supervise his subordinates even after delegation of authority. The advantages of delegation of authority will not be available to the organisation if there is no close supervision and if the subordinates are not made to act independently.

**2. Lack of direction:** The supervisor fails to provide adequate direction to his subordinates. It places the subordinates in a position in which thy do not know what is expected of them.

**3. Lack of accountability:** The efficient use of delegated work cannot be checked by a supervisor. This is a great handicap to the superior. As a result of this, a sense of irresponsibility infuses the subordinates.

## DECENTRALISATION

Decentralisation means that each section has its own workers to perform activities within the department. There will be no general office to provide these services. Under decentralisation, separate staff are allocated to each department for performing those activities which cannot be centralized.

## ADVANTAGES OF DECENTRALISATION

A brief explanation of the advantages of decentralisation is presented below:

**1. Savings of time:** All paper work relating to the basic operations of the business originates from the departmental officers. Decentralisation enables the department staff members to complete the work early.

**2. Greater efficiency and ouput:** The workers of a particular department are well versed in the technology followed in that department. Hence, there is a possibility of increasing their efficiency. The greater efficiency leads to increase in output and minimising the costs.

**3. Maintenance of secrecy:** If the secrecy of the business is disclosed, it may make the organisation realise a loss. Next, if a separate department is put incharge of the maintenance of secrecy under decentralisation, the loss may be avoided and secrecy maintained.

**4. Departmental loyalty:** The staff attached to a particular department for a number of years develop a sense of loyalty to the department. It results in the increase of output and improvement of the performance of the individual.

## DISADVANTAGES OF DECENTRALISATION

The disadvantages of decentralisation are explained below:

**1. No proper division of work:** The work load of the organisation cannot be evenly divided to be given to each department.

**2. Duplication of work:** If the same type of work is performed in more than one departments i.e., duplication of work, separate machines and equipments are used to perform the duplication of work.

**3. No standardisation:** There is no possibility of adopting a standard procedure to perform the same type of work in all departments. Besides, it brings about difficulties in selection and training in each department.

**4. Heavy expenditure:** A large number of staff members and supervisors are required under this department. It leads to increase in the cost of operation.

## RESPONSIBILITY

Responsibility always arises from the superior-subordinate relationship. The essence of responsibilities is obligation. If a person is entrusted with any work, he should be held responsible for the work that he completes.

## MEANING

Responsibility is the obligation to do something. In other words, responsibility is the obligation to perform the tasks, functions or assignments of the organisation.

## DEFINITION

Theo Haimann, "Responsibility is the obligation of a subordinate to perform the duty as required by his superior".

Davis, "Responsibility is an obligation of the individual to perform the assigned duties to the best of his ability under the direction of his executive leader".

Strong, "Responsibility is an obligation to perform certain functions and achieve certain results".

Mc Farland, "Responsibility is the duties and activities assigned to a position or to an executive".

## ELEMENTS OF RESPONSIBILITY

The following are the basic elements of responsibility:

1. It arises from superior-subordinate relationship.
2. It results from contractual agreement.
3. The responsibility cannot be transferred to anybody.
4. It is created by acceptance of authority.
5. There is an essence of obligation.
6. The responsibility may be general or specific.
7. Responsibility is a continuing process by nature.

Delegation of authority and responsibility is necessary for an effective functioning of an organisation. Responsibility without authority is an empty vessel. Authority without responsibility is a very dangerous one. Both authority and responsibility are necessary to an individual.

## MODEL QUESTIONS

1. What is decentralisation?
2. What are the sources of authority?
3. What is meant by delegation?
4. State and explain the difficulties in delegation?
5. Compare and contrast centralisation with decentralisation?
6. What are the types of delegation?
7. What are the different advantages of decentralisation?
8. Explain the various differences between the concept of centralisation and decentralisation?
9. What are the merits and demerits of decentralisation?
10. What are the advantages of centralisation?
11. Describe the term "Delegation".
12. Describe the factors that determine the degree of decentralisation?
13. What are the factors responsible for the absence of delegation on the part of a manager? What are the measures appropriate for promoting delegation in an organisation.
14. Distinguish between delegation and decentralisation.
15. Distinguish between delegation and decentralisation of authority. What are the obstacles to delegation of authority?
16. What are the obstacles to effective delegation? Suggest methods to overcome those obstacles?
17. Discuss the merits and demerits of decentralisation?
18. What is delegation? Explain the factors affecting delegation of authority and its process?

# CHAPTER 11

# DEPARTMENTATION

INTRODUCTION
MEANING
DEFINITION
PROCESS OF DEPARTMENTATION
NEED AND IMPORTANCE OF DEPARTMENTATION
FACTORS IN DEPARTMENTATION
BASIS OF GROUPING DIVERSE ACTIVITIES
BASIS PATTERN TYPES OF DEPARTMENTATION
DEPARTMENTATION BY FUNCTIONS,
DEPARTMENTATION BY PRODUCT OR SERVICE
DEPARTMENTATION BY REGION OR AREA
DEPARTMENTATION BY CUSTOMERS
DEPARTMENTATION BY PROCESS,
DEPARTMENTATION BY TIME
DEPARTMENTATION BY NUMBERS
DEPARTMENTATION BY MARKETING CHANNELS
MODEL QUESTIONS

## INTRODUCTION

Departmentation is a part of the organisation process. It involves the grouping of common activities under a single person's control. The activities are grouped on the basis of a functions of the organisation. This work is done by a chief executive of the concerned organisation.

## MEANING

*Departmentation* means the process by which similar activities of the business are grouped into units for the purpose of facilitating smooth administration at all levels.

## DEFINITION

Koontz and O'Donnell, "A Departmentation is a process of dividing the large monolithic functional organisation into small and flexible administrative units."

Departmentation refers to the classification of activities on operations of an undertaking into functionalised categories.

Departmentation is an essential one in the modern business world. All the business activities cannot be looked after by a single individual. The classified activities bring in specialisation and managerial convenience. It ensures suitable span of control. Departmentation is created in product-wise, process-wise or area-wise. It ensures proper directions to and control on them.

## PROCESS OF DEPARTMENTATION

Departmentation is done through the following process:

1. Identification of work.
2. Analysis of details of each work.
3. Description of the function of the organisation.
4. Entrusting the functions to a separate person who has specialised in the respective field and providing him with suitable staff.
5. Fixing the scope of authority and responsibility of the departmental heads.

## NEED AND IMPORTANCE OF DEPARTMENTATION

Departmentation contributes to the success of the organisation in a number of ways given below.

1. Departmentation increases the operating efficiency of the employees. The reason is that departmentation facilitates the grouping of activities which are of similar nature.
2. There is a fixation of responsibilities to various executives of the organisation. It makes the executive to be alert and efficient in his duties.
3. The departmental heads (manager) are given certain powers and are allowed to take their own decisions. It increases the prestige and skill of the departmental heads.
4. The workings of the various departments are evaluated by the top management and the department which are not managed properly are identified. This makes the departmental heads efficient.
5. There is a possibility of expansion of the organisation because of fixing of the responsibilities to the executives and there is function-wise departmentation.

6. Besides, departmentation gives other advantages such as facilitating budget preparation, effective control of expenditure, attaining specialisation, better co-ordination among the managerial personnel etc.

## FACTORS IN DEPARTMENTATION

The following factors are to be taken into consideration in departmentation:

**1. Specification:** Departmentation should yield the advantages of specialisation. This is the most expected from the modern business organisation. Specialisation may be functional such as sales, finance, production and personnel.

**2. Control:** There should be a proper control under departmentation and simplification of the control process. As a general rule, there should be scope for checking automatically the activity of one person by another person, a separate executive.

**3. Co-ordination:** The whole business activities are grouped department-wise and it requires co-ordination. The purchase department should be located near the production department. The reason is that the purchase department has to render services to the production department. This will make the co-ordination of the work very easy.

**4. Securing attention:** Even an unusually important activity of the business should be given a recognition in the organisation. It is to ensure the success of an organisation. If greater attention is necessary, the activity may be entrusted to a separate division or a higher level of a organisation according to its importance.

**5. Recongnition of local conditions:** The departmentation should take into consideration the local conditions of the place concerned.

**6. Economy:** It should be borne in mind that expenses are incurred in the creation of separate departments. It means avoiding unnecessary expenditure and allowing essential expenditure. The departmental arrangement will be an ineffective one if the departmentation is done with minimum expenses.

## BASIS OF GROUPING DIVERSE ACTIVITIES

Diverse activities should be associated with a relative department in the achievement of the enterprise purpose on the following phases:

**1. Maximum use:** The term *maximum use* means that a given activity will be attached to the major department which makes most use of it. For example, the usage of warehouse and the entire traffic management might be placed within the production department.

**2. Interest:** A superior is requested to look after a new activity if he is also most willing and able to serve. For example, a person who is working in the sales department prefers to work in the accounts department. If such a chance is offered to any person, he can perform the activities with great interest.

**3. Competition:** The prevailing competition among the departments is a desirable one. Team spirit may also be developed whenever the grouping of activities takes place. Here, competition refers to the prevailing competition between two sales departments or production departments within the same organisation.

Sometimes, a sister concern may be engaged in the similar type of business. Competition destroys the enterprise as a whole, if a single person is appointed to work for the elimination of competition between parent and sister concerns. In other words, a single sales manager is expected to perform the sales activities for both parent and sister concerns.

**4. Policy matter:** A particular activity may be assigned to a department which evinces more interest in the unit. For example, the sanctioning of the credit to customer and collection of debt from debtors may be given to the finance department in lieu of sales department as a matter of policy in an organisation.

**5. Separation:** The maximum division of activities involves high cost of operation to the management. But it is essential that a separation is preferable when an activity is complicated by several functions.

**6. Proper attention:** Proper attention should be given to certain activities to keep them from dying under adverse circumstances. If an ordinary activity is assigned to the higher officials who do not consider it important, they will not derive satisfaction in the performance of such ordinary activity. So, this type of ordinary activity should be assigned to somebody else.

**7. Co-ordination:** If the organisation's activities are grouped into several departments, there is a need of co-ordination of various activities. Such a co-ordination work may rest with the general manager.

## BASIS (PATTERN) TYPES OF DEPARTMENTATION

There are certain basic methods of dividing the duties and responsibilities within an organisational structure. They are given below:

1. Departmentation by functions.
2. Departmentation by product or service.
3. Departmentation by regions (area or location) or territory.
4. Departmentation by customers.
5. Departmentation by process.
6. Departmentation by time.
7. Departmentation by numbers.
8. Departmentation by marketing channels.

A brief discussion of the above classified departmentation is given below:

**1. Departmentation by Functions:** The most commonly followed basis of departmentation is by functions. Under this departmentation, the activities are grouped on the basis of functions which are to be performed. The following chart may help to understand the departmentation by functions:

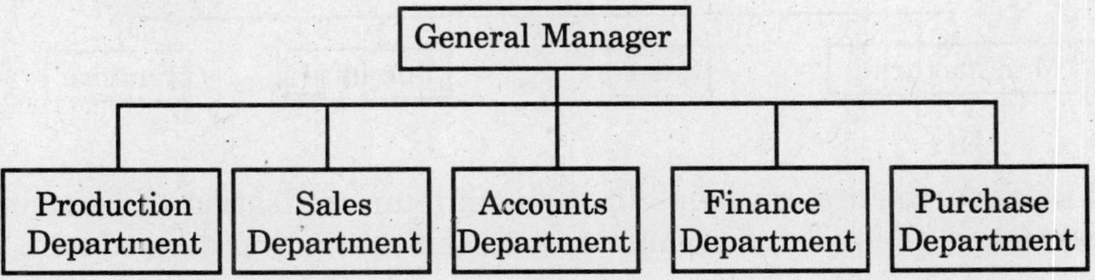


Each department is headed by one responsible person, who is directly responsible to the General Manager. According to George R. Terry, "the functions or activities are the pivot around which effective executives develop effective and efficient organisation".

**Advantages**

1. It is a scientific and time tested method.
2. It follows the principles of specialisation and division of labour.
3. It ensures proper performance control.
4. It preserves the importance of each of the activities of an organisation.
5. It avoids the interruptions of subsidiary groups in the primary activities.
6. Due weightage and prestige are given to the departmental managers and they are respected by top management people.
7. It facilitates co-ordination activity within the department itself and the organisation as a whole.
8. It is economical, simple and easy to understand.
9. It helps the utilisation of manpower and other natural resources of the organisation.

**Disadvantages**

1. It makes the management control work more difficult.
2. The department heads consider themselves to be auto-nomous sections of the organisation. The managers will not look upon the undertaking as a unit.
3. It increases the work load and responsibility of departmental managers.
4. It doesn't offer any scope for training for the overall development of managers.
5. The departmental managers are experts in handling the problems in their departments alone. They may not be able to understand the problems of other departments.

**2. Departmentation by Product or Service:** This type of departmentation is made by the large-scale business unit. A single business unit may manufacture and sell different types of products. Then, each type of product or service is allocated to a separate department. Functionalised units for each product are created within the general structure of the organisation. Manufacturing, sales, finance and personnel functions are arranged separately for each type of product. Each department is responsible for manufacturing a product and selling it to customers. Grouping of all activities are planned in advance within each product section. The co-ordination function is performed by the top management.

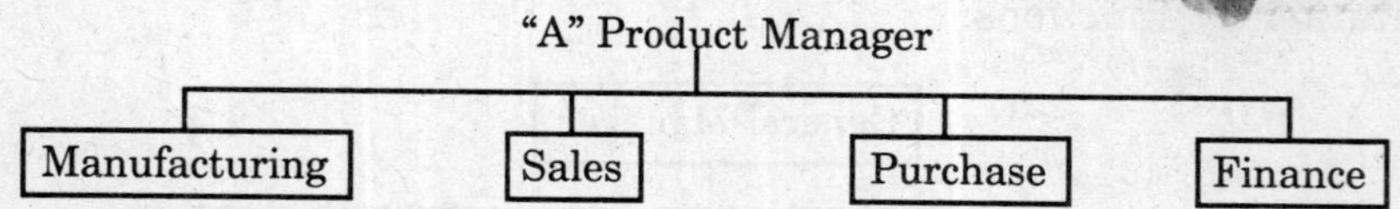


**Advantages**

1. Product departmentation helps in the maximum utilisation of personal efficiency of workers in the area of manufacturing and marketing of product.
2. There is a possibility of gaining economy in manufacturing and marketing of products on account of large scale operation.
3. Better services may be provided to the customer.
4. The profitability of each product is known to the management. So, it is easy to fix the responsibility on the departmental heads.

5. Proper attention may be devoted to the manufacture of a product.
6. All the functions pertaining to the manufacture of a particular product are performed by managerss. Then, there is the possibility of an effective co-ordination and control.
7. A new line of product can be introduced without any difficulty.

**Disadvantages**

1. There is a danger of duplication of work.
2. It increases the number of personnel which in turn increases the cost of operation.
3. It requires additional cost for maintaining a sales force for each type of product.
4. In proportion to the increase in the number of employees, the problem of control at the executive levels become more difficult.
5. Machines and equipments in each product department may not be used fully.

**3. Departmentation by Region or Area:** This method of departmentation may be suitable for a business unit which is wholly dispersed. The business activities are grouped in area-wise and each area is incharge of a single person. The local persons are appointed as salesmen in each area. It will help the business unit to increase the sales. The reason is that the local person is familiar with the local language, the culture and preferences of the customers.

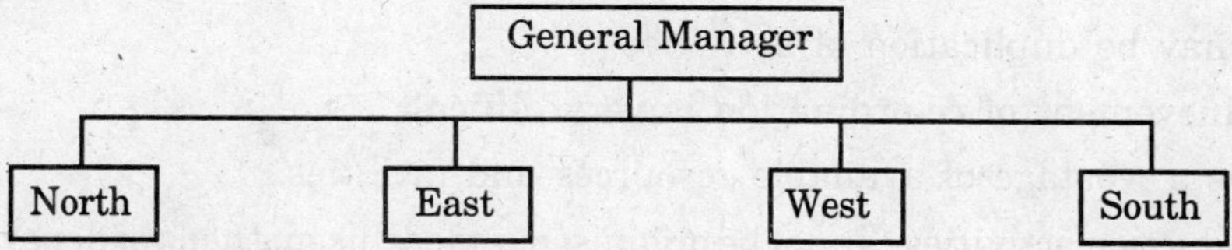


1. It makes possible an effective span of control.
2. It reduces the cost of operation and gains saving in time.
3. The sales may be increased with the help of intimate knowledge about the tastes and preferences of the custom-ers in the local market.
4. Regional managers could win the confidence of customers and remove the competitors from the market.
5. Accounts are prepared area-wise. So, the profitability of each area is known to the management.
6. It provides opportunities to managers to improve their skill in various fields.
7. This type of departmentation is more suitable for a large scale business unit.
8. Control process is very easy to manage.

**Disadvantages**

1. It increases the number of personnel and involves high cost of operation.
2. The control of head office is a less effective one.
3. It may also involve duplication of work.
4. A small business concern cannot manage the high cost of operation.

**4. Departmentation by Customers:** This type of depart-mentation is preferred when the various needs of customers are different in nature. For example, a bank or a financial institution may divide its loan section into number of heads and assign them to various departments, such as loans to businessmen, farmers, professionals and so on. Similarly, the sales department of a business concern could be divided into industrial goods and consumer goods. The consumable goods could again be sub-divided into perishable and non-perishable in nature.

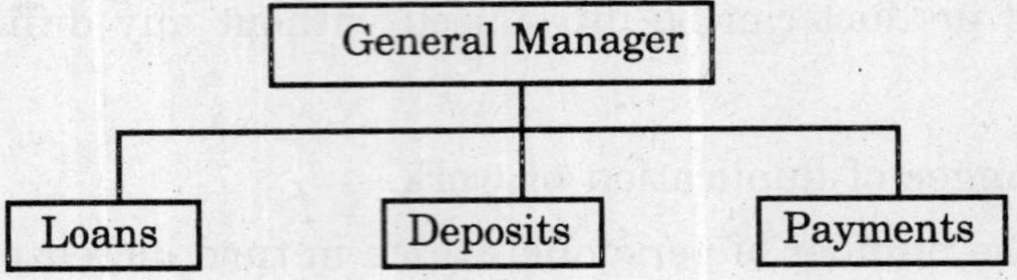


**Advantages**

1. It fulfils the expectations and needs of customers.
2. It develops specialisation among the organisational staff.
3. The out of fashion products can be dispensed with through the departmentation by customers. The reason is that the business unit has intimate knowledge of the customer's tastes and preferences.
4. Each section of the customer is able to get better service from the company and helps the company to win the goodwill, of its customers.

**Disadvantages**

1. There may be duplication of activities.
2. The achievement of co-ordination is very difficult.
3. There is a wastage of available resources and facilities.
4. The production activities cannot be organised under this methods of departmentation. If it is so, the cost of operation will be high.

**5. Departmentation by Process:** This type of Departmentation is followed when the production activities are carried on in many places. For example, a textile mill has many departments such as Ginning, Spinning, Weaving, Dyeing and Printing, Packing and Sales. Each section will be in charge of separate specialised persons.

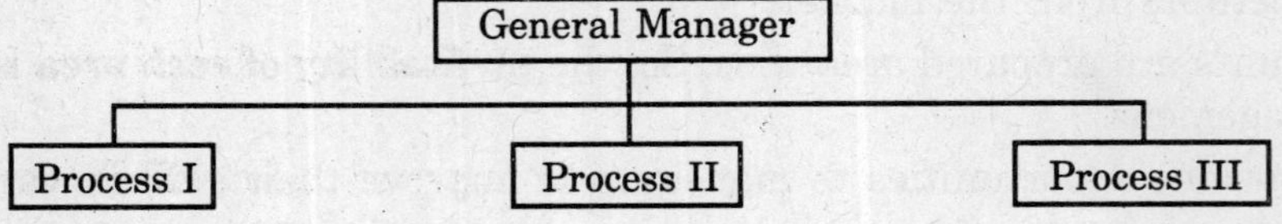


**Advantages**

1. The costlier machines can be used effectively.
2. There is no interruption of the departments or process in other production processes. The requirement and renewals of any process cannot affect the production of other processes.
3. There may be economy in operation.
4. There is no duplication of activities.
5. The principle of specialisation and division of labour is followed under this method of departmentation.

6. This departmentation helps the top management to have effective performance control.
7. This type of departmentation is more suitable to any business unit which manufactures a product passing through a number of processes.

**Disadvantages**

1. Separate rooms for operation and other facilities should be given to all the process. This results in heavy cost of operation.
2. More specialists are essential to each process.
3. It does not give good training to staff members and there is a lack of overall development of the managerial talents.

**6. Departmentation by Time:** The business activities are grouped together on the basis of the time of the performance. If the work is not completed within the normal working hours, extra time will be given to complete it after the normal working hours. Only interested persons are requested to do the job and one person is responsible to supervise them. Whatever be the work performed after the normal working hours, a separate department will be incharge of this type of activity. This type of departmentation is known as *departmentation by time*.

**7. Departmentation by Numbers:** Similar type of duties are performed by small groups. Each group is controlled by a supervisor or an executive. For example, in the Army, soldiers are grouped into squads, battalions, companies, brigades and regiments on the basis of allotment of men to each unit. The principles of span of management, span of control or span of supervision is used under this type of departmentation.

**8. Departmentation by Marketing Channels:** This type of departmentation is adopted on the basis of the channel of distribution chosen by the particular business unit. Normally the channel of distribution is selected by the business unit on the basis of nature of goods and marketability of the product. This method of departmentation has grown in importance as business has become increasingly market-oriented.

## MODEL QUESTIONS

1. Define Departmentation?
2. Why is the departmentation necessary?
3. Discuss the advantages and disadvantages of departmentation by customers.
4. Explain the departmentation by Region?
5. What are the bases for departmentation in a business organisation?. State also the difficulties of delegation.
6. What are the bases of departmentation?
7. What is departmentation?
8. Define departmentation and discuss the different kinds of departmentation?

# CHAPTER 12

# SPAN OF MANAGEMENT

INTRODUCTION
MEANING
FACTORS AFFECTING THE SPAN OF MANAGEMENT
GRAICUNA'S THEORY OF SPAN OF MANAGEMENT
MODEL QUESTIONS

## INTRODUCTION

Span of control, Span of supervision, Span of authority and Span of responsibility are other names for Span of management. It indicates the number of people directly managed effectively by a single person. It is accepted that the large number of subordinates cannot be supervised and their efforts co-ordinated effectively by a single executive. If the number of members is too large, it will be difficult to manage the persons and perform the work effectively. A sound organisation depends upon the effective performance of work by the executive. So, the executive should neither be overloaded nor be idle.

## MEANING

*Span of management* means the number of people managed efficiently by a single officer in an organisation.

It implies that a single executive should not be expected to give guidance to more people. Only limited number of persons are allocated to the executive for dividing the work or duties among the workers. In order to avoid overburden to the officers, it is essential to determine the span of control of the executive officers. In an average firm, an executive can efficiently control upto five or six sub-ordinates. The limit of the number of members for span of control may be increased or decreased according to the levels of management. Normally, the members exercising span of control are decreased at the top level management and increased at the bottom level management.

Many management experts suggested a different number of executives for effective control. According to L. Urwick, the ideal number of subordinates is four in case of higher level management and eight to twelve in case of bottom level management.

## FACTORS AFFECTING THE SPAN OF MANAGEMENT

The following are some of the factors which influence the span of management:

**1. Character of the supervision work:** The span of control may be increased whenever the work is performed and standardised. The reason is that, the supervisor has the opportunity to lay down permanent policies followed in an organisation. It results in the control of more number of subordinates. If the nature of work is a complicated one, the span of control has to be restricted.

**2. Leadership qualities:** The personnal abilities and capacity of a supervisor can influence the span of management. If the supervisor has more skill to control the subordinates, the span of management may be increased and vice-versa.

**3. Qualities of the subordinate:** If the subordinates have enough talent to perform the work assigned to them, the manager or the supervisor can control more number of subordinates.

**4. Time available to supervisor:** Most of the executives or supervisors will spend a lot of time for the operating work and administrative duties like planning and organising activities. They may supervise the subordinates in the remaining available time.

So, they can control lesser number of sub-ordinates than the person who spends full time for their supervision.

**5. Nature of work:** Some of the works are repetitive in nature and does not require any extra-ordinary talent to perform. In such cases, the supervisor or the executive can control a large number of subordinates.

**6. Level of supervision:** Whenever the subordinates perform the work manually, the span of control may be increased. It means that the degree of span of control can be increased at bottom level management and decreased at the top level management.

**7. Delegation of authority:** If the authority delegates the powers of decision making, planning and execution to the sub-ordinates, the span of control may be increased. Whenever an executive performs the planning and executive work in addition to supervision work, the particular executive can supervise relatively more number of sub-ordinates.

**8. Fixation of responsibility:** In case the responsibility of the sub-ordinate is clearly defined, he need not contact the superior for getting guidance and instruction. Then the superior can supervise large number of sub-ordinates.

**9. Using of standards:** Standards are used in an organisation to detect the errors or faults in the performance of work. So, there is no need for an executive to spend more time in watching the performance of the sub-ordinates. Then the executive can control more number of sub-ordinates.

**10. Methods of communication:** Method of communication is also one of the factors which determine the span of control. The method of communication may be divided into two i.e., Oral and Written. Oral communication requires more time and energy and these can be avoided in the written communication.

## GRAICUNA'S THEORY OF SPAN OF MANAGEMENT

A management expert named V.A. Graicunas contributed much to the Span of Management Theory. His theory identified the relationship prevailing between the superior and the subordinates. The relationships are classified into three categories. They are given below:

1. Direct single relationships.
2. Direct group relationships.
3. Cross relationships.

The explanations of the above mentioned three relationships are given below:

**1. Direct single relationship:** *Direct Single Relationship* is one in which a supervisor has direct relationship with his subordinates individually. If A super-vises B and C who are subordinates, there are two direct single relationships. It is explained with the help of the following chart.

SUPERVISOR

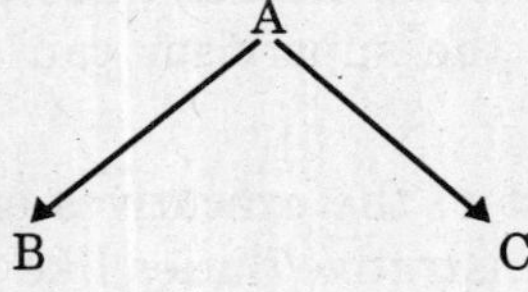


SUBORDINATES

**2. Direct group relationships**

In Direct Group Relationship, a supervisor has direct relationship with his subordinates jointly. It is explained with the help of the following chart.

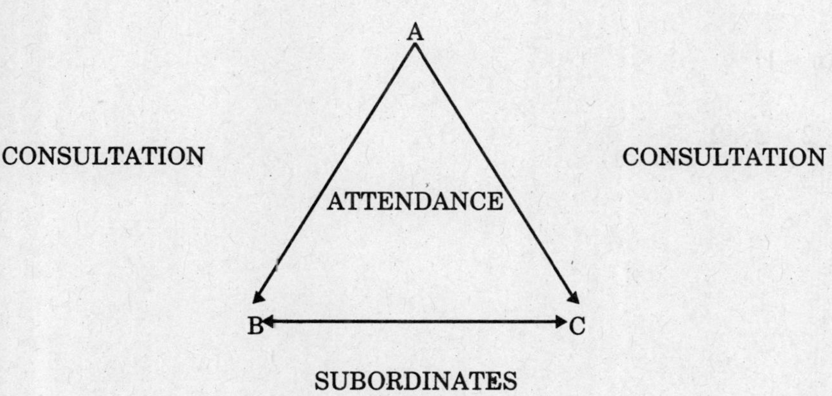


Here, A can consult B while C is present in a situation. In another situation, A can consult C while B is present.

**3. Cross relationship:** In Cross Relationship, a subordinate has relationship with another subordinate mutually. It is explained with the help of the following chart:

SUPERVISOR

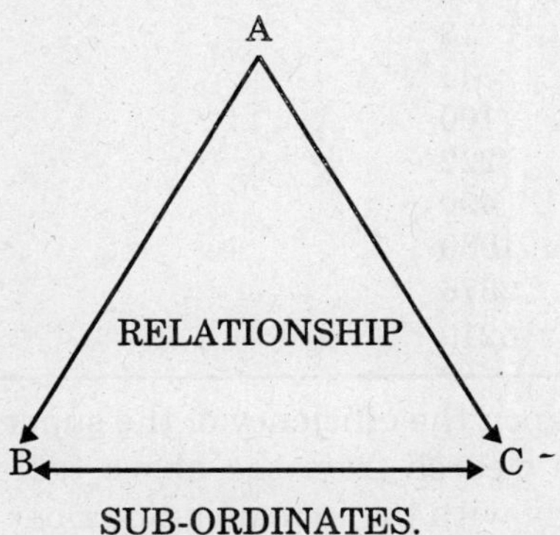


Here, the relationship prevailing between B and C is Cross Relationship.

The number of direct and cross relationships increased geometrically as the number of sub-ordinates under the supervisor increased.

**Formula**

V.A. Graicunas prescribed the following formula to ascertain the number of superiors'and subordinates' relationship.

Number of relationships = $n(2^n/2+n-1)$

Where, "n" refers to the number of subordinates.

For example, the number of subordinates, say 5, the number of superiors' and subordinates' relationships are identified as under:

n = 5

$$\text{Formula} = n \times \frac{2n}{2} + (n-1)$$

$$= 5 \times \frac{2 \times 2 \times 2 \times 2 \times 2}{2} + (5-1)$$

$$= 5 \times \frac{32}{2} + 4$$

$$= 5 \times 16 + 4$$

$$= 5 \times 20$$

$$= 100$$

The number of relationships increases in geometrical progression as shown in the following table.

| *Number of Sub-ordinates* | *Number of Relationships* |
|---|---|
| 1 | 1 |
| 2 | 6 |
| 3 | 18 |
| 4 | 44 |
| 5 | 100 |
| 6 | 222 |
| 7 | 490 |
| 8 | 1080 |
| 9 | 2376 |
| 10 | 5210 |

The effective supervision depends upon the efficiency of the supervisor and the number of sub-ordinates to be supervised. It is cleared from the above table that the number of relationships is increased correspondingly with the increasing number of sub-ordinates. The effectiveness of the supervision decreases if the number of relationships or sub-ordinates is increased. So, the management should fix the number of sub-ordinates to each supervisor according to the nature of work. If the management does so, it can get good results i.e., effective supervision.

## MODEL QUESTIONS

1. What is meant by Span of Management?
2. State the factors in Span of Management?
3. What do you mean by 'Span of Control' and explaining Graicunas theory of Span of Control.
4. What is Span of Control?
5. What is Span of Management? What are the factors that decide the Span of Management?

# CHAPTER 13

# TYPES OF ORGANISATION

## INTRODUCTION

Organisation is designed on the basis of principles of division of labour and span of management. The success of the organisation depends upon the experience and competence of the officers of the organisation. There is a necessity of chalking out the line of authority among the people who are working in an organisation to achieve the desired results. Besides, it involves the determination of duties among the officers and combining the activities of all officers to get the desired results. According to Kimball and Kimball, "The problem of an organisation is to select and combine the efforts of men of proper characteristics so as to produce the desired results."

Nature, scale and size of the business are the normal factors which determine forms of internal organisation. The following common types of organisations find a place in the structure of internal organisation.

1. Line, Military or Scalar organisation.
2. Functional organisation.
3. Line and staff organisation.
4. Committee organisation.
5. Project organisation.
6. Matrix organisation.
7. Freeform organisation.

A brief explanation of the above types of organisations is given below:

## I. LINE ORGANISATION

Line organisation is the simple and oldest type of organisation followed in an organisation. Under line organisation, each department is generally a complete self-contained unit. A separate person will look after the activities of the department and he has full control over the department.

There are certain powers which will be given to line executives to take decisions whenever a need arises. He communicates his decision and orders to his subordinates. The subordinates, in turn, can communicate them to those who are immediately under them.

Such decision making authority is to flow from the top management level to the bottom. The top management people have greater decision making authority than the bottom level executives. It should be noted that in this type of organisation, an executive is independent of other executives of the same level (say departmental heads). In other words, the same level executives do not give or receive any orders amongst themselves. But they receive orders from their immediate boss (general manager) and give orders to their subordinates. Hence, it is known that all the departmental heads are responsible to the general manager. The general manager, in turn, is responsible to the board of directors. The board of directors is responsible to the shareholders who are the owners.

This type of organisation is followed in the army on the same pattern. So, it is called *military* organisation. Under this type of organisation, the line of authority flows from the top to bottom vertically. So, it is called line organisation.

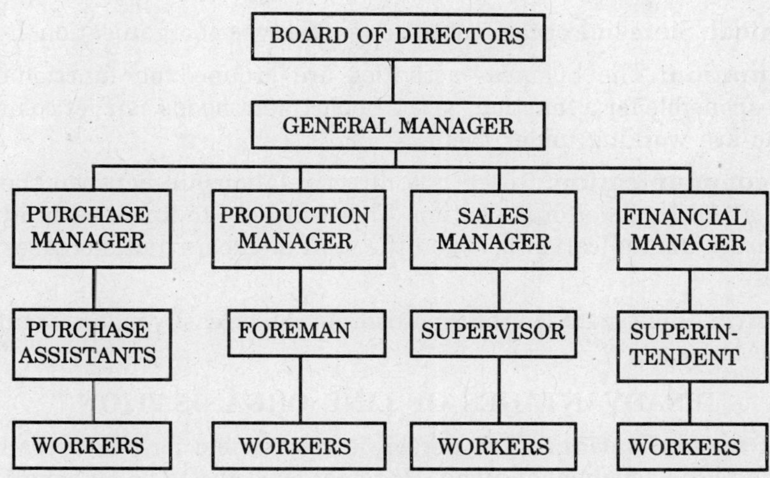


## CHARACTERISTICS OF LINE ORGANISATION

1. It consists of direct vertical relationships.
2. Authority flows from top level to bottom level.
3. Departmental heads are given full freedom to control their departments.
4. Each member knows from whom he would get orders and to whom he should give his orders.
5. Operation of this system is very easy.
6. A senior member has direct command over his subordinates.
7. Existence of direct relationship between superiors and subordinates.
8. Each member knows to whom he is responsible for the accomplishment of objectives of the organisation.
9. The superior takes decisions within the scope of his authority.

## ADVANTAGES OF LINE ORGANISATION

**1. Simplicity:** A line organisation is very easy to establish. Its workers can understand the concept and relationship with others without any difficulty. There is no complication in its ideals.

**2. Division of authority and responsibility:** Each person has his area of authority which is clearly explained to him. So he knows to whom he is responsible for doing the job. No person could share off his own responsilibity after it has been fixed.

**3. Unity of control:** According to unity of control, an individual can receive orders only from one superior. It means, that a subordinate is responsible only to one superior and he gets orders only from him.

**4. Speedy action:** Under line organisation, there is a proper division of authority and responsibility and unity of command. Hence, an individual can take decisions and execute the plans without any delay.

**5. Discipline:** The authority flows from top to bottom. Loyalty and discipline can be maintained among the employees of the organisation without much difficulty.

**6. Economical:** Since line organisation is a single type of organisation, it is economical.

**7. Co-ordination:** The business activities are grouped on functional basis. Each department is responsible for a function, so the department heads can get co-ordination from the workers who are working under them.

**8. Direct communication:** There is a direct relationship between the superior and the subordinate at all levels of organisation. This will help to know each other intimately . This ensures direct cmmunication between the staff members and increases the efficiency of the employees.

**9. Flexbility:** Adjustments in the organisation can be easily made to suit the changing conditions of the business.

## DISADVANTAGES OF LINE ORGANISATION

**1. Lack of specialisation:** Each person is responsible for the overall exhibition of activities relating to his department alone. He is not expected to be an expert in all aspects of managerial task. He simply gives instructions to his subordinates and does not specialise in certain phases of operation.

**2. Over loading:** Whenever the scale of operations or size of the business unit increases, this system gives over work to the existing executives. So, they are not in a position to direct and control the efforts of their subordinates properly.

**3. Lack of initiative:** Since maximum authority is invested with the top management, the departments will lose their initiative to motivate the subordinates.

**4. Scope for favouritism:** Only one person controls the activities of the department when there is a scope for favouritism and nepotism.

**5. Dictatorial:** Under line organisation, a subordinate should carry out the instructions and orders which are given by the superior. If not, he will be penalised. This entails in autocratic and aristocratic approach in administration. So, managers will become dictators and not leaders.

**6. Limited communication:** In normal time, the communication moves downwards but very rarely it moves upwards. The downward communication may be orders, instructions etc. If upward communication is allowed, the management may know the grievances of employees. But upward communication is not preferred by the top management. So it results in limited communication.

**7. Unitary administration:** Each department's activities are looked after by a single executive who takes all the decisions relating to his department. Hence, the successful functioning of that department depends on his abilities.

**8. Subjective approach:** The degree of availabilty of authority is more to the superior than to the subordinates. So the superior takes decision without considering the opinions of the subordinates. The subordinate should follow the decisions taken by the superior.

**9. Instability:** The success of this type of organisation depends mostly on the ability of only few strong men and the failure of this organisation is likely due to the inability of the same persons.

**10. Lack of co-ordination:** The co-ordination among the departmental heads is not eacy to achieve. The reason is that the executive of a department does not consider other departments important. This will result in the lack of co-operation and team spirit.

**11. Unsuitability for large scale enterprise:** This type of line organisation is not suitable for a large-scale enterprise which requires specialisation.

**12.** The business activities may be divided according to the will of the manager rather than according to any scientific plan.

**13.** The system has no means of appreciating the efficient worker and punishing of the inefficient worker.

**14.** Under line organisation, efficient persons are essential to the top management. Practically, it is very difficult to find efficient persons for small organisations.

**15.** The required time and efforts are insufficient formanagerial planning, research and development and controlling activities of the organisation.

**Suitability**

1. This type of organisation is suitable to small size business units.
2. Where the activities are of routine nature or machine based.
3. If the business activities are service minded.
4. Where the number of persons working is small.
5. The business operation is simple in nature.
6. A business unit which has straight methods of operations.

## II. FUNCTIONAL ORGANISATION

Under line organisation, a single person is incharge of all the activities of the concerned department. Here, the person incharge finds it difficult to supervise all the activities efficiently. The reason is that the person does not have enough capacity and required training. In order to overcome the limitations of line organisation, F.W. Taylor proposed a new type of organisation called *functional organisation*.

Under functional organisation, various specialists are selected for various functions performed in an organisation. These specialists will attend to the work which are common to different functions of various departments. Workers, under functional organisation, receive instructions from various specialists. The specialists are working at the supervision level. Thus, workers are accountable not only to one specialist but also to the specialist from whom instructions are received. Taylor advocated this organisation as a point of the scheme of scientific management. Directions of work should be decided by functions and not by mere authority.

The need for functional organisation arises out of:

(i) The complexity of modern and large-scale organisation;
(ii) A desire to use the specialisation in full and;
(iii) To avoid the work-load of line managers with complex problems and decision-making.

## CHARACTERISTICS OF FUNCTIONAL ORGANISATION

1. The work is divided according to specified functions.
2. Authority is given to a specialist to give orders and instructions in relation to specific function.

3. Functional authority has right and power to give command throughout the line with reference to his specified area.
4. The decision is taken only after making consultations with the functional authority relating to his specialised area.
5. The executives and supervisors discharge the responsibili-ties of functional authority.

F.W. Taylor, the father of scientific management, recommended a functional organisation of activities at the top level. According to Taylor, a foreman should not be burdened with looking after all the activities of his work. Instead, he should be assisted by a number of specialists in solving the problems. The following chart will also help to understand the functional organisation.

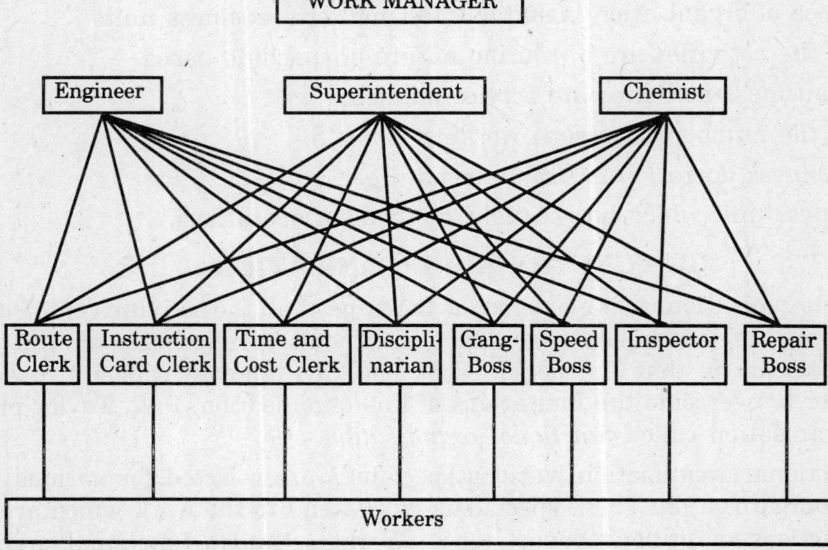


**1. Route clerk:** He is a technical expert. He fixes the route through which each work should travel up to the stage of completion.

**2. Instruction card clerk:** He is expected to draft instructions to workers on the basis of the route fixed by the route clerk. These instructions are written on a separate card.

**3. Time and cost clerk:** This clerk fixes the standard time for each work and the cost incurred for each work. He gives instructions to the workers to record the time actually spent by the workers and actual cost incurred for completion with standard time and cost.

**4. Gang boss:** This worker is expected to see the various machines and materials kept ready for workers to perform the work.

**5. Speed Boss:** He advises the worker to complete the work within the standard time considering the speed of the machines. Besides, the speed boss sees whether each work is completed in time or not.

**6. Inspector:** The Inspector checks up the quality of each work and certifies it as standard. Actually, the accuracy of work is checked with reference to the specification.

**7. Repair boss:** His work starts only after the actual work is performed by the workers. He is concerned with the up-keep of machines and other equipments. It means that the responsibility of the repair boss is the maintenance of machines.

**8. Disciplinarian:** He implements the rules and regulations of the entire organisation. He is a peacemaker of the organisation. He also checks whether each work is performed in a systematic and perfect manner.

The route clerk, the instructions clerk and time and cost clerk work in the planning department. The gang boss, speed boss, inspector, and repair boss belong in the factory section of the organisation. The disciplinarian is not a staff of any section but he is responsible for the workers' conduct.

## ADVANTAGES OF FUNCTIONAL ORGANISATION

**1. Benefit of specialisation:** Under the functional organisation, each work is performed by a specialist. It helps to enhance the efficiency of the organisation. Each work is divided among the workers scrupulously.

**2. Application of expert knowledge:** Planning function and execution function are divided separately and each function is entrusted to a specialist in the line organisation. So, the specialists can use their expert knowledge in the actual performance of work.

**3. Reducing the work load:** Each person is expected to look after only one type of work. It reduces the unnecessary work allotted to them. Hence, the quality of work and effective control over the work are achieved.

**4. Efficiency:** Since each worker is responsible for each work, the workers can concentrate on the work allotted to them. They could assure proficiency in the work.

**5. Adequate supervision:** Each staff member is incharge of a work. So, he can devote enough time to supervise the workers.

**6. Relief to line executives:** Under functional organisation, the instructions are given by the specialist directly to the actual workers. Hence, the line executive does not have any problems regarding the routine works.

**7. Co-operation:** A single person could not have full control over the workers in the organisation. So, there is a possibility of promotion among the executives of the organisation.

**8. Mass production:** Large-scale production can be achieved with the help of specialisation and standardisation.

**9. Economy:** Under functional organisation, each specialist is responsible to the performance of a work. Wastage in the production can be avoided and the expenditure could be considerably reduced.

**10. Flexibility:** Any change in the organisation can be introduced without any difficulty.

## DISADVANTAGES OF FUNCTIONAL ORGANISATION

**1. Complex relationship:** A single worker is working under eight specialists under functional organisation. It is very difficult for the worker to be responsible to all persons. This results in conflict between the workers and the specialist.

**2. Discipline:** It is very difficult to maintain discipline among the workers when a single worker has to serve many masters.

**3. Over specialisation:** The organisation can reap the advantages of specialisation. But at the same time, there might be overlapping of authority and divided responsibility.

**4. Ineffective co-ordination:** The extent of authority of a specialist is not correctly defined. It creates problems while getting the co-operation among the specialists.

**5. Speed of action:** When the control of a worker is divided among the specialists, the speed of action of the workers may be hampered.

**6. Centralisation:** Eight specialists are guiding and directing the workers to perform the work. So, the workers do not have any scope for doing the job on their own. This leads to the centralisation of authority.

**7. Lack of responsibility:** If there is any defect in the performance of work, the management is not in a position to fix the responsibility for it. The reason is that none of the eight specialists is ready to own the responsibility. They may shift the responsibility to any one among themselves for the poor performance of the work.

**8. Increasing the overhead expenses:** The remuneration of the specialist may be higher than that of the foreman or supervisor.

**9. Poor administration:** Since many specialists control the same group of workers, no effective administration of workers could be ensured.

**Suitability of functional organisation**

It is very suitable to a business unit which is engaged in manufacturing activities.

## III. LINE AND STAFF ORGANISATION

There are some advantages and disadvantages both in the line organisation and functional organisation. In order to reap the advantages of both line organisation and functional organisation, a new type of organisation is developed, i.e., line and staff organisation. Under line and staff organisation, the disadvantages of line organisation and functional organisation may be avoided to some extent.

The line officers have authority to take decisions and implement them to achieve the objectives of the organisation. The line officers may be assisted by the staff officers while framing the policies and plans and taking decisions.

In the fast developing industrial world, the line officers are not in a position to acquire the technical knowledge. For example, while taking decisions regarding the production, technical knowledge is needed to take correct decisions.

This type of gap may be bridged with the help of staff officers. The staff officers may be experts in a particular field. Then, the line officers can get expert advice from the staff officers before taking the final decisions. According to Allen, “Staff refers to those elements of the organisation which provide advice and service to the line.”

The authority flows from top level to the lower level of the organisation through the line officers while the staff officers attached to the various departments advise the departments. The staff officers do not have any authority to control anybody in the organisation. Besides, the staff officers are not in a position to compel the line officers to follow the advice given by them. Each department is headed by a line officer who exercises full authority regarding the planning, implementation and control of workers under him with the help of staff officers. There is no connection between workers and the staff officers of any department. The workers get the instructions only from the line officers. Hence, the unity of command and specialisation are followed in this organisation.

## TYPES OF STAFF

**1. Personal staff:** Personal staff means a person who assists another person in the performance of a work effectively. Under such circumstances the work of line officers could not be delegated to others. This type of a person is appointed at the top level of organisation. The personal staff officers do not supervise the subordinates of line officers.

**2. Specialised staff:** The specialized staff officers render service to the line officers at all levels of the organisation. The specialized staff officers offer advice with some limited provisions. These provisions are imposed by the management.

**3. General Staff Assistant:** General staff assistants are a group of persons who are rendering service as advisors to top management in specialised matters. The primary feature of the general staff is that they give advice regarding overall plans and policies of the organisation. But they are not specialized in any area.

## FUNCTIONS OF STAFF OFFICERS

1. The staff officers assist the line officers in the planning of business activity.
2. The board of directors frame the policies of the business on the basis of recommendations given by the staff officers.
3. The managers can get the advise from the staff officers regarding the selection, 'training', placement and remuneration fixation the personnel.
4. The staff officers give advise regarding the method of improving the product, the technique of reducing the cost of production, increasing the profits of the concern etc.
5. The staff officers prescribe the procedures to be followed by the line officers in the execution of policies and programmes.
6. Staff officers of a department help the manager in the preparation of budget of the department.
7. The staff officers may be called to solve the administrative problems encountered by the line officers in general.

In many organisations, the line officers extend their full co-operation to staff officers and vice-versa. This ensures smooth functioning of the organisation. In certain circumstances, conflicts may arise between the staff officers and line officers. When an officer blames the other officers for some lapse, it affects the smooth functioning of the business.

## ARGUMENTS OF LINE OFFICERS AGAINST STAFF OFFICERS

1. The staff officers have only theoretical academic knowledge but not practical knowledge.
2. Frequently, the staff officers go beyond their sphere of activity and assume that they have line officers' authority.
3. Much of the advice given by the staff officers is impractical.
4. Since the staff officers are not responsible for the results they suggest unfruitful ideas.

5. The staff officers unnecessarily increase the paperwork of the line officers.
6. The staff officers give advice without considering the nature of business as a whole.
7. The ideas of staff officers take into consideraration only the objectives of the departments to which they are attached instead of the broad objectives of the business.
8. Staff officers are very much interested in becoming line officers of the organisation rather than imparting advice to them.
9. Staff officers blame the line officers for the failure of the project but keen on getting credit for the success of the project.

## ARGUMENTS OF STAFF OFFICERS AGAINST LINE OFFICERS

1. The line officers completely neglect the advice given by the staff officers.
2. The line officers hesitate to accept new ideas.
3. The line officers do not follow the advice of staff officers properly.
4. Some line officers simply reject the advice without considering its validity.
5. Some line officers are not ready to ask for any advice from the staff offices.
6. The line officers dissuade the management from giving authority to staff officers to implement new schemes.
7. The line officers do not exploit the full services of the staff officers.

## SOLUTION TO THE CONFLICT BETWEEN LINE OFFICERS AND STAFF OFFICERS

The conflict between line officers and staff officers can be settled by the following suggestions.

1. Both line officers and staff officers should clearly understand the nature of relationship prevailing between them.
2. A separate staff member should be appointed to bring about co-operation between the line officers and staff officers.
3. The line officers should be encouraged to use the advice of staff officers.
4. Only qualified persons should be selected and placed as staff officers.
5. The staff officers should be convinced by the line officers if their advice is not accepted.
6. The responsibility for results could be fixed on both line officers and staff officers.
7. Some line officers may resist the change, when it is the duty of staff officers to encourage the line officers to participate in the proposed scheme of change.
8. Only experienced persons alone should be promoted as line executives.
9. The staff officers can give full credit to the line officers for the results obtained.
10. Remove the fear of both line officers and staff officers whether the new ideas or advice would be properly put into use or not.
11. If the favourable results are obtained, the staff officers may be appreciated by the line officers.

12. A special previlege may be given to the line officers to reject or accept the advice given by the staff officers.

## ADVANTAGES OF LINE AND STAFF ORGANISATION

1. It facilitates the workers to work faster and better.
2. Specialisation is attained when the staff officers concentrate on planning function and the line officers concentrate on execution function.
3. It enables the organisation effectively utilise the staff officer's experience and advice.
4. The line officers can take sound decisions with the help of proper advice from the staff officers.
5. A new technology or a new procedure may be introduced in the organisation without any dislocation.
6. A new variety of responsible jobs can be given to skilled workers.
7. The work of line officers would be reduced to some extent if they are relieved of the work of taking decisions.
8. It promotes the efficient functioning of the line officers.
9. The principle of unity of command is followed in the line and staff organisation. Hence, the line officers can maintain discipline among the workers and exercise control over the workers.
10. A very good opportunity is made available to the young persons to get training.

## DISADVANTAGES OF LINE AND STAFF ORGANISATION

1. If the powers of authority pertaining to the line officers and staff officers are not clearly defined, there may arise confusion throughout the organisation.
2. It is very difficult to control the line officers to when they reject the advice of the staff officers.
3. The line officers may reject the advice without assigning any reasons for their action.
4. The staff officers may under estimate the authority of line officers. The reason is that they are superior to the line officers.
5. The staff officers are not involved in the actual implementation of the programme. So, it is not obligatory on their part to give advice with care and caution.
6. The staff officers are not responsible if favourable results are not obtained.
7. It requires the appointment of staff officers who are specialised in various areas. It increases the administrative expenses of the organisation.
8. There is no authority to the staff officers to compel the line officers to accept and implement the advice given by them.
9. There is a communication gap between line officers and staff officers. It reduces the degree of co-operation between them.
10. The differences of opinion between line officers and staff officers will defeat the very purpose of specialisation.

11. The line officers may mis-understand the advice given by the staff officers and proper results cannot be obtained. Sometimes, the staff-officers cannot give unambiguous advice to the line officers.
12. Line officers blame the staff officers for unfavourable results and want to get rewards for fabourable results.
13. Frequently, the line officers want to get advice from the staff officers not only on important matters,but also on ordinary matters. It reduces the effectiveness of control of line officers.

## IV. COMMITTEE ORGANISATION

In the modern business world, some administrative tasks cannot be performed by a single person alone when two or more persons are required to perform the same administrative task collectively. It shapes into a committee of an organisation. A committee is a group of persons to whom certain managerial functions are assigned and from whom some advice or recommendations are expected. According to Hicks, "A committee is a group of people who meet by plan to discuss or make a decision for a particular subject". The duties, responsibilities and authority are fixed by the top management and the committee is accountable to the management.

Terry has defined the committee as "Body of persons elected or appointed to meet on an organised basis for the discussion and dealing of matters brought before it."

Webster's New International Dictionery defines committee as a, "Body of persons appointed or elected to consider, investigate or take action upon and usually report concerning some matter or business, as by a court, legislative body or a number of persons".

Haimahh has defined "a committee as a group of persons either appointed or elected who are to meet for the purpose of considering matters assigned to it".

### TYPES OF COMMITTEE

**1. Advisory committee (or) problem solving committee:** This committee examines the problems which are referred to it.

If a committee is requested to solve a given problem, it should give the best solution. The reason is that the committee members have wide knowledge, offer different opinions and suggest approaches to solve a problem. Before solving a problem, the problem is analysed by the committee members from different angles. A solution is found out by the committee after considering the pros and cons of the proposed solutions.

**2. Fact-finding committee:** This type of committee is formed only for the purpose of collecting information on a particular subject. A detailed report is submitted with recommendations to the management. This is the most common committee formed in any organisation.

**3. Action committee (or) executive committee:** This committee consists of line officers. This committee can take the decisions and it has power to implement the decisions. The committee is permanent in nature. Board of Directors of a company is the best example for the Action committee.

### FUNCTIONS OF A COMMITTEE

1. Collect the necessary information from different sources and arrange the information orderly.

2. The collected information is critically analysed.
3. Draft a detailed report containing the recommondations for the purpose of implementation.
4. Formulate the standard of performance for the purpose of evaluation of actual performance in future.
5. Take a decision if the committee is requested to do so.
6. Framing the policies of the organisation.
7. The committee can select personnel to carryout the business operations.
8. Directing and controlling the officers at regular intervals to achieve the goals said above.

## ADVANTAGES OF COMMITTEE ORGANISATION

1. The committee can take valuable decisions. The committee members can make use of their experience and knowledge while taking decisions.
2. Hasty decisions are avoided by the committee. Normally, the hasty decisions do not give maximum benefit to the organisation. Hasty decisions are not worthy from a long term point of view.
3. The committee members are encouraged to participate in the decision making process. Each committee member can acquire a knowledge of and understand the feelings of the people in other parts of the company. Keeping these in view, the decision is taken by the committee.
4. The committee decisions will certainly be the best one. There is a proverb, "Two heads are better than one".
5. By participating in the decision making process, an officer is persuaded to accept the decision and implement the decision without any delay.
6. Co-ordination between the various departments becomes very easy. The reason is that the committee consists of members from various departments. According to Koontz and O' Donnell, "Committee is a useful device for co-ordinating business planning and the execution of the business policies".
7. The committee members have authority to implement the decisions. If any individual takes a decision, the decision may not be implemented by the committee. The reason is that there is no authority for the committee to implement the decision taken by an individual.
8. If a young person is motivated to participate in the decision making process of a committee, he can get a very good training. It is one way of utilising the opportunity offered to him.
9. Normally the committee consists of specialists from various fields. Then, new ideas may be developed by the committee in the area of production, sales, customer service and the like.
10. Whenever a decision is taken in an organisation, it should be communicated to all the employees. The committee members can disseminate the decision taken by the committee to the employees immediately. It saves a considerable time in communication.

11. The decision taken by the committee reveals the feelings, ideas and thoughts of all the members of the committee. The decision is taken only after having obtained the approval of all the persons who are participating in the decision making.
12. Sometimes, the decision is arrived at after getting the approval of the majority of the members participating in the decision making. So, the committee follows a democratic process in the decision making.
13. Even if a person is opposed to the decision taken, he may accept the decision taken by the committee. He will act so, even though he will not be compelled to accept the decision. It means voluntary acceptance on the part of the concerned persons.
14. Committee members are requested to express their views, ideas and feelings freely. It will minimise the clashes of interests among the employees of the organisation. The discussion may be pertaining to wages, salary, bonus, welfare schemes and the like.
15. The line executives are included in the committee for decision making. It prevents the line executives from feeling that they have not been consulted while taking decisions.
16. If any problem is to be solved by the committee, it can be done by following the principle of division of labour. Each committee member can analyse the problem from various angles at the same time and take fruitful solution.
17. An individual is empowered to take decision and implement it when he has full authority and responsibility. In other words, there is a concentration of authority and responsibility. Concentration of authority and responsibility is avoided in the committee organisation. In this organisation, all the members of the committee have authority and responsibility.
18. Normally, the committee is formed with the interested persons of the organisation.

## DISADVANTAGES OF COMMITTEE ORGANISATION

1. Men from various fields are included in the committee. Each member expresses his own ideas and decisions or solutions. It results in delay in taking a decision.
2. It increases the administrative expenses of the organisation. Expenses are incurred whenever the committee is convened for solving a problem or taking a decision.
3. In case, if there is an absence of mutual co-operation, and the members do not have confidence in the ability of the other members of the committee, they fail to work efficiently and the committee is dissolved without any decision being taken.
4. The secrecy of the committee's decision cannot be maintained under committee organisation. The reason is that there are a large number of members in a committee.
5. The responsibility cannot be fixed on any person if the decision does not produce favourable results to the organisation. Each one blames the other for faulty decision making and unfavourable results.
6. Sometimes, the decisions may be taken on the basis of compromise, when the decision does not reflect the view pionts of the members of the committee.
7. It has been observed that irrelevent matters are at times discussed. The decision should be taken by a committee within a short period of time.

8. In the committee organisation, each member is expected to express his own ideas. It may result in heated argument among the committee members. It does not give any benefit to the organisation.
9. The members of a committee do not use their initiative because of their ignorance, or dominance by the committee members. Thus, the representative character of the decision taken by the committee is not preserved.
10. The committee members who meet frequently, may not be able to devote full attention to their duties.
11. A committee is formed to reap benefits as in a democracy. But, in majority of the cases the committee acts as a puppet of the management.
12. The committee members are not able to develop their own ability or talents individually. Further, it deteriorates the ability of the committee members in various other fields.

## RECOMMENDATIONS FOR EFFICIENT FUNCTIONING OF A COMMITTEE

The following recommendations are given for the successful functioning of a committee type of organisation:

**1. Clear objectives:** A committee can function efficiently if the objectives of the organisation are clearly stated. The scope of the function of a committee should be clearly laid down.

**2. Size of the committee:** The number of members of a committee should not be too large or too small. Only necessary members should be included in a committee. The members who are working at executive levels should not be members of more than three committees. The ideal number of members of a committee is 6 to 8.

**3. Selection of meetings:** The success of a committee depends upon the members of a committee. So, the management should be very careful while selecting a member of a committee. Due weightage should be given to skill, knowledge and experience of the person while selecting a committee member.

**4. Role of committee:** The authority and responsibility of a committee should be clearly laid down. If so, the members of a committee will act according to the regulations of the committee formed.

**5. Role of chairman:** Great care should be taken while selecting the chairman at a committee. Sometimes, the chairman of a committee may be selected by the committee members or nominated by the management. The chairman should act as a man to whom every member at the committee could have easy access and he should encourage the members and extend his cooperation to everyone of the members of the committee.

**6. Preparation for a meeting:** The committee meeting should be periodically convened so as to take prompt decisions and actions to tackle the problems of the management. The flow of work should be maintained by taking correct decisions. It is desirable to collect various essential information necessary to take a decision.

**7. Follow-up:** The minutes of the meeting should be intimated to all the members of a committee . The follow-up procedure is also carried on for the purpose of ensuring proper implementation of the decisions.

**8. Evaluation:** The functioning of the committee should be periodically evalued. If any need arises, certain members may be included in or excluded from the committee.

The benefits accruing the committee should over balance the expenses incurred for the functioning of committee .

9. Selection of subject matter: Certain kinds of subjects can be dealt with by an individual only. This type of subjects cannot be placed before the committee for discussions. Only complicated matters can be handled by the committee.

## V. PROJECT ORGANISATION

The *project organisation* idea was developed after the Second World War. This organisation is developed with the object of eliminating the defects of functional organisation. Delay in taking in decisions and lack of co-ordination are some of the defects of functional organisation.

Project organisation is designed with the object of accomplishing a programme or project. The project organisation is dispensed with after the accomplishment of a programme or project. The project organisation is composed of a core of functional departments in addition to its specific programmes or projects. In other words, project organisation consists of important functional departmental heads.

A project organisation is suitable for the accomplishment of a small number of large projects. According to Middleton, "A project organisation can also be the beginning of an organisation cycle. The project may become a long-term or permanent effort that eventually becomes a programme or branch organisation. The latter may, in turn, become separated from the parent organisation and be established as a full fledged product division functionally organised".

### FEATURES OF PROJECT ORGANISATION

1. The success of the project organisation depends upon the co-ordination of activities.
2. There is a grouping of activities for each project. It leads to the introduction of a new line of authority.
3. The responsibility is fixed for each group with regard to the respective projects and it results in the meaningful control.

### DRAWBACKS OF PROJECT ORGANISATION

1. The professionals are deputed for the project. But there is no assurance of continuous work for the professionals in a project organisation.
2. Under project organisation, there is absence of proper communication and standards for comparing the performance. It reduces the motivation and controls the staff in an organisation.
3. The decision is taken in the project organisation under pressure of the top management. It results in dangerous consequences.
4. The top management does not extend its full co-operation for the effective functioning of the project organisation. Some hindrance may be caused by the top management.

## VI. MATRIX ORGANISATION

There are several departments under Matrix organisation. Each department is assigned with a specified task. The available resources of the organisation can be used by each department along with the co-ordination of other departments in an organisation .

According to Stanley Davis and Paul Lawrence, matrix organisation is, "Any organisation that employs a multiple command structure but also related support mechanisms and an associated organisational culture and behaviour pattern". The matrix organisation may be followed where a large number of small projects have to be managed.

### CONDITIONS FOR EFFECTIVE MATRIX ORGANISATION

The matrix organisation can effectively function if the following conditions are present:

1. The principle of scalar chain of command is not followed in the matrix organisation. A project manager should give his report to more than one superior.
2. There should be an agreement among the managers regarding the authority of utilising the available resources. The term resources includes physical resources, financial resources and human resources.
3. A conflict may arise among the managers regarding the utilisation of available resources. There should be a common willingness among the authority holders to face the conflicts with a view to resolving them.

### MERITS OF MATRIX ORGANISATION

The merits or advantages of a matrix organisation are discussed below:

**1. Achievement of objectives:** The matrix organisation reaps the benefits of functional organisation and line and staff organisation. It ensures the achievement of objectives with technical specialisation.

**2. Best utilisation of resources:** The available resources are used by the managers for the specified project. At the same time, the resources are utilised by the managers — with full understanding among them.

**3. Appropriate structure:** Matrix organisation is an appropriate structure of an organisation to adopt to the external changes. For example, in order to survive the competition, matrix organisation is used to meet customer demands according to the expectations without affecting the marketing of the existing product.

**4. Flexibility:** Matrix organisation is a highly flexible organisation. The rules and procedure are framed on the basis of the experience of the organisation.

**5. Motivation:** If any department is functioning slowly towards the completion of the particular project, Proper motivation is provided to the concerned department.

**6. Personal development:** Matrix organisation gives an excellent scope for training and development of efficient persons.

### DEMERITS OF MATRIX ORGANISATION

The following are the demerits or disadvantages of matrix organisation:

**1. Complex relationship:** The matrix organisation does not follow the principle of scalar chain of command. Here, a single person gives report to more than one superior. It entails in having less opportunity for having rapport with their respective superiors.

**2. Struggle for power:** A subordinate is controlled by many superiors. It means the power is used over the subordinate by many authority holders. It results in delay in the completion of the project.

**3. Excessive, emphasis on group decision-making:** The available resources are utilised by the department for taking group decisions. There is no spirit of accomodation and understanding under the matrix organisation. So, there is delay in taking a group decision. It leads to delay in the completion of the project.

**4. Arising conflect resoultion:** The resolution or the decision is taken under matrix organisation with too much of self analysis of decision makers. The work of decision makers or the managers may be slow in the accomplishment of the project.

**5. Heterogeneous:** A matrix organisation is created by deputing the staff temporarily. They are skilled professionals of various departments. It is difficult to co-ordinate the work of the skilled staff members when there is a lack of unity of command in an organisation.

## VII. FREE FORM ORGANISATION

This type of organisation is formed whenever a need arises to form an organisation, for achieving a particular object. It will be dissolved after achieving the object of the organisation. In many ways, the Free Form Organisation resembles the project and matrix organisation. It is otherwise called *organic* or *adhoc* (ratio) organisation.

The formation of the Free Form Organisation depends upon the external environment of the business. If the business is highly affected by the external environment, the Free Form Organisation will be established.

Decision is taken under Free Form Organisation without following the policies or guidelines which are determined in advance. Normally, the decision is taken in any organisation by following the organisational policies, rules and regulations. These are framed well in advance and followed while taking decisions.

The structure of Free Form Organisation is related to individual expertise used in resolution of the problems at hand. The nature of problems may be changed according to the situations prevailing in the business world. When there is a change of structure of Free Form Organisation, no task is asssigned to it specifically. But tasks are assigned to superiors and subordinates according to their level of experience and competence. So, the authority is available to the persons according to their competence in performing the given task under this organisation.

There is no channel of communication due to the absence of a formal structure in the Free Form Organisation. So, the communication flows in any direction viz., upwards, downwards, and horizontally.

## MODEL QUESTIONS

1. Explain line organisation?
2. What are the advantages of line and staff organisation?
3. Discuss functional organisation?
4. What are the functions of staff officers?
5. What would you recommend for efficient functioning of a committee?

6. Who is a functional foreman?
7. Compare line, line and staff and functional organisation structure.
8. What is line and staff relationship?
9. State the main causes of conflict between line and staff officials in an enterprise. How can they be removed?
10. Explain the salient features of line and staff organisation?
11. What are the characteristics of an organisation?
12. How do you distinguish between line and staff functions?
13. What is line and staff organsiation?
14. What are merits and demerits of the committee form of management?

# CHAPTER 14

# ORGANISATION CHARTS AND MANUALS

INTRODUCTION
MEANING OF ORGANISATION CHART
DEFINITION OF ORGANISATION CHART
CONTENTS OF ORGANISATION CHART
TYPES OF ORGANISATION CHART
CHART REVISION
PRINCIPLES OF ORGANISATION CHART
ADVANTAGES OF ORGANISATION CHART
LIMITATIONS OF ORGANISATION CHART
ORGANISATION MANUALS
MEANING OF ORGANISATION MANUAL
CONTENTS OF ORGANISATION MANUAL
ADVANTAGES OF ORGANISATION MANUAL
DISADVANTAGES OF ORGANISATION MANUAL
MODEL QUESTIONS

## INTRODUCTION

Organisation charts and manuals are prepared for the purpose of describing the organisation structure. These are used as tools of management control. They give full information on a particular organisation. An executive finds out his exact place in the organisation structure from the chart and manuals. It shows the responsibility and authority of an executive. He knows his superior for whom he is responsible and his subordinates whom he has to supervise.

## MEANING OF ORGANISATION CHART

Organisation charts and manuals are devices showing the organisational relationships and activities within an organisation.

## DEFINITION OF ORGANISATION CHART

J. Batty defines, "An organisation chart is diagrammatic representation of the framework or structure of an organisation."

Terry defines, "An organisation chart is a diagrammatical form which shows the important aspects of an organisation including the major functions and their respective relationship, the channels of supervision and the relative authority of each employee who is incharge of each respective function."

According to Henry H. Albens, "An organisation chart portrays managerial position and relationship in a company or a department unit."

According to Mc Farland, "An organisation chart is a type of record showing the formal organisational relationship which executives intend."

Louis A. Allen states that "The organisation chart is a graphic means of showing organisation data. Organisation charts are snap-shuts, they show only the formal organisation and depict it for a given moment only."

## CONTENTS OF ORGANISATION CHARTS

The following are the contents of the organisation chart:

1. Basic organisation structure and flow of authority.
2. Authority and responsibilities of various executives.
3. The relationship between the line and staff officers.
4. Names of components of organisation.
5. Positions of the various office personnel.
6. Number of persons working in an organisation.
7. The present and proposed organisation structure.
8. Ways of promotion.
9. The requirements of management development.
10. Salary particulars.

Proper care should be devoted while drawing the organisation chart. All the essential particulars should be included in the organisation chart and unnecessary particulars avoided. Accuracy, clarity and simplicity are some of the basic characteristics of a good organisation chart.

## TYPES OF ORGANISATION CHART

The following are the some of the organisation charts.

**1. Vertical chart:** The lines of command flow from the top level to the bottom in vertical lines. This vertical chart is in the form of a graph. This type of organisation chart is followed in many companies.

**2. Horizontal chart:** There is no much difference between vertical charts and horizontal charts. The chart in which the lines of command are flowing horizontally is known as *Horizontal* chart. In this chart, the supervisor is on the left side of the chart and the subordinate on the right side or vice-versa. This type of chart is not commonly followed in any organisation.

**3. Circular chart:** It is otherwise called *concentric* chart. The position of the top executive is shown in the centre of the chart. The subordinates of this top executive are shown in all directions outward from the centre. It derivates the status of different levels of subordinates and shows clearly each person's responsibility. It is the best representation of relationship existing among the employees in an organisation structure.

**4. Master and supplementary charts:** Organisation charts can be divided into two kinds. i.e. Master and Supplementary charts. A chart which shows the entire organisation is called *Master chart*. It gives a clear picture of the organisation and major sections or divisions of the organisation. A chart which shows a particular section or division of the organisation is called *Supplementary chart* or *Unit chart*. It shows the details of relationship, authority and duties within the specified area.

## CHART REVISION

Chart revision means keeping the chart up-to-date on the organisation structure. Whenever the changes are made in the organisation, the changes should be recorded in the chart, otherwise the chart becomes obsolete. It should be noted that the chart must reflect the organizational structure correctly. Management can place the responsibility on an individual to maintain the charts up-to-date. He is responsible for maintaining and revision of the organisation charts.

## PRINCIPLES OF ORGANISATION CHART

The following principles of organisation chart should be kept in mind while preparing the chart:

**1. Observation of lines of authority by top executives:** The top management should observe the lines of authority while dealing with subordinates. The top executives should never by pass the lines of authority. If bypassed, the executives will not be expected to hold the subordinates responsible for the work performed by them. So, the executives should give orders or obtain information by following the lines of authority.

**2. Observation of lines of authority by subordinates:** The subordinates should observe the lines of authority while dealing with superiors. Whatever the information needed by the subordinates, they should get the information by following the lines of authority. If there is any failure in this regard, the subordinates will be suspected of their faithfulness and there would not be proper co-ordination among the subordinates.

**3. Defining lines of position:** The position of each individual in an organisation should be clearly stated. The staff should be assured that there would not be overlapping and two persons would not be appointed to the same position when their authorities and responsibilities are different.

**4. Non-assignment of same duty twice:** An individual should not be compelled to work under two masters for the same work performance.

**5. Avoid unique concentration of duty:** All work or maximum work should not be concentrated in a single point. The work should be divided according to the duties and responsibilities of each worker and the administrative relationship with others.

**6.Organisation charts should be above personalities:** A position should not be assigned to a person because he is the son or relative of any one of the top executives of the organisation. Importance should be given more to an organisation than to an individual.

**7. Simple and flexible:** The organisation chart should be simple and understandable even to an ordinary man. Size and nature of the organisation may be changed in course of time. So, need may arise for periodical modification in the organisation chart. Then, the existing organisation chart should permit these modifications.

## ADVANTAGES OF ORGANISATIONS CHARTS

The following are the advantages of organisation charts.

1. They give a clear picture of the organisation in a simple way.
2. They show the levels of authority and relationship prevailing among employees at a glance.
3. Dual reporting relationships and overlapping positions come to light in the preparation of organisation chart.
4. Instructing work is simplified.
5. Newly hired personnel can understand their role in the organisation and behave accordingly.
6. Organisation chart is a starting point for planning organizational changes.
7. The strengths and weaknesses of an organisation are evaluated with the help of organisation charts.
8. Organisation charts act as authoritative sources of information.
9. A person who prepares an organisation chart can understand the organisation thoroughly and provide a best picture of the organisation.
10. The lines of authority and responsibility given in the organisation chart are definite and formal.
11. The lines of promotion can be understood through the organisation chart.
12. Planning is the primary function of the management. Organisation charts help planning.
13. Organisation charts improve communication both inward and outward.
14. Correct methods of checking and balances in the organisation are provided in the organisation charts.
15. The degree of individual contribution to organisation achievements can be identified. The organisation charts provide a basis for this identification.
16. The obstacles to the efficient functioning of the management can be found while drawing the organisation chart.

17. The outsiders of the organisation can have a quick understanding of each department in an organisation.
18. Organisational disputes can be solved with the help of organisation charts.

## LIMITATIONS OF ORGANISATION CHARTS

There are some limitations of organisation charts. They are briefly listed below:

1. Most of the organisation charts are just like photos taken in an instant.
2. The organisation charts create more rigidity of relationship prevailing among the employees of the organisation.
3. It is very difficult to maintain and ensure that the organisation charts up-to-date. The employees of the organisation are very reluctant to put up with the organisational changes.
4. The organisation charts do not show the informal relationship existing among the organisation staff members.
5. If the charts are not correctly prepared, they will lead to misleading inference.
6. There is no differentiation between line officers and staff officers in an organisation chart.
7. The organisation charts produce a psychological complex such as superiors, inferiors etc., in the minds of the employees.
8. A false picture may be developed by following the over simplified organisation structure.
9. The relationship shown in an organisation chart does not actually prevail among the employees.
10. The words and lines used in an organisation charts give different meanings to different persons.

## ORGANISATION MANUALS

*Organisation manual* is a document prepared in an organisa-tion to furnish information on a particular organisation. A brief history of the organisation is given in this manual. It is usually prepared in the form of a small booklet. Any person can have a knowledge of the organisation particulars or information easily. Normally, this type of organisation manual is prepared for the purpose of evolving a plan for the organisation and providing guidance to control the development of the organisation structure.

## MEANING OF ORGANISATION MANUAL

A small book which contains the information regarding the organisation structure, duties and responsibilities of each position, job, description, salaries, prevailing relationships among members including organisation procedures and methods is called *organisation manual*.

## CONTENTS OF ORGANISATION MANUAL

Generally, an organisation manual contains the following information:

1. Full name and address of the organisation.
2. Telephone number of the organisation.

3. Address of the branch office, if any.
4. Address of the showrooms, if any.
5. Name and address of the top executive personnel.
6. A brief explanation regarding the organisation structure.
7. Important sections or departments of the organisation.
8. Duties and responsibilities of the executives.
9. Information regarding the unity of command.
10. Rules and Regulations regarding leave, promotion, transfer and the like.
11. Procedures followed in accounting, costing, etc.
12. Important decisions taken by the management date-wise.
13. Specimen forms used in the office.
14. Company organisational charts.

## ADVANTAGES OF ORGANISATION MANUAL

The well prepared organisation manual gives maximum benefits to organisation in several respects. Some of the advantages are detailed below:

1. The employees of the organisation can get a clear picture of the organisation.
2. The blueprint rules and regulations are followed by the employees and the controlling work is minimised.
3. The decisions taken by the management are given in an elaborate manner. It facilitates the easy functioning of the organisation.
4. Organisation manual contains the standard methods and procedures to be followed in an organisation. Then the organisation goals are easily achieved.
5. Employees of the organisation are selected, placed, promoted and developed only on the basis of information available in the organisation manual.
6. Organisation manual helps the new personnel to know their duties, responsibilities and relationships with others within a short period.
7. The top executives of an organisation can take decisions quickly by referring to the manual.
8. Organisation manual avoids oral instructions. The disadvantages of oral instructions are eliminated with the help of the organisation manual.
9. Organisational conflicts are avoided with the help of organisation manual.
10. Organisation manual may be used as a basis to change the organisation structure in future. These changes may be made if any need arises.
11. It increases the goodwill and concern for the outsiders of the organisation.

## DISADVANTAGES OF ORGANISATION MANUAL

Organisation manual also has some disadvantages. These are briefly explained below:

1. Organisation manual will become outdated very soon. It is due to the continuous changes of the business, behaviour of the employees and the like.
2. The human relationships are defined and described in the organisation manual but they could not be practically followed in an organisation.

3. The organisation manuals are not reviewed periodically. So the relevant changes are not incorporated in the organisation manual.
4. The preparation of organisation manual increases the administrative expenses of the organisation.
5. Much time is necessary to keep the organisation manual up-to-date.
6. The employees of the organisation should follow the procedures mentioned in the organisation manual. It reduces the individual initiative of the organisation.

## MODEL QUESTIONS

1. What is organisation chart?.
2. Explain the organisation chart.
3. Write short notes "organisation chart".
4. What are the types of organisation chart?
5. What are the differnt advantages of organisation chart?
6. Define the term "organisation chart".
7. What is an "organisation chart?" What are its advantages?

# CHAPTER 15

# STAFFING

INTRODUCTION
DEFINITION
ELEMENTS OF STAFFING
FUNCTIONS OF STAFFING
PROCESSING OF STAFFING
PROPER STAFFING
ADVANTAGES OF PROPER STAFFING
RECRUITMENT
SOURCES OF RECRUITMENT
INTERNAL SOURCES
EXTERNAL SOURCES
IMPORTANCE OF SELECTION
STAGES OF SELECTION PROCEDURE
PRE-REQUISITES OF EFFECTIVE TEST
KINDS OF INTERVIEW
PRINCIPLES OF INTERVIEW
PROCESS OF INTERVIEW
PROMOTION
QUALITIES OF GOOD PROMOTION POLICY
MODEL QUESTIONS

## INTRODUCTION

In a new enterprise, the staffing function follows the planning and organising function. In the case of running an enterprise, staffing is a continuous process. So, the manager should perform this function at all times. The staffing function includes recruitment, selection, training, development, transfer, promotion and compensation of personnel.

It is obvious that the management must ensure a constant availability of sufficient number of efficient executives in an enterprise for the efficient functioning of the enterprise. The selected personnel should be physically, mentally and temperamentally fit for the job.

## DEFINITION

According to Koontz and O'Donnell, "The managerial function of staffing involves managing the organisation structure through proper and effective selection, appraisal and development of personnel to fill the roles designed into the structure."

S. Benjamin has defined staffing as, "The process involved in identifying, assessing, placing, evaluating and directing individuals at work."

According to Theo Hainmann, "Staffing function is concerned with the placement, growth and development of all those members of the organisation whose function is to get things done through the efforts of other individuals."

## ELEMENTS OF STAFFING

While performing the staffing function, the manager has to see that men are fit for jobs and jobs are not altered for men. The major elements of staffing are given below:

1. Effective recruitment and selection.
2. Proper classification of personnel and pay fixed for them.
3. Proper placement.
4. Adequate and appropriate training for development.
5. Satisfactory and fair transfer and promotion.
6. Sound relationship between management and workers.
7. Adequate provision for retirement.

## FUNCTIONS OF STAFFING

**1. Manpower planning:** Manpower may be planned for short-term and long-term. The short-term manpower planning may achieve the objectives of the company at present conditions. The long-term manpower planning should be concerned with the estimation of staff members required in future.

**2. Development:** Development is concerned with the development of staff members through adequate and appropriate training programmes. The training is given only to the needy persons.

**3. Fixing the employment standards:** It involves the job specification and job description. These enable the management to select the personnel and train them scientifically. Job description is a systematic and organised written statement of the duties and responsibilities in a specific job. Job specification is a statement of personal qualities that an individual must posses if he is to successfully perform the job.

**4. Sources:** It is concerned with the method by which the staff members are selected. The sources may be internal and external sources. Internal source means that a vacancy is filled up by the company out of the staff members available within the company. The external source means that a vacancy is filled up by the company from outside the company. The person seleted may be unemployed or working in any other company.

**5. Selection and placement:** It includes the process of selection of the staff members. The placement includes giving a job to a person on the basis of his ability, education, experience and the like.

**6. Training:** The training may be arranged by the company itself. In certain cases, the staff members may be sent out by the company to get the training. The expense is borne by the company. The training may be required not only by the new staff members but also by the existing staff members.

**7. Other functions:** The other functions of staffing includes co-ordination, promotion, transfer, record maintenance regarding employees, rating of emplo-yees, motivation, etc.

## PROCESSING OF STAFFING

The selection and placement of personnel involves the following processes. They are briefly discussed below:

**1. Planning:** The term *planning* of staff members includes estimation of the number of staff members required to the company in various grades. It is based upon the size of the company and the policy followed by the company.

**2. Recruitment and selection:** It deals with the selection of qualified applicants to fill the jobs in the organisation. A standard procedure may be followed while selecting the staff members. The procedure may be valid for different types of personnel.

**3. Training of developments:** It is concerned with providing training to new staff members as well as the existing staff members. The working efficiency of the staff members may be developed through the training programmes.

**4. Performance operation:** It deals with assessment of the work performed by the staff members in an organisation. A standard may be fixed in order to evaluate the efficiency of the staff members.

## PROPER STAFFING

Proper staffing means providing adequate qualified staff members for the purpose of effective functioning of office. The chief executive or the general manager undertakes this function. Identifying appropriate staff members is a difficult task. So, some of the staffing functions may be assigned to a separate department in a large concern.

## ADVANTAGES OF PROPER STAFFING

1. It helps in the recruitment of efficient staff members.
2. It helps the proper placement of staff members according to their ability.
3. Proper selection, training and development of staff members, will result in the maximum production in an organisation.
4. Increasing the efficiency of the workers will increase the earning capacity of the workers.

## RECRUITMENT

Recruitment is the process of finding the apt candidates and inducing them to apply for the job in an organisation. The recruitment should be a sound one. If it is not so, the morale of the staff will be very low and the image of the company will be tarnished.

The success of any recruitment depends upon the procedure followed by the company while recruiting the members. Jobs with low salary, uninteresting jobs or difficult jobs cannot be filled up by the company very easily. Every company has to recruit its staff members but the quantum of recruitment may vary from one company to another company. The variation may be due to the size of the company, recruitment policy of the company, nature of the job and the like.

## MEANING

Recruitment means the discovery of the staff members for the present and future jobs in an organisation.

## DEFINITION

According to Dalton E. McFarland, "The term recruitment applies to the process of attracting potential employees of the company".

Edwin B. Flippo, "Recruitment is the process of searching for prospective employees and stimulating them to apply for the jobs in the organisation".

## SOURCES OF RECRUITMENT

The source of recruitment is based on the policy followed by the company. The job can be filled up out of the employees of the company or from outside the company. If the job is filled up out of the present employees of the company, it is said to be the *internal source* of the company.

If the same job is filled up from out of the candidates available in the society, it is said to be the *external source*. A clear picture of the internal sources and the external sources is given below:

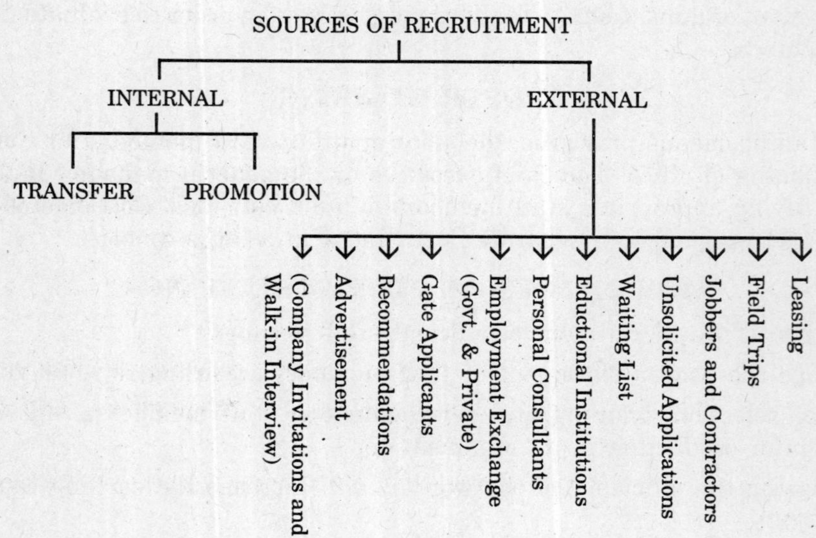

## INTERNAL SOURCES

Whenever a job falls vacant, it can be filled up by giving a promotion to the present employee of the company. It is based on the promotion policy followed by the company. In certain cases, a same cadre staff member is deputed to the job by the company. This is called a *transfer*. This is also based on the transfer policy followed by the company.

**Advantages**

1. It increases the morale among the staff members of the company.
2. Giving promotion keeps the employee happy.
3. It attracts efficient staff members.
4. The training expenses may be reduced to some extent.
5. A person who has got a promotion, inspires the staff members to acquire a thorough knowledge of his job.
6. Internal promotion helps the staff members to derive job satisfaction.
7. A promoted staff member may make use of his past experience in the new post.
8. It increases the security of the job of the staff member.
9. A new responsibility can be entrusted safely to the promoted staff members on the basis of the contents of Service Register.
10. It ensures the continuity of job to the staff members and stability of the organisation.
11. It induces the staff members to work hard to get promotion.
12. Such expenses as on advertisement, recruitment, test and interview are avoided.

## DISADVANTAGES

1. If the higher post is filled internally, the company will not be able to get fresh and original ideas and initiative from the staff members.
2. The outsiders do not have a scope to show their ability in the performance of the work.
3. An underqualified person may be appointed in the higher post.
4. If the promotion is a guarantee to the internal staff members after the expiry of a specific period, the concerned staff member does not care to work efficiently.

## EXTERNAL SOURCES

There are various external sources of recruitment. They are briefly explained below:

**1. Advertisement:** When a company wants to inform the public that it has a vacancy, it puts up an advertisement. The details of the job and the qualification of the candidates are briefly given. The company may receive the applications in response to the advertisement. After that, a interview will be conducted. In certain cases, the walk in interview method may be adopted by the company. In the walk-in-interview method, the applications are received from the candidates. The date and time and place of the interview are mentioned in the advertisement. In this way, a person can be recruited immediately through an advertisement.

**2. Recommendations:** Here, recommendation means appointment of a person on getting a recommendation letter from a person reliable and well-known to the company. In certain cases, an employee of the company may bring the candidates to the company for the purpose of being appointed, when the company does not conduct an interview for selection.

**3. Gate applicants:** The educated unemployed youth may contact the company to get employment. These candidates may not have any recommendations. Even the company might not have issued any advertisement for the post. The candidate personally approaches the appointing authority of the company. If such candidate is found fit for any one of the posts which are vacant at that time, the candidate is appointed.

**4. Employment exchange:** The job seekers register their names with their qualifications with the employment exchange. The company can get a list of candidates who have requisite qualifications to fit in a job. Out of the listed candidates, any one of them can be selected. The employment exchange is of two kinds, *i.e.,* public employment exchange and private employment exchange. The public employment exchange is run by the government. The private employment exchange is run by a private party. The private party can get the a commission both from the job seekers and the company. But the public employment exchange does not demand any such commission both from the job seekers and the company.

**5. Personnel consultant:** Private consultant is a separate specified agency doing the function of recruitment of the personnel on behalf of the company. In other words, the functions of personnel department of any company are performed by the personnel consultants. It receives the applications from the candidates, verifies the applications, conducts interviews and selects the candidates. The personnel consultant receives fees from the company for its service.

**6. Educational institutions:** Universities, colleges and institutions are formed to offer specific courses. The educational institutions make an arrangement for campus interview. The business concerns come to the campus of educational institutions to recruit the students for various posts. The selected students are requested to join the post after completing the course.

**7. Waiting list:** The business concern prepares a waiting list of candidates who have already been interviewed. But, they are not appointed for lack of vacancy. Whenever a vacancy arises, the vacancy may be filled up by the company out of the waiting list.

**8. Unsolicited applicants:** Unsolicited application means the application received through mail from the candidate. The application brings the information regarding the name and address of the candidate, his age, educational qualification, experience, area of interest, etc. If there is any vacancy at that time, the candidate will be recruited for the specified post. Normally, this type of application is considered for the posts at the lower level.

**9. Jobbers and contractors:** The casual vacancy may be filled up by the company through the jobbers and contractors. Normally, unskilled candidates are appointed in this way. They are available at short notice and for a small salary. This type of candidate is brought by the jobbers and contractors to the place of work and they receive some wages from the company for this service.

**10. Field trips:** A company may send a group of experts to the towns and the cities where the various kinds of candidates required by the company are available. In this case, a prior advertisement may be issued in newspapers. The advertisement contains information regarding the date, venue and time of the interview. The interview is conducted in different places. This is the procedure followed to recruit the candidates under field trips.

**11. Leasing:** This type of source of recruitment is followed by the public sector organisation. The reason is that the organisation wants to manage the problems particularly at higher level. Before recruiting the staff members, the period of service is fixed by the company and it is conveyed to the staff members.

## MERITS

There are some advantages to the company if the appointment is made through external sources. These advantages or merits are discussed below:

**1. Choice:** A company can recruit a person out of a large number of applicants. Each and every candidate's plus points and minus points are taken into consideration for the purpose of recruitment. Then, the best candidate can be selected by the company.

**2. New outlook:** If a new person is recruited by the company, a new way of approach may dawn to solve the problem, which will give maximum benefits to the company.

**3. Wide experience:** If the recruited new candidate has experience in various fields, the company can get the benefit of the candidate's experience.

## DEMERITS

The external sources also have some demerits. They are listed below:

**1. Gruging of old employment:** If a candidate is recruited from external sources, the existing staff may have a grudge against him. It results in demoralisation of the staff members.

**2. Lack of co-operation:** The existing staff members do not extend their co-operation to the person who is selected from out of external sources. In addition to this, the existing staff members make the new recruit face the difficulties and try to disorient him in relation to his work.

**3. Expensive:** Recruitment of a person from outside the company requires a lot of formalities. The formalities include issuing advertisement, receiving the applications, screening the applications, despatching the interview letters, fixation of interview date, time and place, formation of an interview committee etc. Completing all the above said procedures involves a lot of expenditure.

**4. Trade union:** If the trade union of the company is very strong, it is very difficult to convince the trade union and recruit a person from outside a company.

**5. Danger of non-adjusttment:** If a newly recruited person fails to adjust himself to the working conditions of the company, it leads to more expenditure in looking for his replacement. Besides, it causes irritation and quarrel between the recruited person and the existing staff members.

## SELECTION

Selection is the device used in an organisation to select a suitable person who has required educational qualifications, skills, abilities, personality and the like. When an organisation gets more number of applications than needed, the applications in excess are rejected. In other words, a screening test may be conducted through which unsuitable candidates may be rejected. Selection procedure starts with the end of recruitment.

## MEANING

Selection is the process adopted by an organisation to select adequate number of persons who are fit for the job.

## IMPORTANCE OF SELECTION

Selection is a tough task at present. The reason is that the available candidates are more qualified than what is required. They have higher education qualifications and experience. So, more care is needed in the selection of proper personnel:

1. Manager is informed about the complexities of selection and the weakness and limitations of various selection techniques. Managers know the probabilities of error.
2. The high degree of education and employment opportunities have made the labour market a buyer's market. The economic security has made it a seller's market.
3. The inexperienced candidates cannot meet the require-ments of today's job. Now, education is developed in such a way that training is given within the study. A person with adequate and desired experience gets selected for the job.
4. Managers know the techniques used to discover the deficiencies in candidates.
5. Today's public policy has imposed many new restrictions with respect to those who can and should be hired and what kind selections are acceptable.
6. If the job specifications are not clearly described, it makes the selection procedure a difficult one.
7. Selection requires high cost but results in a very high rate of return.

## STAGES OF SELECTION PROCEDURE

It may be said that recruitment is a positive function of the management. But selection is a negative function of management. The reason is that eliminating applications is more difficult than selecting them.

Normally, the selection procedure has the following stages:

**1. Receiving and screening of applications:** Prospective employees are requested to submit the applications in white paper or in a prescribed form. In both the cases, full particulars of the employee should be given. Any omission may disqualify the particular candidate. The information relates to the name of the candidate, age, educational qualification, date of birth, experience, parents' name and occupation, address for communication, etc. The same information is kept as a permanent record in the organisation. If the number of applicants exceeds the actual requirement, the organisation may select more candidates than required.

**2. Initial interview:** It is otherwise called *preliminary interview*. The object of conducting this interview is to know whether the applicant is physically and mentally fit for the job. Questions are put to the candidate for evaluation. These questions are related to his qualifications, experience, interest, age, nativity and the like. Only a minimum time is spent for this interview. Candidates who have passed in the initial interview are called for the next selection procedure.

**3. Blank Application:** A specific format is followed by an organisation for this selection process. The nature of the format varies for each job. The same form is not used for all jobs in an organisation. The reason is that different qualifications and skills are required for different jobs. Care should be taken to ensure that the candidates provide brief and pointed answers for queries raised in the form. Besides, irrelevant answers should be avoided and all relevant information should be given in the form.

The advantages of a blank application in the selection procedure are explained below:

**A. Acts as an urgent test device:** The applicants have to find precise answers for the queries raised in the form. This test is used to find the quick understanding capacity and problem solving capacity of the candidate.

**B. Shy candidates:** Some candidates may find it difficult to give answers in the face to face meeting with the employer. They may give answers through this form. Shy candidates and slow candidates may use this process.

**C. Aid to build trust among applicants:** Whenever the applications are issued to applicants for filling up, there is confidence among the applicants as they are for the job in question.

**D. Basis for final inteview:** The answers given in the application form are used as basic things to frame questions for the final interview.

**E. Aid to preparing waiting list:** Candidates may be found fit for the job but they cannot be absorbed immediately. These candidates are placed under the waiting list. The information provided in the form is used for the preparation of this list.

**4. Test:** The test is conducted by the organisation for the purpose of knowing more about the applicants to be selected or rejected. Normally, many organisations ask the applicants questions to know more about their aptitude, interest, general awareness, etc.

Tests can be classified into two kinds. They are Proficiency Test and Aptitude Test. Proficiency Test refers to the testing of the skills and abilities possessed by the candidate. Aptitude Test refers to measuring of the skills and abilities which may be developed by the applicant to perform the job in future.

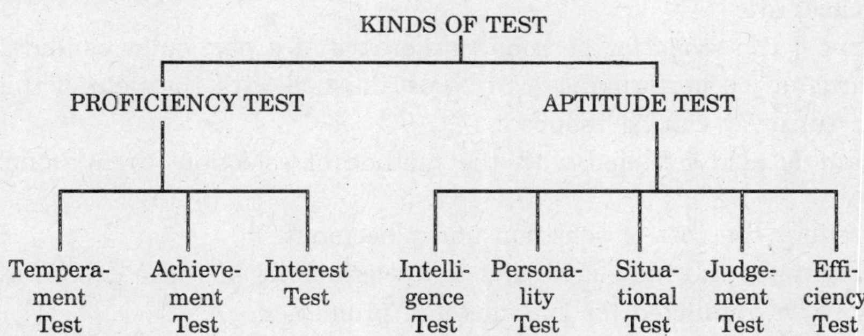


(a) Temperament tests are used to measure the likes, dislikes and habits of an individual. It is helpful to find out whether a particular individual can put up himself in a society or not.

(b) Achievement test is used to measure the level of knowledge for performing the work assigned to an individual. It is otherwise called performance test or trade test. Sometimes, the achievement test is conducted theoretically, i.e., answers are received by putting questions to the individual. For example, an accounting test may measure the accounting performance of an accountant in terms of accuracy and neatness.

(c) Interest test is used to discover the individual's interest in having the work assigned to him/her. It is assumed that an individual who is interested in one type of work does better than the one who is not interested. Interest of an individual may be relating to outdoor activities, accounting, clerical, social service etc. It is otherwise called *Vocational Test.*

(d) Intelligence Test is used to measure the mental ability, capacity and general awareness of the individual. The most common intelligence tests used for management purposes are group tests, individual tests, self-evaluation test, self-administered tests, performance tests, verbal comprehen-sion, word fluency, memory, inductive reasoning, test of reasoning, number facility, speed of perception and the like. The Intelligence Test is conducted agewise. If the management selects highly intelligent people, its training process is easy and training expenses are low.

(e) Personality Test is conducted to measure courage, initiative, emotion, confidence, reaction, ability to mix with others, ability to motivate, general behaviour of the individual, cheerfulness, leadership, patience and domination of character.

(f) Situational Test is conducted to measure the reactions of applicants to a particular situation. Besides, the applicant's ability to succeed in his job in this situation is also measured.

(g) Judgement Test is conducted to measure the ability of an individual in applying the knowledge, intelligence and experience to solve the problems presented before him.

(h) Efficiency test is used to know how quickly and efficiently an individual uses his hands to accomplish the work assigned to him. It is otherwise called *dexterity test*.

**Advantages of Test**

(a) Tests help the employer to find whether a candidate is fit for the job or not.

(b) Besides, tests help in checking candidate's claims in respect of his qualification, experience, etc.

(c) Tests avoid the scope for personal preference of a particular candidate.

(d) Standards of job performance can be established with the help of this test.

(e) Labour turnover can be reduced.

(f) Applicant is also satisfied with the method of selection, even though he is not selected.

(g) Tests reduce the cost of selection and placement.

(h) Tests highlight the hidden talents and overlooking of these can be avoided.

(i) Test may be conducted for transfer and promotion.

(j) Administrative expenses regarding training may be reduced to some extent.

(k) Failure in performing the job is reduced.

**Disadvantages of Test**

(a) Hundred percent best selection is not possible through test. So the test is used as a supplementary method of selection.

(b) Test is more suitable to an organisation where for limited number of jobs, more number of candidates have applied.

(c) If the number of applicants is small, it is desirable to conduct an interview rather than the test.

(d) Test is not able to measure the combination of characteristics required for various jobs.

(e) Some candidates do not reveal their talents through tests.

(f) The actual performances of a candidate cannot be found out through the test.

(g) Test does not provide any basis for motivation.

A test has some advantages and limitations or disadvantages. But it may be stated that more accurate selection is possible through the test. According to Felix M. Lopez, "When tests are used properly, they can help substantially in selection, particularly and most especially in selection for managerial positions. All tests provide clues about an applicant which, when confirmed by other information, enable the assessor to make fairly accurate predictions of job effectiveness. They suggest hypothesis about the applicant's intellectual capacities, aptitudes, vocational attitudes or personality dynamics, each of which must be confirmed or rejected by data drawn from other areas of the applicant's background".

## PRE-REQUISITES OF EFFECTIVE TEST

The limitations of the test can be avoided if the management takes the following precautions while conducting tests:

**(a) Validity:** An effective test has validity. The validity of the tests depends upon the degree of prediction of the job performance successfully. Thus, a test should accurately predict the criteria of job success.

**(b) Reliability:** Reliability of a test refers to getting the same result from any candidate tested for any number of times. So, it is the duty of the management to bear in mind the reliability of a test.

**(c) Norms:** The management should fix the norms for selection. Some companies prescribe minimum marks for selection and some companies prescribe cut-off marks for selection. But, these should be pre-determined.

**(d) No partiality:** Management should ensure that tests have validity. Proper weightage should be given to the scores obtained in tests and personal biases should be avoided.

**(e) Specialisation:** Test administration, scoring and interpretation require technical competence and training in testing. These should be handled by properly trained and competent persons. If not, results may be horrible.

**(f) Supplementary:** A candidate cannot be selected or rejected on the basis of performance in the test. The test should be considered as a supplementary in the selection process. The final selection of any candidate should be based on the information given in the application, performance in the interview, if any conducted, in addition to the test performance.

**5. Checking References:** Sometimes, the applicants are requested to furnish references. References are the norm in society. Applicants may include the name and address of parent educational institutions and the present employer. The information furnished in the applications are checked from these persons. If the referee is a present employer, the applicant's job performance, salary drawn particulars, reasons for leaving the job, etc., are checked.

A letter of recommendation may also be treated as a reference. The prospective employer can collect information about the applicant regarding his character, conduct, ability etc., from the referee. Some management firms do not take much interest in this regard. The verification of references might give correct information about the applicant. Some applicants may give incorrect information regarding experience, past salary drawn and reasons for leaving the job. But these are identified with the help of checking references.

Many managements which do not hold good opinion about the applicant are not ready to give references . At the same time, some applicants have some well-wishers who are considered as potential as reference, and no negative answer is received from those references.

**6. Interview:** Interview is considered as a method of personal appraisal through face to face conversation and observation. The management selects a candidate through a interview by one or more persons. The interviewing persons are experts in the interview technique and they have a thorough knowledge in their respective fields. Interview helps the employer to evaluate the candidate regarding the personality, smartness, intelligence, attitude, etc.

In any interview, the interviewer has a dominant position over the interviewee. The interview is divided into two i.e., preliminary interview and final interview. The preliminary interview has been discussed already. Here, the final interview is discussed. The final interview is conducted only for candidates who succeed in the preliminary interview. The candidate should succeed in two stages of the final interview. In the first stage, the personnel department makes a thorough evaluation of a candidate. In the second stage, the successful candidates from the first stage are sent to the functional department where additional hands are required. The candidate who has successfully passed the second stage is selected.

## KINDS OF INTERVIEW

There are a number of kinds of interviews conducted by the management. Some of the interviews are briefly explained below:

**(a) Direct interview:** Under this type of interview, straight-away questions are put before the applicant to get answers for them. Face to face conversation is the trend towards the interview. The in-depth knowledge of applicant is not observed under this type of interview. But, the skills, character, area of interest and attitudes of the applicant can be identified to some extent.

**(b) Indirect interview:** Questions are not raised directly by the interviewer before the interviewee. The particular applicant is requested to express his views on any topics as he likes. The interviewer carefully listens to what the applicant expresses. The interviewer does not interpret the applicant's views. The applicant has full freedom of expression. The personality of the applicant is easily assessed by the management.

**(c) Patterned interview:** A number of standard questions are framed well in advance which are to be put before the applicant. The answers for these questions are found while framing the questions and answers are written near the questions. These are used for a verification purpose when answers are given by the applicant during the interview. This is the procedure adopted under this type of interview to evaluate the suitability of the applicant.

**(d) Stress interview:** Irritating questions are put before the applicant by the interviewer. If any applicant gets angry when these types of questions are put to him, the particular applicant is evaluated as unfit for the job. For example, the Interviewer may ask, "How many legs does an eight legged insect have? or "Dear Mr. Lakshmanan, what is your name?". These are some questions which irritate any body in normal conditions. If an applicant gets angry over these questions, he/she is rejected as unfit for the job.

**(e) Systematic in-depth interview:** Under this type of interview, the interviewer asks any one of the questions initially. Then, he proceeds step-by-step to get an integrated view of the skills and personality of the applicants.

**(f) Board or panel interview:** A group of persons called interviewers ask the applicant questions in the area of interest of the applicants. Immediately after the interview, they evaluate the performance of an applicant based on the answers given by the applicant.

**(g) Group interview:** It may be otherwise called group discussion or house party technique. A number of applicants are interviewed simultaneously. A common topic is presented before the group. One group consists of six to eight members. Each applicant is allotted a number. They may call other members of the group by calling the concerned member's number. They are restricted to use their names. The applicants are selected or rejected on the basis of performance in group discussion.

## PRINCIPLES OF INTERVIEW

The interview technique should be an effective one. The following principles are adopted by the management in order to make an interview effective:

1. The management should define the specific objectives of an interview.
2. Next, the management has to prepare the procedure followed to achieve the specified objectives.
3. The interviewers should ask the questions which are related to the job to be filled.
4. The interviewer must create a rapport with the interviewee before starting the interview.
5. The interviewees are requested to express their opinions or views freely without any hesitation.
6. The tension or nervousness of the applicants are removed by the interviewer.
7. The interviewer should listen to the answers given by the applicants carefully.
8. The evaluation of the performance of the applicant is done immediately after the interview is over.
9. The interviewer may say 'thanks' to the applicants while closing the interview. This carries much better impression about the interview and interviewer.

## PROCESS OF INTERVIEW

The following procedure may be adopted for an interview:

**(a) Review of background information:** The interviewer has to collect the information regarding the applicant's bio-data *and the* job for which he has applied. This process is known as *review* of background information.

**(b) Preparation of questions:** The interviewer has to prepare the questions in the area in which the applicant is interested. The question is presented by the interviewer in an understandable way. The answers are received from the applicant one by one. The next question is raised only after getting a full answer to the first question. The sub-questions may be raised by the interviewer during the interview, if the need arises.

**(c) Putting the applicant at ease:** There is a mental and emotional strain to the applicants. These may be removed by the interviewer. These are possible through proper understanding of applicants and sympathy with the applicants by the interviewer during the interview.

Outsiders except interviewers and applicants are not allowed to be present in the interview room. All the necessary facilities and comforts are arranged by the management in order to put the applicant at ease. Some mannerisms like causing interruptions through raising number of sub-questions unnecessarily or raising eye-brows or any odd behaviour frequently are avoided by the interviewer.

**(d) Drawing out the best applicant:** Some set of questions are not asked in an interview. So, it is a very difficult task to draw the best applicant out of the interview performance. The interviewer has to follow acceptable norms to select an applicant for appointment. But, the norms should be correct and they should provide a basis to select a suitable person.

**(e) Concluding the interview:** The applicant leaves the room after the interview is over. The interviewer immediately assesses the applicant's performance in the interview. Some interviewers take notes during the interview. These notes may be used to assess the applicant. The next applicant is called for an interview after the process is over.

**7. Final selection:** Finally, a suitable applicant is selected on the basis of performance in the above mentioned test and interview. Only the required number of applicants are selected by the management. The competent authority has to approve the selection of the applicants.

In the case of big organisations, a separate department known as personnel department is in charge of selection. The personnel department manager selects the applicant and approves it. The appointment order will be sent to the applicant without delay. Normally, the applicants are selected provisionally.

**8. Medical examination:** It is otherwise called physical examination. This is carried out for the purpose of assessing physical fitness of the prospective employee. Many organisations do not follow the process of medical examination. The reason is that there is no need for medical examination in certain jobs. Medical certificate is received from the doctor after the medical examination is over. This certificate is attached to the joining report of the new employee. Some applicants may be educationally qualified for the job but physically unfit for the job. For certain jobs, minimum physical fitness is required according to the nature of the job.

**9. Placement:** The applicants are placed on a probation basis only after completing all the formalities. The probation period may vary from one job to another job according to the nature of the job. The maximum probation period for any job is two years. It may be extended to three years in extraordinary circumstances. The new employees are observed keenly over the probation period. These new employees are regularised on the completion of the probation period successfully.

**10. Orientation:** Orientation refers to providing the information regarding the organisation briefly to new employees. The term *information* includes co-workers of new employees, superior, subordinates, location of work place, duties, authorities, responsibilities, and the overall administration of the organisation.

The orientation programme is carried out through lectures or films. The new employees are taken round the offices and plant and they are introduced to the existing employees. Printed literature may also be used to the orientation programme. The orientation programmer helps the new employee to acquire a knowledge of the organisation functioning without any delay. It facilitates the effective performance of a job by the new employee.

## PROMOTION

**1. Meaning:** *Promotion* may be defined as the placement of an employee to a better job which results in extending prestige, salary, powers, duties, responsibilities and it requires more knowledge and skills to perform the job.

Every employee has the aspiration to get promotion and is ready for acquiring the additional qualification and experience fit for the job. Higher posts and key posts are filled up by the management through the promotion policy. This promotion policy persuades the employees to be loyal to the management.

**2. Basis for promotion:** The promotion is given to any employee on a widely acceptable basis. The basis may be seniority or competence. Seniority refers to the possession of more number of years of service in the same organisation than those of the other employees. Competence refers to the accomplishment of a particular job effectively than the other employees.

Senior employees prefer seniority to competence for promotion. Senior people argue that they have more experience in the job than others. So, they demand seniority as the basis for promotion. The juniors and the management people are in favour of competence.

Whenever the management fixes competence as the basis for promotion, all the employees including senior people are ready to increase their knowledge and skills to get promotion. If promotion is denied to senior people, they do not devote their full attention to perform the job. The younger ones may command the old people if the competence is the basis for promotion. It will be just like a son commanding his father.

Unfit persons may also be eligible to get promotion if the management prescribes seniority as the basis for promotion. Besides, senior people are not ready to acquire additional knowledge and skill which are necessary for the jobs to which they seek promotion.

Hence, it is concluded that the same management may follow both criteria for promotion. Seniority is the basis for promotion to a job which does not require much competence. Competence is the basis for promotion to a job which requires professional skills.

## QUALITIES OF GOOD PROMOTION POLICY

A promotion policy followed by any management should have the following qualities or characteristics.

1. Whatever the promotion policy followed by the management, that should be widely published and strictly adhered to.
2. Each and every employee should work in all jobs in an organisation to get thorough knowledge and experience.
3. A detailed and accurate job description should be prepared in each job. The employees can know the qualifications and experience required for each job through job description.
4. Promotion is given to any employee through widest publicity.
5. Employees are permitted to acquire qualifications and experience through job training, vocational courses and the like.
6. Each and every promotion is recommended by line officers and approved by the top executive of the management.
7. An employee has a right to represent his views and opinions regarding promotion if promotion is denied to that employee.
8. The promotion is given to an employee who gives his consent for promotion.

## MODEL QUESTIONS

1. What do you know about proficiency test?
2. What is meant by indirect interview?
3. What are the sources of recruitment? What factors are to be considered while giving promotion?
4. Which is the right basis — seniority or merit for promotion?
5. Describe the steps in recruitment and selection. What should be the features of a sound promotion policy?
6. What are the different methods of selection?
7. Explain staffing?
8. Explain the major steps of the staffing process?
9. Bring out the arguments for and against the promotion system?
10. What is Promotion? What are the basis for promotion?
11. Explain the concept of staffing and brief the significant activities performed in it?

# CHAPTER 16

# PERFORMANCE APPRAISAL

## INTRODUCTION

A member in an organisation expresses an opinion or views about others. The opinion may be about the way of mixing with others, way of working, character, etc. These opinions become a basis for the appraisal of an employee. A superior has some opinion about his subordinates for determining many things like promotion, transfer, training, pay fixation, etc.

## MEANING

*Performance appraisal* means the systematic evaluation of the performance of an employee by an expert or his immediate superior.

Appraisal results in the comparison of more than one person in several directions with others. The very purpose of appraising an employee is for the promotion of the employee. Performance appraisal is used to cover some other activities also. The appraisal is done by the management periodically. The time and venue of the appraisal should be known to both the employer and the employee. The appraisal avoids personal biases and prejudices which tend to lead to an incorrect appraisal of an employee.

## DEFINITION

Edwin B. Flippo, "Performance appraisal is a systematic, periodic and so far as humanly possible, an impartial rating of an employee's excellence in matters pertaining to his present job and to his potentialities for a better job."

The performance of an employee is compared with the job standards. The job standards are already fixed by the management for an effective appraisal.

According to Scott, Clotheir and Spriegal, "Performance appraisal is a record of progress for apprentices and regular employees, as a guide in making promotions, transfers or demotions, as a guide in making lists for bonus distribution, for seniority consideration and for rates of pay, as an instrument for discovering hidden genius, and as a source of information that makes conferences with employees helpful."

## IMPORTANCE OF PERFORMANCE APPRAISAL

Now-a-days, the management uses performance appraisal as a tool. The scope of performance appraisal is not limited to pay fixation and is enlarged to include many decisions:

1. Performance appraisal helps the management to take decision about the salary increase of an employee.
2. The continuous evaluation of an employee helps in improving the quality of an employee in job performance.
3. The performance appraisal brings out the facilities available to an employee, when the management is prepared to provide adequate facilities for effective performance.
4. It minimises the communication gap between the employer and employee.
5. Promotion is given to an employee on the basis of performance appraisal.
6. The training needs of an employee can be identified through performance appraisal.
7. The decision for discharging an employee from the job is also taken on the basis of performance appraisal.
8. Performance appraisal is used to transfer a person who is misfit for a job to the right placement.
9. The grievances of an employee are eliminated through performance appraisal.

10. The job satisfaction of an employee increases the morale. This job satisfaction is achieved through performance appraisal.
11. It helps to improve the employer and employee relationship.

## LIMITATIONS OF PERFORMANCE APPRAISAL

The following are some limitations of performance appraisal:

1. The performance appraisal methods are unreliable.
2. If an employee is well known to an employer, the performance appraisal may not be correct.
3. The inability of a supervision to appraise an employee does not bring out the accurate performance appraisal.
4. Some qualities of an employee can not be easily appraised through any performance appraisal method.
5. A supervisor may appraise an employee to be good to avoid incurring his displeasure.
6. Uniform standards are not followed by the supervisors in performance appraisal.

## KINDS OF PERFORMANCE APPRAISAL

There are many kinds of performance appraisal available. But, the management wants to adopt only one of the types of performance appraisal. The appraisal is done adopting any one of the two approaches. These two approaches are traits and results. The traits approach refers to appraising the employee on the basis of his attitudes. The results approach refers to appraising the employee on the basis of results or his accomplishment of a job. A brief explanation of the types of performance appraisal is given below:

**1. Ranking Method:** This method is very old and a simple from of performance appraisal. An employee is ranked one against the other in the working group under this method. For example, if there are 10 workers in the working group, the most efficient worker is ranked as number one and the least efficient worker is ranked as number ten. All the workers in the working group are ranked as 1, 2, 3 and so on.

**Advantages**

(a) Each employee or worker can be compared with the other person.
(b) A small organisation can get maximum benefits through the ranking method.

**Diadvantages**

(a) A big organisation is not able to get sizeable benefits from the ranking method.
(b) Ranking method does not evaluate the individuality of an employee.
(c) It lacks objectivity in the assessment of employees.

**2. Paired Comparison Method:** This method is a part of ranking method. Paired comparison method has been developed to be used in a big organisation. Each employee is compared with other employees taking only one at a time. The evaluator compares two employees and puts a tick mark against an employee whom he considers a better employee. In the same way, an individual is compared with all other existing employees. Finally, an employee who gets maximum ticks for being a better employee is considered the best employee. The number of comparison is calculated by a formula *i.e.*, n(n-1) /2, where N stands for the number of persons to be compared. The following table illustrates the number of persons compared and the number of paired comparisons.

**Advantages**

(a) This method is suitable for big organisations.

(b) Individual traits are evaluated under this method.

**Disadvantages**

(a) The understanding of this method is difficult one.

(b) It involves considerable time.

| *Number of Persons to be Compared* | *Number of Paired Comparison* |
|---|---|
| 2 | 1 |
| 3 | 3 |
| 4 | 6 |
| 5 | 10 |
| 6 | 15 |
| 7 | 21 |
| 8 | 28 |
| 9 | 36 |
| 10 | 45 |

**3. Forced Distribution Method:** A method which forces the rater to distribute the ratings of the overall performance of an employee is known as *Forced Distribution Method.* Groupwise, rating is done under this method. For example, a group of workers doing the same job would fall into same group as superior, at and above average, below average and poor. The rater rates 15% of the workers as superior, 35% of the workers as at and above average, 35% of workers as below average and 15% of workers as poor. This method is suitable to large organisation. But the individual traits could not be appraised under this method.

**4. Grading:** Certain categories of abilities or performance of employees are defined well in advance to fall in certain grades under this method. Such grades are very good, good, average, poor and very poor. Here, the individual traits and characteristics are identified.

**5. Check List:** The appraisal of the ability of an employee through getting answers for a number of questions is called the method of *check list.* These questions are related to the behaviour of an employee. The evaluation is done by a separate department known as personnel department. But, the duty of collection of check list answers is given to a person who is designated as a rater. The rater indicates the answers of an employee against each question by putting a tick mark. There are two columns provided to each question as yes or no. A model of check list is given below:

***CHECK LIST***

| | *Yes* | *No* |
|---|---|---|
| A. Is the employee satisfied with the job? | ☐ | ☐ |
| B. Does he finish the job accurately? | ☐ | ☐ |
| C. Does he respect the superiors ? | ☐ | ☐ |
| D. Is he ready to accept responsibility? | ☐ | ☐ |
| E Does he obey the orders? | ☐ | ☐ |

**6. Forced Choice Method:** A series of groups of statements are prepared positively or negatively under this method. Both these statements describe the characteristics of an employee. But the rater is forced to tick any one of the statements either out of positive statements or out of negative statements. The degree of description of the characteristics of an employee varies from one statement to another. The following are the positive statements:

(a) The employee completes the job in time usually.

(b) The employee has the ability to complete the job and complete the job as and when there is need.

In this way, the negative statements are also prepared. The final rating is done on the basis of all such statements. But, the rater does not know the statements which are for final rating.

**7. Critical Incident Method:** The performance appraisal of an employee is done on the basis of the incidents occurred really to the concerned employee. Some incidents occurred due to the inability of the employee. But, the rating is done on all the events occurred in a particular period. Some of the events or incidents are given below:

(a) Refused to co-operate with other employees.

(b) Unwilling to attend further training.

(c) Got angry over work or with subordinates.

(d) Suggested a change in the method of production.

(e) Suggested a procedure to improve the quality of goods.

(f) Suggestion of a method to avoid or minimise wastage, spoilage and scrap.

(g) Refused to obey orders.

(h) Refused to follow clear cut instructions.

**8. Field Review Method:** An employee's performance is appraised through an interview between the rater and the immediate superior or supervisor of a concerned employee. The rater is attached with the personnel depart-ment. The rater asks the supervisors questions about the perfor-mance of an employee. The personnel department prepares a detailed report on the basis of this collected information. A copy of this report is placed in the personnel file of the concerned employee after getting approval from the supervisor.

The success of this type of appraisal method is based on the competence of the interviewer.

## BARRIERS TO EFFECTIVE PERFORMANCE APPRAISAL

There are certain barriers to effective performance appraisal. They are briefly explained below:

1. The rater has faulty assumptions about an employee who comes under the performance appraisal system.
2. An employee may act indifferently while being appraised.
3. It is presumed that no appraisal method can provide accurate evaluation of an employee. But, practically the rater assumes that a method which is used in an organisation can provide cent per cent accurate evaluation.
4. Management feels that the personal opinion of an immediate superior is better than the systematic appraisal and review procedure.

5. Employees feel that the opinion of superior is not a valid one. The reason is that the superior may provide inaccurate appraisal.
6. There are some psychological factors responsible for ineffective performance appraisal. The psychological factors include appraisal as an extra work to the appraiser, which arises of conflict with subordinates, and the appraisor unwilling to remark the inefficiency of subordinates and so on.
7. There is no clear cut standard for work pèrformance to compare with actual performance.
8. A rater may be influenced by the ratee's good or bad performance of any type of work. The rater can assess the employee on the basis of first impression for the entire performance as such.
9. The prevailing family or friendship relationship between the rater and ratee.
10. The inability of the superior to evaluate the employee's performance is also one of the barriers to effective performance appraisal.
11. If there is any carelessness on the part of rater, inaccurate evaluation will be obtained.
12. The likes and dislikes of the rater may influence his performance appraisal.

## PRINCIPLES OF EFFECTIVE PERFORMANCE APPRAISAL

Systematic performance appraisal should be an accurate and reliable one. The reliability and accuracy of performance appraisal is obtained whenever the barriers of performance appraisal are overcome by the management. The management may take the following measures to overcome the barriers of performance appraisal:

1. Single employee is rated by two raters. Then, the comparison is made to get accurate rating.
2. Continuous and personal observation of an employee is essential to make effective performance appraisal.
3. The rating should be done by an immediate superior of any subordinate in an organisation.
4. A separate department may be created for effective performance appraisal.
5. The rating is conveyed to the concerned employee. It helps in several ways. The employee can understand the position where he stands and where he should go.
6. The plus points of an employee should be recognised. At the same time, the minus points should not be highlighted too much but they may be hinted to him.
7. The management should create confidence in the minds of employees.
8. The standard for each job should be determined by the management.
9. Separate printed forms should be used for performance appraisal to each job according to the nature of the job.

## MODEL QUESTIONS

1. What do you mean by performance appraisal? Discuss its needs and importance in an organisation.
2. Discuss the relative merits and demerits of policy of "Promotion from within" and "Open competition" for selecting managerial personnel.
3. State the requisites of an effective performance appraisal.

# CHAPTER 17

# TRAINING AND DEVELOPMENT

## INTRODUCTION

The efficient functioning of an organisation depends upon the efficiency or capability of personnel working in that organisation. The capability of an employee is evaluated or identified through some techniques. The need for training is decided by the management on the basis of the performance of an employee. In the Indian context, the process and techniques of management are very complicated. A problem can be solved by providing proper training to the personnel.

The terms 'Training' and 'Development' are used synonymously. But they have different meanings. According to Edwin B. Flippo, "While training is the act of increasing the knowledge and skills of an employee for doing a particular job, the management development includes the process by which managers and executives acquire not only skills and competence in their present job, but also capacities for future managerial tasks of increasing difficulty and scope."

It is concluded from the above definition that training is the process through which the knowledge and skills of an employee to perform the present job accurately increase. But development includes not only the acquiring of knowledge and skills for the present job but also includes increasing capabilities for future managerial positions.

## MEANING

*Training* refers to a programme that facilitates an employee to perform the job effectively through acquiring increased knowledge and skills.

## DEFINITION

Proctor and Thornton define training as, "the intentional act of providing means for learning to take place."

Planty, M.C. Cord and Efferson define, "training is the continuous, systematic development among all levels of employees of that knowledge and those skills and attitudes which contribute to their welfare and that of the company."

## ELEMENTS OF TRAINING

The effective training programme has the following features:

1. Continuous process.
2. Effective utilisation of existing knowledge and skills.
3. Expanding the present knowledge and skills for future requirements.
4. Helping the employee to find his present position and preparing him to accept greater responsibilities.

## IMPORTANCE AND NEED FOR TRAINING

The importance and need for training arises on account of the following reasons:

**1. Non-availability of trained personnel:** It is very difficult to find fully trained workers for all categories levels of jobs in an organisation. Then the organisation selects the persons who are having little training or no training. Adequate training will be given by the employers themselves to the untrained workers.

**2. Suitability for the job:** A worker is assigned a job for which he is not trained. Then a need arises for giving the same special training to the concerned worker. All types of training are not provided in a vocational school. A supplement training is also essential to the worker on the basis of the peculiarity of the job.

**3. Getting knowledge by latest methods:** The rapid develop-ment of science and technology has made it necessary to give training to the workers. The reason is that a worker might have been trained in any one of the methods. It will be useful for a certain period. Further training is essential due to the innovations and inventions of new methods. If proper training facilities are not available to workers, the organisation will face the danger of closing down the business. The adoption of old methods results in increasing administration expenses and other expenses, making it difficult to survive the competition. So, adequate training is essential in latest methods.

## TYPES OF TRAINING

Training is provided to those persons who are eager to take training. Next, training is provided to those persons who have to undergo the training. In this way, training is provided to employees whenever a need arises. This type of training results in the attainment of desired objectives in a better way. Training methods can be deviced according to the mental calibre of personnel in an organisation and the importance of on the job training.

According to the importance of on the job training, the various types of training are given below:

**A. On-The-Job Training**

1. On specific job.
2. Rotation of position.
3. Special projects.
4. Apprenticeship.

**B. Off-The-Job Training**

1. Special courses and lectures.
2. Conference.
3. Case study.
4. Role playing.
5. Management games.
6. Brain-storming.
7. Transactional analysis.

## A. ON-THE-JOB TRAINING

*On-the job training* refers to learning while actually performing a particular work or job. This type of training is more suitable to every type of employee. These are briefly explained below:

**1. On specific job:** A person can learn when he is actually put in a job for which he is selected. This is the most common method of training in every organisation, where the employee can develop his skills for doing the job in a better way. Critical evaluation and correction of the methods are some of the techniques adopted in this type of training. Any individual can learn the job very quickly.

**2. Rotation of position:** A person is given jobs in various sections of the organisation at various levels. The main objective of this type of training is to broaden the knowledge background of the trainee. Working in various sections helps the trainee to develop an integrated view of the functioning of the organisation.

**3. Special projects:** An existing employee is deputed to special projects. He is expected to work under special projects upto the finishing stage. Then he learns the jobs under special projects and he gets an opportunity to move with other different types of persons.

**4. Apprenticeship:** It is otherwise called as *under study*. Here, the trainee is put under the supervision of an expert. Today in India, many organisations provide training to employees under the Apprenticeship Act. These apprentices are used to fill up the places of skilled personnel.

## B. OFF-THE-JOB TRAINING

Under the off-the-job-training system, a trainee is removed from his normal working place and spends his full time for training purpose in any other place. During the training period, there is no contribution of trainee to the organisation. Normally, this type of training is provided outside the organisation and rarely within the organisation but not in the working place. This type of trainings is briefly explained below:

**1. Special course and lectures:** Special course and lectures are some of the knowledge based training methods. The basic concepts and theories, principles and pure applied knowledge of the particular subject are imparted to the participants. This type of training is aimed at giving fundamental information to the trainees.

**2. Conference:** The concept of conference is developed to overcome the limitations of the lectures. Conference emphasises on the one way of communication i.e., trainer to trainee. The trainees are expected to offer their ideas and use their experience for solving the problems with the help of the trainer. Small groups are formed for an intensive discussion of various subjects.

**3. Case duty:** This type of training is more useful to both business executives and management institutes. A case is written in blue print form and circulated among the trainees. The blue print contains the information like the history of business unit, external environment affecting the concerned business unit, internal separation and financial structure. No case contains the full details of the organisation as a reader wishes.

In actual practice, the manager seldom has full details. The reason is that all the information cannot be collected. At the same time collecting full information requires a lot of time. Then the manager takes decisions on the basis of the available information and makes a reasonable assumption on the information not in hand.

Normally, cases are discussed by many groups. The instructor asks each member of the group to present his analysis and critical comment on the views of others. Besides, members of the group should answer the queries of the instructor and members of the other group. This process helps the trainee to develop and improve both analytical and decision-making skills.

**4. Role playing:** Role playing technique is used in a group where different persons are given the role of different managers. They are requested to solve a problem in a situation or arrive at a decision. Discussion among the trainees sparks of spontaneously. At the end of the role playing session, the trainees are given feedback of their role playing. This helps the trainees to develop their efficiency in performing the job, sensitivity among the people and improve better human relations. More number of persons get training simultaneously under this type of training.

**5. Management games:** Management games are used to stimulate the thinking of people to develop their skills to run a company or a department. These games are used to develop the skill in the area of investment, production, sales, collective bargaining, etc. A game consists of situation. Each team tries to win others and only one can win unless there is a draw. A period is fixed for this training and it is made known to all the teams. Various situations are explained to the teams and they are requested to take decisions on such given situations. The decision taken by one team affects the results of another team. The decisions may be in the area of price fixation, sales volume in figures and quantity production, raw materials price and the like. The trainer gives the feedback to every team. Then, each team evaluates its decisions and may change its decisions to arrive at better results.

**6. Brainstorming:** Brainstorming is a technique used to idea generation. Ten to fifteen members are necessary to conduct a brainstorming session. The same level of people is constituted into a group. The reason is that idea generation is the main objective of brainstorming. The participants of the group are connected with a problem directly.

The problem is clearly stated to each member of the group. Besides, the rules and objectives of brainstorming are explained to them. Each member is asked to give more number of ideas to solve the problem. Here, the quantity of ideas of each member is measured instead of the quality of idea. There is no limitation put before the member while generating the ideas. This system avoids social and psychological blocks which may come in the way of idea generation. Osborn has defined brainstroming as, "using the brain to storm the problem".

Webster Dictionery defines brainstorming as, "a conference technique by which a group attempts to find a solution for a specific problem by amassing all the ideas spontaneously contributed by its members".

**7. Transactional Analysis (TA):** *Transactional* Analysis is used to develop interpersonal interactions among individuals. Understanding of personal factors of individuals is the main objective of transactional analysis. Besides, the ego status of individuals are identified. Parent's ego, adult ego and/or child ego of the individuals are understood under the training for transactional analysis.

## CHARACTERISTICS OF GOOD TRAINING PROGRAMME

A large organisation has a separate department to give training. A small organisation may send its employees outside the working place to get training. Whatever it is, substantial finance to spent by the company to provide a training facility to its employees. It is ensured that the training should bring good results to the company. So, in order to get good results, the training programme should have the following characteristics:

**1. Individual differences:** There is a lot of difference among the employees in the learning capacity and the area of interest. So, the management should consider these factors while framing the training programme.

**2. Relating to job requirements:** The training programme should be related to the job for which training is provided.

**3. Determination of trading needs:** The need of training to employees is decided by the management. The method of training to the concerned employee is also decided by the management.

**4. Result-oriented training:** The management can give various levels trainings to its employees. Each and every training should produce favourable results to the company.

**5. Incentives:** Some employees can undergo training very seriously. These types of persons should be identified by the management. Next, adequate monetary as well as non-monetary incentives should be given to these persons.

**6. Support of management:** Top management people should evince interest in and support the training. If the top management supports the training, seriousness of getting training may be increased to some extent.

## MODEL QUESTIONS

1. Explain the various methods of training. Is training essential?
2. What are the different types of training?
3. What are the advantages of training?

# CHAPTER 18

# JOB ANALYSIS AND EVALUATION

## INTRODUCTION

The management can analyse the job for the purpose of solving the problems relating to promotion, selection, training, placement and transfer of employees. Job analysis and evaluation provide a basis to do the above mentioned tasks effectively. A job is assigned to an individual on the basis of his ability, skill, experience, technical knowledge, area of interest, etc. Job analysis and evaluation help to fix the exact pay to each employee. It would avoid bitterness and resentment among employees.

## MEANING OF JOB

A job is a position which contains a certain a degree of variance or similarity in nature with others. For example, the post of a General Manager is a job. There is only one such job in every organisation. At the same time, salesmen, clerks, etc., are some of the jobs which are several in number in every organisation.

## JOB ANALYSIS

Job analysis deals with the contents and characteristics of each job. Job analysis points out the duties and responsibilities involved in each job. Pay is fixed on the basis of job analysis. It determines the degree of skills necessary to perform each job. Job analysis discloses the conditions underwhich each job is performed and the element of risk involved in them. Job analysis helps the management to fix the qualification required for each job and choose the methods or techniques to perform each job.

## PROCEDURE OF JOB ANALYSIS

The following procedures may be adopted to analyse each job:

1. All the job holders are requested to fill up the questionnaire supplied by the management.
2. The job holders are requested to keep a diary. The diary should contain the important particulars relating to the performance.
3. A direct interview with the job holders is held by the management. Then, the job holders have a chance to bring out the possibilities and difficulties in the performance of a job.
4. A separate person is appointed to observe the behaviour of job holders during the performance of a job.
5. Finally, a detailed report is prepared by the management. It may be treated as a job analysis.

Job analysis is done by the management atleast once in two years or three years. The reason is that technical change or social change may affect the behaviour of job holders in the fast changing business world.

## ADVANTAGES OF JOB ANALYSIS

1. Job analysis facilitates the selection and placement, of right personnel in each job.
2. Managemant can provide adequate training to the needy employees.
3. Resonable wage rate is fixed with the help of job analysis.
4. Job analysis helps in job evaluation and merit rating.
5. Job analysis helps the superiors to take timely decisions. The decision may be related to promotion, transfer, selection, etc.

6. Industrial disputes may be put an end to with the help of job analysis.
7. Adequate disciplinary action may be taken by the management.
8. The selection of right personnel ensures job satisfaction and morale among the employees.
9. Job analysis helps in reducing labour turnover, absenteeism and removing inequalities in pay fixation.
10. It provides a basis of performance appraisal and facilitates the control function of the management.

## JOB EVALUATION

Job evaluation is a very useful technique. The wage rate is fixed on the basis of the nature of the job and not for men. Job evaluation is otherwise called as *job rating*. Job evaluation is a systematic procedure which measures the relative importance and value of each job on the basis of skills, duties, responsibilities and the like. In other words, job evaluation is the expression of each job in terms of money. The very purpose of job evaluation is to fix wage rates according to the job done by a man. It means fixing of higher wages rate for highly risky jobs and vice versa. For example, a college lecturer deserves to be paid more than a school teacher.

A person who meets the minimum requirements of a job is recruited by the management. Job evaluation identifies the minimum and maximum requirements of each job.

## JOB EVALUATION PROCEDURE

The following is the procedure of job evaluation:

1. A detailed study of the job-consider education, skill, training, experience and intelligence.
2. Identification of physical and mental efforts necessary and the degree of responsibility.
3. A job description.
4. Consider the characteristics of a job in terms of points, experience and training. If experience is considered twice important as training, experience may be awarded 10 points and training 5 points.
5. Job analysis.
6. Comparison of one job with another.
7. Determine the number of points to be given for each characteristic of a job.
8. Add the points for each job.
9. Rank the jobs on the basis of its points.
10. Expression of the value of job in terms of money according to the points obtained.

## ADVANTAGES OF JOB EVALUATION

The main advantages of job evaluation are as follows:

1. Management may control the labour cost since the pay is fixed on the basis of the nature of job.
2. Ranking of jobs is very easy.

3. Management can fix the same wages for similar jobs. In other words, equal pay for equal job principle is easily applied by the management.
4. There is a possibility of improving morale among the employees.
5. Management can adopt the adequate promotion policy.
6. Job evaluation helps the management in the selection, placement and training of employees.
7. It provides a basis for justifying different rates of pay for different jobs.
8. It improves relations between employee and employer and among employees.
9. Wage for a new job is fixed by the management without much difficulty.
10. Management can prepare proper incentive schemes.
11. Job evaluation minimises the labour turnover.

## DISADVANTAGES OF JOB EVALUATION

The main disadvantages of job evaluation are discussed below:

1. Job evaluation studies the job but not the individual doing the job.
2. Uniformity in pay adversely affects the workers who are above average.
3. Job evaluation is also one of the factors responsible for fixing a wage rate just like other factors.
4. It is very difficult to convert all the factors in terms of money for job evaluation.
5. Points awarded for each characteristic of a job are purely subjective.
6. Job evaluation ignores the labour market condition which is also responsible for wage rate fixation.
7. Job evaluation may not be understood by the workers. So, the workers may suspect the intention of the management.

## PRINCIPLES OF OR GUIDELINES FOR JOB EVALUATION

The following are the general principles of job evaluation:

1. Great care must be exercised by the management since the job evaluation aims at studying the worth of the job estimated by job studies.
2. There should be a mutual co-operation between the management and workers.
3. There are different terms used in the job evaluation process. These are fully explained to workers before the work actually starts.
4. Conclusion of a job is done only after all the raters agree.
5. Size and type of the organisation are also to be considered before setting job evaluation process.
6. The objectives of job evaluation may be determined and they may be explained to these persons who are likely to be affected.
7. The management should take a decision regarding the use of financial resources.

8. The selected job evaluation system and its workings should be communicated to all the concerned parties to avoid misunderstanding.
9. Interested parties are encouraged to engage in the job evaluation system to facilitate smooth functioning.
10. The level of wage rates of jobs must be equal to the same kind of jobs existing in the same company and industry.
11. Company may use the labour grades in the job evaluation programme and make a provision for merit which increses within labour grades and length of service.
12. Short-term over-payments may be made to exhort employee's faith in the job evaluation system.

## METHOD OR SYSTEM OF JOB EVALUATION

The methods of job evaluation are discussed below:

**1. Ranking method:** Under the ranking method, the jobs are graded on the basis of their responsibility and difficulty to perform them. Each job is valued in terms of other jobs and in monetary terms. Ranking method can be applied in small scale organisations successfully. The management can apply this method where more number of similar jobs are performed. This method's main defect is that valuation cannot be done accurately.

**2. Classification method:** It may be called *Grading method.* Initially grades are defined as common to various jobs. Next, the management finds out the various requirements of each job. Then, jobs are graded on the basis of the requirements of each job. For example, class one, class two, class three and skilled, semi-skilled, unskilled etc. This is done usually by a committee.

**3. Factor point scoring:** The management can identify the common factors of each job. Next, points are allotted to each such factor according to its relative importance. Finally, the wage rate is fixed on the basis of total points obtained by each job. Education, experience or skill, responsibility and working conditions are some of the common factors of each job.

**4. Factor comparison method:** This method is more or less similar to factor point scoring method. Under this method also, the management may find some common factors. First of all, the management can select a key job. Great care should be taken by the management while selecting a key job. Wage rate is fixed to the key job through the process of allocation of money in factor wise. For example, education Rs. 4.00, skill or experience Rs. 4.00, physical requirements Rs. 1.50, responsibility Rs. 2.00 and working conditions Rs. 3.50. The total wage rate is Rs. 15.00. Here, education, skill or experience, physical requirements, responsibility and working conditions are common factors. The remaining jobs are compared by factor with the scales of the key job.

### MODEL QUESTIONS

1. What are the components of Job Analysis?
2. What is meant by Job Evaluation? What are the various methods of Job Analysis?
3. Define the term "Job Evaluation".
4. What are the advantages of "Job Analysis" ?.
5. Define the term "Job Analysis".

6. Describe the importance of "Job Analysis".
7. Compare the features of "Job Analysis" and "Job Evaluation".
8. What is Job Evaluation?
9. What is Job Analysis?

# Chapter 19

# DIRECTING

## INTRODUCTION

Direction is a managerial function performed by the top level officers of management. Whenever any decision is taken, it should be properly implemented. If not so, there is no use of taking such a decision. Direction is necessary in order to achieve proper implementation of direction. Every manager gives direction to his subordinates and vice versa every subordinate gets direction from his respective manager.

## DEFINITION

According to Haimann, "Directing consists of the process and techniques utilised in issuing instructions and making certain that operations are carried on as originally planned."

Koontz and O'Donnel, "Direction is the interpersonal aspect of managing by which subordinates are led to understand and contribute effectively to the attainment of enterprise objective."

Urwick and Breach, "Directing is the guidance, the inspiration, the leadership of those men and women that constitute the real core of the responsibilities of management."

J.L. Massie, "Directing concerns the total manner in which a manager influences the actions of his subordinates. It is the final action of a manager in getting others to act after all preparations have been completed."

Earnent Dole, "Direction is telling people what to do and seeing that they do it to the best of their ability. It includes making assignments, corresponding procedures, seeing that mistakes are corrected, provided on-the-job instruction and of course, issuing orders."

## PRINCIPLES OF DIRECTION

Generally, the manager should understand the needs, motives and attitudes of his subordinates. He should change his strategies according to the people and situations. However, the following principles of direction may be useful to the manager:

**1. Harmony of objectives:** Individuals have their own objectives. Organisation has its own objectives. The management should co-ordinate the individual objectives with organisational objectives. Direction should be in such a way that the individuals can integrate their objectives with organisational objectives.

**2. Maximum individual contribution:** Every member's contribution is necessary for the organisation's development. Hence, the management should adopt a technique of direction which enables maximum contribution by members.

**3. Unit of direction or command:** An employee should receive orders and instructions only from one superior. If not so, there may be indiscipline and confusion among subordinates and disorder will ensue.

**4. Efficiency:** Subordinates are requested to participate in the decision-making process. Then, they would have a sense of commitment. This will ensure implementation of decisions. It will increase the efficiency of subordinates.

**5. Direct supervision:** Managers should have direct relationship with their sub-ordinates. Face to face communication and personal touch with sub-ordinates will ensure successful direction.

**6. Feedback information:** Direction does not end with issuing orders and instructions to the subordinates. Sometimes, suggestions given by the sub-ordinates are necessary for the development of the management. So, the development of the feedback system furnishes reliable ideas to the management.

**7. Effective communication:** The superior must ensure that plans, policies and responsibilities are fully understood by the sub-ordinates in the right direction.

**8. Appropriateness of direction technique:** There are three direction techniques available to the management. They are authoritarian, consultative and free-rein. But the direction techniques should be selected according to the situation.

**9. Efficient control:** The management should monitor the behaviour and per-formance of subordinates to exercise efficient control over the sub-ordinates. Effective control ensures effective direction.

**10. Comprehension:** The extent of understanding by subordinates is more important than what and how orders are communicated to them. This is very useful in the proper direction of subordinates.

**11. Follow through:** Direction is a continuous process. Mere issuing orders or instructions is not an end itself. Direction is necessary, so, the management should watch whether the subordinates follow the orders and whether they face difficulties in carrying out the orders or instructions.

## ISSUING ORDERS OR INSTRUCTIONS

An order is used by the management as a tool for direction. An order can be issued only by a supervisor. The supervisor has the right to enforce his order over his subordinates. In the words of Kootnz and O'Donnel, "As a directional technique, an instruction is understood to be a charge by a superior requiring a subordinate to act or refrain from acting in a given circumstance".

## CHARACTERISTICS OF A GOOD ORDER

1. An order should be reasonable and enforceable over sub- ordinates.
2. A clearly defined order should be easily understandable.
3. An order should be such a one as to facilitate the achievement of the objectives of an organisation.
4. An order should be complete in all respects.
5. An order should exhort willingness and acceptance from the subordinates.
6. A written order is preferable to an oral order.
7. Appropriate tone is used by the superior while issuing an order.
8. An order should specify the time within which a job should be completed.
9. An order should be intelligible.

## TECHNIQUES OF DIRECTION

There are three techniques of direction followed by the management. They are briefly explained below:

**1. Consultative direction:** The supervisor or superior has consultation with his sub-ordinates before issuing a direction. The consultation is made to find out the feasibility, enforceability and nature of problem. It does not mean that the superior is not capable of acting independently. Ultimately, the superior has the right to take any decision and give the directions. The co-operation of subordinates is necessary for successful implementation of any direction. Better motivation is available to the subordinates under this direction technique. The supervisor could instill high morale into the subordinates.

**2. Free-rein direction:** The subordinate is encouraged to solve the problem independently under this direction technique. The superior assigns the task generally. The subordinates should take initiative to solve the problem. Only highly educated, efficient and sincere sub-ordinates are required to apply these direction techniques.

**3. Autocratic direction:** This direction is just opposite to free-rein direction technique. Here, the supervisor commands his subordinates and has close supervision. The supervisor gives clear and precise orders to his sub-ordinates and act accordingly. There is no way left to the sub-ordinates to show their initiatives.

## IMPORTANCE OF DIRECTION

Direction is also one of the important functions of management. Direction is necessary to implement the administrative policies and decisions effectively. The subordinates are properly motivated through direction. Direction provides a leadership in a business. Direction is also concerned with getting co-operation among subordinates. Direction is the essence of management and also regarded as a continuous function of management.

1. Direction initiates action.
2. Direction co-ordinates the group efforts.
3. Direction ensures maximum individual contribution.
4. Direction reduces the reluctance to put up with changes in the organisation.
5. Direction provides stability and balance in the organisation.
6. Direction helps to achieve the objectives of an organisation.

## CHARACTERISTICS OF DIRECTION

The characteristics of direction are discussed below:

1. Direction is also one of the managerial functions and so performed by all levels of executives in an organisation.
2. Management initiates action through direction.
3. Direction is continuous throughout the life of the organisation.
4. Initially, direction is started at the top level management. In other words, the subordinates are directed only by superiors.
5. Subordinates do the things as per the original plan.
6. Direction creates link between preparatory functions and the control function of management. The term preparatory functions includes planning, organising and staffing.

## MODEL QUESTIONS

1. What do you mean by Direction?
2. Discuss the principles of Direction.
3. Explain the characteristics of Direction.
4. What are the principles of effective Directing?

# CHAPTER 20

# MOTIVATION

INTRODUCTION
DEFINITION
NATURE OF MOTIVATION
IMPORTANCE OF MOTIVATION
TYPES OF MOTIVATION
THEORIES OF MOTIVATION
THEORY X AND Y
DIFFERENCE BETWEEN THEORY X AND THEORY Y
THEORY Z
FEATURES OF THEORY Z
CRITICISM OF THEORY Z
MASLOW HIERARCHY OF NEEDS
HERZBERG'S THEORY OF NEEDS
MOTIVATIONAL FACTORS
MAINTENNANCE FACTORS
MOTIVATIONAL TECHNIQUES
REQUIREMENTS OF A SOUND MOTIVATIONAL SYSTEM
MODEL QUESTIONS

## INTRODUCTION

Management is the art of getting things done by others. Getting work done is a difficult task. It is related to human behaviour. The success of any organisation depends upon the behaviour and interest of the employees. The organisational goals are achieved through the right direction of human behaviour in a desired manner. Before guiding or directing the employees, the reasons for such behaviour should be identified. The management can strategically motivate the employees based on such reasons.

## DEFINITION

Stanley Vance defines motivation as, "any emotion or desire which so conditions one's will that the individual is propelled into action."

Robert Dubin defines motivation, "as the complex of forces standing and keeping a person at work in an organisation."

Beach defines, "Motivation as a willingness to expand energy to achieve a goal or a reward."

Hodge and Johnson defines, "Motivation as the willingness of an individual to respond to organisational requirements in the short run."

Shartle defines, "Motivation as a reported urge or tension to move in a given direction or to achieve a certain goal."

Owen defines, "Motivation as an ordered way of explaining why a person elects to channel his energies in one direction rather than in another."

The Encyclopedia of Management has defined motivation as, "Motivation refers to the degree of readiness of an organism to pursue some destinated goal, and implies the determination of the nature and locus of the forces inducing the degree of readiness."

Eduir B. Flippo, "Motivation is the process of attempting to influence others to do your will through the possibility of gain reward."

Michael J. Jucious, "Motivation is the act of stimulating someone or oneself to get a desired course of action, to push the right button to get the desired action."

Delton E. Mc Farland, "The concept of motivation is mainly psychological. It relates to those forces operating within the individual employee or subordinate which impel him to act or not to act in cetain ways."

Koontz and O'Donnell, " Motivation is a general term applying to the entire class of drives, desires, needs, wishes and similar forces that induce an individual or a group of people to work."

J.E. Rosenz Weig and F.K. Kast, "Motivation is an inspiration process which impels the members of the team to accomplish the desired goals."

S. Zedeck and K. Blood, "Motivation is a pre-disposition to act in a specified goal directed way."

Scott, "Motivation means a process of stimulating people to action to accomplish desired goals."

## NATURE OF MOTIVATION

Motivation is concerned with the direction of functions of management, so the nature of motivation can be understood from the following points:

**1. Unending process:** A social animal ( a man ) has number of wants. These wants induce a man to work. All the wants cannot be satisfied at one time. If one want is satisfied, then another want emerges. Motivation is also an unending process just like the satisfaction of wants is an unending process.

**2. A psychological concept:** Motivation deals with the psychology of workers. An efficient worker will not perform the work desirably well unless he is properly motivated. So, effective performance requires proper motivation. Proper motivation is possible only through proper analysis of the psychology of workers.

**3. The whole individual is motivated:** An individual is motivated fully and not partly because motivation is related to psychology. Besides, the basic needs of man determine motivation to a great extent. All these needs are interrelated and cannot be separated from each other.

**4. Motivation may be financial or non-financial:** The motivation may be divided into two i.e., financial and non-financial. Financial motivation includes increasing wages, allowances, bonus, perquisites and the like. Non-financial motivation includes recognition, praise, giving more responsibility and inducing to participate in the decision-making process.

**5. Frustrated man cannot be motivated:** If a man does not have his basic needs satisfied, he may be frustrated. He may be mentally ill to some extent. Such a frustrated man cannot be motivated unless his basic needs are satisfied.

**6. Goal are motivators:** Man works to achieve his individual goals. Whenever the goal is achieved, he will be no longer interested to work. So, the management should identify the goals of individuals, and it can persuade them to work by directions.

**7. Unifying force:** Unifying force means the drive to actualise one's own image. The person's self image plays an important role in motivation. If an individual has created an image as a leader, he acts accordingly. So, the unifying force is an important motivating force.

**8. Motivation can be positive or negative:** Positive motivation means use of incentives. The incentives may be financial and non-financial. Pay revision, confirmation of job and the like are positive motivations. Negative motivation means emphasizing penalties. Demotion and termination from the service are some of the examples of negative motivation.

**9. Motivation and job satisfaction are different:** Motivation is goal-oriented behaviour. Job satisfaction is the outcome of a job performance. So, motivation is entirely different from job satisfaction.

## IMPORTANCE OF MOTIVATION

A manager guides the people in a desired manner in order to achieve organisational objectives. Two important things are necessary to perform any job. People have ability to work and willingness to work. Unwillingness to work is of no use. Hence, there is a need for motivation to create willingness in the minds of workers to do a job. So, the performance may be expressed in the following formula:

performance = ability × motivation (willingness)

E.F.L. Brech has explained the importance of motivation as "The problem of motivation is the key to management actions and in its executive form, it is among chief tasks of the general manager. We may safely lay it down that the tone of an organisation is the reflection of the motivation from the top."

The importance of motivation is briefly discussed below:

**1. Maximum utilisation of factors of production:** Workers perform the work sincerely through the inspiration of motivation. This creates the possibility of maximum utilisation of factors of production viz., labour and capital.

**2. Willingness to work:** Motivation influences the willingness of people to work. A man is technically, mentally and physically fit to perform the work but he may not be willing to work. Motivation creates a willingness on the part of workers to do the work in a better way.

**3. Reduced absenteeism:** Financial incentive schemes coerce the workers to work more. Financial incentive scheme is framed in such a way that monetary benefits are given on the basis of number of hours engaged. This reduces absenteeism.

**4. Reduced labour turnover:** Motivation has both financial and non-financial incentive schemes. This helps to retain the existing labourers. The enterprise can plan its activities on long-term basis with the help of reduced labour turnover.

**5. Availability of right personnel:** Financial and non-financial incentives not only retain the existing employees but also attract the employees from outside the enterprise. In otherwords, right people are attracted from outside to work for the enterprise.

**6. Building of good labour relations:** Motivation helps to solve the labour problems of absenteeism, labour turnover, indiscipline and grievances. This ensures building of good labour relations.

**7. Increase in the efficiency and output:** Both workers and management have got benefits from motivational plans. On the one hand, wages of the workers increase corresponding to the increase of output and efficiency. On the other hand, the productivity of the organisation and its profits increases due to consolidated efforts of the motivated people.

**8. Sense of belonging:** A proper motivation scheme promotes closer rapport between enterprise and workers. The workers begin to feel that the enterprise belongs to them and consider its interests as their own. Thus there is no difference between workers and enterprise.

**9. Basis of co-operation:** Efficiency and output are increased through co-operation. The co-operation could not be obtained without motivation, so, motivation is a basis of co-operation.

**10. Helps in realising organisational goals:** Organisational goals are achieved quickly through motivation. Motivated employees have a feeling of total involvement in the performance of organisation task. Employees may work whole-heartedly for the realisation of organisational goals.

**11. Improvement upon skill and knowledge:** Employees have promised efficient job performance or completion. Hence, the employees may improve upon their skill and knowledge required for the job.

## TYPES OF MOTIVATION

The following are some of the types of motivation:

**1. Negative motivation:** Negative motivation is based on force of fear. If the worker fails to complete the work, they may be threatened with demotion, dismissed, lay-off, pay-cut etc. The negative motivation gives maximum benefits in the short-run. In the long-run, there are no such benefits available to the organisation. Negative motivation results in disloyalty to the group as well as to organisation.

**2. Positive motivation:** Positive motivation is based on rewards. According to Flipps, "Positive motivation is a process of attempting to influence others to do your will through the possibility of gain or reward. "Praise, participation in decision-making process, pride and delegation of authority and responsibility are some of the methods of positive motivation.

**3. Extrinsic motivation:** Motivation is available only after the completion of a job. Increase in wages, retirement benefits, rest periods, holidays, health wages, health insurance and the like are examples of extrinsic motivation.

**4. Intrinsic motivation:** Intrinsic motivation is available at the time of performance of work. These motivations provide a satisfaction during the performance of the work itself. Praise, recognition, power, delegation of authority and responsibility, competition and participation in the decision-making process are some of the examples of intrinsic motivation.

**5. Financial motivation:** Financial motivation is directly or indirectly associated with money. The most important financial motivations are wages and salaries. Bonus, profit-sharing, vacation pay, free-medical services, retirement benefits and insurance are some of the other financial motivations.

**6. Non-financial motivation:** Non-financial motivation is that motivation which is not associated with monetary rewards. Praise, job rotation, delegation of authority and responsibility, participation, recognition and power are some of the examples of non-financial motivation. According to Robert Dulin, "Non-financial incentives are the psychic rewards or the rewards of enhanced position, that can be secured in the work organisation".

## THEORIES OF MOTIVATION

Prof. Douglas McGregor has introduced two theories in his famous book, 'The Human side of Enterprise.' They are called 'X' theory and 'Y' theory. A brief explanation of 'X' theory is given below.

**1. X-theory:** This theory is based on 'papa knows best.' In other words, a manager has thorough knowledge and excludes workers from decision-making process. A manager has authority or power to take decisions. The workers should follow whatever decisions are taken by the manager.

**2. Assumptions of theory:**

1. Workers have an aversion to work inherently.
2. Workers may find a way to postpone the work completion in laziness.
3. Workers may do the job half-heartedly.
4. Fear of punishment can motivate the workers into action.
5. The worker may know the hazards of non-performance of a work.
6. No worker is ready to accept any responsibility.
7. There is a need for explaining the consequences of being inactive.
8. Workers are not interested in achievement. They prefer to maintain *status quo*.
9. A worker prefers to be directed by others.
10. Workers hate to improve their efficiency. The reason is that they fear losing their present job.

11. Worker is also one of the factors of production and does not deserve any special treatment.
12. Worker lacks integrity.
13. Worker avoids taking decision whenever necessary.

X-theory is regarded as the means to supervise and control the workers. Decision-making in all the fields is entrusted with the managers. Workers are allowed to express their suggestions and emotions. But the decisions are taken by managers and workers are forced to follow the decisions.

**3. Y-theory:** Y-theory is just opposite to X-theory. So, X-theory is considered as traditional theory and Y-theory is considered as modern theory. Y-theory emphasises the importance of workers in the accomplishment of enterprise objectives.

## ASSUMPTIONS OF Y-THEORY

1. The average human being has the tendency to work. A job is as natural just like a play.
2. Once the worker understands the purpose of job, he may extend his co-operation for job completion.
3. Worker can put in his best efforts for the accomplishment of enterprise objectives early.
4. Worker has self-direction, self-motivation, self-discipline and self-control.
5. If right motivation scheme is prepared by the management, the worker is ready to accept extra responsibility.
6. The existing worker has competence to work and can take right decisions.
7. A worker expects recognition of the successful accomplishment of task.
8. A worker may exhibit his efficiency even for non-monetary rewards such as participation in decision-making, increased responsibility etc.
9. The potentialities of human beings are not fully utilised by any industry.

According to Y-theory, a worker has integrity and readiness to work hard. He is willing to participate in the decision making process and shows a sense of creativity and imagination. So, X-theory may be said to be a negative and pessimistic one and Y-theory may be said to be positive and optimistic.

## THEORY Z

Prof. William G. Ouchi has developed theory Z. This theory is based on the comparative study of Japanese and American management practices. Theory Z describes how Japanese management practices can be adopted to the environment of other countries especially in the United States. This theory focuses attention on the organisational behaviour side of management. Theory Z can be treated as a model for motivation. This theory believes in the philosophy of management. Both major and minor decision are taken through consensus in the truly democratic and dynamic management. Besides, family relationship prevails between the employer and employees. In other words, close, Co-operative and trustworthy relationship prevails among workers, managers and other groups.

| THEORY X | THEORY Y |
|---|---|
| 1. Workers dislike to work by themselves. | 1. Workers feel that work is as natural as play. |
| 2. Workers are not ready to accept responsibility. | 2. Workers are ready to accept responsibility if proper motivation is available to them. |
| 3. Workers prefer to be directed by others. | 3. Workers are directed by them-selves. |
| 4. Workers are unambitious | 4. Workers are ambitious. |
| 5. Workers by nature resist changes and want security. | 5. Workers are ready to cope with changes. |
| 6. Workers lack creativity and fail to solve organisational problems. | 6. Workers have a high degree of creativity and succeed in solving organisational problems. |
| 7. It focuses the lower level needs of workers i.e., physiological and safety. | 7. It focuses not only the lower level needs but also higher level needs i.e., social, esteem and self-actualisation of workers. |
| 8. Strict control is necessary to achieve organisational objectives. | 8. Workers exercise self-control and self-direction to achieve organisational objectives. |
| 9. Authority is not delegated. | 9. Authority is delegated. |
| 10. Autocratic leadership is followed. | 10. Democratic leadership is followed. |

Theory Z emphasis external control of human behaviour. Mutual trust reduces conflict among the employees and ensures team spirit. In practice, the management people workout their own style of management on the basis of the type of people dealt with and the nature of work performed.

## FEATURES OF THEORY Z

The distinguishing features of theory "Z" are briefly explained below.

1. Trust: The existence of trust and openness between employees, workers, trade unions and management executives avoids conflict at the maximum. Besides, employees extend their co-operation fully to achieve the objectives of the organisation. According to William G. Ouchi, trust, integrity and openness are necessary to an effective organisation.

**2. Life-Time Employment:** Life time employment should be given to all employees in order to promote a strong bond between employees and organisation. Shareholders or owners of the company should forgo their dividends or profits to avoid retrenchment of workers during adverse business conditions.

**3. Involvement of Employees:** Involvement of employees means participation of employees in decision making process. Participation of employees is not necessary in all decisions. But at the same time, any decision affecting employees in any way should be taken jointly. If the management wants to take a decision independently, the employees should be informed the position of management so that the employees do not feel ignored. Such involvement generates a sense of responsibility.

**4. Integrated Organisation:** An integrated organisation gives importance to job rotation. The reason is that job rotation improves understanding of interdependence of tasks. This type of understanding leads to team spirit.

**5. Restricted Promotions:** Promotion of worker is restricted to the maximum. The reason is that promotion leads to saturation in the adoption of latest technology. The promoted workers are not ready to cope with changes. Instead, the management gives importance to the horizontal movement of workers so that workers do not have a sense of stagnation in the same post for a long time.

**6. Co-ordination:** The role of any leader is to co-ordinate the efforts of employees and create class feeling in the organisation. The leader should have a discussion with each and every employee and analyse the problems.

**7. No Formal Structure:** There is no formal structure to the organisation as per theory Z. At the same time, there should be a perfect team-work with co-operation, ideas, strategies, plans and information. For example, A cricket team plays well and solves problems with no formal reporting relationships.

**8. Motivation:** If workers are allowed to work with their superiors or on specific projects they will be motivated. The reason is that there are the prospects of greater income in future due to their involvement.

**9. Informal Control System:** Organisation should make the control system an informal one. So, importance is given to mutual trust and co-operation rather than superior-sub-ordinate relationship for this purpose.

**10. Working Environment:** The stable working environment is necessary to the workers for increasing their satisfaction.

## CRITICISM OF THEORY Z

Theory Z is not considered as a motivation technique. Hence, it has been criticised on several grounds. The criticisms are listed below:

1. Theory Z is based on the Japanese management practices. Japanese management practices have emerged from that country's culture. Theory Z can be applied where Japanese culture prevails. Culture of one country differs from that of another country. So, theory Z cannot be applied universally.
2. Theory Z lacks empirical research. So, the practical utility of this theory is very limited.
3. Theory Z fails to give guidelines relating to the time at which it may be applied in an organisation.
4. One of the features of theory Z is that there is no formal structure. The absence of formal structure creates some operational problems if the organisation wants to implement theory Z.
5. Life-time employment is not possible as per theory Z. The reason is that an employer is not ready to retain an employee who is otherwise unproductive, there is also easy availability of substitutes.
6. Theory Z emphasizes on a class feeling within the organisation. It is very difficult to achieve this. The reason is that employees differ in habits, having food, dress, language and the like.

7. In India, Owners or Shareholders will not accept less profit or less divided to avoid lay-off.
8. If upward promotion of workers is restricted, an organisation will have to face a lot of problems created by trade unions.
9. Horizontal movement of workers is not very easy. A skill needed for a particular job cannot be transferred to another job.
10. An organisation is not in a position to reap the advantages of specialisation if it follows the restriction in upward promotion.

In a nutshell, theory Z does not present any solution of problem to the management. A perfect solution is necessary at the present fast developing computer world.

## MASLOW'S HIERARCHY OF NEEDS

Basically, needs are classified into two classes ie. innate needs and acquired needs. Innate needs are inherent in nature. For example, anger, hunger, sexual desire etc. Innate needs are otherwise called as *natural* needs. Acquired need are based upon experience. For example, if a student, in the as neighbourhood, has a 'Bajaj M80' vehicle, other students will want to have the same vehicle. This is called *acquired* need.

Another way of classification of needs are primary needs and secondary needs. The primary needs are necessary to survive and for preservation of life. e.g., food, water, air, etc. Secondary needs are concerned with mind and spirit, e.g., recognition, love, affection, etc.

Dr. Abraham H. Maslow classified the various needs of human beings in a definite order. This order is widely accepted. In this way, Dr. A.H. Maslow was the pioneer in the proper classification of human needs. According to Maslow, human wants are innumerable and never ending. If one want is satisfied, another want emerges in that place.

The satisfied wants do not motivate the workers. Only unsatisfied wants induce the man to work hard. Maslow is of the opinion that wants or needs are satisfied in an order. Hence, Maslow classified needs as lower level needs and higher level needs in the diagram next page:

## MASLOW'S HIERARCHY OF NEEDS

**1. Basic physiological needs:** The basic physiological needs are concerned with Breeding, shelter, sexual gratification, clothing etc. These needs are inherent in nature. These are necessary both to man and animals. If these needs are not satisfied, other needs will not emerge. Man lives by food alone. These needs are a powerful motivating force than others.

**2. Safety and security needs:** Safety and security needs emerge only when the basic physiological needs are satisfied. Safety needs are concerned with physical danger or loss of existing basic physiological needs. Security needs are concerned with loss of job, support, illness and the like. Hence, the workers attempt to get job security, insurance, pensionary benefits and so on.

**3. Belonging and social needs:** Man is a social animal. He wants to love and be loved in a society or in a family. Exchange of feelings and grievances, love, sociability, recognition, conversation and belongingness are some of the examples of social needs.

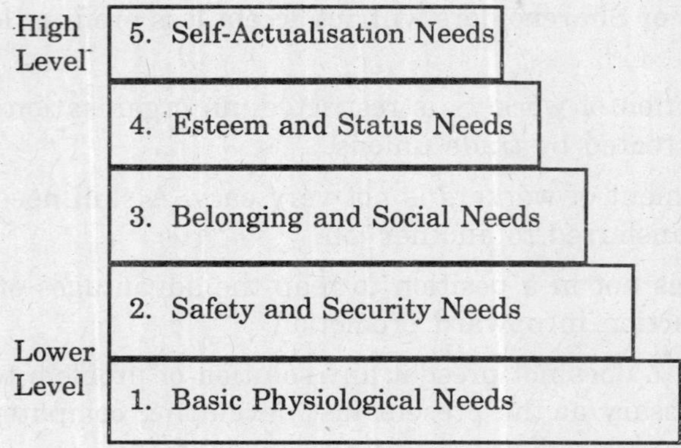


*Maslow's Hierarchy of Needs*

**4. Esteem and status needs:** Esteem and status needs are otherwise called *ego needs* or *egoistic needs*. Self-confidence, independence, achievement, competence, knowledge, status, recognition and appreciation are some of the examples of esteem and status needs. Most of these are rarely satisfying.

**5. Self-actualisation needs:** Self-actualisation needs are otherwise called *self-realisation needs*. Self-actualisation refers to the desire to become everything that one is capable of becoming. For example, a doctor thinks that he is capable of saving the life of a patient. A teacher thinks that he is capable of giving best teaching to students. In other words, a maximum level of excellent performance is done by the individual.

Of the above mentioned five needs, the first three needs (i.e., basic physiological needs, safety and security needs and belonging and social needs) are regarded by Maslow as lower level needs. The remaining two needs (*i.e.,* Esteem and status needs and self-actualisation needs) are regarded as higher level needs by him. The lower level needs are satisfied through monetary and non-monetary compensation. The term non-monetary compensation includes good working conditions, love, recognition, etc. The higher level needs are satisfied through allowing in decision-making process, delegating authority and responsibility, greater freedom, opportunities for advancement and so on.

## CRITICAL APPRAISAL OF MASLOW'S HIERARCHY OF NEEDS

The hierarchy level of needs help the management to understand the behaviour of workers and motivate them. But Maslow himself accepted that the hierarchy level of needs are not rigid ones and can be changed from one person to another person. So, Maslow's hierarchy of needs theory has the following weaknesses:

1. Maslow's hierarchy of needs is not applicable at all times, in all places and in all circumstances.
2. Some people do not require social needs because they might have lost love during their childhood.
3. The level of needs of different people are not equal. The reason is that there is a long experience in the lower level needs. The people of lower level needs may lack ambition and not expect higher level needs.
4. The perceptions, expectations and experience of an individual are responsible for his behaviour. These do not result in the needs classified by Maslow.

5. A single need cannot motivate any individual. There is a need of several needs to constitute proper motivation.
6. Some needs do not motivate all the workers. A need may motivate one worker. It may not motive another worker.

## HERZBERG'S THEORY OF NEEDS

In the late 1950s, Frederick Herzberg had conducted a study on motivation. The study has developed a theory of work-motivation. This theory has broad implications for management in the effective utilisation of human resources. So, this theory is known as Herzberg Motivation theory of needs. It is otherwise called Maintenance Theory of Motivation, Hygiene Theory or Two-Factor Theory of Motivation.

Herzberg tried to understand from his studies the motivation problem and to identify the human behaviour, nature and needs which are invaluable to organisation and individuals. In this study, he interviewed 200 engineers and accountants from 11 industries in Pittsburgh area. He asked these persons to think of the time when they felt good and bad about their jobs and describe the conditions which caused such feelings.

The study reveals that the factors responsible for job satisfaction are quite different from those responsible for job-dissatisfaction. These two feelings were not obverse of each other. If a factor is responsible for job satisfaction, the absence of such a factor would not mean job dissatisfaction but it might be called the job-satisfaction.

Similarly, a factor is responsible for job dissatisfaction. The absence of such a factor would not mean job satisfaction but it might be called no job-dissatisfaction. Thus, this theory is based on two types of factors. They are factors leading to job satisfaction and factors leading to job dissatisfaction.

According to Herzberg motivational factors are responsible for job satisfaction. Hygiene or maintenance factors are responsible for job-dissatisfaction.

## MOTIVATIONAL FACTORS

The presence of some factors creates motivation to the workers and at the same time absence of such factors does not cause dissatisfaction. They are called motivation factors. Herzberg identified some motivational factors as (i) achievement, (ii) recognition, (iii) advancement, (iv) work itself, (v) possibility of growth, and (vi) responsibility.

## MAINTENANCE FACTORS

The presence of some set of factors motivate the workers but the absence of these factors caused serious dissatisfaction. In other words, the presence of these factors prevent dissatisfactions. Herzberg called these factors as maintenance of hygiene factors.

In his study, *Herzberg*, identified the following factors as maintenance factors. They are (i) company policy and admini-stration, (ii) technical supervision, (iii) inter personal relations with sub-ordinates, (iv) salary, (v) job security, (vi) personal life, (vii) working conditions, (viii) status, (ix) inter-personal relations with supervisiors, and (x) inter-personal relations with peers.

Intrinsic factors are internal rewards which are available at the time of performance of work. So, the workers are directly motivated and they have self-motivation.

Extrinsic factors are external rewards which are available only after the performance of job. Retirement benefits, holiday pay, leave, insurance, etc., are some of the extrinsic factors. Here, the workers are motivated but not directly.

After Herzberg's research, organisational managers paid more attention on the intrinsic factors because often they produced good results. He came to a conclusion from his studies. The workers may be motivated:

1. If job is challenging;
2. If there is a possibility of growth;
3. If there is possibility of achievement;
4. If the workers have enough authority and responsibility;
5. If the workers receive recognition; and
6. If the workers are able to advance in the profession.

## MOTIVATIONAL TECHNIQUES

Some of the motivational techniques are briefly explained below:

**1. Monetary incentives:** The term *monetary incentives* includes pay revision or increase, fringe benefits, bonus, etc. Monetary incentives have more motivation power than non-monetary incentives.

**2. Job-based techniques:** Job-based techniques cover job simplification, job rotation, job enlargement, job enrichment, job analysis and evaluation. Job enrichment increases the awareness of purpose of performing a particular job. Job rotation reduces the monotony of the work to some extent. Job enlargement develops the number of operations.

**3. MBO technique:** Both workers and managers participate in the determination of the area of responsibility and the expected results. They used MBO as guidance for operation and assessing their contribution towards organisationl development.

**4. Leadership techniques:** Autocratic, democratic and persuasiveness are some of the styles of leadership. They have their own implications for workers' motivation in the short-run as well as in the long-run.

**5. Sensitivity training:** This type of training is given to groups of managers. They, in turn motivate their subordinates after receiving sensitivity training. Sensitivity training helps the managers to understand themselves better, develop insight into work situations, scientific thinking and acquire behavioural skills in dealing with sub-ordinates.

## REQUIREMENTS OF A SOUND MOTIVATIONAL SYSTEM

A sound motivational system brings maximum benefits to the organisation. So, proper care should be taken in framing a motivation system. The following are some of the requirements of a sound motivational system:

1. A motivational system should balance the objectives and philosophy of organisation workers.
2. Motivational system should be understood by the members of the organisation in the right direction.
3. The motivational system should cover all the activities of the workers.
4. The motivational system should have corresponding relationship with efforts and rewards.

5. The motivational system should be flexible. It means that some changes are incorporated in the motivational system from time to time according to the requirements.

**MODEL QUESTIONS**

1. What is meant by motivation?
2. Explain Maslow's theory of motivation.
3. Explain the importance of motivation.
4. What are the types of motivation?
5. What are the advantages of motivation?
6. Explain the different types of motivation.
7. Define motivation and why is it important?
8. What are the characteristics of motivation? Explain the various methods of motivation?
8. Motivation is the Core of management. Discuss?
9. Define the term motivation and point out its importance.
10. Explain McGregore's 'X' and 'Y' theories.
11. Discuss the various kinds of motivation.
12. Write a note on the contribution made by Douglas McGregor?
13. Bring out the importance of motivation in business enterprises? List out different motivation tools that a business enterprise can adopt to motivate its employees?

# CHAPTER 21

# LEADERSHIP

## INTRODUCTION

Success of a business concern is dependent upon the ability of its leadership. Leadership exists in any type of organisation. Whenever and in whatever situation if someone tries to influence the behaviour of another individual or a group, there is leadership.

In an organisation, wherever an individual has subordinates, he may act as a leader. The efforts of subordinates (followers) are to be channelised in the right direction. As leaders, they are not only the responsible for directing their followers but also responsible for the attainment of goals of the organisation. It is believed that leaders are born and not made. At the same time, a few people also believe that leaders are not born but made. But generally, leaders are born and also made.

## DEFINITION

Koontz and O'Donnell said, "Leadership is generally defined as influence, the art of process of influencing people so that they will strive willingly towards the achievement of group goals."

Allen, "Leader is one who guides and directs other people. He must give effective direction and purpose."

According to the Encyclopedia of Social Sciences, "Leadership refers to the relation between an individual and a group around some common interest and behaving in a manner directed or determined by him (the leader)."

George R. Terry says, "Leadership is the activity of influencing people to strive willingly for mutual objectives."

In the words of Peter F. Drucker, "Leadership is the lifting of man's visions to higher rights, the raising of man's performance to higher standards, the building of man's personality beyond its normal limitations."

Robert C. Appleby defines, "Leadership is a means of direction, is the ability of the management to induce subordinate to work towards group ideals with confidence and keenness."

Alford and Beatty Opines, "Leadership is the ability to secure desirable actions from a group or followers voluntarily without the use of coercion."

Ordway Tead asserts, Leadership is that combination of qualities by the possession of which one is able to get something done by others, chiefly because through his influence, they become willing to do so."

Haimann Theo fact that, "Leadership can be defined as the process by which an executive imaginately directs, guides and influences the work of others in choosing and attaining specific goals by mediating between the individual and the organisations in such a manner that both will obtain maximum satisfaction."

Chester I. Barnard holds, "It (leadership) refers to the quality of the behaviour of the individual whereby they guide people on their activities in organised efforts."

R.T. Livingston believes, "Leadership is the ability to awaken in others the desire to follow a common objective."

## NEED OR IMPORTANCE OF LEADERSHIP

**1. Perfect organisation structure:** An organisation structure cannot provide for all kinds of relationships. That is why, informal relationships are made to exist within the framework or formal organisation structure. But the organisation structure is complete or perfect with the help of effective leadership.

**2. Directing group activities:** The personal conduct and behaviour of a leader can direct others to achieve organisational goals. The main responsibility of a leader is to get the work done effectively by the followers. The followers cannot work hard and effectively without leadership. A leader alone can consolidate the efforts and direct them towards the goal.

**3. Technological, economic and social changes:** There is frequent change in technology, economic and social structure in the present computer world. So, the organisation should change its operation and style. This is possible only with the help of effective leadership. If the changes do not take place, the organisation cannot survive.

**4. Better utilisation of manpower:** A leader treats with equal importance, plans, policies and programmes of an organisation. The plans, policies and programmes do not work themselves. There is a need for a leader. The leader implements the plans, policies an programmes to utilise the available manpower effectively and get highest production with minimum human cost.

**5. Avoiding imbalances:** An organisation grows in size and complexity with the imbalances. Complexity arises due to the introduction of new functions. The reason is that the introduction of new functions resulted in increased levels of management. So, there is a problem of command, co-ordination and control. A leader can tackle these problems and maintain balances.

**6. Source of motivation:** Simply, the existence of leadership does not motivate the workers. The leadership style should be utilised to motivate the workers according to the situations prevailing. The achievement of goals is doubtful in the absence of leadership.

**7. Reconciliation of goals:** An organisation has its own goals. The employees of the organisation have their own goals. They are working mainly for achieving their goals instead of achieving organisational goals. An effective leadership can reconcile the goals of organisations and employees. It is necessary for the success of an organisation.

**8. Developing good human relations:** Human relations represent the relations between the leader and the followers (subordinates). An efficient leader can develop the skill of the followers and promote self-confidence apart from motivation. Next, the leader creates opportunity to show their abilities and induces the followers to work towards the accomplishment of goals. In this way, the leader promotes the co-operative attitude of workers and maintains better relations with them.

**9. Promoting the spirit of co-ordination:** A dynamic leader can co-ordinate the activities of the subordinate. In an organisation, workers are working in groups, so there is a need for co-ordination among the group members. A leader promotes the spirit of co-ordination among the workers.

**10. Fulfiling social responsibilities:** Social responsibilities refer to the high standard of living to workers, higher productivity and income to the organisation, more revenue to the government, reasonable price to consumers and fair return on investment to the investors. These could be achieved with the help of effective leadership. Only an efficient leader can get work done to fulfil social responsibilities.

## APPROACHES OR THEORIES OF LEADERSHIP

The various approaches or theories of leadership are discussed below:

**1. Traitist's approach or theory:** *Trait* means quality. According to this theory, leadership behaviour is influenced by certain qualities of a person (leader). In simple words, leadership behaviour is sum total of traits. Studies were conducted to identify the qualities of past and present leaders in terms of their education, experience, character, family background, etc. Another way of finding leadership quality is to enquire how the leader considers himself different from others in a particular situation.

Researchers have found out a number of qualities of leadership from their study. A successful leader has the following qualities: (i) Good personality; (ii) Tirelessness; (iii) Ability to take quick decision; (iv) Courage to face competitors; (v) Persuasion; (vi) Lesson out of experience; (vii) Intelligence; (viii) Different thinking; (ix) Reliability; (x) Physical fitness etc.

Initially, most of the persons thought that leadership qualities were inherited but later they concluded that the acquired qualities could be developed by experience and training. So, leadership qualities are not only born but also developed. This theory was mostly accepted during 1930s and 1950s.

## WEAKNESSES OF TRAIT'S THEORY

Trait's theory suffers from the following weaknesses:

***No common equalities list:*** The qualities of a successful leader are listed by various thinkers. But the list of the qualities of a thinker may not tally with the list of qualities in another thinker. At the same time, no thinker has listed the qualities in order of importance. The list of qualities have confused the readers often.

***Measurement of quality:*** Thinkers simply provide the list of qualities. They fail to give the scale to measure the qualities. Besides, it is very difficult to specifiy the qualities which are necessary for an effective leader.

***No scope for future development:*** Trait's theory focuses on the inborn qualities of an individual. These inborn qualities cannot be developed or acquired. But, the inborn qualities can be developed. It has been practically proved. But, trait's theory does not give any scope for future development of inborn qualities. The reason is that the theory assumes that leaders are born but not made.

***No consideration for situational factors:*** Thinkers do not take into consideration the situation which influences the leaders. The quality of the leader comes to light only when a situation arises. If there is no situation present, there will be no scope for the use of trait or quality.

***No need of uniform traits:*** Different qualities are necessary for different levels of manage-ment. There is a direct contact between the leader and the followers at the lower level management. So, there is a compulsory need for technical knowledge. The policy of the management is interpreted at middle level management. Here, better human relations are necessary between the leaders and followers. Top management people frame the policy of the organisation. They require more skills than others. So, it is concluded that the same leadership qualities are not necessary to all the management people.

Next, leadership role is very limited in the case of large organisation and vice versa.

**2. Behavioural approach or theory:** Thinkers diverted their attention to study leaders' behaviours instead of leaders' qualities. The reason is that trait's theory has many weaknesses. Behaviour Theory had popularity during 1950s. So the behaviour approach study emerged after 1950s and 1960s. The basis of behaviour theory lies in the fact that how the management viewed the workers.

Behaviour theory assumes that people are lazy aand irrespon-sible by nature. So there is a need of an instrument to give motivation to workers. Here, leadership acts as an instrument. Manager is an instrument holder. Therefore, the manager should be directive. F.W. Taylor finds the behaviour of workers through his scientific management approach. Elton Mayo and his associates have conducted Howthorne experiments and identified the workers' behaviour. They came to the conclusion that human behvaiour is mainly reponsible for effective leadership.

Autocratic , democratic or supervisory styles are some of the leadership styles. Behaviour approach theory developed these leadership styles which produce different and conflicting results. Different and conflicting results were obtained due to changes in the behaviour of leaders and followers. Both leaders and followers change their behaviour according to the situations.

Behaviour theory concentrated on explaining the behaviour of leaders. The behaviour of the followers changed according to the changes in the behaviour of the leaders. So, what the leader does is the main concern.

**3. Situationalist approach or theory:** Trait theory explains the characteristics required for an effective leader. But it does not specify the person who should possess particular traits to be a leader. In case of behaviour theory, it explains the leadership styles available to leaders but fails to recommend the last best leadership style. Both these theories initiated further researches and accepted that situation is also an important element. During 1970s the situation theory was developed.

The usefulness of traits and behaviours is tested in a particular situation. Some traits and behaviours are effective in a particular situation and ineffecitve in another situation. As per the situation theory, a leader is strongly affected by the situation in which he works. Situation helps the persons to develop their leadership qualities and emerge as leaders. Here, traits or behvaiours are supporting elements to the leaders. Situation theory believes that there is an interlink between the group of workers and its leaders. Some group of workers have aspirations. They follow the leaders who one capable of realising their aspirations. Thus, it is the situation that shapes the leadership qualities.

**4. Follower's theory or acceptance Theory:** According to this theory, only followers decide whether a person is a leader or not. Followers take a decision analysing the qualities of the person who helps to have their needs fulfilled. Here, there is a need for forming a group and fulfilling some needs of such a group. This theory cannot be applied without a group of followers.

Traits and behaviour are not considered as essential elements of leadership. Under this theory, if followers accept a person as their leader, he becomes a leader irrespective of his qualities and behaviour. Modern managers are of the opinion that Acceptance theory plays a significant role in managing the people at present. In the political world also, a person who satisfied the needs of his followers will become a leader. Followers disown their leader when he fails to satisfy their needs. The needs of the group are the crucial and guiding factor in determining the leader.

**5. System theory or a path-goal theory:** System theory is focused on a person's act rather than his traits or behaviour. A leader co-ordinates the efforts of his followers. The process of co-ordination is done by a person (leader). It is termed as person's act. The process of co-ordination stimulates the people to achieve the goal in a particular situation. System theory considers all the variables. The term variable includes the leader, followers, situation, leadership traits, environment goals and group's nature, characteristics and needs, role behaviour of the leader and co-ordination efforts of the leader. So this theory is considered as modern theory of leadership.

## FUNCTIONS OF A LEADER

The functions of a business leader are briefly explained below:

**1. Taking initiative:** A leader has to take all initiatives to lead the business activities. He should not except others to induce him to take initiative. He himself should come in the field and take all steps to achieve pre-determined targets.

**2. Representation:** A leader is a representative of an organisation. The leader represents the purpose of organisation to workers and outsiders.

**3. Guide:** The leader has the primary duty of guiding others. Proper direction should be given by a leader. If he does not do so, the organisation will not succeed. The leader should issue instructions and orders whenever needed. These instructions and orders should be properly communicated.

**4. Encouraging others:** The leader is the captain of a team. The leader must win the confidence of his colleagues before winning in a competition. The leader cannot succeed without teamwork. Encouragement is necessary to build up teamwork.

**5. Arbitrator and Mediator:** The leader can settle the disputes arising among the workers. Besides, he can create a smooth relationship among the workers. He performs these duties in a friendly manner. Generally, people accept friendly advice. Sometimes, the leader can act as a friend.

**6. Planner:** The type of activities or type of work is to be decided by the leader. The leader can decide when a work is to be done, where it should be done and by whom it should be done. This planning work is completed by the leader.

**7. Rewards and Punishments:** There is a standard for some set of work. Some workers perform their work within a standard time and properly. The leader can give rewards to those who have completed the work as per the standard. The leader can punish the worker who does not complete the work as per the requirements of job.

**8. Integration:** Each individual does a part of a whole work. They perform the work according to their specialisation. Here, there is a need for integration. So the leader integrates the efforts of all workers. In this way, integration is one of the functions of the leader.

**9. Communication:** Communication is necessary to every organisation. Nothing will succeed without effective communication. An effective commu-nication system conveys the authority and responsibility to each individual so that he may come to know what he is to do and what not. An individual understands his authority and responsibility from organisational policies, procedures and programmes. The leader should arrange for an effective communication system in an organisation.

**10. Production:** A leader is expected to show high production figures. A production oriented style is followed by the leader. He should take all necessary steps to increase production.

## QUALITIES OF LEADERSHIP

A leader should have some leadership qualities in order to provide effective leadership. According to Henry Fayol, a leader should have the qualities of: *(i)* health and physical fitness, *(ii)* mental vigour and energy, *(iii)* courage to accept responsibility, *(iv)* steady, persistent thoughtful determination, *(v)* sound general education, and *(vi)* management ability embracing foresight and the art of handling men.

The important qualities of a leader are discussed below:

**1. Physical appearance and strength:** The leader has to put in hard work physically. He should have a capacity to work for long hours than others. It proves the diligence of the leader to his followers easily.

**2. Mental vigour:** The leader is also strong mentally. It means that the leader is expected to withstand strain in finishing the work properly.

**3. Emotional stability:** The leader should not be moved by emotion or sentiment. He should analyse the problem rationally and take a decision without bias. The leader should not have short temper. Besides, he should show firmness in his decision and not show despair or indecision on his face.

**4. Sense of judgement:** A leader should know the human psychology. He should understand the behaviour, needs, thoughts, motives etc. of his followers. This will help him to take a strategic decision and get it recognised by his followers. Besides, he can set right his actions.

**5. Goodwill:** A leader should be able to understand the feelings of others. He takes decision on the basis of expectations of his followers. If he does not do so, he will not win the goodwill of his followers.

**6. Motivation:** A leader should know the motivation techniques and how to use them. If a person is forced to do his job under the threat of getting punishment, he will not perform his work properly. At the same time, if the same person is motivated, he will perform his job more than the expectations of his leader.

**7. Communication skill:** Whatever the information needed to workers, it should be passed through the leader. So, the leader should communicate the information to the workers. Now, the leader is acting as an effective speaker and writer. If the leader has communication skills, he will direct his followers effectively.

**8. Guiding ability:** The leader acts as a teacher to new workers. So the leader helps his followers to learn their work. He should train the workers by work and deed to complete the job effectively.

**9. Sociability:** An able leader can easily mingle with the workers. The workers should be encouraged to discuss their problems and difficulties with their boss. The leader should also meet the workers frequently. The leader should show his keen interest to develop the ability of workers.

**10. Technical knowledge:** A leader should possess a thorough knowledge of the theory and practice of his job. Besides, he should know the current developments in his job along with technical knowledge. For example, a computer department manager should know all the latest developments in computers.

These are some qualities of a leader. Besides, he should be honest, sincere and fair. Sincere, fair and honest people are mostly liked by others and their leadership is accepted by one and all.

## TYPES OF LEADERS

Leadership cannot exist without followers. The characteristics of the followers play a vital role in the exercise of leadership. The behaviour of a leader is based on the maturity levels of the followers. Here, maturity level refers to job enrichness and psychological maturity (motivation) of followers. Thus, the leader has to adopt task behaviour if he has low level maturity followers and tell them what, when, where and how the given work is to be completed. In other words, if the leader has high level maturity followers, he can adopt assigning behaviour and the entire work along with freedom to complete the work.

The types of leaders are classified on the basis of behaviour of leaders. They are briefly explained below:

**1. Autocratic leader:** A leader is one who wants to run the organisation all by himself. He frames the objectives of the organisation and requires the followers to achieve the objectives. These objectives are expected to be achieved within the time limit fixed by him. Besides, he gives specific directions to his followers and he is regularly informed of the progress in work.

A leader thinks that his followers do not have much ability to do a job effectively. So, he avoids discussions with his followers regarding job completion. The leader does not delegate any authority to his followers. He has close supervision and control over his followers. He uses the technique of giving rewards and/or punishments to his followers. If any follower completes his job according to the expectations of the leader, he will be rewarded. On the other hand, if any follower fails to complete his job as per the requirements, he will be penalised and the punishment may be in the form of company action or dismissal.

**2. Intellectual leader:** A leader wins the confidence of his followers by his intelligence. Generally, the advice of a leader is sought in big business concerns. He gives advice on the matter in which he is expert. He may be a specialist in sales, personnel management and the like. He gets results through others. He excels as a leader because he uses his superior knowledge.

**3. Liberal leader:** A leader is one who permits his followers to do their job howsoever they want to do. The leader has not framed any policy or procedure which the followers are expected to follow in their jobs.

The liberal leader would not exercise any influence over his followers and vice versa. Wide scope and opportunities are available for free discussion which aims at performing the job effectively. The followers should have a high degree of maturity. High degree of maturity means the followers have both the ability and willingness to work. If the followers have low maturity, the leader cannot succeed in his position. In other words, whenever the liberal leader has low maturity followers, he is not able to make his followers understand what, how, when and where to perform.

**4. Democratic leader:** A leader acts according to the wishes of his followers. The leader does what his followers want. The leader frames the policy or procedure according to the opinion of the majority of his followers. He acts as a representative of his followers to management. The leader holds his leadership because he is loyal to his followers. He is always interested in protecting the interests of his followers. The leader is a friend of his followers and he is helpful to them.

**5. Institutional leader:** A leader exercises his power over his followers because of his position held in the organisational hierarchy. He exercises authority with which his post is invested. The leader can control the activities of his followers in order to achieve the objectives.

The leader may or may not be an expert in his field. If he is an expert, he will have relationship behaviour with his followers. If he is not so, he has task behaviour with his followers. The followers prefer relationship behaviour to task behaviour. Whenever the leader adopts task behaviour, the followers are frustrated.

**6. Inducing leader:** The leader is one who influences his followers with his personality and persuades them to join him in doing a work. He loves and is loved by his followers. The followers have confidence in him and want his goodwill.

The leader gets things done by others through speaking nice words. The whole gang responds to the words of the leader.

**7. Paternal leader:** An individual who has become the leader in the place of his father as leader has close relationship with his followers and comes to their rescue ever so often.

Paternal leader has job maturity followers only. The reason is that the followers may be lacking only in their psychological maturity. They are not permitted to show their initiative. The leader lays certain conditions under which the followers are expected to work. So the followers are not aware of their potential fully.

**8. Creative leader:** The leader is one who encourages his followers to suggest new ideas, thoughts or ways. Sometimes, the leader himself puts forward new ideas. Whenever more than one new idea flows from the group, the leader will select the best one among them without personal bias. He controls his followers just like other leaders and makes them to achieve the specific goals. According to Ordway Tead, the followers adopt the big idea but not the big.

## TECHNIQUE OF LEADERSHIP

A leader can use a number of techniques to extract work from his followers. Some of the techniques are discussed below:

**1. Securing co-operation:** A leader should get co-operation from his followers. Unless he enlists their co-operation, he cannot succeed. There must be a willingness on the part of both parties. The leader must convince each follower to extend co-operation. Both leaders and their followers must have interest in the growth of an enterprise. First, the leader himself extends his co-operation to his followers. The leader must treat his followers as co-workers and not as followers.

**2. The use of power:** Leadership goes with power. It cannot exist without power. So the leader must use his power which subsequently results in getting things done by others. At the same time, the leader should use power only to safeguard the interests of the enterprise. Some leaders expect more powers than required. It is not advisable. On the other hand, a leader can achieve the goals with the available power.

**3. Co-ordination:** A leader can co-ordinate the activities of his followers through orders or commands. Definite, flexible and open orders alone co-ordinate the activities. Definite order means that an crder is not oral and the terms used in definite order have unequivocal meaning. In the case of flexible order, only goals are communicated. Next, the followers achieve the goals by using the pre-determined time. A leader specifies the goals and leaves the other details to his followers in open order.

An order fulfils its purpose only when it is properly received and understood. The receiver must know the expectation of the issuer. Then only proper results will be obtained.

**4. Discipline:** Discipline is nothing but the adherence to rules, regulations and procedures. Discipline should be maintained to achieve the objectives. Individuals are restricted from doing things which are detrimental to the group interests. If a particular follower is violating the rules, he may be penalised. The very success of leadership and organisation depends upon the maintenance of discipline.

**5. Morale:** Leighton has defined morale, as the capacity of a group to pull together persistently and consistently for a common goal. *"Morale is the attitude of an individual and group growing out of the conditions under which he or they complete the job effectively."* The leader should create confidence in the minds of his followers. Here, confidence is necessary to both the leader and the followers. A leader has confidence in his followers and vice versa. Mental maturity plays an important role in creating confidence. Having confidence ensures effective performance of a job.

## CHARACTERISTICS OF LEADERSHIP

Following are some of the characteristics of leadership:

**1. There must be followers:** A leadership cannot exist without followers. If a leader does not have followers, he cannot exercise his authority. Leadership exists both in formal and informal organisations.

**2. Working relationship between leader and followers:** There must be a working relationship between the leader and his followers. It means that the leader should present himself in a place where the work is actually going on. Besides, the leader should be a dynamic person of the concerned group. If he is not so, he cannot get things done.

**3. Personal quality:** The character and behaviour of a man influence the works of others.

**4. Reciprocal relationship:** Leadership kindles a reciprocal relationship between the leader and his followers. A leader can influence his followers and, in turn, the followers can influence the leader. The willingness of both the leader and the followers is responsible for the influence and no enforcement is adopted.

**5. Community of interests:** There must be community of interests between the leader and his followers. A leader has his own objectives. The followers have their own objectives. They are moving in different directions in the absence of community of interests. It is not advisable. It is the leader who should try to reconcile the different objectives and compromise the individual interests with organisation interests.

**6. Guidance:** A leader guides his followers to achieve the goals of the organisation. A leader should take steps to motivate his followers for this purpose.

**7. Related to a particular situation:** Leadership is applicable to a particular situation at a given point of time. It varies from time to time.

**8. Shard Function:** Leadership is a shared function. A leader is also working along with his followers to achieve the objectives of the organisation. Besides, the leader shares his experience, ideas and views with his followers.

**9. Power relationship:** A leader has powers to exercise over his followers. The leader derives these powers from the organisation hierarchy, superior know-ledge, experience and the like.

## LEADERSHIP STYLES

The success of a business unit depends upon the leadership styles followed by the leaders. Leadership style describes how a leader has relationship with his group. Some of the leadership styles are discussed below:

**1. Positive style:** A leader motivates his followers to work hard by offering them rewards. A rule is framed in such a way that a reward will be ensured to those who show high efficiency. Positive leaders promote industrial peace. For example, higher bonus (bonus linked with wages) will certainly increase efficiency of the workers. Wages are payable under piece rate system.

**2. Negative style:** A leader forces his followers to work hard and penalises them if the work is not upto the organisation's standard. The penalty is given according to the performance. The penalty will be a severe one if the performance has more short comings. For example, if the manager gives ousting order for continuous absence from duty for ten days even though the worker is absent due to unavoidable circumstances. It is a negative style.

Negative style has high human cost. But, it is necessary in some circumstances. Under negative style, everybody tries to shift his responsibility over to others. Negative style leaders act more as bosses than leaders.

**3. Autocratic or authoritarian style:** Under this leadership style, the leaders have full power or authority to take a decision. The leaders create a work situation under which the subordinates are expected to work. They will work no more or less than the instruction of the leader. So, the leaders have full responsibility.

The followers are not aware of organisation goals. Besides, the followers feel insecure and are afraid of the authority of the leaders. The reason is that these leaders have the desire to wield loving more powers.

The leader uses his power for the interest of his group and motivate his followers. Then the productivity is increased and the followers get full satisfaction from their job.

### Advantages

1. This leadership style provides strong motivation to the followers.
2. Quick decision is possible. The reason is that the leader himself takes decision for the whole group.
3. Less talented followers can perform their job effectively.
4. Followers need not take any decision.
5. Decision-making, planning or organising need no initiative.

### Disadvantages

The autocratic leadership style has some disadvantages. They are given below:

1. Most of the people dislike this style. The reason is that this style has a negative motivation approach.
2. Frustration, low morale and conflict develop easily under autocratic leadership.
3. New ideas or creative ideas of the followers will not have a scope to be applied and benefits of these could not be obtained under autocratic style.
4. The followers have no opportunity for development.

### Suitability

Autocratic style is not suitable to all business organisations. It is suitable to those organisations in which the followers are uneducated and unskilled. The reason is that they are unable to take decisions. If the organisation follows the punishment principle, this leadership style may be suitable.

**4. Democratic style:** It is otherwise called as *participative* style. It is just opposite to autocratic style. The authority is decentralised. So, the followers are permitted to take decisions under this style. The decisions are taken wholeheartedly. The reason is that the superior has consultation with his subordinates before taking a decision. The subordinates know the goals of the organisation, so, they offer fruitful ideas during discussion. If a leader follows this style, he can use the force to control his followers instead of using authority.

Generally, most of the leaders follow this style. At present, the worker's participation in management is gaining popularity.

### Advantages

1. Consultation gives satisfaction to the followers. Followers are consulted before taking a decision.
2. Due recognition is given to the followers. So, they show more interest in increasing the company's productivity.
3. Followers are aware of the activities in the organisation.
4. A leader can improve his decision-making ability through consultation with his followers while taking a decision.
5. Followers get opportunity to show their ability or talent.

### Disadvantages

1. Decentralisation of power is used only when consultation is made for taking a decision. Nothing more than that is done.
2. Taking a decision and the implementation of it require more time. The reason is that several members are involved in taking a decision.
3. Followers can dominate the leader.
4. A leader can easily shift the responsibility to his followers for failure in taking and implementing a decision.
5. It requires communicating skill on the part of the leader. If does not have it, unfavourable things may happen in an organisation and the organisation may be financially and status-wise ruined.

**5. Free-rein style:** The leaders have no authority and responsibility under this style, so the followers themselves take decisions for which they get authority. This style is employee-centred. Employees (Followers) are free to establish their own goals and chart out the course of action. The employees train themselves and they are self-motivated.

The leader acts as a laison officer between the employees and the outside world. He brings the information which is needed to the employees. The information is utilised by the employees to do their job. Here, the leader fails to motivate his followers (Employees).

### Advantages

1. Morale and job satisfaction of the followers are increased to some extent.
2. The talent of the followers is properly utilised.
3. The followers get full opportunity to develop their talents.

### Disadvantages

1. The leader does not care to motivate his followers.
2. The contribution of a leader is nothing.
3. The leader does not support the follower and no guidance is available to the former.

## MODEL QUESTIONS

1. State the qualities of a good leader.
2. What are the different types of leadership?.
3. Explain the qualities of a leader.
4. What is the definition of "Leadership"?
5. Define the term 'Leadership.'
6. What is leadership? 'State its necessity in business organisation.'
7. Define the term 'Leadership.'
8. What are the qualities of good leadership?
9. Define leadership and explain the characteristics of a successful leader.
10. Discuss the different styles of leadership, pointing out merits and demerits of each.
11. What do you mean by "situational leadership"?

# CHAPTER 22

# SUPERVISION

## INTRODUCTION

*Indian employees* have hardly paid full attention to their work. Besides, managerial talents are in short supply in India. So, the management often cries for good managers and executives. Good managers oversee the performance of workers. It is necessary to oversee the performance to achieve early objectives.

Overseeing of performance is done at all levels of manage-ment. (from top to bottom). Top management and middle management members oversee the performance of the management members. But, bottom management members oversee the performance of non-management members *i.e.,* workers. Bottom management members are directly dealing with actual workers. High degree of overseeing is necessary to bottom management members. So, they are called, *first line managers*. First line managers supervise the actual production. Hence, supervision means overseeing employees at work.

'Supervisor' refers to a person who is responsible for overseeing the performance of employees at work. Supervisor has different names. They are: foreman, departmental head, chargehand, depart-mental incharge, overseer, sectional head, head clerk, chargeman, chief clerk, head assistant, inspector, superintendent or section officer, etc.

## FUNCTIONS OF SUPERVISOR

Supervisor's work is directly concerned with the workers' activities which are responsible for achieving the objectives of an organisation. So the supervisor is regarded as a *Key man* in management. Generally, the supervisor performs the following functions:

1. He gives orders, instructions and implements the rules.
2. He converts the goals, programmes, policies, and resources into products or services.
3. He creates a proper climate or working conditions in the working places.
4. He arranges work assignments, determines procedures and prescribes methods.
5. He arranges tools and materials for workers.
6. He provides technical knowledge to workers.
7. He motivates the workers as to how well they can do their jobs.
8. He acts as an example to his group members or sub-ordinates.
9. He hears the grievances and complaints of his sub-ordinates and helps to solve them.
10. He can communicate the feelings or problems of his sub-ordinates to the top management, if needed.
11. He controls the performance of workers.
12. He recommends promotions, transfers and pay increase of his subordinates.

## RESPONSIBILITIES OF SUPERVISOR

The position of the supervisor is that of a key position in every type of organisation. He is in charge of workers who are directly engaged in basic operations' of an organisation. So the supervisor is primarily responsible for the successful accomplishment of operation. The machines and equipments are effectively utilised through proper placing of workers by the supervisor.

The responsibilities of the supervisor are classified under the following heads:

A. Responsibilities towards workers or subordinates.

B. Responsibilities towards management.

C. Responsibilities towards his own functions.

D. Responsibilities towards his colleagues.

**A. Responsibilities Towards Workers OR Subordinates**

1. Supervisor issues orders and instructions to his workers or sub-ordinates.
2. Supervisor works to win the confidence of his sub-ordinates.
3. Supervisor must develop a sense of team-spirit among the workers.
4. Supervisor must prescribe work methods, procedures and schedules.
5. Supervisor must listen to the complaints and problems of his sub-ordinates and must help to solve them.
6. Supervisor must arrange training facilities to newly appointed workers.
7. Supervisor must motivate his sub-ordinates and appreciate the efficient performance of any work.
8. Supervisor must act as a model to his sub-ordinates.
9. Supervisor must ensure discipline among the workers.
10. Supervisor must listen to the suggestions given by the sub-ordinates and in turn, give suggestions to his sub-ordinates according to the circumstances.
11. Supervisor must explain the objectives of organisation clearly to his subordinates.

**B. Responsibilities Towards Management**

1. Supervisor must inform the management about the progress of the assignment.
2. Supervisor must inform the management of the problems and difficulties faced by the sub-ordinates.
3. Supervisor must extend his co-operation to his superiors and accept more responsibility, if needed.
4. Supervisor must ensure that work is performed according to the desires of his superiors.
5. Supervisor must act as a good liaison officer between the management and workers.
6. Supervisor should take steps to be economical in operation.

**C. Responsibilities Towards His Own Functions**

1. Supervisor must properly plan his work which is assigned to him.
2. Supervisor must allocate the work to his subordinates according to their ability and willingness.
3. Supervisor must implement the policies and programmes of management.
4. Supervisor must procure the materials and tools and inspect them regularly.
5. Supervisor must acquaint himself with the latest production techniques and implement them in time.

6. Supervisor must organise the labour force.
7. Supervisor must supervise the work of his workers and give suggestions for further improvement.
8. Supervisor must take all initial steps to implement the plans and policies of the management.
9. Supervisor must take steps to improve the productivity of his subordinates.

**D. Responsibilities Towards His Colleagues**

1. Supervisor must extend his co-operation to his colleagues.
2. Supervisor must consider and accept the criticism of his plans, posed by his colleagues.
3. Supervisor must accept his transfer from one department to another department.
4. Supervisor must supply essential information to other departments, if required.

The responsibilities of the supervisor are changed from time to time. In the 19th Century, the personnel matters were handled by the supervisors. Now, personnel matters are looked after by the personnel department. Personnel matters are concerned with hiring, chiding, compensation, discipline, training, placement and promotion of employees. Recognition of the responsibility of the supervisor is justified by the effective utilisation of human efforts.

## QUALITIES OF SUPERVISOR

The foregoing discussion of responsibilities of the supervisor gives importance to his qualities. Besides, maximum production with minimum cost is the main consideration of the supervisor. So the supervisor must perform his work with honesty and devotion. The following points highlight the qualities of a supervisor:

**1. Technical knowledge:** The supervisor should have sufficient technical knowledge which is necessary to his post. Next, he should know how this technical knowledge is to be applied suitably to his work.

**2. Knowledge of the organisation:** The supervisor should know the principles of organisation to do his job properly. The supervisor should know the degree of delegation of authority that benefits the organisation, the number of members effectively supervised, functions that required specialisation etc.

**3. Ability to talk well:** A supervisor should know the art of talking. He must speak in simple words to be understood. He should convey accurately what he means. Changes in tone can effectively convey more ideas than many spoken words. The supervisor must use the words and language which are known to his subordinates.

**4. Administrative ability:** The supervisor should have the ability to administer. He should know the art of getting co-operation or co-ordination from his subordinates or workers.

**5. Ability to listen:** Listening is necessary to the supervisor. The reason is that the supervisor should receive information from his subordinates, share experiences with them and understand the problems faced by them. The subordinates should not have a feeling that the supervisor will turn a deaf ear to their words and be callous about their complaints.

**6. Honesty:** The supervisor should be a man of principle and honesty. The nature of his decisions and dealings should prove his honesty and integrity.

**7. Ability to memorise:** The supervisor should remember the orders received from his superiors and the orders communicated to his subordinates. The supervisor is not expected to remember all the information but he should remember all vital information.

**8. Understand and respect the feelings of others:** The supervisor's approach should be a gentle one. If there is any problem conveyed by his subordinates, he should understand the feelings and convey the problems to the top management for being solved, i.e., respect for feelings.

**9. Ability for orderly thinking:** The supervisor has to perform the functions of planning, organising, direction, co-ordination and control. So, he should know the orderly execution of work. Orderly execution of work is possible through orderly thinking.

**10. Complete information:** The supervisor should have complete information about his subordinates. Ability, qualification, interest, experience and willingness of each subordinate should be known to the supervisor.

**11. Ability to judge the people:** The supervisor should have the ability of fair assessment of workers. It helps the supervisor to secure the accomplishment of his tasks.

**12. Physical appearance:** The physical appearance of the supervisor should be commanding than his subordinates.

**13. Patience:** The supervisor should not lose his temper when mistakes are committed by his subordinates. The supervisor should correct the mistakes instead of punishing his subordinates. The supervisor should explain the consequences of the mistakes to his subordinates and he should not be angry with them.

**14.** A supervisor should be self-motivated, failing which so, he cannot motivate his subordinates effectively.

**15.** The supervisor should not express his frustration regarding his job, salary and working conditions in the presence of his subordinates. If he does so, his subordinates will also be frustrated.

**16.** The supervisor should have self-confidence and nourish the self-confidence of his subordinates.

## PRINCIPLES OF SUPERVISION

The principles of supervision are explained below:

1. The effective utilisation of supervision ensures the achieve-ment of the objectives of organisation.
2. Effective supervision is a function of the supervisor.
3. The definition of the role of the supervisor and the acceptance of the organisation are responsible for the efficiency of the supervisor.
4. Supervisor should analyse his group and decide which course of action helps to achieve the objectives of organisation. This facilitates effective supervision.
5. The success of any supervisor depends upon the effective fulfilling of group needs.
6. Group's survival and its progress towards its objectives are the parameters to judge the efficiency of the supervisor.

## TYPES OF SUPERVISION

The types of supervision are classified on the basis of ways adopted by the supervisor. In this way, supervision is classified as follows:

**1. Autocratic or authoritarian supervision:** Under this category, the supervisor has full power and full responsibility for group action. The supervisor does not have any consultation with his subordinates. but expects only obedience. Here, the supervisor repeatedly tells the subordinates what to do, how to do, etc. In otherwords, the supervisor may be said to be 'do-this, do-that' boss.

**2. Free-rein or independent supervision:** Here the supervisor does not interfere with his subordinate's performance. He wants to exercise minimum control. The supervisor is mainly looking after the procuring of raw materials, receiving information from the top management regarding rules and regulations and conveying them to his subordinates. The sub-ordinate's problems may be solved by the supervisor as a mediator.

**3. Democratic supervision:** It is based on democratic principles. The supervisor takes a decision only after receiving ideas and suggestions from his subordinates. The supervisor has free discussion and consultation with them. In other words, the supervisor has confidence and full control over his subordinates.

## KINDS OF SUPERVISORS

The kinds of supervisors are classified on the basis of the type of supervision followed by him. Prof. R.K. Burns has classified supervisors into the following categories:

**1. Bureaucratic regulative:** The supervisor has framed (or) followed the rules and regul-ations. The personal touch with subordinates is very rare. The supervisor avoids communication with superiors or subordinates to the possible extent.

**2. Autocratic — directive:** One way communication is followed by the supervisor. Who wants to get more power and responsibility. The supervisor has strict control over his subordinates and he is superior on the technical side of the job. He wants to get more work done and he does not consider the subordinate's attitudes. The supervisor exercises more authority on the subordinates. So, the subordinates extend little respect to the supervisor.

**3. Idiocratic — manipulative:** The supervisor has close contact with the top management and subordinates. He knows how to manage the subordinates. He cares about his security and advancement. Here, the subordinates have selfish mentality. The supervisor is of easy going type.

**4. Democratic — integrative:** The aim of this type of supervisor is to build a real work-team. The supervisor wants to get recognition, advancement and security for both his subordinates and himself. He follows the give-and-take policy with his subordinates. A sincere two way communication is followed by the supervisor. The supervisor is motivated by group interest.

## SUPERVISORY TECHNIQUES

Supervisory technique is a method or procedure to be adopted in the work of supervision. Supervisory technique is applied on the basis of attitude of the subordinates. Supervisory technique determines the type of supervision. Some of the supervisory techniques are discussed below:

**1. Consultative or democratic technique:** A supervisor takes decision regarding methods or procedures to be adopted only after consulting his subordinates. All the democratic principles are adopted under this technique. An opportunity is given to the subordinates to express their opinions. The supervisor develops a sense of confidence and recognises the subordinates.

**2. Authoritarian or dictatorial technique:** This technique is adopted by the management which has centralisation of authority. Hence the supervisor exercises more authority over his subordinates. Whatever the methods or procedures are fixed by the management, they should be strictly adhered to by the subordinates. This technique is not suitable to the modern business world but suitable where the labour is not properly organised.

**3. Non-interfering or fee-rein technique:** The subordinates are allowed to select methods or procedures available within the organisation. The supervisor gives importance to quality and quantity of the product. The supervisor acts as a consultant and helps the subordinates in solving their problems. Hidden talents are exposed by the subordinates under this technique.

## MODEL QUESTIONS

1. What are the functions of the supervisor?
2. Discuss the responsibilities of the supervisor towards his management and subordinates?
3. Explain the principles of supervision?

# CHAPTER 23

# COMMUNICATION

## INTRODUCTION

Communication is the passing of information. Communication is necessary for better performance of job. A manager works through the co-operation of others. Therefore, he should communicate the policies, plans, programmes of management to the workers. Communication ends only when it reaches the destination. Communication is also a part of the function of management.

The term 'Communication' is derived from the Latin word *'communis'* which means common. Thus, information common to a person should be communicated to him. Literally, communication means to inform, to tell, to show or to spread information. It creates confidence among human beings and enhances good industrial relations.

## MEANING

Communication is a process through which an information idea or opinion is transferred to more number of persons. If information is communicated to only one person, it will also be termed as communication. But, the essential element of communi-cation is that the communicated information should be understood correctly and transferred in the right direction.

## DEFINITION

According to Louis A. Allen, "Communication is the sum of all the things, one person does when he wants to create understanding in the mind of another. It involves a systematic and continuous process of telling, listening and understanding."

Charless E. Red Field, "Communication is the broad field of human interchange of facts and opinions and not the technologies of telephone, telegraph, radio and the like."

Newman and Summer, "Communication is an exchange of facts, ideas, opinions or emotions by two or more persons."

M.W. Cunning, "Communication is the process of conveying messages (facts, ideas, attitudes and opinion) from one person to another so that they are understood."

Keith Davis, "Communication is defined as the process of passing information and understanding from one person to another."

It is essentially a bridge of meaning between people. By using this bridge of meaning, a person can safely cross the river of misunderstanding that separates all people."

Theo Haimann, "Communication, fundamental and vital to all managerial action, is the process of imparting ideas and making oneself understood by others."

Billy J. Hedge, "Communication can be thought of as an attempt to achieve as complete and as accurate an understanding as possible between two or more people. It is an act characterised by a desire in one or more individuals to exchange information, ideas or feelings. This desire is implemented by using symbols, signs, actions and pictures as well an other verbal and non-verbal elements in speaking and writing."

William Scott, "Communication is a process which involves the transmission and accurate replication of ideas ensured by a feed back for the purposes of eliciting actions which will accomplish organisational goals."

D.K. Mc Farland, "Communication may be broadly defined as the process of meaningful interaction among human beings. More specifically, it is the process by which meanings are perceived and understanding is reached among human beings."

Fred G. Meyer, "The act of making one's ideas and opinions known to others."

Herbert A. Simon, "Communication may be formally defined as any process whereby decisional premises are transmitted from one member of an organisation to another."

Cyril I. Hudson, "Communication in its simplest form is conveying of information from one person to another."

Koontz and O'Donnell, "Communication is an intercourse by words, letters, symbols or messages and is a way that one organisation member shares meaning and understanding with another."

C.G. Brown, "Communication has been defined as the transfer of information from one person to another, whether or not it elicits confidence. But the information transferred must be understandable to the receiver."

## IMPORTANCE OF COMMUNICATION

The implementation of policies and programmes of management is possible only through effective communication. We can understand the importance of communication from the following:

**1. An aid to managerial performance:** A manager can take appropriate decisions with the help of communication. The problems may be solved without much difficulty by the manager. The manager can get things done by sub-ordinates through communication. He can impart the objectives of organisation to the subordinates through communication.

Thus, communication acts as a tool of management.

**2. Achieving co-ordination:** A large-scale business organisation employs a large number of workers. They are working on the basis of division of work and specialisation. There is a need for co-ordination among such workers to attain organisation goals. The co-ordination is obtained through communication. According to Mary Curling Nilen, "Good communi-cations are essential to co-ordination. They are necessary upward, downward and sideways, through all the levels of authority and advice for the transmission, interpretation and adoption of policies, for the sharing of knowledge and information and for the more subtle needs of good morale and mutual understanding".

**3. Helps in smooth working:** Communication helps the workers to know the real situation prevailing in an organisation. Subsequently, workers perform their duties without any delay, which leads to the smooth functioning of an organisation. According to G.R. Terry, "communication serves as the lubricant fostering for the smooth operations of the management".

**4. Increase managerial efficiency:** Out of the total time available to the manager, the manager nearly spends 80% of his time in transmitting the information to others regarding the business targets, rules, programmes, policies, etc. Communication helps the manager discharge his duties systematically and facilitates him to increase his efficiency.

**5. Helps in decision-making:** Good communication system provides all the necessary information, which enables the manager to take quality decisions in the proper time. Again, these decisions are communicated to those who are in need of them. According to Chester Barnard, "the first executive function is to develop and maintain a system of communication".

**6. Maintaining industrial peace:** The main reason for industrial unrest is lack of communication or improper communication. This creates a strained relationship between the management and the workers. Communication helps both management and workers to understand each other and facilitates industrial peace.

**7. Aid to leadership:** Management uses the communication as transmitter to forward its ideas, feelings, suggestions and decisions to the employees. In the same way, the employees express their responses, attitudes and problems through communication to the management. Under this two way communication, the management can assume itself as a leader of its employees.

**8. Aid to job satisfaction:** If the employees know what would be done and for what purpose, they can perform in a better way and efficiently. Employees know the expectations of the management. If their perform-ance is not upto the standard, they can improve it. Employees may wish to know how their performance is correlated with the achieve-ment of objectives. These are possible through effective commun-ciation. If effective communication exists, employees can get job satisfaction.

**9. Saving in time:** Effective communication results in the saving of time. A manager can communicate easily to all his subordinates by sitting in his room. There is no need for the manager to meet all the sub-ordinates personally.

In turn, the manager can get all the information from his sub-ordinates. This results in the savings of time and effort for both of them.

**10. Aid to public relation:** The term *public* includes customers, potential customers, shareholders, members of the public, state government, central government and the like. The management can create good image among the public through effective communication. In this way, the management can maintain better public relations.

## EFFECTS OF COMMUNICATION

The very purpose of communication is to bring in some changes in the attitude, behaviour and actions of the receiver. The efforts of the sender may produce the following effects:

**1. Successful communication:** Successful communication refers to the changes desired by the sender in the receiver's action, behaviour or attitude. It may be otherwise called as *effective communication.*

**2. No communication:** *'No communication'* means that the communication has not brought any changes in the behaviour, action, attitude of the receiver. Here the efforts of the sender are totally a waste.

**3. Miscommunication:** *'Miscommunication'* refers to the undesirable changes in the receiver's action, behaviour or attitude. The changes may be contrary to what the sender expected. Hence, the miscommunication may produce total waste and adverse effects.

Thus, successful communication brings desirable effects and no effects emanate from no communication. But, adverse effects may be produced by miscommunication.

## FEEDBACK

The management should assess the effects of communication. As stated above, the effects of communication may be assessed by observing the behaviour of the receiver. Sometimes, the facial expressions also give the indications. The observation of the effects of communication on the receiver is called *feedback*.

## OBJECTIVES OF COMMUNICATION

The following are the main objectives or purpose of communication:

**1. Communicating right information:** The information should be communicated to the concerned person. The receiver should understand the information correctly so that he may translate it into practice effectively.

**2. Co-ordination of efforts:** Co-ordination is one of the functions of management. Communication is an effective tool of co-ordination. Management cannot get co-ordination without proper communication.

**3. Development of managerial skill:** Communication helps the manager understand the behaviour of his subordinates. Manager may receive the information regarding the facts, ideas and opinions from his subordinates. So, the manager can know the happenings as and when they occur. This will develop managerial skill.

**4. Better industrial relationship:** The management can communicate the ideas or views to its employees and vice versa. Each one tries to understand the other's view. It may reduce misunderstanding and develop better industrial relations.

**5. Effectivness of policies:** Policies and programmes should be communicated to the persons who are responsible for their execution. These are necessary to achieve the objectives of the organisation. Effectiveness of policies depends upon effective communication.

The above discussed objectives of communication are necessary to ensure the success of the organisation.

## ELEMENTS OF COMMUNICATION

A communication which is transmitted from one person to another in any organisation has the following elements:

**1. Information:** The term *'information'* refers to the content of communication which is to be transmitted. The information is supplied to the staff and workers.

**2. Sender:** A person who is supposed to pass on the information is called *'sender'*. Normally, he may be the manager or the top executive.

**3. Receiver:** A person who is supposed to receive the information is called *'Receiver'*. Normally, the receiver may be the subordinate in the organisation.

**4. Communication channel:** Communication channel is the way through which the information is passed from the sender to the receiver. There are a number of communication channels available now a days.

**5. Symbols:** The sender can correctly transmit the information with the help of symbols. Symbols include spoken or written words, signs, play cards or even gestures. The sender cannot produce desired changes in the receiver without using symbols. Sometimes, written words are more effective than spoken words and vice versa. So, the sender may use the symbols according to the circumstances prevailing.

**6. Feedback:** There is a need for using a technique to know the effect of transmitting the information. In other words, the sender should know how far the receiver has understood the information in the right sense.

## BARRIERS TO COMMUNICATION (OR) PROBLEMS OF COMMUNICATION

There may be filtering or distortion of information while it is being communicated. If such a thing happens, the object of communication will not be achieved. The barriers to communication or problems of communication are given below:

**1. Noise:** There is a possibility of noise interruption while communicating information. The noise may be produced by the conversation of somebody-else nearly or by the machine operation and the like. In such circumstances, the communicator takes an extra effort to overcome the noise. The communicator must also use right vocabulary which is easily understood by the receiver.

**2. Missing information:** The communicator may miss some of the information. It may be caused due to giving undue emphasis to a few pieces of information. Sometimes, the communicator may fail to supply the required information if he communicates the information in a hurried manner.

**3. Alteration of information:** The information is altered if the communicator sends the information through a third party. The third party may twist or alter the information according to his convenience. It may be done intentionally or unintentionally. Normally, this is possible in the case of upward communication. The reason is that the third party wants to earn a good name from his superiors.

**4. Overloading:** This barrier arises due to an increase in the number of messages to be sent. There is a need for the introduction of communication channel to reduce workload. If it is not done, the messages do not reach the correct persons or places in time. So, the manager should make a special arrangement to send the urgent and important messages.

**5. Lack of facility:** Sometimes, meetings and conferences are necessary to impart the information to the employees or else the communication will not be an effective one. If the management does not have any facility to conduct meetings and conferences, there will be no possibility of conveying the information to employees correctly.

**6. Inadequate policies, rules and procedures:** The management should adopt the communication policy which is adequate to meet all the present and future requirements of the organisation. The communication policy should be a flexible one. This is necessary to meet any contingency. The rule of *'through proper channel'* may be relaxed if important messages are to be passed during emergency periods. If it is not done so, the information cannot be passed in time. It means that there is a delay of communication.

**7. Status patterns:** Problems may arise due to the status prevailing between the superiors and subordinates. Superiors have executive chair and table, phone connection and a separate room to indicate then status. But the subordinates have only chairs and tables. This differential treatment widens the communication gap between the superior and subordinates. The trend has however, changed, following the emergence of a strategic global communication network.

**8. Lack of attention:** The receiver does not pay any attention in grasping the information. This attitude of the receiver may be caused by the receiver's immersion in his own thoughts, his difficulty in understanding the idioms and phrases or his having no belief in the information. Sometimes, the receiver may think that the information is not worth paying attention to.

**9. Quick conclusion:** The receiver comes to a conclusion without giving due weightage to the information. Besides, he has his own opinion and belief. So, the quick conclusion may not be a correct one.

**10. Lack of confidence over the communicator:** The receiver may feel that the communicator is not able to effectively extend the information. Then, the receiver does not believe the information which he gets. This may defeat the very purpose of the communication ultimately.

**11. Improper state of mind:** At times, the receiver may not be in a sound state of mind to receive the information accurately. If he is mentally upset, it will definitely affect the free flow of information.

**12. Lack of time:** The opportunity to communicate is limited because of the lack of time the communicator has at his disposal.

**13. Badly expressed messages:** If there is no coherence of information and no clarity of information, then the receiver will not be in a position to understand the information correctly.

**14. Technical language:** There are large number of special languages as computer, system analysis, operation research and the like. Different types of vocabulary are used to communicate the message. A single word may have different meanings.

**15. Poor retention:** Generally, the employees retain only 50% of the information which they receive, so poor retention is also one of the barriers of communication.

## METHODS OF OVERCOMING THE BARRIERS

There is no possibility of eliminating the above discussed barriers altogether. But some managerial actions may minimise the effect of barriers to some extent. So the management should take necessary steps to overcome the barriers. They are explained below:

1. The management should clearly define its policy to the employees. It should encourage the free flow of information. Then, the employees at all levels of management can realise the full significance of communication.
2. The management sets up a system through which only essential information could be supplied. Besides, these are supplied in a prescribed manner.
3. All the information should be supplied through a proper channel. But, it should not be insisted upon always. The reason is that in the case of emergency, proper channel process may cause a delay in the supply of information. Proper channel system can be insisted on only for routine information.
4. Every person in the management shares the responsibility of good communication. Top management people should check from time to time whether there is any barrier or not in the free flow of information. It can be achieved only if there is strong support from the top management.
5. Adequate facilities should be provided by the management. In other words, the available communication facilities should be properly utilised.
6. Communication is an inter-personal process. Each person has confidence in another person. There should be mutual understanding. In large organisations, the disparity status pattern may be reduced through forming good frendship between the superior and the sub-ordinates.

7. The communication should be in a known language for both the receiver and the communicator. Ambiguous words should be avoided while supplying the information.

## CHARACTERISTICS OF EFFECTIVE COMMUNICATION

The effective communication has the following characteristics.

**1. Complete communication:** There are two persons necessary for complete communication *i.e.,* a sender and the receiver. Besides, the receiver should understand the message. For example, if a person shouts in a locked room without anybody present, at the top of his voice, he will communicate nothing. Here there is no complete communication.

**2. Understanding in the same sense:** The receiver should understand the message in the same sense i.e., in right direction. If he does not understand it, there will be no effective communication. For example, if a message is written in uncommon words, the receiver will not be able to understand it correctly.

**3. Message to have substance:** The receiver can take ideas, information or facts out of the message. It means, only related information is communicated to the concerned persons. If it is not done, the receiver will not evince any interest in receiving the message.

**4. Communication may be oral, written or a gestural:** Information may be communicated orally, in writing or through gestures. These three modes of communication have equal importance, so, the apt mode should be selected for effective communication. Rolling of eyes and movement of lips are some of the gestures used by the sender.

**5. Communication may be formal or informal:** An information passed through proper channel is referred to as formal communication. For example, a manager informs the matter to the supervisor and in turn, the supervisor communicates the same message to the subordinates and vice versa.

If the messages are not passed through proper channels, they will be referred to as informal communication. These pieces of information are passed through personal contact. The sender communicates the information to other members of the organisation whenever he meets them.

**6. Vital to managerial function:** Communication is not only necessary to the planning function of management but also necessary to organising, staffing, directing, controlling and decision-making. So, communication is vital to all the functions of management.

**7. Continuous process:** Communication is a regular process just like blood circulation in our body. Communication fulfils its purpose when the receiver understands the message. No organisation, business or management survives without communication.

**8. Mutual understanding:** Management can achieve its objectives with the help of group efforts. Group efforts are obtained through mutual understanding. Only communication facilitates mutual understanding.

## PROCESS OF COMMUNICATION

There are two persons necessary irrespective of the mode of communication. They are the sender and the receiver. The sender may be called as *resource* person. A communication process comes to an end only when the receiver understands the message as the sender communicates.

The following is the process of effective or proper communication:

**1. Ideation:** The sender can create an idea to communicate. In simple words, a sender decides what is to be communicated and how? This is the content of communication.

**2. Encoding:** The sender can decide the series of symbols which are necessary to communicate the information. Besides, the symbols facilitate the understanding of the receiver. Encoding includes the selection of the methods of communication. Different words are used in different methods of communication to extend the same information. Some methods to initiate a conversation or action are showing a green signal to start a train etc.

**3. Transmission:** Transmission confirms the channel of communication. The term channel of communication includes a letter, telegram, telephone and the like. A lengthy information cannot be transmitted through a telegram. As such, confidential matters and important matters are not to be transmitted by telephone. When confidential matters are sent, it is better to use an envelope marked 'Confidential' or 'Personal matter' etc. The selected channel should be free from any barrier to communication.

**4. Receiving:** Receiving the message is the fourth step in the process of communication. The receiver should pay great attention in this regard. The reason is that all the relevant information should be received and all unnecessary information neglected. Mere listening is not enough. The receiver should understand the entire information.

**5. Decoding:** Decoding means translation of symbols encoded by the sender into the message for understanding. The receiver may misunderstand the message. The reason is that the perception of the sender may be different from the perception of the receiver. The communication will be an effective one, if the receiver understands the message correctly.

**6. Action:** The receiver has the responsibility to see that the received message reaches its destination. The receiver may ignore the message he receives. There is a need for action to complete the process of communication. Sometimes, the message may be a direction to *'stop the work'*. It means that there should be some reaction on the part of the receiver.

## PRINCIPLES OF EFFECTIVE COMMUNICATION

The communicator or the sender should observe the following principles for effective communication in all types of communication.

**1. Language:** The sender must use simple language and the language should be known to the receiver. Simple language means using 'familiar words' while transmitting the information.

**2. Clarity:** The message should be transmitted in clear words. There should be unambiguous language. The sender should give the meaning of words instead of making the words speak for themselves.

**3. Purpose of communication:** The basic purpose of any communication is to elicit a behaviourial response from the receiver. The next stage is that the order should be accepted by the subordinate. So, the sender or communicator must make efforts to achieve the objective of this response.

**4. Physical and human setting:** Physical setting refers to the person to whom the message is communicated. The receiving person may be an individual, concerned department personnel or organisation as a whole. Human setting refers to the circumstances under which the message is communi-cated. So, the communicator or the sender should bear in mind the circumstances and the receiving persons while communicating the message.

**5. Consultation:** It is necessary to seek the participation of others in planning a communication. It helps the sender to get additional insight into and objectivity of the message. Moreover, those who participate and help communication planning will give active support to you.

**6. Content of message:** The communicator should decide his tone of voice with reference to the content of the message. Sometimes, the communicator may make his voice loud or shrill in order to make the communication effective.

**7. Follow-up action:** Follow-up action is necessary to find out whether the receiver has understood the message correctly. The receiver may take some action after receiving the message. The sender should know the type of action taken by the receiver.

**8. Time and opportunity:** The sender should consider the interest and needs of the receiver of message. It helps him to find out the correct time when the message is to be communicated. In this way, the sender uses the opportunity to convey the message for enduring and immediate benefits to the receiver.

**9. Training to the communicators:** Proper training is essential to the communicators to develop their communication skills. This helps in increasing the effectiveness of communication considerably.

**10. Action support communication:** The actions or attitudes of the sender should support the message. For example, the sender may raise his hand to convey the message of *'stop the work'*. So, the actions of the sender should not contradict his words or message.

**11. Personnel co-operation:** Co-operation of the personnel is necessary to make effective communication. The communication results in strengthening the business concern through the co-operation of managerial personnel.

**12. Listening:** Listening is one of the most important tasks of the sender. Here, listening refers to the reactions of the receiver. The sender must learn to listen with the inner ear. The sender can gather useful information through listening for further communication. So, the sender should stop talking, because without stopping the talking, one cannot listen.

## FACTORS DECIDING THE COMMUNICATION PROGRAMME

The top management has responsibility to implement a communication programme in an organisation. The manager should select a communication programme. The following factors will influence while selecting a communication programme:

**1. Cost:** The cost of a communication programme is considered initially. The cost should be within the limits of the financial burden of the company. Besides, the utility of a communication programme should be more than the expenses or the cost incurred on it.

**2. Secrecy:** Whatever the information is, it should not be leaked out. Communication programme should ensure secrecy. The absence of secrecy in a communication programme is equal to a pot with a hole. Nobody can fill this pot with water.

**3. Accuracy:** The communication programme is arranged in such a way that there is no scope for miscommunication. The success of communi-cation depends upon the accuracy.

**4. Speed:** The message should arrive in time to the needy persons. If it does not arrive in time, it may go waste. Now, public use the *'speed post'* and *'courier service'* for speedy communication.

**5. Convenience:** The proposed communication programme should be conve- nient to those who handle it. If there is any cumbersome feature in a communication programme, information will not be available to needy persons.

**6. Suitability:** No single programme can be suitable for all enterprises or for all times in the same enterprise. So, the communication programme should be capable of adjusting to the needs of the enterprise and the existing situation.

**7. Proper recording:** All communication should be properly recorded. It is a must. The same communication may be required in future for reference or to take a strategic decision.

**8. Expressive:** The receiver of the communication should get a good impression of the communication programme. If it is so, there may be desirable changes in receiver's actions. The sender may get satisfaction out of the communication. The communication process will thus serve its purpose.

## MEDIA OF COMMUNICATION

Passing of information is a routine matter in an organisation. There may be an upward or downward communication. The downward communication channel is used by the top management. The upward communication channel is used by the workers or the lower level management. The following are some of the media of communication:

**1. Bulletin:** Information regarding promotion, posting and transfers are published in the bulletin. This media is also adopted by the government. Initially, the information is communicated to concerned persons. Then, it is made known to the public in general. All the employees are informed of the recent changes in administrative level in this way. This is a very essential one. Each employee can know with whom he will have dealings thereafter.

**2. Annoucements:** There are a number of decisions taken in board meetings or department managers' meetings. These decisions are communicated to workers through an announcement. This will induce workers to work well. This announcement is made in addition to circulars.

**3. Meetings:** Personal communication has more effect than that of other media of communication. Management can arrange a meeting for a specified section of workers, and the workers can put forward their views and resentments. If the management arranges general meetings with target audience of workers, cordial relationship can be maintained with workers. This will ensure smooth running of the enterprise.

**4. Suggestion/grievance boxes:** Often employees are hesitating to express their ideas directly to the management people. This can be avoided with the help of suggestion/grievance boxes. Sanctions and suitable ideas will be available to the management. Management can award the employee who gives the best idea. It is one way communication *i.e.,* upward communication. The irregularities of fellow workers and supervisors will also be obtained and made known to the management. Suitable action may be taken by the management in this regard.

Whenever a grievance is placed before the management, necessary steps should be take to redress the grievance. The real working environment is known to the management.

**5. Company publications:** A company may publish a magazine. The magazine contains the information pertaining to the working results and benefit scheme of workers. Each worker desires to know the working results of the company. The publication of various benefit schemes of workers will arrest the prevailing rumours among the workers. The morale of the workers may be strengthened through the company publications.

## TYPES OF COMMUNICATION

Types of communication can be classified on the following basis:

### *I. ON THE BASIS OF ORGANISATIONAL RELATIONSHIP*

**1. Formal communication:** The communication flows through the formal channel. Formal channel refers to the way in which the information is passed and it has a recognised position in the organisation structure. Sometimes, it may be termed as 'through proper channel'. Through proper channel is an attempt to regulate the flow of communication and to ensure smooth, accurate and timely passing of information. Thus, formal communication facilitates effective functioning of an organisation.

**Advantages of Formal Communication**

1. The authority and respect of senior staff members are protected through formal communication. Nobody is allowed to by-pass anybody while communicating information.
2. An organisation can fix the responsibility easily.
3. The information is available to the right person.
4. The formal communication helps the boss and the sub-ordinates to understand each other's attitude and behaviour well.
5. Good morale and discipline are maintained among the employees.

**Disadvantages of Formal Communication**

1. There is a possibility of filtering of information in formal communication.
2. Future is uncertain. So action-based information cannot be formalised.
3. Formal communication increases the work load of the line officers. The reason is that the line officer has to take action on all the downward and upward communications are passed through him.When he has many little time to perform his executive functions effectively.
4. An information is passed through a number of persons to arrive at a right person. It entails to delay in communicating the information. Besides, an information may be miscommunicated.
5. There is no close contact between top executives and lower level workers. So, the intention and attitude of the top executive are not known to the lower level workers and vice versa. Hence, there is an absence of cordial relationship between them.

**2. Informal communication:** An information is passed not in accordance with any formalities and rules and regulations of an organisation. Most executives use the informal communication as a supplement to formal communication. Most of the informal communication is oral. Often, informal communication proves very effective.

The formal communication is the result of the natural desire of the people to communicate with each other. Information, under this system, may be passed by a simple glance, gesture, smile or mere silence too. Personal matters are also discussed and passed under informal communication. It is also known as 'Grapevine'.

## Grapevine

Grapevine is the primary source of upward communication. Under the grapevine system of communication, there is no clear cut way for transmitting the information. They (information) may pass it as they like. The term information includes the workings and feelings of employees in a particular situation and what they think about the management.

Generally, grapevine operates like a cluster chain.

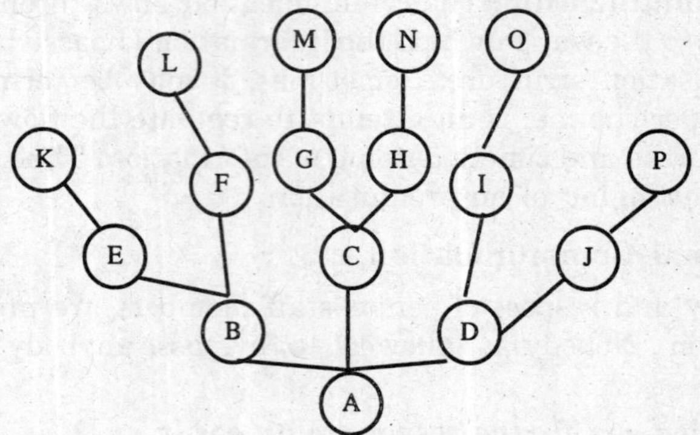


CLUSTER CHAIN

For example, A tells something to three of his well-known persons. In turn, they (three persons) tell something to two of their (three persons) known persons. Then, they (two persons) tell something to only one of their (two persons) known persons. The receiving persons are gradually reduced in number. The reason is that the information becomes stale and those who know it do not retransmit it. It should be remembered that only a few persons are very active in the grapevine system of communication. These active communicators are called 'Liaison agents'.

## Advantages of Informal Communication

1. The information is passed very quickly.
2. There is a social sanction for informal communication. Information is transmitted without any difficulty. Both the sender and the receiver exchange their information freely.
3. There is no channel of command. A senior staff of one department may transmit the information to a lower level staff of another department. It promotes sound co-operation among the employees.
4. Informal communication may go to any extent. It means there is no limit for passing information under the informal communication system.

## Disadvantages of Informal Communication

1. It is not in order.
2. Informal communication carries inaccurate information very often. So it is of no use.
3. Sometimes, it may create a lot of confusion or mis-understanding among the employees.

4. It is very difficult to fix the responsibility under the informal communication system. The reason is that it is hard to pinpoint the person who first communicates the information.
5. If the information reaches the chief executive, it may be completely distorted.

Both the systems exist in all organisations together. Some prefer formal communication and others informal communication.

### *II. ON THE BASIS OF DIRECTION OF FLOW OF COMMUNICATION*

The following types of communications are classified on the basis of the direction of their flow. They are discussed below:

**1. Downward Communication:** A communication which starts from the top level executive and ends with the lower functionaries through middle management is known as *downward* communication. While communicating the information, scalar chain is followed. The adoption of the scalar chain ensures proper communication.

#### Objectives of Downward Communication

The major objectives of downward communication are listed below:

1. To provide job instructions specifically.
2. To supply the information regarding the rules and regulations and organisational procedures.
3. To give information regarding the relationship of one job with another job and the importance of each job.
4. To give information regarding the job preference of the subordinates.
5. To provide the information which facilitates the achievement of goals.

#### Advantages of Downward Communication

1. This system of communication helps in explaining organisation rules and regulations to the new staff members and third parties.
2. It helps to exercise control over subordinates.
3. It helps to motivate and extract maximum work from the subordinates.

#### Disadvantages of Downward Communication

1. The information passed is interpreted and re-interpreted at every level of management people.
2. The information passed may be distorted.

**2. Upward Communication:** Upward communication is just the reverse of downward communication. Passing of an information which starts with the lowest level i.e. subordinates and ends with the chief-executive is known as *upward* communication. The information should be passed through the middle level executive.

There are two types of upward communication. First, there is a feedback of information, in response to original communication. An executive can understand the subordinates' feelings about their jobs and working environment. Besides, he can know the extent of performance of work done by adopting the orders and instructions issued. Secondly, the information is given by the subordinates voluntarily. This voluntary information may be relating to complaints, new ideas, different opinions, suggestions of subordinates, etc. The real picture of the functioning of the organisation is known to the top executives through upward communication.

**Advantages of Upward Communication**

1. The grievances of the subordinates may be redresed at an early date.
2. Upward communication helps the management to take decisions promptly.

**Disadvantages of Upward Communication**

1. Superiors may ignore the information given by the sub-ordinates.
2. The information may be distorted.
3. Sometimes, top executive are unwilling to listen to the grievances and redressing them.

**3. Horizontal Communication:** Horizontal communication refers to the passing of information among the executives who are at equal level in an organisation. It is otherwise called as *lateral* communication. Both the receiver and the sender may be in the same department or different departments. The very purpose of horizontal communication is to co-ordinate the activities of various departments or persons.

**Advantages of Horizontal Communication**

1. Horizontal communication helps the management to co-ordinate the activities of different departments.
2. It avoids duplication of work. It ultimately leads to reducing wastage of time, money, material and labour.

**Disadvantages of Horizontal Communication**

1. There is a possibility of arising difference of opinions among the executives. The reason is that each person has a different approach. It may have an impact on productivity and efficiency of the organisation.
2. The receiver does not give due importance to the message.
3. The sender does not have any control over the receiver of information.

4. Diagonal Communication: Diagonal communication is between two or more persons who are neither in the same section nor on the same level of organizational structure. Generally, it comes into operation when other systems of communication fail to convey the information effectively. For example, the auditor has responsibility to check and verify the cash balance at the end of the accounting year, so, the auditor may be authorised to get information from the cashier directly. It is diagonal communication. The cashier need not send the information to the auditor. This communication system violates the principle of unity of command.

## *III. ON THE BASIS OF WAY OF EXPRESSION*

These types of communication are classified on the basis of the way of expression. They are discussed below:

**1. Oral Communication**

It is otherwise called verbal communication. Oral communi-cation is used when the contents of the communication are little. Generally, in the case of emergency, oral communication is adopted. The reason is that there is no time available to print or type the information. The real meaning is conveyed to the receivers by manner or tone of the voice. Sometimes, the sender can communicate the information effectively through facial expressions and attitudes. The receiver's understanding is coloured by their (senders) emotions and attitudes.

**Forms of Oral or Verbal Communication**

1. Face to face orders, instructions, responses, informations and observations.
2. Talks on telephone or on intercom.
3. Lectures.
4. Conferences.
5. Meetings.
6. Interviews.
7. Group meetings of workers and management people or executives.
8. Television and news magazine through cinema.
9. Radio.
10. Message through tape-recorder (It is normally followed in big sized business units).
11. Calling.
12. Whistling.

These are some of the forms of oral communication.

**Advantages of Oral Communication**

The following are the main advantages of oral communication:

**1. Economical:** Oral communication is very cheap. The reason is that the oral communication saves time, labour and stationery.

**2. Personal touch:** Oral communication eliminates intermediaries. The information is passed from one person to another person personally. They can discuss the matter in a relaxed manner.

**3. Effective:** In case of oral communication, the receiver not only listens to the words but also observes the reactions of the sender in his face, eyes and hands, out of which, the receiver can fully understand the information. The physical movements of the sender ensures effective communication.

**4. Better understanding:** Whenever a doubt is raised in the mind of the receiver, he can clear his doubt by getting more clarifications. The sender himself can assess the understanding of the receiver. The sender may give maximum information for better understanding.

**5. Immediate motivation:** If the chief executive has close touch with his subordinates, he can motivate them easily. Oral communication enahances the personal touch of the chief executive with his subordinates. So, there is a possibility of immediate motivation.

**6. Flexibility:** Oral communication provides for greater flexibility, The sender is always free to change his comments. As there is no printed record for oral communication, the entire information may be altered without any difficulty.

**7. Spending the information:** During emergencies, no other communication is as useful in speeding up information as oral communication. For example, if fire breaks out in the business premises, oral communication alone will speed up the information and can rescue the employees without delay and injury.

**Disadvantages of Oral Communication**

Oral communication has some disadvantages also. They are listed below:

**1. Physical distance:** It will be very difficult to adopt oral communication if both the sender and the receiver are located in far off places. Even though telephone is used to transmit the information, it does not hold good.

**2. No evidence:** In oral communication, the words used by the sender may motivate others to do something. If the act goes wrong, the person who motivates, is not held liable. The reason is that there is no evidence for motivation. The affected party may be the receiver of information. In future, nobody could be motivated without written communication.

**3. Lengthy information:** If the message is very long, it cannot easily be transmitted through oral communication. Much time is required to convey the information. Top executives are not ready or are unable to spend more time for conveying the information to others.

**4. Creates unnecessary problems:** Oral directions may be understood by the receiver at the time of communication and he may forget it thereafter. Then, the receiver acts according to his willingness. It creates unnecessary problems in an organisation. They arise due to the absence of record.

**5. Not useful to large number of receivers:** Some information is transmitted to a large number of persons. The oral communication may not produce the desired results. Then it is better to use written communication.

**6. Filtering the received information:** The receiver may omit the received information. If the receiver is out of mood, he cannot fully receive the information. It cannot be assessed by the sender. In that case, the entire information may not be communicated.

**7. Misunderstanding:** The sender should use the terms which are generally in practice. If he does not do so, the receiver may take the words to mean different than the original. Besides, the poor verbal (or) oral expression of the sender may lead to misunderstanding. So, it is advised that ambiguous words should be avoided and the best oral expression be used for proper understanding.

**2. Written Communication**

This type of communication is followed to transmit any information. Written communication is an essential one, not only to a small organisation but also to a large organisation. The communication which is recorded in black and white, is called *written* communication. Written communication is followed whenever the information is passed to a far off place. Written communication blinds both the supervisors and the sub-ordinates.

**Forms of Written Communication**

The following are the forms of written communication:

1. Graphs.
2. Diagrams.
3. Pictures.

4. Circulars.
5. Notes.
6. Manuals.
7. Reports.
8. Bulletin.

**Advantages of Written Communication**

The main advantages of written communication are discussed below:

**1. Binding the authorities:** Generally, the written communication binds the sender and the receiver. Nobody escapes from the responsibilities.

**2. Covering distance:** If the proposed receiver of the communication is far away from the sender, the sender is, indirectly compelled to use written communication. So, the written communication can reach any place.

**3. Useful for lengthy information:** Maximum information may be passed through written communication.

**4. Reaches large number of persons:** A circular, a form of written communication, brings the infor-mation to numerous persons.

**5. Permanent record for future reference:** Written communication contains policy matters, rules and regulations, secret matters, service conditions, orders, instructions and the like. These are necessary for future reference. In this way, written communication helps the authority to take timely decisions and action.

**6. Reduce dispute:** Written communication avoids or reduces disputes among the employees. The reason is that each person has his own copy of information and he uses it whenever needed.

**7. Helps to analyse the matter:** The receiver can analyse the matter after receiving the information. Written communication gives time to the receiver to think, to analyse and to decide the future course of action.

**8. Avoiding alteration:** Unauthorised alterations are avoided through the use of written communication. Every alteration should be attested by the issuing authority. Generally, altering the information is not allowed in an organisation.

**Disadvantages of Written Communication**

Even though the written communication is the best type of communication, it suffers from the following weaknesses:

**1. Costly and time consuming:** Time should be spent for preparing the draft of information and printing or typing the information. All this work requires more than one staff member and it involves maximum paper work. It results in high cost of conveying the information and much time.

**2. Red-tapsim:** It is not flexible and results in red-tapism.

**3. No secrecy:** In written communication, no secrecy is maintained. The reason is that everything is put in black and white. Besides, written communication is passed through the typist. Thus, the message does not remain a secret, at all.

**4. No flexibility:** Written communication lacks personal touch. Once the information is transmitted, it cannot be withdrawn easily.

Even though the written communication has some limitations, it is the best one. The secrecy may be maintained by the superior, if he types the matter himself.

## MODEL QUESTIONS

1. State and explain the barriers of communication.
2. What are the important media of communication?
3. Explain the different barriers to communication.
4. What is horizontal communication?
5. What is meant by communication? How can communication be made more effective?
6. Enumerate the importance of communication in management. Describe the types of communication on the basis of organisational structure?
7. What is 'grapevine' communication system?
8. What are the barriers of communciation?

   What steps can be taken to overcome the barriers?

# CHAPTER 24

# CONTROLLING

## INTRODUCTION

Control is the last function of management. The controlling function will be unnecessary to the management if other functions of management are performed properly. If there is any imperfection in the planning and actual performance, control will be needed. The deviations are set right by the controlling function. This function ensures desired results. Planning identifies the activities and controlling regulates the activities. Success or failure of planning depends upon the result of success or failure of controlling.

## DEFINITION

Earnest Dale, "control envisages a system that not only provides a historical record of what has happened to the business as a whole but, pinpoints the reasons why it has happened and provides data that enables the chief executive on the departmental head to take corrective steps if he finds he is on the wrong track."

E.F.L. Brech, "Control — checking current performance against pre-determined standards contained in the plans, with a view to ensure adequate progress and satisfactory performance, also recording the experience gained from the working of these plans as a guide to possible operations."

Billy E. Goetz, "Management control seeks to compel events to conform to plans."

Knootz and O'Donnel, "Controlling is the measurement of accomplishment against the standards and the correction of deviations to assure attainment of objectives according to plans."

Henry Fayol, "Control consists in verifying whether everything occurs in conformity, is with the plans adopted, the instructions issued and principles established. It has for its object to point out weaknesses and errors in order to rectify them and prevent recurrence."

George R. Terry, "Controlling is determining what is being accomplished, that is, evaluating the performance and if necessary, applying corrective measures so that the performance takes place according to plans."

Robert N. Anthony, "Management control is the process by which managers assure that resources are obtained and used effectively and efficiently in the accomplishment of an organisation's objectives."

Mary Cushing Niles, "Control thus viewed, is an aspect and projection of planning whereas planning sets the course to the chosen courses or to an appropriately changed one."

Haynes and Massie, "Control is any process that guides activity towards some pre-determined goal. The essence of the concept is in determining whether the activity is achieving the desired results."

J.K. Rosen, "Control is that function of the system which provides direction in performance to the plans."

Dalton E. Mc Farland, "The presence in a business of that force which guides it to a pre-determined objective by means of pre-determined policies and decisions."

## AREAS OR SCOPE OF CONTROL

The term *control* covers all the activities of a business concern. The main areas of control are as follows:

1. Control over the policies of the concern.
2. Control over organisation.
3. Control over the personnel employed in an organisation.
4. Control over capital available to the concern.
5. Control over capital expenditure.
6. Control over production.
7. Control over wages and salaries paid to the employees.
8. Control over the cost of production.
9. Control over public relations.
10. Control over research and development.
11. Control over tools and equipments.
12. Overall control.

## STEPS IN CONTROL PROCESS

Control points out the deviations of the plans and suggests remedial action to improve future plans. Some of the procedures are to be found defective because of human limitations. So, control is necessary and it has the following steps:

**1. Establishing standards:** It is necessary to find the results which are desired. It is very useful to setting the standards. If it is not, useful control will not be possible. Standards may be quantitative or qualitative. Most of the standards are expressed in terms of quantity. Number of units produced, number of men, hours employed, total cost incurred, revenue earned, the amount of investments etc., are some of the examples of quantitative standard. If expression of standards in quantitative terms is not possible, they will be expressed in qualitative terms such as goodwill, employee's morale, motivation, etc.

The standards should have some characteristics to produce effective performance. The characteristics may be time, cost, efforts, result oriented, quantitative terms expressed, accurate, periodical revision and the like.

**2. Measuring performance:** The performance should be compared with the established standards. So, necessary information should be collected about the performance. The effective management information system provides the necessary information *i.e.,* performance particulars. If standards are expressed in quantitative terms, quantitative information can be collected. In other words, if standards are expressed in qualitative terms, qualitative informations can be collected. Several techniques are used by the management to measure the performance.

**3. Comparison of actual with standards:** Whenever the actual performance is compared with standards, the deviations are known to the management. Then, the management may find the extent of deviations and identify the reasons for deviations. Comparison is very easy when standards are expressed in terms of quantity. If results are intangible or qualitative, personal observation will be used to find out the extent of deviation.

When the actual performances are equal to the standards, there is no need for further action. Control process comes to an end with this stage. However, if the standards are not achieved, the management has to decide the type of corrective action.

All the deviations need not be reported to the management. Deviations which are beyond the reasonable limits should be reported to the top management. This is termed as control by exception or management by exception. Then, the reasons and causes for the deviations are analysed. The causes may be controllable or non-controllable. The management has to take necessary corrective action only in case the causes are controllable. However, no need will arise to the management to take corrective actions if the causes are uncontrollable.

**4. Taking corrective action:** Management has to find out the causes of deviation before taking corrective action. The causes of deviation may be due to ineffective and inadequate communication, defective system of wage payment, defective system of selection of personnel, lack of proper training, lack of motivation, ineffective supervisions and the like. The management has to take necessary corrective action on the basis of nature of causes of deviations.

## REQUIREMENTS OF EFFECTIVE CONTROL SYSTEM

There are certain requirements of effective control system. They are briefly explained below:

**1. Feedback:** *Feedback* is the process of adjusting future actions based upon the information regarding past performance. If feedback practice is followed by the management, the control process will be very easy.

**2. Objective:** Control should be objective. It means there is a certainty of control. The impartial appraisal of performance is necessary for certainty of control.

**3. Suitability:** The control system should conform to the nature of deviations. The control technique may be used, if there is any need.

**4. Prompt reporting:** The deviations from standards should be informed without any delay. If there is any delay caused, exercising control will be of no use.

**5. Forward looking:** Effective control system must focus how the future actions will conform to plans. In other words, the control system should provide an aid in planning.

**6. Pointing out exceptions:** The control system points out the deviations. But, all the deviations do not have equal impact. If the deviations have high impact, the control system should pay direct attention to them. Then, the management can take corrective actions.

**7. Flexible:** The standards or criteria should be altered from time to time. The reason is that the standards should conform to the present requirements. Hence, the control system should be flexible in accordance with the changed standards or criteria.

**8. Economy:** The benefits derived from the control system should be more than the cost of exercising such a control system.

**9. Intelligble:** The control system should not be a complicated one. The control system should be easily understood by an ordinary layman of the organisation.

**10. Suggest remedial action:** The effective control system should disclose the places of failure, persons for failure and how they have been dealt with.

**11. Motivation:** A good control system should be employee centred. The control is designed to secure positive reactions from employees. If large deviations are found, the employees will be properly directed and guided instead of being punished. The very purpose of control is prevention and not punishing.

## TECHNIQUES OF CONTROL

Various methods are used by the management for controlling the various deviations in the organisation. Let us study them briefly. The nature and use of managerial control techniques are discussed below.

**1. Statistical control reports:** These type of reports are prepared and used in large organisations. Reports are prepared in quantitative terms. Then, the variations from standards are easily measured. In this way, control is exercised by the management. A periodical report of sales volume is an example of statistical control reports.

**2. Personal observation:** Using this technique, the manager personally observes the operations in the work place. The manager corrects the operations whenever the need arises. This is the oldest method of control. Employees work cautiously to get better performance. The reason is that they are personally observed by their supervisor. Personal observation is a time-consuming technique and the supervisor does not have enough time to afford personal observation. Personal observation technique is disliked by the honest and efficient employee. The observer may be biased in performance evaluation.

**3. Cost accounting and cost control:** Profit of any business depends upon the cost incurred to run a business. Profit is maximised by reducing the cost of operation or production, so, the business concern gives much importance to the cost accounting and cost control. Management uses a number of systems for determining the cost of products and services. The cost accounting procedures and methods differ from one industry to another according to the nature of industry. They are used for effective cost control and cost reduction.

**4. Break-even analysis:** It is otherwise called as *'cost volume profit analysis.'* It analyses relationship among cost of production, volume of production, volume of sales and profits. Here, total costs are divided into two *i.e.,* fixed cost and variable cost. Fixed cost will never change according to the changes in the volume of production. Variable cost varies according to the volume of production. This analysis helps in determining the volume of production or sales and the total cost which is equal to the revenue. The excess of revenue over total cost is termed as *profit.* The point at which sales is equal to the total cost is known as *'Break Even Point'* (BEP). In other words, the break-even point is the point at which there is no profit or loss.

The break-even point is calculated with the help of the following formulae:

$$\text{BEP} = \frac{\text{Fixed cost}}{\text{Selling price per unit} - \text{variable cost per unit}}$$

(or)

$$\text{BEP} = \frac{\text{Fixed cost}}{\text{Contribution per unit}}$$

Contribution per unit = Selling price per unit – variable cost per unit

The break-even point analysis helps in managerial control in several ways.

**5. Special control reports:** This report may or may not contain statistical data. Using this technique, a particular operation is investigated at a specified time for a particular purpose. This is done according to the requirements of management but not in regular basis.

The deviations from standards are paid additional attention and corrective action is taken. Handling complaints of damage is an example of this type of control technique.

**6. Management audit:** Management audit is an independent process. It aims at pointing out the inefficiency in the performance of management functions such as planning, organising, staffing, directing, controlling and suggesting possible improvements. It helps the management to handle the operations in an effective manner. Management audit is not a compulsory audit and not enforced by law.

**7. Standard costing:** Standard costing is used to control the cost. The following are the steps involved in standard costing:

A. Determination of cost standards for various components such as material, labour and overhead.

B. Measurement of actual performance.

C. Comparison of actual cost with standard cost to find variations.

D. Finding the causes of variations.

E. Taking measures to avoid the variations in future.

**8. Return on investments:** Return on investment is also known as return on the capital employed. Using this technique, the rate of profitability is identified by the management. The amount of profits earned by the company is different from the rate of profitability of the company. The difference between the cost and revenue is profit. The rate of profitability is the earning capacity of the company. Return on investments is calculated by dividing the net profit with the total investment or capital employed in the business organisation.

**9. Internal audit:** Internal audit report is prepared at regular intervals, normally by months. It covers all the area of operations. This report is sent to the top management. The management takes steps to control the performance on the basis of the report. Internal audit report emphasises the degree of deviations from the expectations. It is very useful to attain the objectives on timely basis.

**10. Responsibility accounting:** The performance of various people is judged by assessing how far they have achieved pre-determined objectives. The objectives are framed section-wise, department-wise and division-wise and assessed similarly. Costs are allocated department-wise rather than product-wise. Each department, section or division, is fixed as reponsibile centres. An individual is responsible for his area of operation in a particular section, department or division.

**11. Managerial statistics:** Using the managerial statistics technique, the manager compares the past results with current results in order to know the causes for changes. These are very useful to the management in planning and decision-making for the future. According to Kenit O. Hauson, "Managerial statistics deal with data and methods which are useful to management executives in planning and controlling of organisation activities."

**12. Performance evaluation and review technique (PERT):** This technique is used to solve the problem which crops up once or a few times. It is not useful in tackling the problems which come up continuously. The PERT was developed by Booz, Allen and Hamiltan. They used this technique in Polaris Submarine Project under the sponsorship of U.S. Navy. The PERT technique is very useful for construction projects, publication of books etc.

**13. Critical path method (CPM):** This technique also follows the principle of PERT. The technique concentrates on cost rather than duration. CPM assumes that duration of every activity is constant. Time estimate is made for each activity. CPM technique was developed by a group of employees of DU de Nemours company.

**14. Gantt milestone chart:** This technique was a old one and at present, it is not in use. The reason is that this technique emphasises only on production scheduling but not on product quality. This technique was propounded by Henry I. Gantt.

**15. Production control:** The production control technique is necessary for smooth functioning of an organisation. Production control involves planning of production, determination of stock level of raw materials, finished goods, selection of process, selection of tools in production, etc. According to Spreigel, "Production control is the process of planning in advance of operations, establishing the exact route of each individual item, part or assembly, setting, starting and finishing dates for each important item, assembly and the finished product and releasing the necessary orders as well as initiating the required follow up to effectuate the smooth functioning of the enterprise."

**16. Managment information system:** Relevant information is collected and transferred to all the persons who are responsible to take decisions. A communication system is developed through which all levels of persons are informed about the growth of the organisation. Whenever the deviation is found, the corrective or control action is taken by the responsible person. The management information system emphasises the need for adequate information in time for taking the best decision. Thus, management information system helps the management in managerial decision-making by giving the right information at the right time and in the right form.

**17. External audit control:** External audit is a must to all the joint-stock companies under the purview of statutory control. So, it is otherwise known as *statutory audit* control. This type of audit protects the interests of the shareholders and creditors of the company. The external auditor certifies that all the books of accounts are kept as per the requirements of law and supplies all the necessary information for the purpose of audit and the balance sheet presents a true and fair view. The external audit is conducted by the qualified auditor. The qualifications of such type of auditor is fixed by the Central Government.

**18. Zerobase budgeting:** This is a new technique and has become popular within a short period. It is a new approach to budgeting. Zerobase budget is prepared without considering the previous year's figures. This technique requires the recalculation of all organisational activities to ascertain which should be eliminated or reduced or increased. In other words, the funds are estimated at current requirements. It means finding out how much amount is necessary to complete an ongoing project.

**19. Standing orders:** Standing order covers rules and regulations, discipline, procedure and the like. Rules and regulations are framed according to the requirements of administration. For example, no employee should leave the office before office time without getting prior permission in writing.

**20. Budgetary control:** The preparation of budget is also one of the control techniques followed by the management. The detailed discussion of this technique is presented in the forthcoming pages in this chapter.

## PERT/CPM

PERT Stands for programme Evaluation and Review Technique or Project Evaluation and Review Technique or Performance Evaluation Review Technique. CPM Stands for Critical Path Method. PERT was developed from Gantt Chart by Booz, Allen and Hamilton Inc. In response to the need of U.S.A. Navy in 1957-58 in connection with Polaris Weapons System. CPM was developed by engineers at the Du Pont Company, U.S.A. There is a basic difference between PERT and CPM, eventhough, both utilise the same principle. The basic difference is that PERT focus on time only and CPM focus on cost and time. Both PERT and CPM are used as control techniques to know time spent in completing a Project.

PERT is used as a planning tool and as a controlling tool. As a planning tool, PERT is used to compute the total time required to complete a project and identify bottleneck activities which can make a delay in the project completion date. As a control tool, PERT helps the management to closely watch the entire performance of a project to find any deviations if any. PERT/CPM expresses total events and activities and their interrelationships with each other. Optimum time can be find out for each event and activity in order to find out total time required to complete a project.

### Suitability of PERT/CPM

PERT/CPM is a very important control technique for project management. This technique is best suitable for the following projects.

1. Large weapon system
2. Ship building.
3. Construction of a building or olympic site.
4. Reinforcing weakdam.
5. Planning and launching a new project.
6. Air port facilities building.
7. Installation of computer system.
8. Launching new products.
9. Creation of Road facilities.
10. Creation of model village/town.
11. Creation of picnic spot.
12. Creation of colony.

### Advantages of PERT/CPM

The application of PERT/CPM Control techniques brings the following advantages.

**1. Ensures Planning:** PERT ensures actual planning. A manager is compelled to prepare a plan under PERT. He is requested to findout all key events and activities. Besides, the manager should identify the sequencing of events and activities and their interrelationships. Manager should compute the most likely time by considering all possibilities, uncertainties and pit falls.

**2. Identification of favourable factors:** Computation of most likely time eliminates surprises and wastages. This helps the management to find the favourable factors which are responsible for the successful completion of the project in advance.

**3. Savings of cost and time:** CPM focus on the events which requires maximum attention. It leads to savings of cost as well as time.

**4. Taking preventive or corrective actions:** PERT/CPM disclosed the bottlenecks and potential trouble spots well in advance. It is enough to take some preventive measures or corrective action.

**5. Attention on critical activities:** Serious attention can be devoted on critical activities and it is possible to speed up these activities.

**6. Everything at right:** It emphasis the right action at right time in the completion of a project.

**7. Making awareness of responsibilities:** It makes every manager fully aware of his responsibilities. It is possible by understanding the relationship of one work with other works.

**8. Securing Co-operation:** The PERT/CPM is constantly reviewed and updated on the basis of feedback. It helps the management to get co-operation of all departments.

**9. Facilitates decision-making:** Management can analys the effects of various alternate decisions instead of conducting expensive operations. It facilitates improved decision-making.

**10. Improved communication:** Each critical path and sub-critical paths are graphically represented. For each employee (Designers, Contractors, Project manager etc.) can understand his role in the proposed project from the graphic representation. It results in improved communication.

**11. Simultaneous performance of works:** It ensures simultaneous performance of different parts of the work. The whole project is divided into various different parts of work. Each work is performed by different persons separately.

**12. Advance control action:** PERT/CPM discloses how a delay in one activity affects all the succeeding activities. It helps the management to take a control action well in advance.

**13. Timely completion of a project:** The management can get an opportunity to shift its attention to any critical task so that the entire project is completed in time.

### Limitations of PERT/CPM

The PERT/CPM has certain limitations also. They are given below.

**1. Error in estimation of time and cost:** Future is uncertainty. Three times are estimated i.e. optimistic pessimistic and normal. Eventhough, it is very difficult to estimate accurate time required to complete a project. So, PERT is an unreliable as a control aid.

**2. Application:** PERT has to be applied only to one-time non-repetitive projects. It does not help the management to exercise control on continuous performing work.

**3. Time consuming and expensive:** A lot of data have been collected to prepare PERT net work. It requires a lot of time and consume some amount of expenses also before implementation of a project.

### Distinction between PERT and CPM

The basic principles and steps involved in both PERT and CPM are one and the same. Eventhough, there are some differences between PERT and CPM. They are briefly discussed below.

1. Three time estimates are made for each activity.

   The duration of each activity is constant. So, only one time estimate is made for each activity.

2. PERT gives importance on time.

   CPM gives importance on cost.

3. PERT is suitable where activity timings are not known.

   CPM is suitable where times are well known.

4. PERT is event oriented

   CPM is activity oriented.

Thus, PERT/CPM is used as a best control technique applied by the management over a period of time. Events and activities are the basic building blocks of a PERT network. Each event is numbered and connected by activities. The connection of activity with an event disclose the fact of preceding and succeeding events very clearly. A typical PERT network may help the management a lot to exercise control over the project implementation.

## CHARACTERISTICS OR FEATURES OF CONTROL

The main characteristics or the features of control are briefly discussed:

**1. Controlling process:** Controlling is also a continuous process just like other functions of management. The superior has continuous watch over the entire operations. Besides, he ensures that all the efforts are made to achieve the desired objectives and if not, necessary control action will be taken to correct them. According to Koontz and O'Donnell, "just as the navigator continually takes reading to ascertain whether he is relative to a planned course, so should the business manager continually take reading to assure that his enterprise or department is on course".

**2. Universal:** Control is applied at all levels of management and irrespective of the organisation. The manager of business and non-business concern uses control to regulate the on-going activities to obtain desired goals. The nature, scope and limit of control exercised by the manager vary according to the levels of management.

**3. Forward looking:** Control has links with future. How? Past cannot be controlled. But, the future activities may be controlled on the basis of past experience. The presence of control reduces the wastages, losses and deviation from standards.

**4. Dynamic process:** The control technique is changed according to the nature of deviations. The same technique is not followed throughout the year or a particular period. Besides, the control results in changes in the performance of other functions of management.

**5. Control involves management:** Control recommends the future course of action on the basis of evaluation and measurement. Evaluation and measurement are the eyes of the control process.

**6. Influencing factor:** The behaviour of a responsible person is influenced by the control process for the effective performance of activities. Control avoids the undesirable happenings and shapes the future plan. Control influences the people to conform to the norms and standards in performance.

**7. An essence of action:** The corrective action should be taken by the management on the basis of information available. If it does not do so, the purpose of control will not be achieved. The corrective action will be taken if there is any deviation from the standards.

## NEED OF CONTROL

Control is necessary as other functions of management. The control is necessary on account of the following reasons:

**1. Judging the accuracy of standards:** The actual performance should be compared with the fully accurate standards. But, it is very difficult for a large and complex organisation to establish the fully accurate standards because of the lack of timely information. In such a case, the control is necessary to judge the accuracy of standards.

**2. Minimise dishonest behaviour:** A honest person may tempt to misbehave in the absence of control. Only an efficient control minimises the dishonest behaviours or maintains honest behaviour on the part of employees.

**3. Better performance:** Employees will become lazy in the absence of control. Control facilitates to get better performance and regulate the efforts of the employees.

## ADVANTAGES OF CONTROL

A good control system gives the following benefits to the management:

**1. Adjustments in operation:** Every organisation has certain objectives. These objectives are achieved only when the plans are properly implemented. If it is not done so, objectives cannot be achieved. Control provides a clue to find whether the plans are properly implemented to achieve the objectives. The deviations from standards are corrected immediately. Thus control makes necessary adjustments in operation.

**2. Verification of policy:** The management frames the policies and plans to help the organisation function smoothly. The organisational performance is reviewed in the light of these policies. The organisational performance might deviate from the plans (standard) on account of many internal and external factors. These factors may force the organisation to deviate from the original plans. Constant review of plans helps to revise and update them. Thus, the management can verify the policy through the control process.

**3. Managerial accountability:** Managerial personnel are assigned responsibilities from top to bottom. A superior may delegate his authority to his subordinates. But the superior is responsible (or accountable) for the performance of his subordinates even after the delegation. It is quite natural that the superior has control over his subordinates. Besides, it is specified that the superiors should not misuse their authority. Control flows throughout the organisation from top to bottom as the existence of relationship between the superior and subordinates. Everyone, whether superior or subordinate, has responsibility for the work assigned to him.

**4. Psychological pressure:** Better performance is obtained by the management through the control process. It is achieved psychologically. The reason is that each person's performance is evaluated and linked with rewards. So, the employees will work hard to achieve the standard set for them.

**5. Maintaining morality:** Control creates an atmosphere of discipline in the organisation. Everybody is responsible for the work assigned to him. The workers are expected to make best efforts to complete the work and to the satisfaction of the management. These are not possible in the absence of control.

**6. Co-ordination:** Control gives unity of direction. Proper performance of all managerial functions is necessary to achieve co-ordination. A manager has to co-ordinate the activities of his subordinates with the help of control. Control helps to maintain an equilibrium between means and ends.

**7. Efficiency:** As responsibility is fixed for each individual, effective performance is possible. Control indirectly induces the employees to perform the work efficiently. They are well aware that defective performance is linked with punishment.

## LIMITATIONS OF CONTROL

Control process has some limitations. They are briefly explained below:

**1. Absence of perfect standards:** Standards cannot be fixed in all the cases. In some areas, quantitative standards cannot be expressed. In the absence of quantitative standards, the performance cannot be measured accurately. This indicates the ineffectiveness of control process.

**2. Uncontrollable factors:** Some of the factors cannot be controlled by the management or organisation. Changes of government policy, strategy of competitors, introduction of new substitute products in the market, technology changes, consumer preference changes could not be controlled by the organisation or management. These are external factors of organisation.

**3. Difficulty in fixing responsibility:** Normally, control reduces the freedom of employees. So, the employees resist the exercise of control. Then the control loses its effectiveness. Thus, the management has to face the difficulty of fixing responsibility.

**4. Expensive process:** The control process has several stages. They are (i) collecting information for fixing standards; (ii) actual fixation of standards; (iii) measuring the actual performance; (iv) finding deviations; and (v) taking corrective or control actions. These processes involve much paper work and are time consuming. A small organisation cannot afford these expenses.

## TYPES OF MANAGERIAL CONTROL

**1. Standardising control:** Controls are used to standardise performance for increasing efficiency. Costs may be reduced by time and motion studies, inspections and work schedules.

**2. Preserving control:** Company assets are protected or preserved through the allocation of responsibilities. Proper accounts are maintained for assets and usage of assets are controlled and put under strict supervision.

**3. Delegation of authority control:** Control puts some limits to the usage or delegation of authority. The approval of the top management is necessary to use the delegation of authority. Policy manual, procedure manual and internal audits are some of the techniques included in this control.

**4. Measurement control:** Controls are used to measure the job performance. Performance is measured through special reports, budgets, standard cost and production per hour or per employee.

**5. Motivating control:** Controls are designed to motivate the employees of organisation. Motivation includes promotions, rewards for best opinions and operation, profit sharing and the like.

## BUDGET

The term, *'Budget'* is derived from the French word *'Budgette'* which means small leather bag. Budget is not only looking forward as planning but also expresses what should be the future course of action in quantitative terms. Budget is prepared with the help of past experience. The past is the parent of the present as the present is the parent of future. This principle is followed in budget preparation. In simple words, budget is a control tool used by the management in planning its future activities. Thus, a budget may be said to be an instrument of planning, laying down the results desired to be achieved within a given period.

## DEFINITION OF BUDGET

Institute of Costs and Works Accountant of England said that, "Budget is a financial and/or quantitative statement, prepared prior to a defined period of time, of the policy to be pursued during that period for the purpose of attaining a given objective."

Hary L. Wlise, "Budgets are finished products — they are formal programmes of future operations and expected results. Budgets result from forward thinking and planning."

G.R. Terry, "A budget is a plan for income or outgo or both, of money, personnel, purchased items, sales items, or any other entity about which the manager believes that determining the future course of action will assist in the managerial efforts."

Professor Landers, "The essence of a budget is a detailed plan of operations for some specified future period followed by a system of records which will serve as a check upon the plan."

Brown and Howard, "A budget is a pre-determined statement of management policy during a given period which provides a standard for comparison with the results annually achieved."

Wneldon, "A budget is thus a standard with which to measure the actual achievements of people, departments, etc."

Knootz and O'Donnel, "Budgeting is the foundation of plans for a given future period in numerical terms. As such, budgets are statements of anticipated results, in financial terms — as in revenue and expenses and capital budgets or in non-financial terms — as in budgets of direct labour hours, materials, physical sales volume, or units of production."

Bartizal, "A budget is a forecast in detail, of the results of an officially recognised programme of operations based on the highest reasonable expectation of operating efficiency."

Prof. Saunders, "The essence of budget is a detailed plan of operations for some specific future period, followed by a system of records which will serve as a check upon plan."

Clearance L.Von Sickle, "The budget is an estimate prepared in advance of the period to which it applies."

## BUDGETARY CONTROL

Budgetary control is a tool used by the management to obtain the objectives expressed as in the form of budget. The actual results are compared with the budgeted figures. If there are any deviation, they can be remedied by either adjusting or correcting the cause of difference. Budget is concerned with policy making whereas budgetary control results from the implementation of such a policy. Budgetary control is a continuous process but budget is an end process. The preparation of budget is finished within a stipulated time. Budgetary control starts only after preparing the budget.

## DEFINITION OF BUDGETARY CONTROL

G.R. Terry, "Budgetary controlling is a process of finding out what is being done and comparing these results with the corresponding budget data in order to approve accomplishment or to remedy differences by either adjusting the budget estimates or correcting the cause of the difference."

J. Betty, "Budgetary control is a system which uses budgets as a means of planning and controlling all aspects of producing and/ or selling commodities or services."

R.C. Davis, "Budgetary control is an important means of establishing accountability for a satisfactory discharge of this responsibility for expenses. Budgetary control depends on budgetary planning."

Institute of Cost and Management Accountant, London, "Budgetary control is the establishment of budget relating to the responsibilities of executives to the requirements of a policy and the continuous comparison of actual with budgeted results, either to secure by individual action the objective of that policy or to provide a basis for its revision."

Gien A. Welsch, "Budgetary control involves the use of budgets and budgetary reports throughout the period to co-ordinate, evaluate and control day-to-day operations in accordance with the goals specified by the budget."

Brown and Howard, "Budgetary control is a system of controlling costs which includes the preparation of budgets co-ordinating the departments and establishing responsibility, comparing actual performance with budgeted and acting upon results to achieve maximum profitability."

Marry Cushing Niles, "Budgetary control is an important tool of management. It is, in fact, a tool in the hands of planning which reaches through co-ordination into control and ties the three aspects firmly together. It stimulates thinking in advance by requiring specific planning and the anticipation of operating problems."

Walter W. Bigg, "The term budgetary control is applied to a system of management and accounting control by which all operations and output are forecast as far ahead as possible and the actual results when known are compared with the budget estimates."

## OBJECTIVES OF BUDGETARY CONTROL

Budgetary control is a tool of management. It's very purpose is the estimation of the development of organisation activities and watching whether the present performance confirms to the budgeted figures. If there are any deviations, the causes will be identified and corrective action recommended. The corrective actions are taken not only to rectify the present deviations but also to avoid the occurrence of such deviations in future. The main objectives are discussed below:

1. Fixation of the income and expenditure department-wise.
2. Defining the goals or objectives of the organisation for a stipulated period.
3. Helping the decentralisation work. Sometimes, budgets are prepared department-wise.
4. It establishes a measure of performance for each division or section of the organisation.
5. Co-ordination of the work of various departments or sections of the organisation.
6. Assisting in terms of data, the top management for policy determination.

7. Forecasting the financial position of the company.
8. Eliminate departmental accumulation of cost and performance data for control purposes.
9. Increasing the efficiency of the employees and minimising the expenses at every level of the organisation.
10. Determining the capital expenditure of the company.
11. Helping the preparation of fund flow and cash flow statements.
12. Indicating the area where action is necessary to take corrective action.
13. Checking the over-capitalisation or under-capitalisation of the company department-wise or section-wise.
14. Centralising the management control. Budgets are prepared department-wise but control vests with the top manage-ment.

## CHARACTERISTICS OF BUDGETARY CONTROL

The various characteristics of Budgetary control are explained below:

1. The activities of the organisation are presented department-wise or section-wise.
2. Budgets give the extent of expenditure through which cost control is achieved.
3. The co-ordination of various departmental activities helps to prepare the master budget.
4. The future is planned on the basis of past experience.
5. Recording the present performance for comparing purposes with the pre-determined standards.
6. Clear-cut and specific requirements of the organisation are expressed in quantitative terms.
7. Determines the deviations by comparisons and identifies the causes of such deviations.
8. Recommends and implements the corrective actions whenever necessary.

## ADVANTAGES OF BUDGETARY CONTROL

The activities of the organisation are pre-planned in monetary terms as the preparation of budget. The actual achievements are compared with pre-planning. Budgetary control helps the management to achieve the pre-plan. Some of the advantages of Budgetary control are discussed below:

**1. Tool for planning the activities:** Budgets are prepared department-wise or section-wise, following which the department managers will know their activities. Thus, each department has a plan of its future course of action.

**2. Thinking in advance:** A budget is prepared, normally, for a year in advance. The top management people could develop forward looking strategies and thinking with the help of budgets. They, think in advance as to how to market the product, how to solve production problems, finanical difficulties and the like.

**3. Co-ordination of efforts:** Policies and objectives provide a basis for the preparation of a budget. Each department personnel are well aware of the link of the policy with the budget. Then, the top management may easily co-ordinate the efforts of various departments.

**4. Control of expenditure:** The expenditure of various departments are clearly fixed in the budget. So unnecessary expenditures are avoided.

**5. Solving financial difficulties:** The budget forecasts the probable cash receipts and expenses. Temporary financial accommodation is arranged with the financial institutions or with banks. In this way, financial difficulties of the enterprises are solved.

**6. Delegation of authority and responsibility:** There is an automatic sanction of work whenever the budget is prepared. There is no need of getting permission from the top management for the second time. Delegation of authority and responsibilities become easier.

**7. Better utilisation of resources:** The term *resources* includes money and raw materials. Adequate amount is allocated to buy the raw materials, make salary payment, purchase fixed assets and the like. Economic order quantity principle is followed in buying the raw materials. Proper control is exercised over the usage of raw materials in the production place.

**8. Promotion of efficiency:** Production per hour, production per day and production per man are fixed with the Budgetary control technique. It encourages the employees to increase their efficiency. According to Mr. Blocker, "Budgetary control is planned to assist management in the allocation of responsibility and authority, to aid in making estimates and plans for the future, to assist in the analysis of the variations between estimated and actual results and to develop bases of measurement of standards with which to evaluate the efficiency of operations."

**9. Achievement of goals:** Under budgetary control system, each person can know what he is expected to do. This offers an opportunity to the management to achieve the goals or objectives.

**10. Criteria of self-examination:** Budgetary control system points out the deviations and causes of such deviations. These are very well known to the employees. In this way, Budgetary control acts as a criteria of self-examination.

**11. Promoters balanced activities:** A department activity is correlated with another department activity. One department's results are the basis of other department's functioning. Balanced activities of different departments are possible under the budgetary control system. For example, production department's activities are based on those of sales department. Likewise, the purchase department's activities are based on those of production department.

**12.** Budgetary control system discovers the areas of operation where improvements can be suggested.

**13. Ensures proper communication:** Management's policy and the objectives of preparing the budgets are communicated to all the managers. Again, the managers are requested to send the report of actual performance against budget. The managers are informed of the type of action to be taken to correct deviations. Thus, budgetary control ensures proper communication.

**14. Fixation of responsibility:** Responsibility of deviations can be fixed easily. Sales budget fixes the responsibility of sales department. Likewise, the production budget fixes the responsibility of the production department.

**15. Encourages exchange of information:** Functional budgets are prepared by the enterprise normally. It requires the free flow of information from one department to another department. Purchase budget cannot be prepared unless production figures are available.

## DISADVANTAGES, LIMITATIONS OR PROBLEMS OF BUDGETARY CONTROL

Budgetary control facilitates planning, controlling and co-ordination. Yet it has some limitations, and they are given below:

**1. Inaccuracy:** Budget figures are expressed in monetary terms. So, a budget is based on the price level at a particular point of time, and inflation or deflation leads to inaccuracy of budget. Besides, future is uncertain. The standards are fixed on the basis of past experience. So, the budget may go wrong.

**2. Personal bias:** The preparation of budget is subject to imperfection in human judgement and shortcomings.

**3. Non-availability of co-operation:** Inefficient employees hesitate to extend their co-operation to implement budgetary control. The reason is that the deviations occur on account of inefficient employees.

**4. Rigidity:** An enterprise is running on certain conditions and circumstances. These conditions and circumstances are static at a certain time and flexible at another time. Under such situations, budgetary control cannot be implemented effectively. It means that, it is very difficult to attain flexibility in budget preparation.

**5. Results are not attainable:** Adequate information is necessary to prepare and implement the budget. At the same time, the available data should be properly interpreted and evaluated. The budgeted results may not be attainable because of defective analysis of data.

**6. Consistency:** The budgets are not prepared afresh every year. The new budgets are prepared by adjusting figures in the previous budget. It may happen that an important event of the past would not be considered important for future budget.

**7. Time consuming process:** Initially, management constitutes a budget committee and prepares the budget manual. The budget committee receives the data from all the employees of the organisation and consults all the departmental heads. Then the committee prepares the budget. It requires much time.

**8. Ineffective budgetary control:** Proper arrangements should be made for adequate supervision and administration. These are not possible at all times. In such circumstances, budgetary control will be an ineffective one.

**9. Discourage the initiative:** The departmental heads are discouraged from doing extra activities for which a provision has not been made in the budget. It automatically minimises the initiative of the employees of the organisation.

**10. More paperwork:** The implementation of budgetary control involves more paperwork. The paperwork includes receiving information from the employees, preparation of budget manual, setting up of standards, the actual preparation of budget, recording of actual performance and taking corrective actions, if any. So, maximum managerial work suffers because of much paperwork.

Inspite of the above mentioned limitations and problems, budgetary control is the best tool of management for planning and controlling and so, the management should take necessary steps to make the budgetary control system more effective.

## ESSENTIALS OF EFFECTIVE BUDGETING SYSTEM

A sound budgetary control system is necessary for effective managerial control. The essentials of effective budgeting system are discussed below:

**1. Efficient organisation:** The effective organisation depends upon the proper fixation of responsibility and clearly defined authority. An efficient organisation alone can adopt effective budgeting systems.

**2. Preparing master budget:** Normally, the budgets are prepared department-wise or section-wise. These budgets should be assembled and integrated in the form of master budgets.

**3. Quick reporting:** The actual performance reports should be prepared by the subordinates and sent to the top management without any delay. It will help the top management executives to analyse the report and take necessary action immediately.

**4. Flexible:** The budgets should be flexible as far as possible. The reason is that future is uncertain and the budgets regulate the future course of action. Sometimes, the management may prepare a flexible budget which has flexibility to some extent.

**5. Support of top management:** The adoption of budgetary control system should be supported by the top management. If it does not do so, there will be no seriousness on the part of subordinates. It will weaken managerial control.

**6. Based on reasonable assumptions:** Budgets forecast the sales, production, purchase, profit, expenditure and the like. On the basis of some of the assumptions, these are forecast. So, the assumptions should be reasonable and reliable ones.

**7. Reward and punishment:** The employees whose performances are according to the budget plans are rewarded. At the same time, the situation can be totally different.

**8. Appropriate authority:** Appropriate authority should be given to those employees who are responsible to implement the budgetary control system. These employees will not be able to fulfil their responsibilities if there is a lack of appropriate authority and they will not be in a position to take strong decisions.

## TYPES OF BUDGETS

Budgets may be classified on the basis of the purpose for which they are prepared. Some of the budgets which are classified on the basis of purpose are described below:

**1. Master budget:** Master budget has detailed planning of the entire business in one budget. Most of the business organisations involve themselves in the preparation of the master budget. Master budget shows how each department budget promotes the business as a whole. Other budgets are subsidiary budgets of master budget.

**2. Sales budget:** Sales budget is the first of the subsidiary budgets. Without preparing the sales budget, no budget can be prepared by the business organisation. Sales budget is prepared on the basis of data available from market research. Population trends, consumer's taste, consumers' purchasing power, competitors trend and production capacity are considered while preparing the sales budget. Sales budget may be prepared area-wise or product-wise. If the company sells more than one product, the sales budget will be prepared product-wise and area-wise. If it is not so, sales budget will be prepared only area-wise.

**3. Cash budget:** Cash budget discloses the probable cash receipts and cash payments for a specific period. Cash budget helps the management to arrange the finance accomodation from financial institutions and/or commerical banks if need arises. In this way, it avoids the lack of finance. In other words, the amount is received from the concerned party at the appropriate time. It minimises the bad debts. It is otherwise called financial budget and revenue and expenses budget.

**4. Production budget:** Production budget is prepared on the basis of sales budget. In addition to that, the company considers the production capacity, number of skilled employees available, availability of power and space and warehouse facility while preparing the production budget. A great degree of co-ordination is required in the sales programmes and production budget.

Production budget helps to produce the goods of a desired quality at minimum cost. Production budget shows the production in quantitative terms. In simple words, the production budget aims at maximising the utilisation of available resources.

**5. Physical property budget:** The term *physical property* includes building, machinery, furniture and fitting, plant and inventories and equipments. These have permanent investment. This budget indicates the amount required to replace the existing physical property and to make additions during the budget period. Sometimes, this additional amount is raised without paying any dividends as ploughing back or sale of additional stock or bonds. These budgets are usually tied with long-range planning. It is otherwise called *capital expenditure budget*.

**6. Time and material budget:** Most of the budgets are expressed in monetary terms and few in quantitative or physical terms. In the next stage, the physical terms are converted into monetary terms. Here, the budget figures are expressed as direct labour hours, machine hours or units or material required to produce a product.

**7. Selling and distribution cost budget:** This budget includes the selling and distribution cost such as packaging expenses, storage, insurance, transportation, advertisement expenses, sales commission, marketing research expenses and the like. Selling and distribution cost budget is prepared by the sales department manager. It helps the management to control the costs of selling and distribution.

**8. Balance sheet budget:** Balance sheet budget is prepared to utilise the working capital. Working capital is nothing but the excess of current assets over current liabilities. This budget indicates how the current assets can be utilised to pay-off the current liabilities.

**9. Supplies budget:** The term *'supplies'* does not represent the raw materials. Raw materials are formed as part of the finished product. But, the supplies do not form a part of the finished product but are consumed in manufacturing operations. These are of small value, but these are necessary in production process. So, the management should prepare a separate budget for supplies and ensure continuous supplies.

**10. Production cost budget:** Production budget provides a basis for preparing the production cost budget. Production cost budget indicates the expenses to be incurred in the production process during budget period. Production cost budget may be sub-divided into raw materials budget, production overhead budget, etc.

**11. Production overhead budget:** Production overhead budget lays down all the production overheads to be incurred in production during the budget period. The overheads may be sub-divided into fixed overheads, variable overheads and semi-fixed or semi-variable overheads.

**12. Research and development budget:** This type of budget is prepared by the large organisations. Research is carried on to invent new products or to improve the existing products. It is necessary to survive in the market. Marketing risk may be reduced to some extent with the help of research. Research and development expenditure is in the nature of insurance.

Budgets may be classified on the basis of nature also. They are discussed below:

**1. Fixed budget:** The budget figures remain unchanged irrespective of the level of activity. The level of activity is unknown obviously. The actual performance is more deviated from the standard.

**2. Flexible budgets:** A budget is prepared at various levels of activity in columnar form. The expenses are divided into three categories such as fixed, variables, or semi-fixed or semi-variable. This type of budget very useful to the management in taking corrective actions if there are any deviations.

## PREPARATION OF A BUDGET

There are some steps involved in the preparation of budget. These steps are outlined below:

**1. Sound forecasting:** Every budget is prepared on the basis of forecast. Top executives of management must judge the future market and take decisions regarding financial requirement, purchase of machinery and inventories, advertising expenses and selling expenses in the light of their analysis. Then, they may use the statistical data with their assumptions. However, sound forecasting is necessary for a reliable budget.

**2. Developed accounting system:** Costing information is necessary for effective budget preparation. These costs are properly recorded in the well-developed accounting system. Only developed accounting system alone supplies the adequate and desired information to the top management executives. They can convert this information into reality as a budget.

**3. Fixation of responsibility centres:** The attainment of budget objectives lies with the departmental heads. So, there is no need for raising questions regarding the man who is responsible to fix the amount of expenditure and produce definite results. Adequate authority should be assigned to those who are responsible to complete the task assigned.

**4. Formation of budget committee:** The preparation of a budget is a group effort. An accountant will be enough to prepare the budgets in a small organisation, if he has close contact with the general manager and departmental heads. This is not possible in bigger organisations.

A budget committee is formed in bigger organisations. The budget committee consists of all the departmental heads and is headed by an experienced officer who may be designated as Budget Officer. The budget committee will receive all the information from the various departments whose services are used in the preparation of the budgets. The budget committee has full responsibility to prepare all the departmental budgets. Periodical reports are collected by the budget committee.

The budget committee has to compare the actual performance with budgeted figures. If there is any deviation, the budget officer may consider revisions of budget to meet the changed business conditions.

**5. Clear definition of business policies:** The top management must clearly define the business policies and communicate them to the departmental heads. If it does not do so, the hard work of departmental heads will be a waste and the budget figures cannot be achieved. So, it is the duty of the top management to circulate the business policies to the departmental heads before preparing the budgets.

**6. Statistical information:** Necessary information regarding each department must be available in the form of figures. Production budget is prepared with the help of sales budget. Purchase budget is prepared with the help of production budget. These budgeted figures are recorded in the accounting records with more details for sales and profit control.

**7. Support of top management:** The preparation of budgets require the support of the top management. There should be cordial relationship between the top management and various departmental heads.

**8. Budget period:** The period to be covered in the budget depends upon the type of business. Normally, the budget is prepared for one year. But, anyhow, the length of the budget period covers the seasonal fluctuations of business, production operations and financial implications. One year budget may be broken down into half-yearly, quarterly and monthly. These facilitate control. The budget must be prepared before the commencement of the year.

Budgets are prepared by all the business units. The objectives of business organisation are presented in quantitative terms as a budget. Then, the objectives are easily achieved. Besides, budget facilitates the control process.

## MODEL QUESTIONS

1. State the basic requirements of good controlling.
2. What are the various good qualities of efficient controlling system?
3. What are the objectives of 'control'?
4. What is the need of controlling?
5. What is the need of fixing standards ?
6. Bring out the importance of control as a function of management. Write a brief note on various types of controls exercised at different levels of management.
7. Narrate the importance and short-comings of control?
8. Define control and describe the process of control?
9. Explain the various steps involved in control process?

# CHAPTER 25

# CO-ORDINATION

## INTRODUCTION

Various departments or sections are assigned different tasks to perform. They are assigned on the basis of their specialisation. Employees of each department perform their duties with a view to achieving common objectives collectively. It is co-ordination. Co-ordination is the process which ensures smooth interplay of the functions of management. Common objectives are achieved without much wastage of time, efforts and money with the help of co-ordination.

A modern enterprise consists of a number of departments. In olden days, the enterprise was divided into departments such as purchase, production, sales, finance and accounts. But, now a days, the enterprise is divided into the following departments: purchase, production, sales, finance, account, personnel, research and development, public relations and the like. The classification of departments is very large at present. So the importance of co-ordination has subsequently increased.

## DEFINITION

J. Lundy, "Co-ordination involves the development of unity of purpose and the harmonious implementation of plans for the achievement of desired ends."

Henry Fayol, "To co-ordinate is to harmonise all the activities of a concern so as to facilitate its working and its success. In a well co-ordinated enterprise, each department or division, works in harmony with others and is fully informed of its role in the organisation. The working schedules of various departments are constantly tuned to circumstances."

Alan C. Reiley and James D. Mooney, "Co-ordination is the orderly arrangement of group effort, to provide unity of action in the pursuit of common purpose."

Orduray Tead, "Co-ordination is the effort to ensure the smooth interplay of the functions and forces of all the components and parts of an organisation to the end that its purpose will be realised with a minimum of friction and a maximum of co-operative effectiveness."

Koontz and O'Donnel, "It seems more accurate to regard co-ordination as the essence of managership for the achievement of harmony of individual efforts towards the accomplishment of group goals as the purpose of management. Each of the managerial functions is an exercise in co-ordination."

G.R. Terry, "Co-ordination deals with the task of blending efforts in order to ensure the successful attainment of an objective. It is accomplished by means of planning, organising, actuating and controlling."

Newman, "Co-ordination is a part of all phases of administration and that it is not a separate and distinct activity."

E.F.L. Brech, "Co-ordination is balancing and keeping the teams together by ensuring a suitable allocation of working activities to the various members and seeing that these are performed with due harmony among the members themselves."

## FEATURES OR CHARACTERISTICS OF CO-ORDINATION

**1. Not a separate function of management:** Co-ordination is necessary in all functions of management. So, co-ordination is not a separate and distinct function of management.

**2. Managerial responsibility:** Every departmental head is responsible to co-ordinate the efforts of his subordinates. It is inherent in the managerial job and responsibility.

**3. Provides unity of action:** Unity of action is necessary to obtain common objectives. So, unity of action is considered to be the heart of the co-ordination process.

**4. Co-ordination is necessary to all levels of organisation:** Co-ordination is not brought by force or left to chance. So, the top executives should take deliberate efforts to bring co-ordination.

**5. Relevant of group efforts:** Group efforts rather than individual efforts are necessary to bring co-ordination. An individual cannot work without affecting the functions of others. It emphasises the group efforts.

**6. Continuous and dynamic process:** Co-ordination starts with the planning process and ends with controlling process. In every organisation, a certain kind of co-ordination exists. Special efforts should be taken by the management to achieve high degree of co-ordination.

**7. System concept:** An organisation is a system of co-operative efforts. Each department functions are different in nature and have inter-dependence in the organisation system. The organisation runs smoothly with the help of co-ordination. Thus, co-ordination is a system-concept.

## NEED AND IMPORTANCE OF CO-ORDINATION

The effective performance of managerial functions require co-ordination.

**1. Unity in diversity:** Effective co-ordination is the essence of good management. There are large number of employees and each has different ideas, views or opinions, activities and background in a large organisation. Thus, there is a diversified activity in a large organisation where these diversified activities will be inefficient in the absence of co-ordination. So, co-ordination is the main element of unity in diversity.

**2. Term work or unity of direction:** The efforts, energies and skills of various persons should be integrated as group efforts to achieve the objectives of organisation. In the absence of co-ordination, the group efforts may be diversified and fail to achieve the objectives. Besides, co-ordination eliminates the duplication of work which leads to economic and efficient management.

**3. Functional differentiation:** The organisation functions are divided department-wise or section-wise or division-wise. Each department performs different jobs. They are necessary to achieve the general objectives. Co-ordination ensures definite achievement of objectives. Each department tries to perform its function in isolation from others. It may create a problem. Therefore, co-ordination is necessary to integrate the functions of the related departments.

**4. Specialisation:** There is a high degree of specialisation in the modern indus-trial world. Specialists know thoroughly about their respective fields. They are able to judge the scope, nature and kind of work they perform. But they fail to know the job of others and the importance of others' performances. This tends to cause dispute among the specialists. Disputes may be solved with the help of co-ordination.

**5. Reconciliation of goals:** Each department or division has its own goals to achieve within the stipulated time. There are general goals in relation to an organisation. The employees who are working in the organisation also have their own goals. Individuals or employees give more importance to their own goals than to the department and organisational goals. The department members give more importance to their own departmental goals than to the organisation goals. Therefore, co-ordination reconciles the employee's goals with both departmental and organisation goals.

**6. Large number of employees:** Large number of employees are working in large organisations. They have different habits, behaviour and approaches in a particular situation. Sometimes, they do not act rationally. Their behaviour is neither always well understood nor completely predictable. So, there is every possibility of problems arising in a complex organisation. All this makes co-ordination more essential.

**7. Congruity of flows or congruent flows:** Congruity of flows refers to the continuous flow of similar information from one direction to other directions. Information regarding the utilisation of resources, activities, using of authority and output is made to flow in an organisation. Co-ordination ensures the smooth and continuous flow of information.

**8. Empire building:** Empire building refers to top portion of line organisation. The line officers always expect co-operation from staff officers. But the line officers are not ready to extend their co-operation to staff officers. It creates conflicts between line officers and staff officers. Therefore, co-ordination is necessary to avoid conflicts between line officers and staff officers.

**9. Differentiation and integration:** The whole activity of every organisation is classified into two units. They are specialised and homogeneous units. Authority is delegated to the various levels of organisation. This is necessary to achieve group efforts. Co-ordination facilitates this process.

## PRINCIPLES OF CO-ORDINATION OR ESSENTIALS OF EFFECTIVE CO-ORDINATION

In order to ensures effective co-ordination, the co-ordination should be based on certain principles. They are briefly explained below:

**1. Early start:** The co-ordination should be started even from the planning function of management. The management should prepare the plan after consulting the concerned officials. By this, the preparation of a plan and its implementation will be very easy for the management. Then, there will be no resistance from the concerned officials.

**2. Personnel contract:** Oral communication brings two persons very close. It means, there is a possibility of personal contact. An agreement may be arrived on methods, actions and achievement of objectives through personal contact. Ideas, views, opinions, recommendations, feelings, etc. are conveyed to the receivers effectively through personal contact. Personal contact avoids controversy and misunderstanding. Thus, co-ordination is achieved through co-operation and mutual understanding and not by force, order or coercion.

**3. Continuity:** Co-ordination is a must so long as the organisation continues to function. Co-ordination is the key stone of the organisational structure. So, co-ordination starts with planning and ends with controlling.

**4. Reciprocal relationship:** This principle states that all factors in a situation are reciprocally related. Each factor influences other factors and are influenced by the other factors. Thus, the action of one employee influences the action of other employees and vice versa. So, there is a need for integration of all efforts, actions and interests.

**5. Dynamism:** The external environment of business influences the internal activities of the business. Besides, the internal activities and decisions are changed according to the circumstances prevailing. So, co-ordination is modified according to the external environment and internal actions and decisions. Co-ordination should be a dynamic one.

**6. Simplified organisation:** *Simplified* organisation also facilitates effective co-ordination. The management can arrange the departments in such a way, to get better co-ordination among the departmental heads. If two sections or two department's functions are most similar in nature, these two departments are put under one executive incharge. This facilitates to get better co-ordination. Somebody recommended that if there are dissimilar functions between two sections or departments, these two departments should be handed over to only one executive. This will also ensure better co-ordination between the two departments. According to Keith and Gabelin, "even though certain activities are dissimilar, management may put them under a single executive because they need close co-ordination".

**7. Self co-ordination:** According to this principle, the function of one department affects other departments and in turn, is affected by the functions of other departments. The same department modifies its functions in such a manner that it may affect other departments favourably. In this way, co-ordination is achieved. There is a need for effective communication to get self-co-ordination. Effective communication facilitates a department to appraise the functions of another department.

**8. Clear-cut objectives:** The departmental heads should know clearly the objectives of the organisation. So, the management must take necessary steps to explain the objectives to the departmental heads. This is very useful in achieving the common objectives of the organisation collectively. Clear-cut objectives and clear explanation of objectives are bound to produce uniformity in action.

**9. Clear definition of authority and responsibility:** The management should clearly define the authority and responsibility of each individual and of each department. This will facilitate effective co-ordination in an organisation. Besides, it will reduce conflicts among the individuals. The department manager has enough authority to exercise over the subordinates who have violated the limits and other irregularities.

**10. Effective communication:** Effective communication is necessary for proper co-ordination. The individual and departmental problems can be solved with the help of co-ordination. In addition, the efforts of a staff are effectively utilised to achieve the objectives of the organisation.

**11. Effective supervision:** Effective leadership also helps in proper co-ordination. Leadership creates confidence in the minds of subordinates and increases the morale of the subordinates.

**12. Effective supervision:** Top executives should supervise the work of subordinates to ensure successful performance as planned. Top executives may entrust this type of work to the supervisors. When, the top executives find any deviation, they may take immediate steps to correct them with the help of supervisors. So, there is a need for co-ordination between the supervisors and the top executives. Thus, supervisors play an important role in co-ordination.

## TECHNIQUES OF CO-ORDINATION

Supervisors can use a number of techniques to enlist co-ordination. Some of the techniques of co-ordination are discussed below:

**1. Clearly Defined Objectives:** Each and every organisation has its own objectives. These objectives would be clearly defined. Then, the employees of the organisation should understand the objectives of organisation well. Unity of purpose is a must for achieving proper co-ordination.

**2. Effective chain of command:** In each organisation, the line of authority decides who is responsible and to whom. If the line of authority and responsibility are clearly defined, the superior has proper control over his sub-ordinates. Then, the superior or manager can co-ordinate the efforts of his subordinates by means of his authority. If the line of authority is clearly defined, the superior could decrease the conflicts and get co-ordination.

**3. Co-ordination through group meetings:** The common group of problems of an organisation are discussed by the officials in group meetings. Such group meetings help in achieving co-ordination. The group meetings are easily convened. The reason is that there is an obligation on the part of group members to extend their co-ordination.

**4. Harmonious policies and procedures:** Rules and regulations, procedures and programmes are used as guidelines for taking a decision in a consistent manner. It ensures uniformity in action at every level of management.

**5. Effective communication:** Effective communication promotes mutual understanding and co-operation among the various officials in an organisation. The communication should be direct as far as possible. The direct communication alone avoids any misunderstandings and misinterpretation. Quick communication can facilitate the performance of activities in time. Then there is a possibility of performance of other activities which are to be co-ordinated.

**6. Sound organisational structure:** Sound organisational structure integrates the activities of different units and sub-units in an organisation. Besides, horizontal co-ordination is achieved with the help of sound organisational structure.

**7. Co-ordination through a liaison officer:** A person who acts as a link between two persons is called *a liaison officer*. The external co-ordination is obtained through him. Many large organisations depend on this officer to maintain cordial relations with government and outsiders.

**8. Co-operation:** Co-operation is the result of better relations among the employees of the organisation. The sound policies and procedures provide a basis for better relations. Informal contacts are also encouraged to ensure co-ordination through co-operation.

**9. Self co-ordination:** There are different functions in an organisation which are inter-linked. So, the arrangement of different departments' functions are in such way that each department benefits by the functioning of others. Self-co-ordination may be achieved through this process.

**10. Co-ordination by leadership:** A manager uses his leadership skills to induce the subordinates to co-ordinate willingly. A leader can motivate the subordinates and identify the interests of individuals. These are used to get co-ordination. Many conflicts and unpleasant situations may be avoided with the help of good leadership.

**11. Incentives:** The term *'incentives'* includes only monetary incentives. They are increments in the scale of pay, bonus, profit sharing and the like. These schemes of incentives promote better team spirit which subsequently ensures better co-ordination.

## TYPES OF CO-ORDINATION

Normally, the co-ordination is divided into two types. They are explained below:

**1. Internal co-ordination:** It is the establishment of relationship with a view to co-ordinate the activities of all the managers, executives, divisions, sub-divisions, branches and other workers.

Internal co-ordination is also sub-divided into the following two types:

**(i) Vertical co-ordination:** Vertical co-ordination refers to that co-ordination in which a superior authority co-ordinates his work with that of his sub-ordinates and vice versa. Sales manager co-ordinates his work with the activities of the sales supervisor. Similarly, the sales supervisor is required to have co-ordination and cordial relationship with his superiors.

**(ii) Horizontal co-ordination:** Horizontal co-ordination refers to the establishment of a relationship between the persons of the same status. For example, co-ordination between the departmental heads, supervisors, co-workers, etc.

**2. External co-ordination:** External co-ordination is the establishment of a relationship between the employees of the organisation and outsiders of the organisation. This relationship is established for the benefit of the organisation as a whole. The following are the outsiders with whom an organisation has to establish better relationship:

(i) Market agencies.

(ii) General public.

(iii) Competitors.

(iv) Customers.

(v) Union government, state government, local self- governments and other government agencies.

(vi) Different institutions rendering auxiliary services.

(vii) Financial institutions.

(viii) Different Industrial organisations.

(ix) Technological Agencies.

(x) Different commercial organisations.

The work of the establishment of a relationship between the employees of the organisation and the outsiders is entrusted to a person who is designated as public relations officer.

## PROBLEMS OF CO-ORDINATION

Co-ordination is necessary for the smooth and successful functioning of the management. But in practice co-ordination faces certain problems listed below.

**1. Natural hindrances:** Co-ordination is not an effective one due to some natural hindrances. The term *'natural hindrances'* includes flood, earthquakes, fire, etc. These affect the behaviour of individuals and the group as a whole. It results in ineffective co-ordination.

**2. Lack of administrative talent:** Lack of administrative talent arises due to the selection of inefficient candidates. They do not understand the administrative procedure properly. This results in ineffective co-ordination.

**3. Lack of techniques of co-ordination:** Management is not interested to find out new techniques for effective co-ordination. The reason is that it is good enough for the development of an organisation. If the management uses a number of techniques of co-ordination, the problems of co-ordination can be easily tackled.

**4. Ideas and objectives:** Each management has its own objectives and finds ways (ideas) to achieve those objectives. But, the managers confuse these objectives with ideas. It poses the problem of co-ordination.

**5. Misunderstanding:** There are a number of personnel employed in an organisation. They should have mutual understanding with each other. But, the problem of co-ordination creeps in due to misunderstanding among employees very often.

## STEPS FOR EFFECTIVE CO-ORDINATION

In order to overcome the above mentioned problems of co-ordination and get effective co-ordination, the management should follow the following steps:

1. There should be a proper delegation of authority and responsibility at all levels of management.
2. The whole or entire activities of the organisation should be divided department-wise or section-wise according to the size of the organisation.
3. Preparing and adherence to rigid rules and regulations, procedures, policies, etc.
4. Establishment of an effective communication system.
5. Establishment of employees' grievances cell.
6. There should be a proper system for reporting.
7. Skilled workers are to be rewarded adequately.
8. The management should induce the employees to take active part in meetings, committees, conferences, seminars and the like.
9. The management should encourage the employees to have friendly relationship with others.
10. Managers should have opportunities to get training in the area of leadership, co-ordination, planning, staffing and the like.

## CO-ORDINATION AND CO-OPERATION

Co-ordination and Co-operation are the two terms widely used in the business organisation. They are different from each other. They are discussed below:

| *Co-ordination* | *Co-operation* |
|---|---|
| 1. It is one of the functions of management. | It is not a function of management. |
| 2. Co-ordination is an orderly arrangement of group efforts. | Co-operation is willingness to work with others or help others. |
| 3. The early success of an organi-sation depends upon the degree of co-ordination. | Co-operation is the basis for co-ordination. |
| 4. Co-ordination is obtained officially. | Co-operation is a voluntary service. |
| 5. There is a direct link between the achievement of objectives and co-ordination. | There is no such direct connection between co-operation and the achievement of objectives. |

## MODEL QUESTIONS

1. What are the problems involved in co-ordination? What are your suggestions for effective co-ordination?
2. What is the importance of co-ordination?
3. What are the different problems of co-ordination?
4. What is effective co-ordination?
5. Define the term "co-ordination".
6. Discuss the technique for achieving co-ordination. What problems are to be encountered in the process?
7. Bring out the importance of co-ordination in a business organisation. What are the methods of achieving co-ordination?

# CHAPTER 26

# MANAGEMENT AUDIT

## INTRODUCTION

Management Audit is of recent origin as compared to statutory audit. Management Audit is otherwise called *Operational Audit*. When the functions of the statutory auditor expanded, the need arose for the review of the management process. Initially, the statutory auditor was required to state whether the Balance Sheet and Profit and Loss account were prepared according to the Companies Act and furnish a correct and unbiased picture of the state of affairs of the company. The statutory auditor never goes beyond this limit. The reason is that the growing size and complexity of the business organisation resulted in developement of new audit *i.e.,* Management Audit. Besides, the statutory auditor is not expected to verify whether policies laid down by the management are properly put in to practice or not; to evaluate the execution of various management fuctions and processes in order to improve its efficiency; to find out whether a change in the method of purchase is beneficial to the company; he is not expected to suggest that a change in the system of running the business would be beneficial to the company.

The success or failure of a business or a company depends fully on the quality of management. Management Audit is an overall scientific appraisal of the quality of management. In our modern business world, it is necessary that the management auditor should consider the factors of production and various elements of costs. The reason is that each company wants to minimise the cost of production by eliminating wastage and utilising full manpower to make a mark in the competitive business world.

In the present computer world, the company wants to get management consultancy services to locate deficiencies in the performance of management functions. Competent staff members are not available to business concerns in the management cadre or some specialised areas such as operation research, electronic data processing, production control and the like. If a person has specialised in these areas, he will not be willing to work in a business concern. He wants to practise as a Management Consultant. At the same time, he wishes to work as Management Auditor and demand high fees. The client is ready to pay him high fees because the client can earn profits more than what he actually spends on consultation.

Management Audit is a new concept in the field of auditing. The expansion of internal audit is now called *Management Audit*. However, some differences are pointed out between Management Audit and Internal Audit.

## MEANING

Management audit means the examination, review of various policies and action of the management on the basis of certain specified objectives.

The management audit is conducted to critically evaluate the activities and efficiency of the management. It is an independent appraisal activity.

## DEFINITION

It will be useful to study a few definitions of management audit to understand the concept. Some of the definitions are given below:

William P. Leonard defines, "Management audit is a compre-hensive and constructive examination of an organisational structure of a company, institution or branch of Government, or of any component thereof, such as a division or department, and its plans and objectives, its means of operations, and its use of human and physical facilities."

The Institute of Internal Auditors Inc. defines, " A Management audit is a future-oriented, independent and systematic evaluation of the activities of all levels of management for the purpose of improving organizational profitability and increasing the attainment of other organizational objectives through improvements in the performance of the management function, achievement of programme purpose, social objectives and employee's development. Included are an evaluation of the management control system in terms of existence, compliance and adequacy; the management decision- making process in terms of existence, compliance and relevance to the attainment of organizational objectives; the management decision itself in relation to the organizational objectives and the quality of management. The resultant audit report both identifies problems, recommendations and solutions."

H. Washbrook, "The total examination or part of it, include checks on the effectiveness of managers, their compliance with company or professional standards, the reliability of the management data, the quality of performance of duties, and recommendations for improvement. These are variously termed as management audits, administrative audits, opreations audits, or management and administration audits. Management and administration audit is an independent assessment of the soundness of the business unit and its ability to face the business problems of the future."

Leslie R. Howard, "Management audit is an investigation of a business from the highest level downward in order to ascertain whether sound management prevails throughout, thus facilitating the most effective relationship with the outside world and the most efficient organisation and smooth running of the internal organi-sation."

To the American Institute of Management, "Management auditing is a diagnostic appraisal process for analysing goals, plans, policies and activities in every phase of operation to turnover unsuspected weaknessess and to develop ideas for improvement in areas that have escaped management attention."

Taylor and Perry, "Management auditing is a method to evaluate the efficiency of management at all levels throughout the organisation, or more specifically, it comprises the investigation of a business by an independent body from the highest executive level downwards, in order to ascertain whether sound management prevails throughout, and to report as to its efficiency or otherwise, with recommendations to ensure its effectiveness where such is not the case."

William F. Kelly, "A management audit is a critical review of an organisational structure and administration. Its purpose is making recommendations for adjustment and improvement. An audit may involve a whole company structure or be restricted to one of its parts such as division or department."

Michael Stephen R., "The business counterpart of human physical examination is the management audit. In many ways, it is like a financial audit in which the finanacial operations of the company are tested against commonly accepted standards and practices. In the same way, Management Audit is an examination of the administrative operations and organisational arrangements of a company using commonly accepted standards of good management for evaluation."

Federal Financial Officers' Institute, Canada defines, "A systematic independent appraisal activity within an organisation for a review of the entire departmental operations a service to management. The overall objective of operational auditing is to assist all levels of management in the effective discharge of their responsibilities by furnishing them with objective analyses, appraisals, recommendations and pertinent comments concerning the activities reviewed."

Roy A. Lindberg and Theodore Cohn define, "A technique for regularly and systesmatically appraising units or function effectiveness against corporate and industry standards by utilizing personnel who are not specialists in the area of study with the objectives of assuring a given management that its aims are being carried out and/or identifying conditions capable of being improved."

A careful analysis of the above definitions of experts, enables to ascertain that management audit covers the following areas:

1. Examination of organisation structure in full or part thereof.
2. Checking the operations of management and its effectiveness.
3. A critical appraisal of activities of management executives.
4. Examination is to be carried on independently by experts.
5. Evaluation of the functioning of the management board.
6. Analysing goals, plans, policies and activities of the management.
7. Evaluation of the earning capacity of the management.
8. Identification of management weaknesses and suggesting suitable measures for rectification.
9. Making management to face or tackle any problem effectively in future.

## OBJECTIVES OF MANAGEMENT AUDIT

The basic objectives of management audit are given below:

1. To identify the level of achievement of the main objectives of the organisation.
2. To identify the defects or irregularities of management executives.
3. To ensure that the management is going to achieve the objectives.
4. To help the management to do efficient administration of the operations.
5. To help the management executives in the effective discharge of their responsibilities.
6. To suggest to the management the ways and means available to achieve the objectives.
7. To improve the profitability of the organisation.
8. To obtain or utilise the full efficiency of the management.
9. To help the management executives in the effective discharge of their duties.

## SCOPE OF MANAGEMENT AUDIT

The scope of management audit will depend upon the objectives of management audit and requirements of the management. Management audit covers the review of the activities of the entire organisation or only a part of it. The scope of manage-ment audit is briefly explained below:

1. Review of objectives, goals, plans and policies of management.
2. Review of the results of various operations department-wise.
3. Review of the planning process and appraisal of planning.
4. Review and appraisal of utilisation of finance and human resources.

5. Review of organisation structure.
6. Review of management decisions and appraisal of the results of such decisions.
7. Review of the process of delegation of authority and fixing responsibility by management executives.
8. Review and appraisal of physical processes and activities.
9. Review of rules, regulations and methods *i.e.,* systems and procedures of the organisation.
10. Review of management information system and appraisal of its effectiveness.
11. Review of office operations and appraisal of its effectiveness.
12. Review of personnel policies adopted by management.
13. Review of management control systems and control techniques followed by management.
14. Review of selling and distribution system and appraisal of its effectiveness.
15. Review of purchasing operations and appraisal of their effectiveness.
16. Review of production operations and appraisal of their effectiveness.

## NEED FOR OR IMPORTANCE OF MANAGEMENT AUDIT

There are several factors which make management audit important and the need of the hour. Management Audit has become necessary on account of the following main reasons:

1. Management audit examines whether the policies laid down by the company are carried out properly or not.
2. It helps in the improvement of the performance of the various managers including the general manager.
3. Management audit offers suggestion to eliminate wastage or reduce the cost of production.
4. It helps the general manager or the managing director to analyse the performance independently.
5. Management Audit points out the ways available to maximise profit and for optimum utilization of all resources.
6. It finds out the weaknesses or shortcomings which are responsible for inefficient performance and brings improvement in performance.
7. Management Audit can ascertain the financial soundness of the company.
8. It helps the management to sort out financial and non-financial incentive schemes and link them with the performance.
9. Banks and financial institutions may require management audit to find out whether the loan amounts have been properly utilised or not.
10. Management Audit assists the foreign collaborators to assess the progress and performance of the management of the concern with which collaboration has been undertaken.

11. In India, public enterprises follow the rules and procedures but do not evince interest in their achievement and results. Management Audit suggests to the public enterprises that they should change their outlook and insist on improving their efficiency.
12. The management audit is necessary to find out the best methods of improving efficiency.

## QUALIFICATION OF MANAGEMENT AUDITOR

There is no prescribed qualification for a management auditor. The reason is that management audit is the latest development of internal audit and laws do not insist on it. So, it is said that thé internal auditor himself can carry out the management audit also. As such, the management audit work can be assigned to the internal auditor on account of the following reasons:

1. Internal auditor has a good knowledge of the organisation structure, nature of business, real problems of management and the like. Therefore, it is possible for him to offer valuable suggestions.
2. The internal auditor finds an opportunity to gain knowledge of the performance of management in all aspects.
3. The inter-relationship of the personnel is well known to the internal auditor.
4. The personal strength and weaknesses of the employees are well-known to the internal auditor.
5. The internal auditor examines the flows in the working of all the departments of an organisation.
6. The internal auditor can easily undersand the factors which necessitate management audit.

Some express the view that the management audit work should be assigned to a person other than the internal auditor on account of the following reasons:

1. An external auditor can look after the affairs of the company in a different way or from a different point of view.
2. He is not a paid employee of the company. So, he fearlessly offers suggestions to remove the bottlenecks in the performance.
3. He would have rich experiences in various fields. He knows very well the best methods which help to improve the efficiency of the personnel.
4. He has technical knowledge.

These two views have sound reasons to be upheld. It is very difficult to find out who will do management audit very efficiently and economically. In any case, the management audit does not come under the purview of statutory audit.

Now-a-days, there is no statutory body which prescribes any qualification for a management auditor. Management experts are invited to conduct management audit. They are designated as management consultants. The management should consider the technical proficiency of the management consultants while appointing a management auditor. It is advisable to appoint a person other than the internal auditor and statutory auditor as a management auditor. If the management follows this practice, it is sure to get valuable suggestions for improving the efficiency of the management executives.

## APPROACH OF MANAGEMENT AUDIT

A management auditor should frame a audit programme before starting management audit. If the management auditor follows the undermentioned approaches, he can perform his duties efficiently with the help of a good audit programme:

1. He should evaluate the formal organisation structure and organisation charts.
2. He should appraise the management information system in operation.
3. He should study the various policies followed by the management.
4. He should review the extent of authority assigned to the management executives and the responsibilities fixed on them.
5. He should study leave rules and procedures.
6. He should observe the inter-relationship of various management executives.
7. He should study the existing layout of the organisation.
8. He should review the various standards fixed by the management.
9. He should assess the impact of decisions taken by the management executives.
10. He should study the statutory regulations followed for the running of the company.
11. He should review the working conditions and working environment of the management executives.
12. He should study the main objectives and subsidiary objectives of the company.
13. He should review the various levels in the organization hierarchy.

The success of management audit is fully based on the skill and the competence of the management auditor.

## PRELIMINARIES OF MANAGEMENT AUDIT

A single person cannot possess the various skills required for conducting management audit. The management audit should be conducted by a team of experts in order to produce best results. Therefore, the management audit team should consist of members who are experts in different fields such as accounts, engineering, science, psychology and the like. These persons should undergo proper training. Top management should extend all co-operation and provide necessary facilities to them to acquire skills required to appraise the various areas of management.

The management auditor should perform certain duties *i.e.,* preliminary work before commencing the auditing work. These are briefly explained below:

1. He should observe organisation climate.
2. He should study the nature of appointment of management executives.
3. He should study the psychology of management executives.
4. He should identify the inherent talents of management executives.
5. He should find out the degree of involvement of management executives in the performance of work.
6. He should fix the standards for various types of activities.
7. He should observe the treatment of executives and workers by management.

8. He should find out the extent of freedom given to management executives in the performance of work.
9. He should find out the control techniques applied by the management.
10. He should identify the level of job satisfaction available to management executives.
11. He should find out the adequacy of staff members.

Management Auditor should get proper authority from the management to authenticate his appraisal activities. In other words, he should have obtained a clearly defined authority from the management.

## DUTIES OF MANAGEMENT AUDITOR

It is very difficult to fix the duties of management auditor. However, he shall deal with a few areas of work. The management auditor may proceed to check the following items:

1. Purchasing practices followed by the management.
2. Sales practices *i.e.,* receipt of order and its execution.
3. Critical analysis of the manufacturing process.
4. Inspection of a factory *i.e.,* neatness in the production place.
5. Storage facilities.
6. Safety measures with regard to raw materials, finished goods and various assets of a company.
7. Internal transport system with regard to men and materials.
8. Maintenance of records.
9. Customer service.
10. After sales service.
11. Treatment of complaints made by customers.
12. Publicity.
13. Quality inspection practices with regard to raw materials and finished goods.
14. Communication system prevailing between production department and sales department.
15. Efforts adopted to minimize the cost of production.
16. Channel of distribution followed by the company.
17. Cash payment made to creditors.
18. Cash collection got from debtors.
19. Approval of bad debts and the procedure of writing off these bad debts .
20. Safety measures available to workers in the production place.

## MANAGEMENT AUDITOR'S REPORT

The management auditor should make a correct assessment of the working of the organisation. For this puropose, he should prepare a report which contains findings and conclusions of the management audit. He should present his report lucidly without any ambiguity.

The statements which are included in the report should be correct. The correctness of the statement is based on the information received by the management auditor while engaged in the audit work. He should not hesitate in criticising the management.

The management auditor presents his report with courtesy and avoids unnecessary pungency in words. He should express his views regarding the relationship prevailing between the management and the staff. Generally, the following matters have to be dealt with in the report:

1. Express opinion about the returns on investments.
2. Comparison of the actual performance with the standards set by him or the management.
3. Comment on the operating costs of the company.
4. Express opinion about the utilisation of plant and machinery.
5. Recommendations for improvement.
6. Findings and conclusion.

## ADVANTAGES OF MANAGEMENT AUDIT

The main advantages of management audit are discussed below:

1. It helps to identify the present and potential strength and weaknesses in management. With this information, major improvements or rectification of defects can be made.
2. It assists in establishing and reviewing the system of planning in an organisation. Then, it allocates responsibility for planning.
3. It helps to improve the communication and control system. Effective management information systems can be followed. Proper control system ensures no deviations from standards.
4. It reviews the decision-making-process and the quality of decision. It helps the management to bring about more objectivity in decision-making.
5. It protects the interests of the organisation by continuous review of all aspects of organisation and improving the performance.
6. It helps the management to ensure free flow of communication between the responsibility centres.
7. It assists the management in identifying the opportunities through innovations in the light of changes in the business world.
8. It helps the management to improve co-ordination and to evaluate the control techniques.
9. It assists the management in pinpointing the inhibiting factors which affect the profitability and the ways to remove them so that the profitability may improve.
10. It suggests to the management to bring about better efficiency and overall improvement.
11. Human resource is crucial in every organisation. Management audit helps the management to improve performance appraisal system and to develop human resources.
12. It relieves the management of pressure. Thus, the management can devote more attention to important and special matters.

## DISADVANTAGES OF MANAGEMENT AUDIT

Management audit is not free form limitaions or disadvantages. It has some disadvantages also:

1. The scope of management audit is not well defined.
2. Management audit is not conducted every year. So, it is not possible to improve anything during the interval period.
3. Management audit has no standard techniques of its own.
4. It is very difficult to get a competent and expert management auditor to conduct management audit.
5. Management audit may create complexity in authority relationship.
6. Inter-disciplinary knowledge is essential to the management auditor. In practice, it is very difficult to get an auditor with such knowledge.
7. Management does not like to have its policies and actions appraised.
8. Management audit expense is an additional one to the business unit. So, almost all business units consider it unnecessary to meet these additional expenses.
9. In practice, the management audit discourages the initiative of executives rather than encouraging them.
10. It is not possible for a large concern to undertake intensive management audit. Hence, the results are not reliable ones.
11. Management executives are not ready to face criticism of the management auditor. So the management executives are not in favour of the management audit being conducted.
12. Management auditor is not in a position to assess the competence of management executives.
13. Management auditor may try to find fault with others in order to justify his appointment.
14. The suggestions of the management auditor may create an occasion for arousing controversies. There is no consensus of opinion among the management executives. Bradford Cadmus has stated that, "unless the auditor is assigned this project as a special study, he is not in a position to make definite recommendations as to change his primary responsibility which is fulfilled when he has brought the results of the policy to attention through his report — which should present the facts in such manner that the situation may not be overlooked or dismissed without adequate review at a appropriate management level".
15. Management Auditor makes recommendations casually or carelessly. In that case, the desired results may not be obtained.
16. Management does not implement the recommendations as such. It makes some changes in the recommendations before implementation. So, the purpose of the management audit is defeated.
17. Manager will always pay attention to keep the books of accounts correct instead of concentrating on more production and efficiency.

Under these circumstances, the management audit is an effective and efficient tool for the management to exercise control if the management audit is properly conducted. The company can derive more benefits if the management adopts a system to link incentives to the efficiency of the management executives who will also favour the management audit assessing their performance.

## DIFFERENCES BETWEEN MANAGEMENT AUDIT AND STATUTORY AUDIT

There are many similarities between the statutory audit and the management audit. However, there are some differences. The important differences are discussed below:

1. Management auditor reviews and evaluates the policy and performance of the management to ensure its future prosperity. The statutory auditor examines the books of accounts in order to know the past performance.
2. The purpose of management audit is to ensure improvements in the performance of the management. The purpose of statutory audit is to find out whether the books of accounts are properly maintained or not.
3. Management auditor reports the performance of executives for a particular period. Statutory auditor reports the financial position of a company on a particular date.
4. Management audit takes preventive measures. Statutory audit is a post-mortem examination.
5. Management audit suggests ways and means to achieve the pre-determined objectives in the days to come. Statutory audit does not offer any opinion about the state of affairs of the company.
6. Management auditor receives the data both from internal and external sources. Statutory auditor receives the data only from internal sources.
7. Management audit begins when the statutory audit ends. Statutory audit begins at any time.
8. Management audit is not required by law. It is a discretio-nary one. Statutory audit is compulsory as per law.
9. There are no clear cut rules and regulations governing the conduct of management audit. Legal rules and regulations have to be observed while conducting statutory audit.
10. Management audit does not only consider the financial aspects but also considers non-finanacial aspects such as organisation structure, production process, purchase policy and the like. Statutory audit takes into consideration only the financial aspect.
11. There is no prescribed qualification for the management auditor. The qualification of the statutory auditor is prescribed in the Companies Act.
12. Management standards or norms are observed in the case of management audit. Accounting principles, conventions and postulates are followed in the case of statutory audit.
13. Management audit can cover only a part of an organisation. Statutory audit should examine the accounts of the entire organisation.
14. Management audit is conducted as and when required. Statutory audit is conducted once every year.

15. Management auditor submits his report to the management. Statutory auditor submits his report to the shareholders.
16. Management auditor is appointed by the management. Statutory auditor is appointed by a majority of the share holders.
17. The remuneration of the management auditor is fixed by the management. The remuneration of the statutory auditor is fixed by the shareholders.
18. There is no prescribed format to present the report by the management auditor. Statutory auditor should prepare and present the report as per the standard or in the prescribed form.
19. The management auditor cannot be held criminally liable. Statutory auditor is criminally liable under the Companies Act, 1956.

## MODEL QUESTIONS

1. Define management audit?
2. Discuss the benefits and limitations of management auditing?
3. "The deficiencies of financial audit has led to the growth of management audit." Critically examine this statement?
4. State the points which should be borne in mind by the management auditor before he commences the management audit?
5. What points should be incorporated in the management audit report?.
6. What is management audit?

CHAPTER

27

# BUSINESS ETHICS

## INTRODUCTION

Business ethics is concerned with the behaviour of a businessman in doing a business. Unethical practices are creating problems to businessmen and business units. The life and growth of a business unit depends upon the ethics practiced by a businessman. Business ethics are developed by the passage of time and custom. A custom differs from one business to another. If a custom is adopted and accepted by businessmen and public, that custom will become an *ethic*.

Business ethics is not only applicable to any particular type of business but is applicable to every type of business. The social responsibility of business requires the observing of business ethics. A businessman should not ignore the business ethics while assuming social responsibility.

## MEANING OF ETHICS

The word *'ethics'* is derived from *'ethos'*, which to refers character. In literature, *ethics* means a set of principles or morals. The adoption of morality results in forming an ethic in the performance of a work.

## DEFINITION OF ETHICS

P.W. Wright defines, "Ethics is that branch of philosophy which is the systematic study of reflective choice, of the standards of right or wrong by which it is to be guided and of the goods towards which it may ultimately be directed."

Webster defines ethics as "the discipline dealing with that which is good and bad and with moral duty and obligation."

Hurley defines, "Ethics as a system of moral principles."

## MEANING OF BUSINESS ETHICS

Business ethics means the behaviour of a businessman while conducting a business, by observing morality in his business activities.

The behaviour of a businessman has more impact within the business organisation than outside. So, he should obey the laws even though he may personally believe them to be unjust or immoral. If the businessman feels that the provisions of laws are unjust, he can take steps to change the provisions instead of disobeying them.

A businessman should observe morality not only in business activities but also in non-business activities. Such observation of morality is not required out of fear for punishment. He should observe ethics inspired by his own interest in his business and society as a whole. The reason is that there is no distinction between a businessmen and his business. According to Drucker, every individual and organisation in society should abide by certain moral codes and that there is no separate ethics of business.

## DEFINITION OF BUSINESS ETHICS

There is no unanimity of opinion about what business ethics is? Eminent authors define business ethics in their own way. Some of the important definitions of business ethics are given below:

Wheeler 'Business ethics is an art and science for maintaining, harmonious relationship with society, its various groups and institutions as well as reorganising the moral responsibility for the rightness or wrongness of business conduct."

T.M. GARRETT "Business ethics is primarily concerned with the relationship of business goals and techniques to specifically human ends."

Business ethics may be defined as a set of moral rules and principles to protect the interest of customers, employees, society, business unit and the industry as a whole.

## NEED FOR BUSINESS ETHICS

The development of a business has an impact on the lifestyle of a businessman. The behaviour of a businessman has close relationship with his lifestyle. Hence, it is necessary to observe business ethics for the following reasons:

**1. Survival of the business unit:** Businessmen should consider the interest of the business unit. Unethical practices of businessmen will lead to the closure of business unit. The closure of a business unit does not only create problems to business but also to employees and the society in general. Normally, good behaviour is rewarded and bad behaviour is punished. Since, a business is an economic institution, it aims at maximising profits. Businessmen do not maximise the profit at the cost of existence of a business unit. The behaviour of a businessman is affected by some of the factors such as leadership qualities, integrity, knowledge, skills, influence and exercising power. Businessmen are expected to protect their units in all respects.

**2. Growth of business unit:** The next reason for observing business ethics is that it ensures the growth of a business. Whenever a businessman observes ethics strictly, definitely the particular business unit will get developed. A business could not be run in such a manner as is detrimental to the interest of society or business itself. So, it is argued that there should be some business ethics for the growth of a business.

**3. Earning goodwill:** The prime objective of any business is to earn profit. At the same time, no business is allowed to earn profit without following business ethics. If business ethics are properly followed by a business, automatically that particular business unit earns a good name among the public.

**4. Improving the confidence:** Business ethics are necessary to improve the confidence of the customers, employees and the like. If confidence is infused, they (customers and employees) will popularise the name or excellent consumer services of the particular business unit. For example, by speaking well of its merits and pointing out its flaws.

**5. Maintaining Inter-relationship:** No business functions separately or independently. Each business has close relationship with another business even though the nature and size of the other business differs. The proverb "No tree can be considered as a forest" attests this fact. It is expected that each business unit should have a smooth relationship with others. The inter-relationship of business is maintained by adopting business ethics.

**6. Solving social problems:** If a businessman observes ethics in his business, the public have no difficult in having their wants fulfilled. There is no bargaining between the businessman and public. There is a fair treatment of an employee by him. This will avoid social problems like strike, lockout, etc.

## PRINCIPLES OF BUSINESS ETHICS

Following are some of the basic principles of business ethics. They are briefly explained:

1. Service motive should be in the first place rather than profit motive, even though the very purpose of any business is to earn profits.
2. There is no discrimination against any particular group of people, say the rich, the poor, the high, the low, the caste, the religion, etc.

3. Fullest satisfaction should be available to consumers.
4. There is no lack of consideration for clean environment.
5. Human feelings are properly considered while rendering service.
6. There is no wastage or misuse of available scarce resources.
7. Business must be a dynamic and efficient one.
8. Business should provide quality products at reasonable price.
9. Business must maintain or improve standard of living.
10. There must be healthy competition.
11. Employees have no fear regarding the security of job. In other words, there should be job security to employees.
12. Businessman must be sincere in payment of fair wages.
13. Better working conditions or environment should be provided.
14. Efficient employees are properly motivated and recognised.
15. Employees are requested to participate in management.
16. Monetary and non-monetary incentives must be available to employees.
17. Businessman must pay taxes promptly and obey other obligations promptly.
18. Business unit must avoid unfair trade practices like hoarding, black-marketing, etc.
19. There should be no formation of cartel agreements to control production, price, etc.
20. Businessman must disclose all relevant information to needy persons.
21. Businessman must prepare genuine books of accounts and presents before all authorized persons as and when required by them.
22. He should protect the interests of its members at the time of amalgamations, absorption and the like.
23. He should be ready to extend mutual co-operation and mutual help.
24. Business should act as a partner in the development of nation.
25. He should follow proper communication system at all levels.
26. He should not make promises that could not be fulfilled
27. Business assets should not be utilized by its owner or employees for personal use.
28. Employees are allowed free speech in the work place.
29. Business unit should follow proper personnel policy with regard to promotion, transfer and the like.
30. Businessman should not indulge in politics.

## REGULATIONS OF BUSINESS ETHICS

Business ethics are observed by a businessman because of the consequences that would result due to their non-compliance. Here, some of the regulations are presented briefly:

**1. Legislative measures:** Enforcing the legislative measures is one of the ways of making businessmen follow business ethics. The purpose of enforcing the acts is to protect the public interests including the business and the businessmen. The Company's Act, Consumer Protection Act, M.R.T.P. Act and the like are some of the legislative measures.

**2. Goodwill of business unit:** Generally, businessmen have to work hard to earn goodwill by adopting business ethics. Thereafter, the same practice is followed to maintain the earned goodwill.

**3. Social status of businessman:** Businessman thinks that he gets recognition from the public in a place where he does business. It is always ethical for a businessman to keep social status. Then, he wants to enjoy social status continuously and avoid unjust or immoral business activities.

**4. Trade union:** There are number of trade unions functioning in India. A trade union may be a registered or unregistered one. Here, the trade union has to suffer a break if business ethics is not properly followed. Trade union acts as a watchdog to ensure observation of business ethics.

**5. Business association:** Outside agency like the business association guides the business as how to observe business ethics, stating the reasons for doing so. A business unit may be isolated from the business association if the particular business unit fails to comply with ethics.

**6. Consumer movement:** Now-a-days, the consumer movement has developed so much to protect consumer interests. As a matter of fact, business ethics deals with morality in the business environment. Nevertheless, consumer movements take active part in the adoption of business ethics. For example, if a purchased product is not upto the stan- dards as specified, the consumer movement claims damages or takes steps to replace the product to the consumer and insists the business unit to maintain the quality as specified by it.

## FACTORS AFFECTING BUSINESS ETHICS

Business ethics reflects its responsibility, authority and dignity. So, the business organisation wants to conduct its business without affecting the interest of society and the business itself by assuming responsibility, exercising authority and maintaining dignity. But there are some factors affecting the observation or adoption of business ethics. They are briefly explained below:

**1. Unhealthy competition:** Businessmen adopt unfair trade practices to have an edges over other competitors. This will ruin business in the long-run. Unhealthy competition is not preferred by gentleman-businessman.

**2. Abnormal profit motive:** The very purpose of starting a business unit is to earn profit. Only a lesser amount of profit is earned during the initial period of business. But, the businessman wants to earn more profits by economising establishment expenses.

**3. Political interference:** Political parties approach the businessman to get donation. Now, the businessman is not ready to deny it as it would affect the smooth running of business. The donation given to a political party is considered unnecessary expenses from the business point of view. This will affect profit and the smooth running of business.

**4. Political uncertainty:** The policy of government affects the business ethics to some extent. If a number of governments are in power for short periods, there is every chance for changes in the policies of the government. A Stable Government alone does not affect business ethics.

**5. Unjust legislation:** An act is passed only after thorough discussion. But, the person who participates in the discussion does not know the practical difficulties and practices and no business experience. So, a legally right practice may not be ethically right.

**6. Corruption:** A business is regulated by the government through its officials. Straightforward and able officals are working in the government departments. However, the approach or behaviour of some government officials are not appreciated by the businessmen.

**7. Lack of ethical attitude:** A businessman wants to stand out distinctly from other fellow businessmen. At the same time, he does not prefer to practice business ethics inspite of his sound knowledge of them.

**8. Lack of education:** Here, education refers to the knowledge of ethical values. Businessman wants to follow business ethics strictly but he does not know what is the business ethics relating to his business.

**9. Non-co-operation of workers:** Workers or employees do not care about the business ethics. They want, just, to do their work as quickly as possible for remuneration. The impact of non-adoption of business ethics affects the business and not the workers or employees.

**10. Red-tapism:** The existence of red-tapism also affects the business ethics. Business unit should get prior permission of the government for all its proceedings at every stages of development. Red-tapism is found to be at its maximum in the issue of licenses and in the taxtion policy.

## BENEFITS OF BUSINESS ETHICS

A business may be conducted according to certain self-recognised business ethics. If so, certainly, the following benefits are available to the concerned groups. The benefits of business ethics are listed groupwise:

**1. Customers**

1. Receive quality goods.
2. Pay reasonable price.
3. No difficulty in obtaining goods.
4. No price discrimination.
5. No price fluctuation.

**2. Employees**

1. Fair wages.
2. Better working conditions and working environment.
3. Recognising human fellings.
4. Reward for efficiency.
5. Job security.
6. Participation in management.
7. Proper personnel policy.

**3. Industry**

1. Healthy competition.
2. Better co-operation and co-ordination.
3. Steady growth.

**4. Business**

1. Adequate Profit.
2. Fast growth.
3. Fast diversification of business.
4. Less labour turnover.

**5. Society**

1. Better utilisation of resources.
2. Improving standard of living.
3. No pollution problem.

**6. Government**

1. Prompt collection of taxes.
2. Development of nation.
3. Easy implementation of legislation.

## BUSINESS ETHICS IN INDIA

In India, most of the businessmen believe in good business ethics. They realise their responsibilities towards various segments of the society. Novertheless, they find it difficult to translate business ethics into practice. The reason is that the business environment changes every second. Businessmen are ready to cope with changes at any cost by giving up business ethics.

Large number of businessmen wish to earn large profits, through short-cut methods. Books of accounts are prepared by recording focus expenses in order to show less profit to elude tax liability. Next, goods are invoiced at cheaper rate to lower taxes. Reduction in selling price is announced only after increasing the actual selling price. Price discrimination is followed to different types of people, say, known and unknown, educated and uneducated, rich and poor, gents and ladies and the like.

Businessmen are not ready to pay even minimum wages. The health condition of employees is not considered by the businessmen and they are reluctant to pay medical expenses if needed. In some cases, the medical expenses borne by businessmen is deducted from the wages. Businessmen get acknowledgement from the employees for a higher amount than the amount actually paid. This type of practice cannot be controlled by anybody without the whole hearted co-operation of businessmen. The observation of business ethics is only in the hands of businessmen.

## MODEL QUESTIONS

1. Explain the responsibilities of directors and professional managers in the business ethics and management association?
2. Explain business ethics?
3. What is business ethics? Is it a necessary condition for the economic development?
4. What do you understand by ethics of business?
5. Explain briefly about business ethics?

# CHAPTER 28

# OPERATION RESEARCH

INTRODUCTION
MEANING
DEFINITION
CHARACTERISTICS
ROLE OF OPERATION RESEARCH
OPERATION RESEARCH TECHNIQUES
— QUEING THEORY, LINEAR PROGRAMMING,
GAME THEORY AND SIMULATION METHOD
ADVANTAGES OF OPERATION RESEARCH
LIMITATIONS OF OPERATION RESEARCH
MODEL QUESTIONS

## INTRODUCTION

Operation research (OR) technique is used to solve the existing problem in the decision-making process. So, the operation research is otherwise called management science. In a decision-making situation, all variables are quantified for the purpose of analysis. Quantification of variable means that the available information is converted in terms of money, kilogrames, litres, hours, days, months and the like.

OR considers which is best for the company or organisation or management as a whole, not for an individual, a department, section, division or branch. OR was developed during the early years of second world war. Through the analysis of possible consequences of different solutions OR makes an attempt to diagnose and tackle a problem for arriving at the best solution.

## MEANING

Operation research is a technique used to solve all kinds of business, management, industrial and military problems with optimum utilisation of resources.

OR applies mathematical method to solve a problem. So, it eliminates differences of opinion. The solution given by OR is being accepted by all without questions. The overall interest of the management is taken into consideration before selection of a solution.

## DEFINITION

American Encyclopedia of management states that, "The quantitative study of an organisation in action carried out in order to find ways in which its functions can be improved is called operations research."

According to Morse and Kiball, "Operations research is a scientific method of providing executive departments with a quantitative basis for decisions regarding the operations under control."

C.W. Churchman, R.L. Acroff and E.L. Amoff say that, "Operations research is the application of specific methods, tools and techniques to operations of system with optimum solution to the problems."

The definitions of operation research reveal that the nature of problem is expressed in numerical terms, and the existing relationship among the elements of problem are analysed so that a wise decision could be taken on the basis of the analysis made. Operation research is applied where optimum solution is required. Basically, it was developed in order to find ways of allocating scarce resources (men, money and material) in an effective manner to various production operations and to the activities within each operation in order to maximise profit.

## CHARACTERISTICS

The essential characteristics of operation research is discussed below:

1. Presentation of problem quantitatively.
2. Identification of elements of problem.
3. Finding of the existing relationship among various elements of problem.
4. Operation research gives importance to models. Model means representation of events, processes or systems of a problem.
5. Solution is found out on the basis of model.

6. Identification of constraints in the way of proposed solution.
7. Weighing the proposed solution in such a way that a degree of achieving goals is determined.

Operation research techniques are used to solve problems of both routine and non-routine problems i.e. strategic nature. Routine problems are repetitive in nature. They are production problem, inventory problems, repairs to machinery, labour problem, amenities and the like.

## ROLE OF OPERATION RESEARCH

Originally, the operation research has been developed in order to solve the problem of complex decision making. The complexity of business decision is increased by increasing the size of business, competition, laws, consumerism etc. In a complex situation, the basic problem, before most of the managements, is how to optimise business activities for achieving best results. In the present fast developing internet world, business managers face the problem of earning maximum profit at any cost with limited resources. In this situation, operation research helps the business manager to optimise business activities.

1. The operation research techniques cover the entire business activities. The operation research technique can be utilised with regard to production planning, and tackle problems related to labour, materials control, finance, channel of distribution, marketing and the like.
2. Resources can be allocated in the best manner with the help of operation research techniques. Resource allocation is a big problem to a large size business unit because each section of the large size business unit has a tendency to work autonomously and it may require higher resource allocation.
3. Operation research techniques help the management to take quick decision to avail market opportunities at national and international level.
4. A manager can quantify different variables by using operation research techniques.
5. Operation research techniques cover various disciplines such as mathematics, statistics, computer, economics, engineering, management and the like. This type of combination facilitates analysing the problem with greater details and finding out more precise answer of the problem.

The best solution or optimum solution is necessary in every walk of life to get success. In the case of business also, concrete and best solution is essential because of competitive environment.

## OPERATION RESEARCH TECHNIQUES

Operation Research Techniques are developed in order to find optimum solution. Some of the techniques are described below.

## QUEING THEORY OR WAITING LINE THEORY

This theory is applicable to waiting line solution. So, this theory has the name of waiting line. In our fast moving world, people come across waiting line every day at Bus stand, Railway Station, Bank, Park, Beach, Movie House, Hospital, Grocery shop etc. Delay in service at these centres creates loss of customers.

The queing models help the management to take a wise decision. Here, the additional cost of reducing or eliminating waiting time is taken into account. Two factors are considered before taking a final decision. The first factor is additional cost and the second factor is the cost of idle capacity. Idle capacity comes to light when a facility is created by incurring additional cost to reduce or eliminate waiting.

A facility created with low cost, forces the customers to pay high cost of waiting. At the same time, a facility created with high cost, has a high idle capacity cost. An optimum solution that minimises the sum of these two (additional cost and ideal capacity cost) types of cost is necessary.

A facility is created by considering the following points:

1. Rate of arrival of customers.
2. Probability of waiting time
3. Service time.
4. Cost of losing a customer.
5. Number of facilities available.
6. Servicing order i.e. First come First served policy of service.
7. Priority of services-Emergency case is attended to in Hospital.

Quewing theory helps the management in arriving at a decision regarding the provision of optimum facilities.

## LINEAR PROGRAMMING

Linear programming is used to maximise a profit or minimise a loss. This technique is applied when there are several variables affecting the achievement of the objectives of an organisation. Here, the problem arises in choosing the best combination of values for these variables. There is a relationship prevailing between the objectives and each one of the variables. The nature of relationship is linear. It means that a slight change in anyone of the variable would lead to a change in the attainment of objectives.

Scarce resources of an organisation can be effectively utilised by applying linear programming technique. The scarce resources may be money, materials, machines hours and the like. The available resource is found out in its maximum quantity at any given point of time. The quantity of any resource cannot be increased to maximum immediately but it may be possible in the long run. Under linear programming, the management has to take a decision regarding the manner in which those limited resources are to be properly alloted and effectively utilised.

According to Ferguson and Sargent, "Linear Programming is a technique for specifying how to use limited resources or capacities of a business to obtain particular objective, such as least time when those resources have alternative uses." Thus, linear programming is the maximisation of earnings or minimisation of losses subject to certain conditions. Besides this, linear programming gives a lot of information to management for making a more effective decision regarding the resources under control.

## FEATURES OR CHARACTERISTICS OF LINEAR PROGRAMMING

Linear programming has certain features or characteristics. These are briefly discussed below.

**1. Objective function:** The objective of an organisation can be achieved through the application of linear programming. So, it can be termed as objective function.

**2. Quantifiable:** Resources are expressed in terms of quantity. For example Human resources are expressed as number of labour hours, production capacity is expressed as number of units and the like. The objectives of an organisation is also to be expressed quantitatively, say, profit in terms of rupees.

**3. Restrictions:** There are number of restrictions imposed on decision-making process. The restrictions may be in the availability of raw materials, power, labour force and the like.

**4. Certainty:** The outcome of all decisions is known with certainty.

**5. Positive factors:** The linear programming can find out the positive factors in an organisation. There is no possibility of negative factors. Positive factors are responsible for the attainment of the objectives of an organisation.

**6. Optimum utilisation of resources:** Scarce resources are properly alloted and utilised. Nothing will be a waste.

**7. Linear relationship:** Linear relationship means direct relationship. There is a linear relationship between two or among more variables. In other words, a certain proportion of additional inputs will produce the output in the same proportion.

**8. Selection of best course of action:** The decision maker has choice of a number of feasible courses of action instead of a single course of action. Out of several courses of action, the decision maker has to select the best course of action.

**Formulation of Linear Programming Model**

Assume that a company has to produce two types of products viz. G and S. The profit from product G is Rs. 10 per unit and from product S is Rs. 15 per unit. Both products can be produced in the same production process which has a total capacity of 1000 machine hours. The total amount of time required to produce single unit of G is 3 hours and single unit of S is 2 hours. The maximum demand for product G is 225 units and for product S is 200 units in a given period of time. The products of G and S can be sold at any other combination which gives best results subject to the above mentioned restrictions of constraints. The purpose is to find out the best combination which gives the maximum profit by selling these two types of products.

This issue can be solved by applying linear programming model.

**I Choice**

| | | | | |
|---|---|---|---|---|
| G | = | 225 units × 3 hours | = | 675 Hrs. |
| S | = | 162 units × 2 hours | = | 324 Hrs. |
| | | | | 999 Hrs |

Note: One hour is idle time.

Profit from first choice

| | | | | |
|---|---|---|---|---|
| G | = | 225 units × Rs. 10 per unit | = | Rs. 2250 |
| S | = | 162 units × Rs. 15 per unit | = | Rs. 2430 |
| | | | | Rs. 4680 |

**II Choice**

| | | | | |
|---|---|---|---|---|
| G | = | 200 units × 3 hours | = | 600 Hrs. |
| S | = | 200 units × 2 hours | = | 400 Hrs. |
| | | | | 1000 Hrs. |

Profit from second choice

| | | | | |
|---|---|---|---|---|
| G | = | 200 units × Rs. 10 per unit | = | Rs. 2000 |
| S | = | 200 units × Rs. 15 per unit | = | Rs. 3000 |
| | | | | Rs. 5000 |

Note: No idle time

**III choice**

| | | | | |
|---|---|---|---|---|
| G | = | 201 units × 3 hours | = | 603 Hrs. |
| S | = | 198 units × 2 hours | = | 396 Hrs. |
| | | | | 999 Hrs. |

Note: One hour is idle time

Profit from third choice

| | | | | |
|---|---|---|---|---|
| G | = | 201 units × Rs. 10 per unit | = | Rs. 2010 |
| S | = | 198 units × Rs. 15 per unit | = | Rs. 2970 |
| | | | | Rs. 4980 |

In the case of first choice, full opportunity of product G is utilised. Here, one hour is idle time with a profit of Rs. 4680. In the case of second choice, full opportunity of product S is utilised. Here, no idle time is involved with a profit of Rs. 5000. In the case of third choice, product G has be an concentrated since it has more demand than product S. But, an hour is idle with a profit of Rs. 4980. So, it is to be learnt that the second choice is the best one with highest profit and no ideal time.

## SUITABILITY OF LINEAR PROGRAMMING

The linear programming techniques have been successfully used in the following areas.

**1. Allocation of limited resources:** Available limited resources should be properly utilised in order to increase the total output with profit through proper allocation of resources. It involves decisions on allocation of limited resources. Linear programming helps the management to take a valuable decision.

**2. Selection of best combination:** Best combination can be selected in order to achieve the best results at a minimum cost. Combination may be in the area of sales or production, labour force (skilled, unskilled or semi-skilled) etc.

**3. Distribution of products:** A given product can be sold throughout the world. Long distance market requires high cost of transportation which leads to decrease in profit. The profitability of nearby market can be compared with long distance markets. At this junction, the problem with regard to distribution of products can be solved.

**4. Make or buy decisions:** Large scale organisations are usually facing the problem i.e. whether to make a product themselves or buy it in the open market. Here, linear programming techniques can be applied to decide which products should be produced, which should be purchased and the like.

## LIMITATIONS OF LINEAR PROGRAMMING

Linear programming is a highly useful technique for solving peculiar problems, even though, it has some limitations. These limitations are specified below.

1. Linear programming assumes that there is a direct relationship between two variables. But, in practice, there is no such relationship especially in business and industrial problems.
2. The linear programming does not take into consideration of the effect of time and uncertainty. Most of the business or industrial problems are not constant. At the same time, the results or outcome of any solution is not definite.
3. Linear programming deals with single objective of increasing profit or total output. In actual practice, the business or industrial problem has more than one objective. It means that the management does not only consider the increase of profit but also considers labour force, production capacity and the like. The linear programming model cannot handle the multi-objective problems. So, linear programming cannot be applied in the present fast developing internet world.

## GAME THEORY

John Van Neumann and Oskar Morgenstern have developed Game Theory. Game theory tries to anticipate rationally the behaviour of people in competitive situations. The action of an individual has an impact on the behaviour of others. In business, an entrepreneur wants to know the reactions of competitors by offering a special discount or offering gift for bulk purchase, marketing the existing product with new design and the like. Besides, the same entrepreneur wants to know the reactions of consumers by the introduction of a new product, a new advertising campaign and the like. In this situation, Game theory helps the management to develop new strategies for success.

A rational course of action is necessary to get success in competitive situations. Besides, the whole outcome of any action is not only based on the individual action but also on the actions of others. The other members are also facing the same type of problem.

The term "game" refers to a conflict between two or more persons. A game is framed by a set of rules. The set of rules lay down clearly, what should be done and what should not be done by each player in a set of circumstances. Each player has a lot of choice in every movement of other fellow-players. Finally, one player has to win and others have to lose. A logic behind in every game is finding an optimum winning strategy for a particular competitive situation. Each player should realise that his opponent i.e. fellow-player is motivated similarly. The reason is that each player has the sole aim i.e. winning.

## FEATURES OR CHARACTERISTICS OF GAME THEORY

A competitive situation can be termed as game if the same has some of the following features or characteristics.

1. Each player is expected to act rationally.
2. There is a conflict of interests among players. Here, the conflict of interest refers to the goal i.e. winning.
3. Each player plays logically.
4. There is only one winner.
5. Every movement is to maximise his gains and minimise his losses in a competitive situation.
6. The strategy adopted by a player affects the strategies followed by other players.

7. Each player has a lot of methods to be chosen for a win.
8. Set of rules of a game are constraints to the strategies followed by all the players.
9. No player knows the strategies of other players until he has decided his own course of action.
10. There is no direct communication between the players.
11. Each player knows the competitive situation.

The basic objective of game theory is to provide a basis for taking a decision in the light of competitive situation and actions of the competitors. The game theory can be applied to elections, military, war, marketing strategies and the like. The difficulty of application is compounded because the competitive situations and relationships are dynamic and constantly fluctuating. The reason is that the action of one person sets off a chain of reaction in others. Besides, other people are changing their actions also. However, Game theory helps the management to predict the future events with a reasonable degree of accuracy.

## SIMULATION METHOD

Simulation is not a procedure but a model. The model represents reality. Under simulation, a situation is to be described instead of searching for an optimal solution. Description of situation helps the management to take a valuable decision. According to Chase, Richard B. and Nicholas J. Aquilano, "Simulation is the use of digital computers to assist in performing experiments on a model of a real system."

This method can be applied whenever there are several variables affecting results and the same variables are themselves uncertain. Simulation is not a separate tool. But, it is used along with mathematical tool if the problem is too complex in nature. Simulation models have been successfully used in plant location, selection of a space for branch, space flights and the like.

## ADVANTAGES OF SIMULATION

Some of the advantages of simulation method are discussed below.

1. The expenses of simulation model is very low.
2. Simulation model can answer any type of questions.
3. Risk of adopting simulation model is very low. The reason is that a trial and error approach is followed to frame a model.
4. The problem can be thoroughly studied. It helps the management to frame a best model.
5. Simulation model can be used to verify solutions obtained through analysis.

Even if the above mentioned advantages are available, there is no possibility of getting optimum model for any problem. This is the demerit of simulation model. A simulation model cannot be applied to study, to analyse other problems than the specified one.

## ADVANTAGES OF OPERATION RESEARCH

Some of the advantages of operation research are given below.

1. Sound decisions can be taken by the management.
2. By analysing operation research models, management executives have to pay close attention to several variables which are affecting the decisions.

3. Operation research is not a decision. But, it helps the management in decision-making process.
4. A systematic approach is made instead of avoiding rules of thumb approach while taking a decision.
5. A tough problem is to be broken into several small parts so that the problem can be easily diagnosed and found a suitable solution.
6. An experimentation of any solution is carried on before implementation. This process makes the solution as the best one.

## LIMITATIONS OF OPERATION RESEARCH

Operation research has some limitations also. A manager or decision-maker should be well aware of these limitations while taking a valuable decision.

1. Operation research requires heavy expenses because taking a single solution or decision involves a long process.
2. Operation research tries to give best solution by taking into consideration all the variables related to the problem. This is not possible in this present business world. It is very difficult to find the number of variables affecting a problem.
3. Operation research cannot be applied to many situations where human qualities and interpersonal relationship are responsible for a problem.
4. There is a gap between the decision-maker and an operation research analyst. A decision-maker is not in a position to be conversant with the operation research techniques. At the same time, the operation research analyst may not be aware of the nature of problems. This type of gap impair the quality of the decision.
5. Operation research is based on the quality of statistical information. If the statistical information is far from exact, the decision taken with the help of operation research may turn out to be faulty.

Over and above the limitations operation research technique can be used to find the best solution. Individuals can also adopt operation research techniques for solving the problems related to their private affairs.

## MODEL QUESTIONS

1. Define operation research?
2. What are the advantages of linear programming?
3. How Game Theory helps the management to solve a problem?

# CHAPTER 29

# MANAGEMENT INFORMATION SYSTEM

INTRODUCTION
MEANING
DEFINITION
INFORMATION AND DATA
OBJECTIVES OF MANAGEMENT INFORMATION SYSTEM
ELEMENTS OF MANAGEMENT INFORMATION SYSTEM
AREAS OF MANAGEMENT INFORMATION SYSTEM
IMPORTANCE OF MANAGEMENT INFORMATION SYSTEM
FACTORS AFFECTING THE MANAGEMENT INFORMATION SYSTEM
TYPES OF INFORMATION
PER-REQUISITES FOR DESIGNING MANAGEMENT INFORMATION SYSTEM.
DESIGNING THE MANAGEMENT INFORMATION SYSTEM
PROCESS OF MANAGEMENT INFORMATION SYSTEM
ADVANTAGES OF MANAGEMENT INFORMATION SYSTEM
CAUSES FOR POOR MANAGEMENT INFORMATION SYSTEM
GUIDELINES FOR IMPROVING MANAGEMENT INFORMATION SYSTEM
MODEL QUESTIONS

## INTRODUCTION

Management requires complete reliable information to solve any problem and exercise effective control by taking a timely decision. The complete reliable information is received by proper collection, handling and providing the right information to the right person in right time. The proper management information system it not only reduce the risk of wrong decisions but also work as an effective controlling techniques. Managers at every level require important information with speed, brevity and economy in order to discharge their functions effectively.

Due to the complexity of business and industrial operations, the management information system (MIS) gets more importance. Government regulations are to also create the need of supply of more reliable information accurately within short span of time. This clearly shows that the management executives are entering into an "Information Age".

## MEANING

Management Information System is a planned, organised and systematic collection of relevant, accurate, precise and timely information which are properly processed and supplied to required persons economically for the purpose of achieving organisational objectives.

## DEFINITION

Walter J. Kennevan defined Management Information System as, "a formal method of collecting timely information in a presentable form in order to facilitate effective decision-making and implementation in order to carryout organisational operations for the purpose of achieving the organisational goals."

James A.F. Stoner defined Management Information System as, "a formal method of making available to management accurate and timely information necessary to facilitate the decision-making process and enable the organisation's planning, control and operational functions to be carried out effectively."

Management Information System Committee of the Financial Executive Institute defined, "An Management Information System is a system designed to provide Selected decision-oriented information needed by management to plan and evaluate the activities of the corporation. It is designed within a framework that emphasises profit planning, performance planning and control at all levels. It contemplates the ultimate integration of required business information sub-systems both financial and non-financial within the company."

## INFORMATION AND DATA

Information is different from data. Data means facts that are not currently being used for decision-making purposes. Data may provide a basis for the decision-making process. On the other hand, information means a processed data which is used directly in the decision-making process. Simply, data can be converted into an information. Likewise, an information can be converted into data. But, data cannot be a substitute of information and *vice versa*.

The term data includes number of persons employed, production and sales details, sundry debtors, sundry creditors, bonus details and the like. This data can be processed, prepared and presented in such a way that in making decisions regarding planning and control of operations of the organisation. The available data has to be converted into a desirable form. The transformation of data involves *six* functions. They are collecting of data, processing the data, analyse the data, storing of data, evaluation and supply of data to the needy persons.

Since the human beings is going to use the information to take decisions such information can be carefully handled without losing any useful aspect. The reason is that large amount of information can be processed on a daily basis with growing of business. According to Louis E. Boone, "Daily computer printouts provide thousands of details about production schedules, current inventory positions of raw materials, goods in process and finished products, output levels by plants, shifts and departments; and cost and sales analysis by territory, product, customer, sales division and order size, etc."

## OBJECTIVES OF MANAGEMENT INFORMATION SYSTEM

An effective Management Information System can achieve the following objectives.

**1. Facilitates decision-making:** Management executives at all levels are taking large number of decisions by receiving the best possible current information. Accurate, reliable, precise and timely information facilitates the decision-making process very easy.

**2. Avoid duplication of work:** Major portion of the organisational operations are computerised and procedures are simplified. This type of system reduces unnecessary work and eliminate the performance of duplication of work.

**3. Savings of time:** Efficient methods are applied in the execution of assigned activities and proper direction is available to the employees of an organisation. Standard time is fixed for each work separately. In this way, there is a possibility of savings of time.

**4. Establish uniform procedures:** Nature of work is different from one department to another department or one section to another section, but standard and uniform procedure is followed in the performance of a work. Uniform procedures ensures proper flow of data from the concerned department of section.

**5. Fixing responsibility:** Data have to be supplied immediately after execution of work. Hence, it is the responsibility of concerned executive to provide data. In this way, MIS fixes responsibility each executive.

**6. Improving service:** Necessary training is to be imparted to the executives before installing Management Information System. Hence, improved service is rendered by the executives in an organisation.

The Management Information System should be flexible in nature to incorporate revisions and include additional sub-systems in order to achieve above mentioned objectives.

## ELEMENTS OF MANAGEMENT INFORMATION SYSTEM

The term Management Information System consists of three words. They are Management, Information and System. If one understands the meaning and nature of these three words, properly, he can have thorough understanding the concept of Management Information System.

### Management

Management is the process of planing, organising and controlling of the physical and human resources in order to achieve the objectives of an organisation. Managers can prepare the plan in order to achieve the objectives by selecting best course of action. He can indentify the task which are emerged under the operation of an organisation and organised into homogeneous groups. The completion of the task is to be controlled by setting performance standards and avoid deviations from such standards. In this place, management facilitates the executives for taking number of valued decisions with regard to planning, organising and controlling the performance of task and functions of the business.

**Information**

Information can be defined as a tangible or intangible facts which are used to reduce or avoid uncertainty of future events. Information is necessary to every management to plan and control the business operations effectively.

Information is derived from the data out of the available data, information is developed and used for decision making purpose. There must be a proper transformation of data into information. The presentation of information in such a way that is current and in a readily usable and easily understood format.

**System**

A system can be defined as a set of interrelated elements working towards for achieving general objectives of an organisation.

There may be many sub-system in an organisation and all such systems are parts of large systems. There is a need of application of principles of system in a business organisation. If so, there is a possibility of integration of the sub-systems through information inter proper change. The system concept of MIS is therefore one of optimising the output of the organisation by connecting the operating sub-systems through the medium of information exchange.

## AREAS OF MANAGEMENT INFORMATION SYSTEM

There are three areas of management information system. They are decision-making, planning and control. These areas are briefly explained below.

**Decision-making**

MIS is designed to generate and free flow of information collected from internal and external sources for sound decision making in all functional area of business. Management should have well organised system to collect information and maintain upto date information to take prompt and timely decision. MIS is an integral part of decision-making process at all levels of management.

The main aim of MIS is to help the managers to take timely decisions in their areas of responsibility irrelevant information should be avoided while taking a decision.

**Planning**

Top management wants information for planning purpose. Planning is the primary function of management. The primary function is effectively carried on by the managers under well designed management information system. Sometimes, the MIS can be hooked up to various corporate models for planning. The uncertainty can be converted into a certainty through proper planning. This is possible only with the help of management information system.

**Control**

The MIS informs the decision-maker about the performance of work with standards set for them. If the information is better, more complete, more reliable and timely, it is easier for manager to exercise effective control. Additionally, a system of controls must be developed so as to ensure proper control.

## IMPORTANCE OF MANAGEMENT INFORMATION SYSTEM

An effective management information system is very important on account of the following reasons.

**1. Complexity of business operations:** The business operations will be changed into complexity due to dynamics of the environment. The MIS helps the managers in this situations, to look upon the business operations without much difficulty.

**2. Size of business unit:** Most of the business units have grown in size. This results in management being removed from the scene of the operations. Now, MIS plays in vital role to solve operational problems.

**3. Changes in economic structure:** Rate of inflation and unemployment, changes in interest rate GNP and the like are affecting the smooth functioning of a business unit. Hence, these type of information should be collected and helps the managers to take a valid decision.

**4. Technological changes:** These include changes in the operations of a business unit. Whenever there is a changes in technology, there is a problem to the management. This type of problem can be easily solved with the help of effective MIS.

**5. Social changes:** These include higher level of education,. changes in consumer tastes, usage of computer at home, preferences of job etc. this type of information is maintained upto date. If so, running of a business unit is very easy.

**6. Determination of training needs:** In large scale enterprise, the operations are decentralised so that more information is needed about the operations of units. The performance of all units should be closely watched and steps must be taken if there is a poor performance of units. It means that training needs can be found out in order to improve the performance of units. Here, MIS can be effectively used for measuring performance and decide the training needs for better performance and achieve organisational goals and plans.

**7. Wide use of computer:** The computers are widely used since the operation requires less expenses and have more capacity to store and supply more information. This has made information handling easier.

## FACTORS AFFECTING THE MANAGEMENT INFORMATION SYSTEM.

There must be a free flow of information from one place to another place within organisation. If so, every employee knows what is happening in an organisation and try to change his activities. Even though, some factors affecting the free flow of information. They are listed below.

**1. Availability:** Availability of information refers more accurate and relevant information. All decisions are made out of available information. If decisions are made out of inadequate, inaccurate and irrelevant information, the results are highly uncertain. But, there is no parameter available to access the information as accurate or inaccurate, relevant or irrelevant and adequate or inadequate. Hence, the managers are forced to take decisions out of available information

**2. Quality:** Quality of information describes its compactness and accuracy. Sound decisions are taken only out of quality information. Accordingly the information should be precise and highly reliable.

**3. Quantity:** Too much information cannot be processed very easily by the management within stipulated time and difficult to get accurate information. On the other hand, too little information may leave relevant, reliable and accurate information which are necessary to take useful decisions.

**4. Timeliness:** Information must be available when needed. Sometimes, some important decisions can be delayed due to non-availability of necessary information properly in time and the results missed opportunities. At the same time, the time gab between the collection of data and the presentation of the proposed information should be reduced as much as possible. Besides, the information should be presented before the decision-maker when needed and not on a periodic and cyclic basis.

## TYPES OF INFORMATION

The various types of information needed to the management. They are briefly discussed below.

**1. Operating information:** It includes various operation of unit. Details of production and sales, number of persons employed, overtime worked in terms of production and man hours, wastage's in terms of unit of measurement etc. are the examples of operation information

**2. Status information:** The status of certain work on a particular point of time is given. Work in progress in terms of unit of measurement, stage of major project, stage of construction work etc., are the examples of status information

**3. Resource information:** It includes the resources of an organisation. Own capital, borrowed capital, skilled human resources, semi-skilled human resource, unskilled human resources, materials, power etc. are the examples of resource information.

**4. Resource allocation information:** It includes allocation of available resources within organisation own capital used for purchase of fixed assets and current assets, borrowed capital used for purchase of fixed assets and current assets or clean of old debts, employment of personnel in departmentwise etc., are the examples of resource allocation information.

**5. Planning and control information:** Top management can prepare the plan and control for each activity production and sales budget, cash budget production schedule, capital budgeting, zero base budgeting etc., are the examples of planning and control information.

**6. Government information:** It includes the fiscal policies of the government. Government present the budget every year which affects the business to some extent. The extent of affect and ways of affect are to be accessed and presented to the Government information.

**7. Social information:** It includes demographic details. population in urban area wise and rural area wise, sex wise, industrial workers wise, religion wise, community wise etc. are social information.

**8. Economic information:** It includes economic condition of a nation. Rate of inflation, rate of interest, cost of inflation index, money value standard of living, per capita income, GNP, etc. are the economic information

**9. Technology information:** The technology adopted by the organisation for each activity is kept in a separate file. Besides, the technology available in the market, technology adopted by other similar units and the gab between latest technology available and technology adopted by the organisation are included in technology information.

**10. Competition information:** Competition with regard to sales, labour force and raw materials suppliers are included in competition information. The list of competitors and their strength and weaknesses are also collected as information for taking sound decisions.

## PER-REQUISITES FOR DESIGNING MANAGEMENT INFORMATION SYSTEM

Management Information System should be effective. So, proper care has been taken by the management executives to design management information system. The following pre-requisites are necessary for designing effective management information system.

1. Top management should define, decide and describe the types of information needed to the decision-maker.
2. Information format is also decided well in advance for quick supply of information.
3. Management can identify the problems connected with free flow of information within organisation. These problem should be solved to remove the constraints involved with supply of inadequate information.
4. The sources of information should be clearly defined and explained to the concerned persons who are responsible to collect the information.
5. Management information system has the alternatives to the long range plans by considering environment conditions.
6. The management can select the best MIS pattern. The management should consider cost, feasibility, flexibility and implementability while selecting the best MIS pattern.
7. High degree imagination and foresight are the important factors responsible to design effective management information system. Hence, the management should employ such type of personnel while designing MIS.
8. The designed MIS should cope with the needs, goals and environment of the organisation.

## DESIGNING THE MANAGEMENT INFORMATION SYSTEM

Under management information system, a set of procedures is systematically followed to collect relevant data, processing the data and presented in a required format as information. When the management can take sound decisions and necessary actions for running the business. A well developed system should be designed in the following manner.

**1. Supplies complete, accurate and timely data:** Effective planning and decision-making is possible by availing complete, accurate and timely data. The MIS would solve the problems connected with inconsistent, incomplete and inaccurate data,

**2. Identify and quantify inter-related operations:** Production and sales are independent variables, but, these variables have close relationship within each other. Production is depending upon the demand for the product i.e. sales volume. So, the information of production develops a relationship with sales. This can be projected to forecast future trends.

**3. Measure and control the performance:** Production data can be presented in monetary terms. If so, production costs can be measured and control the performance which can be closely monitored.

**4. Identify needs of decentralised organisation:** In large scale enterprise, there is a decentralisation of authority and departmentation. The needs of such decentralised units and departments can be properly noted to avoid duplication and waste of efforts. It means that a pool is created to collect the data from such units and departments.

**5. Information in summarised form:** Information is presented in such a manner that action can be initiated and/or decision can be taken without further interpretation and analysis. It reduces the time, efforts and volume of information. Management by exception principle is followed here by the top management.

**6. Flexibility:** The management information system should be flexible as much as possible so that the system can be changed or revised whenever necessary.

## PROCESS OF MANAGEMENT INFORMATION SYSTEM

The transformation from data to information involves six stages. These six stages have been briefly explained below.

**1 Assembling:** It means finding and collection of data and recorded in a set of files. The well defined sources of information facilitates the collection of data.

**2. Processing:** It means that the collected data has been summarised, edited and processed. During editing, the irrelevant and inaccurate data have been eliminated from the records.

**3. Analysing:** It means that the data has been analysed to develop or calculate percentages, ratios etc. percentages and ratios are providing useful information to the decision-maker.

**4. Storage and retrieval:** Indexing, coding, filing and location of information are coming under the process of storage. Provisions have been made to quick relocation of such information and retrieval when it is necessary.

**5. Evaluation:** It means the determinations of usefulness of information in terms of accuracy, precise, and relevance. The degree of accuracy, precise and relevance is based upon the needs of the decision-maker.

**6. Dissemination:** It means supplying the required information in the specified format at the right time to the decision maker.

## ADVANTAGES OF MANAGEMENT INFORMATION SYSTEM

The effective management Information System contributes in the following ways to the management

**1. Facilitates planning:** Planning requires reliable, relevant and accurate information. These are possible under the effective management information system. The MIS keeps the executives aware of changes in the environment of business. In this way, MIS facilitates the planning function carried on by the executives.

**2. Reduce information overload:** All the data collected by an organisation is not required to managers. Under effective MIS, the data has been divided into relevant and irrelevant. The irrelevant data may create confusion in the minds of managers. Hence, the irrelevant data has been avoided with the help of effective MIS and reduced information overload

**3. Simplifies control:** MIS is acting as a bridge between planning and control. It helps the managers to take a sound decision which simplifies control function.

**4. Assists co-ordination:** MIS is an integrated approach to planning and control. MIS facilitates co-ordination by keeping each department/section aware of the problem, status, importance and needs of other departments/ sections. It links all decision centres in an organisation.

**5. Improves decentralisation:** Monitoring work is also done under the effective MIS. This type of arrangement helps the management to delegate authority without losing control.

## CAUSES FOR POOR MANAGEMENT INFORMATION SYSTEM

Management Information System is to make an effective with the help of computer capabilities. Eventhough, there may be some causes for poor management information system. They are given below:

**1. More information is better:** Effective or sound decision can be taken only out of more information. This is a fallacy. But, the real fact is that only relevant, accurate and precise is enough for taking effective decision and not more. Generally, more information will over burden the decision- maker and even creates a confusion. This process may lead the decision-maker into an unwanted place. Besides, he cannot be able to absorb all information. Hence, mere accurate and relevant information is enough.

**2. Lack of managerial involvement:** Effective MIS requires top management support. Moreover, the decision maker has to be encouraged so that MIS has been properly utilised. If not so, no use following MIS.

**3. Poor communication:** The managers must be provided with relevant current information. Then, the managers should be trained to recognise the basic nature and utility of computer. The computer specialist must design a system in which every decision maker is going to use the computer to avail better communication. But, in practice, the computer is used for generate data and results poor communication.

**4. Computers cannot do everything:** Computer can process the data and provide at the information in a specified format. But, it does not compensate managerial judgement. Besides, computer can be used as a tool and not a substitute of decision maker.

**5. Human acceptance:** The success of the MIS depends upon the acceptance and involvement of employees of the concerned organisation. Generally, the employees can oppose the MIS because the system may increase the workload or decrease the importance of human being.

## GUIDELINES FOR IMPROVING MANAGEMENT INFORMATION SYSTEM

The management information system can be improved by adopting the following guidelines.

1. There must be a involvement of top management in the design of MIS. This involvement leads to greater acceptance on the part of employees of an organisation.

2. There must be a close relationship between the designer and user of MIS. This is created by motivating employees to design the MIS themselves. Employees know the ground reality of an organisation. Hence, employees can design the MIS very effectively.

3. Master plan can be developed. The master plan is not only covers current needs but also covers future needs of an organisation. The master plan avoid the uncertainties connected with MIS development.

4. Both designees and users are held responsible and accountable for the success of MIS on cost benefit analysis basis. The accountability cannot be changed so that benefits exceeds costs.

5. Management should take all efforts to create confidence in the minds of employees to accept it as an aid rather than a replacement.

## MODEL QUESTIONS

1. How do you differentiate data from information?
2. What is management information system?
3. "Information itself is a resource for optimum utilisation by management." Comment.
4. What are the symptoms of an inadequate MIS design?

# APPENDIX A

# CASE ANALYSIS

**Case Analysis 1**

Analyse the following case and write your report:

**Inter-personal Communication**

Ms. Shina, was incharge of administrain branch of a big firm. There were a large number of women typists. They were all efficient in their job and finished the entire work assigned to them for that day before leaving office. There was no overtime requirement for typing work in this section.

One day the Managing Director of the firm sent for the Manager of the Administration Department, Mr. Mohan and informed him that 'persons in his department have started taking liberty in regard to punctuality in the office.' He said that on a particular day, when he was coming to office at 9.40 a.m. in the morning, he found two typists/stenos coming late and that it was not the first time that he had seen this. He wanted that his supervisors should be made wise in this respect.

Mr. Mohan listened to the instructions of the Managing Director and promised to ensure punctuality.

Mr. Mohan called Ms. Shina and told her about the incident of the two late comers and the Managing Director's observations. He also stated that punctuality should be observed at all costs. Ms. Shina, replied that she was aware of the situation and did not feel the necessity of taking any action. She said that the stenos/typists are very hard working and that they do not mind even sitting late for an hour or so in the office if there was pressure of work. They were intent in finishing the day's work before leaving the office and that they were not habitual late comers and they usually observe punctuality. She also pleaded that probably because of some personal reasons, one or two typists may be late by ten or fifteen minutes, sometimes, and this should not be taken cognizance of in the interest of good working.

Mr. Mohan, however, insisted that she should act according to the instructions of the Managing Director.

Ms. Shina got perplexed. She went back to her section and communicated the entire story to her typists and told them that the Managing Director wanted them to come to the office in time and that he is against any relaxation in this matter. She also told them that action will be taken against the late comers.

The typists did not relish this Ms. Sarla and Ms. Rama discussed this matter during lunch as they were the typists who came late that day. They felt that they had not been given proper treatment.

Ms. Sarla said, 'It is very strange that things have been taken too far. I have now decided that if I am asked to sit late, I won't, I shall leave the office at 5.30 p.m. leaving the work where it is.'

Just after two days, the Private Secretary to the Managing Director sent some urgent typing work to Ms. Rama at 5.15 p.m. Two typists would require atleast one hour to type that entire material. The Managing Director was to see the Chairman in the evening with these important papers. He wanted the typed matter back to him in any case by 6.30 p.m.

Ms. Shina assigned the work to Ms. Sarla and Ms. Rama, but both of them expressed their inability to undertake the job as it would take complete one hour, whereas they could stay in the office atmost for fifteen minutes. The office closes at 5.30 p.m. Both the typists did not fail to remark that, if 'the officers sometimes wanted them to sit late, why such hue and cry should have been made when someone was late by a few minutes and that too on a few occasions?'

It became a problem for Ms. Shina to get the papers typed. She was afraid that other typists may also give the same reply. So, she went back to the Private Secretary to the Managing Director stating that the Private Secretary and herself may have to share the work and do it, though the Private Secretary had some other work of priority.

## QUESTIONS

(a) What do you think about the behaviour of Ms. Shina, Ms. Sarla and Ms. Rama?
(b) Has the communication failed somewhere? If so, where and how?
(c) How can you improve such a situation?
(d) What do you feel about the Managing Director's attitude?
(e) What do you feel about Mr. Mohan's attitude?
(f) How would you react in such a situation?

*(B.B.A., M.K. University, Nov. 1997)*

**Case Analysis 2**

Analyse the following case and write your report:

### Punishment and Discipline

Mr. X, a commerce graduate with management qualifications, is a junior officer in an organisation where there are more white-collared than blue-collared workers. Mr. X is extremely dedicated to his work and can be called a workaholic. He adopts all modern management techniques to get results; a go-getter and a trouble shooter. He is respected and loved by his subordinates for his approach and knowledge and the workers would go to any length to complete the job given by him.

Mr. Y is a middle level manager in the same organisation. Though not formally qualified in management, he adopts management techniques suited to the organsiation. His style of functioning has been extremely successful. He is an extremely knowledgeable person and has the right pulls at right places to get things done. His approach towards his subordinates is parental and towards his bosses is one of 'reaching organisational goal at any cost.' His motto towards his junior officers is 'freedom, independence and protection' and hence Mr. X has taken him to be his mentor.

Mr. Z is the top manager in this ladder. As General Manager, he is good in his approaches, listens and take decisions based on his own judgements. He generally does not believe in severe reprimands and punishments (though occasionally shows his annoyance) but is very lavish in his praises particularly towards his subordinates. He is also known for his 'extreme liking' for disciplined behaviour.

Whenever some good work was done by Mr. X, Mr. Z, the General Manager had showered praises and expressed his appreciation to Mr. X on many such occasions during discussions between Mr. X and Mr. Z. On some such occasions even Mr. Y had also been present.

There have been some occasions when Mr. Y let out his temper in public and has taken up with Mr. X for some mistakes, in front of his colleagues. Mr. X has also been argumentative on such occassions and has been insisting that what he had done is right and that there was only a communication gap or that Mr. Y has not understood the problems correctly.

On one particular occasion Mr. Y really became furious on Mr. X and reprimanded him severely publicly. Mr. X felt hurt and the matter was taken to the top level.

Mr. X was arguing with Mr. Z, the top boss that 'praises should be given in public and reprimand in private' and that Mr. Z was praising Mr. X in private while Mr. Y was reprimanding in public and hence both were making things worse for Mr. X and doing a disservice to the organsiation.

Mr. Z explained that he was lavish in praises in private to Mr. X, mainly to encourage and motivate him for better results and never failed to put in a word of appreciation about Mr. X at the appropriate higher levels at appropriate time. Also, if Mr. X was praised in public, this might create jealousy amongst colleagues and may create problems for him by their non-co-operation in conveniencing him in day-to-day functioning for want of proper horizontal interaction.

With regard to the action of Mr. Y, he explained to Mr. X that a reprimand given publicly will be taken seriously and he will make amends besides making others feel that Mr. Y is not partial or have no peculiar attachment to Mr. X and Mr. Y's position will be clear before the other colleagues and subordinates.

This will also reduce jealousy towards Mr. X by his colleagues and may even result in some sympathy towards Mr. X and there would be better results. If any reprimand or other disciplinary action is taken privately, others will not know whether that action was fair or not, and it cannot have a constructive influence on the future behaviour of others.

Mr. X being a qualified management graduate and having always been told that 'reprimand should be given in private and praises in public' did not agree with the views of both the bosses.

The points that arise from the above case study are:

## QUESTIONS

1. With whom do you agree and why?
2. How will you avoid the gap being widened?

*(B.B.A., M.K. University, April 1998)*

## Case Analysis 3

Analyse the following case and write your report.

### The Case of the Controversial Person

S & Co. Ltd. was an organisation manufacturing consumer durables. The company had a large number of workforce white collared for office and factory management and blue collared for factory work. There were a number of technical supervisors in the factory. While the managers at all levels were at the corporate office, the technical supervisors of the factory has also had a channel/avenue for promotion to the management cadre in the corporate office provided the corporate office had a separate wing dealing with any special aspect of a particular shop. There were some shops like the finished product section, millright, sample testing sections etc., which fell in this category. Mr. Ram, who has also specialised in Human Resource Development was the Personnel Manager of the Company (in the middle management cadre-directly reporting to the top). Mr. Krishna is a colleague of Mr. Ram. dealing with technical matters of the company and belonging to a different department. Whenever any promotion is sought to be given by the company to any of the posts in the category of lower level managers, the recommendations of these two are required to be submitted which the top brass considers and orders the promotion.

There arose one vacancy of lower level manager in the finished product division at the corporate office. This section was dealing with the problems of workers of that section in the factory, apart from other work and this work was entrusted to that manager. Recommendations were to be made.

Mr. Prasad and Mr. Kumar were the eligible, entitled contenders for that post. Papers were accordingly put up, stating that both of them were good in their work. Mr. Prasad was a go-getter, used to take quick decisons (sometimes wrongly also) while Mr. Kumar was a non-interfering type permitting decisions to be taken at lower levels.

There were also reports that on one or two earlier occasions Mr. Prasad was sought to be charged owing to his cetain unpalatable decisions, which could not ultimately be implemented. Work turnout under his supervision was very good and a number of workers liked him for the simple reason that he used to take decision one way or the other without procrastination, though some subordinate branded him as a controversial person.

Mr. Kumar, apart from being a non-interfering, non-controversial person, also wanted, whenever required, others in the organisation to come to him for guidance but not to quote him anywhere (particularly to the top or whenever his guidance has resulted in something going wrong).

Mr. Ram the Personnel Manager wanted to recommend Mr. Prasad on the ground that he was a go-getter and good at decision making. Mr. Krishna, however, wanted to recommend Mr. Kumar for that post on the ground that he was non-interfering. The Personnel Manager argued with his colleague in favour of his recommendation stating that, in an organisation, particularly at the level of Manager in a section be it lower, middle or higher decision making is very important. Decisions, he argued, depend upon many factors including circumstances, and may be unpalatable to some at times and this cannot be avoided. Mr. Krishna, argued that Mr. Prasad is a controversial person since he used to show his authority and assert himself and this was not advisable in the present day context and present position where he had to handle a very important section of blue collared staff. Mr. Ram did not agree with this view and argued that since Mr. Kumar is one who plays safe and avoids, whenever occasion permits, taking decision, he may not be a good manager. Also that Mr. Kumar looks in the eyes of Krishna as good, since he was not keen in enforcing the systems and thus not causing inconvenience to any one which was not good for the organisation in the long run. Mr. Ram also argued that no management is free from controversial persons. It is human nature that some persons cannot keep quiet without commenting on others and others action and they have to say something bad or adverse about the performers and thus make them controversial. In fact, a controversial person is always better for the organisation since there will, otherwise, be no competitiveness with consequential higher production, particularly in our Indian context, the Japanese style of co-operative leaderhsip and co-operative ego cannot be expected as only individual ego produces results in this country. Since they did not see eye-to-eye, they sent in their recommendations separately recommending both Mr. Prasad and Mr. Kumar, respectively, giving inter-alia the reasons mentioned above leaving the choice to the head.

As the 'head' if you are to take the decision whom will you select and why?

*(B.B.A., M.K. University, April 1998)*

**Case Analysis 4**

Read the following case carefully and answer the questions given at the end.

**Role Shifting**

AL Group of companies had six sister concerns and EF Ltd. was one of its associates. Each concern had a General Manager. For the main Company, AL Ltd., the other five companies including EF Ltd. were supplying ancillary parts. The relationship between the Managing Directors of the various companies of the group were quite cordial. Mr. Swami, was the Managing Director of the EF Ltd. EF Ltd. had a recognised union belonging to one particular ruling party of the State. The other five companies including the main AL Ltd. had unions belonging to various political parties. The relationships between the unions and administration including the one belonging to EF Ltd. were generally cordial. The production of EF Ltd., at the time when Mr. Swami was the Managing Director was 200 per cent more than the targeted production with the result that AL Ltd. had also, increased their production level with appurtenant benefits in the perks to the employees. The unions contribution in the increased production level was no less in due measures. On a particular occasion, during one of the co-ordination meetings, there was a difference of opinion between the Managing Director of EF Ltd., and the Managing Direcotr of AL Ltd. The Managing Director of AL Ltd., being the main body of the entire group, had a better say. He and the members of the family had a major share in the companies. Mr. Swami the Managing Director of the EF Ltd., as also others on the rolls of the Company were actually paid Managing Directors. Mr. Swami, was respected for his uprightness, forthrightness and also his wide knowledge on account of his high qualifications in Management and Engineering and also because of his experience which he had gained by his extensive travelling abroad. Nonetheless, in one of the meetings, his technical advice was not considered, and some serious difference of opinion had cropped on account of this. The Managing Director of AL Ltd., was supported by the other four Managing Directors of the group and Mr. Swami was told in no uncertain terms that his technological advice would not hold water. Mr. Swami felt insulted and offered to quit.

Frayed tempers persisted and Mr. Swami left the organisation. Since no new Managing Director had joined, the Executive Director was co-ordinating with the organisational work. Though more than the targeted level of production was maintained during Mr Swami's time, the level had fallen down considerably after Mr. Swami had left, but the minimum target level was maintained.

After about a month, a meeting between the Union of EF Ltd., and the Management was fixed. It was a surprise for the Management, including the Managing Director to see Mr. Swami, sitting in the opposite bench as the Chairman of the Union of EF Ltd. Mr. Swami assured the Management of a very cordial relationship. He, however, presented six demands to the Management. Mr. Swami put forward as a suggestion from the Union, the same technical advice which he tendered as Managing Director and pointed out that if the suggestion was implemented, the production would not fall down. The Management did not agree. After about a month, when the question of payment of bonus to the employees came up, the Management pointed out that the production of EF Ltd. had fallen by 20 per cent, less than the targetd production, i.e., by 180 per cent, of the previous level. It was also pointed out that the main group AL Ltd., is also suffering on account of the low production of EF Ltd. The Management insisted that this state of affairs is mainly on account of the Union's non-co-operation. The Union pointed out that there has absolutely been no change in their attitude and that it is because of the intention of the Managing Directors of the other groups as also the Executive Director and other Directors of the AL Ltd., that the production has gone down.

The question that arise from the above case study are:

(a) Do you agree with the Union's stand?
(b) Analyse the behaviour of Mr. Swami as Managing Director and as Chairman of the Union.
(c) Analyse the behaviour of the Managing Director of AL Ltd., the main company.

*(B.B.A., M.K. University, Oct. 1998)*

**Case Analysis 5**

Analyse the following case and write your report:

**Recruitment and Selection**

The Southern Steel Company manufactures tin plated steel primarily for sale to canning companies. It employs about 5,000 persons. The company applies modern scientific methods wherever possible.

The personnel department applied one such scientific method in the selection of management trainees. A battery of tests was used to determine the interests, emotional stability, general intelligence and personality of the candidates. The tests were applied by an agency which has an excellent reputation in preparing and analysing tests. The company purchased the tests from the agency, gave them to the applicants and returned them to the agency for grading and analysis.

In addition to the tests, the personnel director analysed the data on the application forms. The applicant with the highest grade on the tests and with satisfactory application rating were selected for interviews with the personnel director. After the interviews, selections were done.

By the end of one year, the company had hired 30 applicants by this method. Upon evaluation of these trainees, the company was surprised to find that 14 of them did not have the qualifications considered necessary for executive personnel. The total expenditure on these unqualified trainees amounted to approximately Rs. 26,000.

The personnel department then took steps to evaluate the testing and hiring procedure. It found that the tests had been used successfully by other steel companies. It found no fault in the tests or in the administration. The personnel director was undecided as to what to do. He referred the problem to the executive committee comprising eight departmental heads. The head of the Industrial Relations Department suggested that error was in the tests and that they should abandon them and set-up another method for selecting management trainees.

**QUESTIONS**

(1) What are the short-comings in the company's hiring procedure?
(2) On the basis of the information given what actions should the company take to solve the problem of selection.

*(B.B.A., M.K. University, Nov. 1998)*

**Case Analysis 6**

Analyse the following case and write your report.

The modern spring company makes springs according to manufacturers specifications. It makes leaf springs, tension springs and bumper springs. Most of the springs are supplied to manufacturers of cars, trucks and buses.

The company has been experiencing misunderstandings in its line and staff relationships in recent months. The Chairman-Cum-Managing Director of the company, is searching for a suitable approach to line-staff understanding and co-ordination.

Unlike many concerns where the line does not make any use of staff help and advise, and the staff find its expedient to assume line authority, the line officers at modern appear to be subtle victims of informal staff authority. It is quiet common for the line officials to accept staff ideas and advise strictly on the basis of assumed technical competence. For example, the director of R & D completed his Ph.D. degree last year and acceptance of his ideas by line personnel is approaching 100 per cent.

Many of the staff men report directly to the managing director. The line officers in many instances interpreted the advise and counsel of these staff men as command through status. For example, the personnel manager had no difficulty last year in convincing the plant manager that the training of all employees should be part of the personnel function.

Most of the staff personnel are college trained, personable and good salesman. It has become increasingly evident to top management that command through personal qualities is operative between line and staff. For example, the publicity and public relations manager has been in particular instances authorised to act for and in the name of line management. However, it appears that unauthorised authority gravitates to this department and is used by the manager for personal advantage.

The staff personnel at modern have not found it necessary to spread the best ideas before top management. The managing director is a firm believer in the staff function. Line management has on occasion interpreted this as command through sanction. For example, the sales manager has in recent years of the companies vigorous growth been dealing more and more with the managing directors staff assistant in matters of special projects, developing plans and suggesting policies rather than with the managing director himself.

## QUESTIONS

1. How would you describe the staff way of thinking in an organization?
2. Analyse informal staff authority as it is used at the company. Why does this implied authority work in many situations? Is it good or bad?
3. Suggest to the managing director a suitable approach to line-staff understanding and co-ordination.

*(B.B.A., M.K. University, Nov. 1998)*

**Case Analysis 7**

Analyse the following case and write your report.

Southern Manufacturing Company has been engaged in the produciton of colour television sets which have a greater demand in the market. The company finds difficulty in meeting the demand in terms of giving timely delivery. Amirthalingam joined the Southern Manufacturing Company Ltd. two months ago as a General Manager. He was forced to take suitable measures to see that sales delivery schedule is to be followed strictly. He had to examine the facts in the company to see the causes for delay in delivering the products.

Amirthalingam finds that the manufacturing department shows a picture of rising costs, failure to meet delivery dates and increasing number of quality complaints. At once, he called the works manager Mr. Bhaktavasalam for discussion to analyse the facts so as to have a solution to the problem. Bhaktavasalam admitted to poor performance but said that his failure to meet the delivery schedule is due almost entirely to the fact that the sales department makes unrealistic promises and does not bother to check manufacturing schedules. He attributed most of the quality problems to the incessant flow of engineering changes that come without warning and with no time to work out the production problems present in all new products. Amirthalingam himself admitted that he had approved the last set of engineering changes.

As a sequence, Amirthalingam called Deeran, the Engineering Manager, to his chamber for discussion. He explained Deeran the problem of implementing the approved engineering changes into production. Mr. Deeran explained that the engineering changes with the approval of the top management comes to him one after one with a gap of number of days and hence there is difficulty in implementing them altogether. Hence, Amirthalingam asked Deeran to put all the approved changes into production immediately so as to enhance production to meet the time schedule of the sales department.

In the course of problem solving exercise Amirthalingam called Mr. Nayar, the sales manager who is the man responsible to adhere the sales schedule for discussion. In the task of following sales schedule strictly Mr. Nayar admitted that he had no knowledge of the manufacturing schedules. He also made a complaint that the engineering department had changed product specifications many times without consulting and informing the sales department. He also made a further complaint that the finance department tightened the credit requirements without giving previous intimation to the sales department which caused delay in delivering the goods.

Amirthalingam again realises that it is the same engineering change which caused trouble for the sales department and made obsolete the existing stock of replacement parts. He also finds that at his request, due to an unusually short cash position, the finance department tightened up the credit requirements.

## QUESTIONS

1. Define the major co-ordination problem facing Amirthalingam.
2. What caused the problem?
3. How can co-ordination between different departments of the company be maintained?

*(B.B.A., M.K. University, April 1999)*

### Case Analysis 8

Analyse the following case and write your report.

## Problem of Personal Conflicts

Hariharan, 53, had more departmental seniority than any other employee, including Muthusamy, the departmental manager in a major transport company. Hariharan was considered one of the more capable employees. He was extremely conscientious and worked very hard. As a result of his ability and seniority, he normally received the choice work assignments and was the highest paid employee in the department. Although there was no formal designation of various "special" projects as belonging to Hariharan, he handled them as a matter of course.

A problem developed when Muthusamy employed, Neelakandan, 23, a personable, intelligent and deligent employee. Neelakandan's two years previous experience in closely related work made it possible for him to catch on to work routine much more rapidly than was customary for a new employee. He was both hard working and aggressive. On several occasions, Muthusamy became aware of tension developing between the two employees i.e. Neelakandan and Hariharan. However, he did not wish to intrude into personal conflicts, and the work was being accomplished on schedule.

One afternoon, the tension reached the boiling point when Hariharan decided his personal duties were being taken over far too extensively by the new employee Neelakandan. He practically pulled Neelakandan to the front of Muthusamy's desk and demanded, "Will you please tell him once and for all which projects are mine and which are his?" The office suddenly became quiet as every one awaited Muthusamy's reply. The abrupt confrontation made further no procrastination impossible.

## QUESTIONS

1. In what way has the managers organising function contributed to this problem? Could it have been avoided by the better organization? How?
2. Evaluate Muthusamy's performance as an organizer.
3. How should Muthusamy respond to the demand of Hariharan?

*[B.B.A. M.K. University, April 1999]*

**Case Analysis 9**

Analyse the following case, write your report.

### The Human Aspects of Personnel

Mr. Ramlal, owner of a three star hotel at Muradabad employed 50 persons to man various jobs in his hotel in 1980. Almost all of them were educated upto $10^{th}$ Standard. The salaries paid by Ramlal were high compared to other hotels at Muradabad. He provided various benefits including free boarding, lodging, medical and recreation to all employees. He was rated as the best employer in the hotel industry in Muradabad. But he never allowed any two of the employees to interact with each other while at work or off the work except work transaction. He did not allow even the Accountant and Manager to share their personal or family problems. He however used to discuss work-related issues with every worker quite seriously.

But he never asked or allowed them to speak about their needs, desires, sentiments, values etc. as he thought that he was the model employer in hotel industry in Muradabad and he was meeting all the needs of his workers.

Another three star hotel was started in 1985 in Muradabad under the ownership of Mr. Rajesh Sethi. Mr. Sethi offered comparatively lesser wages and benefits. Even then surprisingly, 35 employees working with Ramlal including the Manager and Accountant joined Sethi's hotel.

## QUESTIONS

(a) Do you feel that the workers of Mr. Ramlal were really satisfied with their jobs? If Yes, why? If not, why did they keep quiet until 1985?

(b) Why did 35 workers leave Mr. Ramlal despite higher wages and better benefits compared to all other hotel employees at Muradabad?

(c) Do you find any impact of change in the trends towards human resources management on human desires in this case?

*[B.B.A. M.K. University November 1999]*

**Case Analysis 10**

### Inter-personal Relations/MBO

Analyse the following case carefully and answer the questions given at the end:

Vikas Pvt. Ltd., an engineering firm with 50 years of success behind it has become a household name in India for its quality products. Although it had started its business in a modest way, it became a dominant supplier of spares and equipments of critical nature needed by the Transport and Engineering Industries in a short span of 10 years. Later, with the advent of industrial planning initiated by the Government of India, and by virtue of its position in the engineering business, it made rapid strides in many product lines, including electronics. In 1960, its assets were of the order of Rs. 200 crores with a total employment of over 10,000 spread over, all important industrial centres in India. With the growing complexity of management, the top management, time and again, discussed the need for reorganising the entire business on functional lines, and finally introduced decentralised administration on April 1, 1974.

Mr. Vasudeva, an MBA graduate from Harvard with a Mechanical Engineering background was incharge of the Mechanical Engineering Section since 1964. He was promoted as the Chief Executive of the Division in April 1974. This was in recognition of his outstanding contribution to the development of new product lines, especially in the area of compressor-cum-vacuum pumps. In fact, the firm earned a good name in the export market and also bagged an export award during 1973-74. Moreover, Mr. Vasudeva was known for his honesty, integrity, leadership and decisiveness. He was a brilliant engineer and always worked hard to be a step ahead of his competitors in the field. He was virtually a thing ' tank, and the management was very proud of him.

For the last six months he spent long hours redesigning the export model-T compressor-cum-vacuum pump set. In his discussions with his foreign collaborators, he was convinced that with a little more effort, the company could successfully redesign the model, thus saving production costs as well as improving the efficiency by 16-20 per cent. He depended entirely on Mr. Hanuman, a foreman of exceptional ability and tenacity. Moreover, Mr. Hanuman was good at human relations and commanded respect from his immediate subordinates. Since the fabrication of the new model was in its infancy, everyone concerned felt it undesireable to let others know what was happening on the shop-floor. Moreover secrecy was the style of operation, and therefore it was clear to both the foreman and the persons working under him that this matter would not be brought to the notice of Mr. Keshav, the new Works Manager, and a recent induction into the company. They were one with their new job and always delighted in any words of appreciation from their chief, Mr. Vasudeva, when he visited the shop-floor.

Mr. Keshav, was young and energetic with a flair of Mechanical engineering products. He had no knowledge of management, but had attended a few courses in materials management and productivity control. He always laid stress on proper supervisory activities, knew his job well and always expected others to perform their duties as scheduled. He could never tolerate indiscipline. His colleagues had nicknamed him "the real fire-brand" of the company.

One evening, before going home, Mr. Keshav went to the shop-floor where he found six machinists, and helpers engaged in fabricating a spare part of the pump set as per the order of Mr. Vasudeva. Mr. Kesav was happy to see people working under him so involved in their work.

However, his enthusiasm vanished like morning mist when he saw that, what they were engaged in was not a normal part of their work. "Damn it. What the devil are you upto?" he asked in annoyance.

The workers were perplexed, they did not know what to say. However, Mr. Hanuman soon appeared on the scene and explained the on-going project and the benefit its success would bring.

The Works Manager got very angry with Hanuman and reprimanded him severely. In fact, he was admonished in the presence of his subordinates and technicians working on the shop-floor.

Mr. Hanuman felt confused and hurt. As though this was not enough he received a show cause notice from the Works Manager demanding an explanation within 24 hours. This was adding insult to injury. He had no alternative but to report to the chief, but to his chagrin, he found that Mr. Vasudeva had already left on foreign tour and was expected back a month later.

Mr. Hanuman felt that he was approaching a dead end, harassed, he went from pillar to post no help or advice was forthcoming. Exaspernated and hurt he went to the General Manager and handed him his resignation letter.

Mr. Hanuman was known for his honesty, simplicity and hard work. Only by the dint of hard work, had he developed his skills and risen to the position of foreman from the level of an ordinary helper within a span of 10 years. Everyone knew the role he played in developing a new prototype of Model-T, vacuum pump set. His one weakness was that he was very sensitive and would never compromise on issues affecting his personality and dignity. On the whole, he was respected by all.

News of his resignation spread like a wild fire. The workers, technicians and others sympathetic to his cause were alarmed, and eagerly awaited the outcome.

The issues arising from the case are:

1. Was the GM right in accepting Mr. Hanuman's resignation?
2. Was it well advised to keep Mr. Keshav in the dark about the on-going project, especially since he was the Works Manager?

3. Did Mr. Keshav act hastily in reprimanding Mr. Hanuman?
4. What action should be taken now?
5. What repercussion would this incident have on all involved?

*[B.B.A. M.K. University November, 1999]*

**Case Analysis 11**

Read the following case carefully and answer the questions given at the end

**The Goldmine Scheme**

Sterling & Co. had an incentive scheme for its factory personnel on piece rate basis, amounting to Rs. 10 per good unit manufactured. For the year ending 31st March, 1987, the company recorded an average monthly production of 18,000 good units. Excluding 2,000 nits per months, which had to be scrapped, after all the manufacturing operations, due to the vigorous quality control standards maintained by the company. The realisable value of scrap is Rs. 20 per unit. The unit pricing structure of the product is as follows:

Variable Manufacturing cost (exclusive) of the piece - rate incentive to the workers Rs. 80

| | |
|---|---|
| Selling and distribution cost | Rs. 25 |
| Selling price | Rs. 160 |
| Fixed expenses | Rs. 3,60,000 per month |

Mr. Lal, labour union leader approached, Mr. Patel, the Managing Director of the company for a better incentive scheme which would substantially benefit the workers. After considerable deliberations and discussions, it was mutually agreed between the Union and the Management that the incentive amount shall be increased to Rs. 15 per good unit manufactured, subject to a minimum achievement of 20,000 good units per month. It was further agreed that the new incentive scheme shall be initially tried for a period of three months and subject to review by Mr. Patel thereafter, it shall be extended for a period of three years. At the time of such a review, Mr. Patel shall be at liberty to impose any further conditions, without increasing the monthly target of 20,000 units, which shall be duly accepted by the union.

All the workers were very happy about the new scheme, which increased their incentive amount by 50% and they were quite confident of achieving the monthly target. They enthusiastically named the new scheme as "Goldmine," which became quite popular in the company.

During the trial period of three months, the average monthly production of good units increased to 21,000. At the same time, 3,000 units had to be scrapped per month. Mr. Patel was extremely cheerful to see the stepping up of the production of good units. However, after a little thought, the sudden hike in the rejected units worried him very much. Due to severe competition, no increase in selling price was possible, though fixed cost per month increased by 10% on account of increased production level.

**QUESTIONS**

(a) Has the company been benefited by the introduction of the "Goldmine" Scheme?
(b) Do you find any lacunae in the framing of the "Goldmine" Scheme?
(c) What should be the future course of action by Mr. Patel?

*[B.B.A., M.K. University October, 1999]*

**Case Analysis 12**

Read the following case carefully and answer the questions given at the end:

Joseph Mahoney, General Manager of Universal Automotive, Inc., Chicago, recommended a sales contest to improve declining sales performance. This was his response to first-quarter results that san sales fall substantially below quota. Mahoney believed that a sales content would, among other things, provide the incentive to get sales up to or beyond territorial quotas.

Universal manufactured and distributed a complete line of automotive parts and accessories. It sales force of sixty persons operated out of nine district offices located throughout the United States. The sales force's compensation plan consisted of a basic salary and a bonus. The bonus was based upon the territorial quota, which was set by the general sales manager in consultation with the branch sales manager.

Mahoney proposed a sales contest that he believed would motivate sales personnel to achieve their quotas. He felt that the sales people's spouses should be involved in the contest. The proposed contest would run thirteen weeks and each sales person would be assigned a weekly sales volume quota, determined by the general sales manager and the district manager. In addition, each of the nine sales districts would have a district sales volume quota.

Each week, a $ 200 cash bonus would go to the sales personnel exceeding their quota by the greatest percentage, although Mahoney had seriously considered using total sales volume instead of a percentage. Each salesperson achieving quota for the thirteen-week period would get a $ 300 bonds. The person exceeding the thirteen-week quota by the greatest percentage would receive an additional $ 400, with $ 250, $ 200 and $ 100 bonuses for salespeople in second, third and fourth places respectively.

Spouses would also participate in the sales contest proposed by Mahoney. For each $ 100 worth of bonus earned by a salesperson exceeding his or her weekly or quarterly bonus, the sales person's spouse would receive five chances to win a merchandise prize.

All quota-making salespeople and their spouses would attend a three day convention at the Chicago headquarters. The three days would mix business and pleasure, culminated by a gala dinner dance and drawing for the merchandise prize.

In the competition among the sales districts, the district exceeding quota by the greatest percentage would receive an $ 800 price with the money to be divided among that district's salespersons. Second, third and fourth places for the districts would be worth $ 600, $ 400 and $ 200 respectively.

When Mahoney formally proposed his plan for a sales contest several criticisms were voiced. Objections centered around that disappointments and frustrations of those people who did not win, the over aggressiveness that might result from ambitious salespeople striving to win at all costs, the distribution of normal activities caused by the convention, and the temporary nature of the stimulation provided. Several executives opposed the contest, arguing that the negative aspects out weighted the possible benefits.

Mahoney countered that a contest would help correct a poor sales performance, it would appeal to the sales force's competitive spirit, it would enable sales people to earn some recognition, and it would raise the morale of the entire sales force.

Inspite of the lack of agreement, Mahoney scheduled a meeting of his staff of eight people to discuss the advisability of conducting a sales contest:

## QUESTIONS

1. Should Universal Automotive Inc. have held a sales contest to motivate its sales personnel to better sales performance? Why (or) why not?
2. What is the purpose of including spouses in the contest? Would working and non working spouses be likely to react differently?

*(B.B.A., M.K. University, October 2001)*

**Case Analysis 13**

Analyse the following case write your report

**Ethnic and Religious considerations**

Sri Rama Paper Mills Ltd., was established at Rajahmundry (A.P.) in 1954. The company was located here due to the availability of raw material and labour. The company employed most of manual labour from the scheduled caste communities, technical staff from the Muslim community and supervisory staff from other communities. The company has Saturday off as weekly holiday as majority of the employees (almost all manual labour and supervisory staff) belong to Hindu Religion. Hindus, especially in AP Religion, worship Lord Venkateswara on Saturdays. The company's performance had been above the targets including industrial relations during 1950s, 1960s and 1970s. Christianity had spread in the villages particularly among the scheduled caste people during 1980 to 1985. Consequently almost all the manual workers (belonging to scheduled caste) converted themselves as Christians. They found that it had been much difficult for them to attend the factory on Sundays as they go to church. They demanded the management to declare Sunday as weekly holiday instead of Saturday. The Management did not accept this demand as all the directors of the board and executives belong to Hindu Religion. Employees belonging to Hindu religion organized demonstrations and demanded the management to keep the Saturday as weekly holiday. In the meanwhile the technicians belonging to Muslim community requested the management to consider their demand for Friday as weekly holiday. Management did not consider any of these demands. Suddenly, all the manual workers did not attend to work on the Sunday. This resulted in closure of the factory on that day and Management introduced the policy of 'no pay - no work' and discontinued the services of all the temporary workers. Immediately all the manual workers formed a Union and Organised strike against the Management's action and were pressing for their demand for declaring Sunday as weekly holiday.

**QUESTIONS**

1. What is a root cause for the tension between labour and management?
2. How would you solve the problem if you were the Managing Director of the company?
3. What would you suggest to the Managing Director if you were the Personnel Manager of the company?

*(B.B.A., M.K. University, November 2001)*

**Case Analysis 14**

Analyse the following case and answer the questions.

ABC company is a producer of a specialized pulverizing equipment. Almost all of its products are made to customer's special order, and vary from small units suitable for making face power to huge machines used to pulverize rocks.

The company uses in its machines a number of bearings that are relatively expensive and that must be ordered from three to six months before the date they are needed. Because of the required lead time it has been the practice to keep a considerable inventory of bearings on hand. Under the circumstances it is almost impossible to predict future usage, but the general intent is to keep a six months supply of bearings on hand at all times. Despite this considerable investments in bearings, however, it still has not prevented the delay of a number of orders as a result of an inadequate supply of the right kind of bearing for a specific job.

One difficulty seem to stem from the fact that frequently, when the store room clerk is busy with other work, the machine assemblers help themselves to the bearings needed. The assemblers, being more interested in machine assembly than in paper work, will seldom leave requisitions for the bearings they take.

## QUESTIONS

1. Summarise the case and identify the probelms.
2. Analyse the causes of the problem.
3. What steps can be taken to ensure that bearings will be on hand when needed?
4. Is there any way the investment in bearing inventory can be reduced?
5. Choose the best alternative course of action. Justify.
6. Present the suggestions in a report form.

*(B.B.A., M.K. University, April 2002)*

**Case Analysis 15**

Analyse the case and answer the questions given at the end of the case:

ATAT company, a major integrated petroleum company headquartered in Mumbai, introduced in late 1977 a new premium motor oil, priced 24 percent above its previous best grade. The new product, called ATAT graphite, differed strikingly from traditional lubricating oil for motor vehicles because it contained graphite, a form of the element carbon that is widely used to reduce friction in such mechanical devices as locks. It had taken the company four years to develop the product, although graphite had long been combined with oil. The problem was to keep it from separating from motor oil while not being agitated, tests had shown that ATAT graphite would conserve fuel by between 1.0 percent and 8.7 percent. Another Plus was its ability to reduce wear and tear.

In addition to price, there was another serious marketing problem. ATAT graphite was naturally pitch-black. The public thought that even slightly muddy motor oil was old or worn out and not to be used any longer, and it considered black motor oil even less desirable. Company management thought that the marketing problems could be diminished by disseminating good objective publicity at the same time the product went on sale. Assistance was sought from the Vice President (VP) for public relations and the media relations manager, who reported to the manager of communication and resources. The public relations objective was to develop way to "illustrate and simplify this rather complex technical story" for the media and then to spread that story drawing a single five –day week in 12 major cities across the country.

The decision was to use visual media and to divide the 12 cities into 2 groups – on principally eastern and the other western – and have two teams make essentially identical presentation in both areas. Three types of visual media were to be used:

(a) Exhibits of full- sized cut away engines used by auto schools and manufactures.

(b) Three dimensional props such as large chunks of petroleum coke from ATAT's refineries (this being the graphite used), enabling demonstration of the flaking properties of graphites and supplies of both regular oil and ATAT graphite with beakers for use in demonstrations:

(c) A one minute, 16 mm. Animated colour film.

For sake of credibility, professional performers were avoided and two of the company's research scientists who had been involved in development of the new product were enlisted to make the presentation to media. On each of the teams (East and West) were several persons from marketing and two from public relations. With the help of the public relations office in each area the public relations people arrange the logistics, invited and followed up on invitations to the media guests, and resided at the conference with them. A press kit was provided to each media person who attended a conference. Alongwith the kit each guest was given two (2) ounce plexiglas vilas, one filled with ATAT graphite and the other with ATAT's previously premium oil, supreme. The physical arrangement at each conference were designed to facilitate the operations of both TV crews and print media representation.

The first two conference were held 90 minutes apart in Mumbai and Chennai city so as to enable media on both the west and east coasts to get story at approximately the same time.

## QUESTIONS

(a) Summarise the cases facts and identify the issues.
(b) Analyse the causes of the problem.
(c) State various alternative courses of action along with their merits and demerits.
(d) Should ATAT have used public relations media other than those described in this case? Why?
(e) Was proper research conducted before media strategy was determined? What other research might have been conducted?
(f) Write a report, on the case in the Standard format?

*(B.B.A., M.K. University, April, 2002)*

**Case Analysis 16**

Read the following case carefully and answer the question given at the end:

Henry Hull opened a container of "Hearthside" brand bouillon cubes and rolled them across his desk. As the small foil – wrapped shapes tumbled on his blotter they reminded him of unmarked dice. Actually, the illusion merely reflected Henry's anxiety concerning the solution to a major problem which, at the moment, seemed just as risky and elusive as guessing the roll of dice at a gambling table.

Six months ago Henry had been hired as Marketing Manager of Instant soups, Inc. an old, established and reputable food manufacturer located in the Midwest. The firm produced and distributed high – quality bouillon cubes on a nation wide basis. At the present time they made both beef and chicken – flavoured cubes and Marketed them in packages containing 5, 12 and 25 units, which generally retailed at 12, 13 and 41 cent respectively. The firm originally sold only locally but gradually expanded its sales perimeter and, until the last two years , had consistently enjoyed increasing sales and profits. During the past decade a number of regional and national competitors had entered the industry and these firm were successful in slicing off substantial positions of some of instant soup's markets.

In a few areas, even with stepped – up advertising appropriations and newly designed aggressive promotional techniques, Instant soups lost considerable ground. Henry felt that the major problem was that the bouillon cube, as a product, was nearing the end of its maturity segment in the product lift cycle. Everything he observed seemed to point in that direction. Price cutting was rampant, specific brand names were aggressively advertised, and promotional activities were greatly intensified. Besides, a number of significant mergers in the industry indicated that other bouillon cube manufacturers seemed to be experiencing similar difficulties.

Instant soups had used the same advertising agency for the past five years, and Henry felt it was trying to do a good job. As a matter of fact, its research staff had recently conducted a study which appeared to confirm Henry's belief about the product life cycle. Bill English, purchasing manager for Instant soups, mentioned recently that several salesmen, who sold raw materials to the firm, were complaining bitterly about their own lower sales figures this year. This, of course, merely indicated prevailing conditions throughout the industry. In addition, several of instant soups brokers had commented in their correspondence that some major customers were threatening either to devote less shelf.

Case prepared by Prof. W.F.Rohrs, Wagner college, reproduced with permission. Space to instant soups' bouillon cubes or possibly drop the line completely. Infact, one large retail chain based in St. Louis announced that in the future it would stock only the 25 – unit size.

Quite obviously there were some serious problems ahead for instant soups. Henry realized the firm had been too complacent for too long – its market was eroding. Something had to be done, and done quickly. He decided to try to think of ways to extend the product life cycle in order to augment and stimulate instant soup's sales.

## QUESTION

1. What should Henry Hull do to stimulate instant soup's sales and thus extend the product's Life cycle?

*(B.B.A., M.K. University, May 2002)*

**Case Analysis - 17**

Analyse the following case and write your report.

**Management Education at the Harvard Business School**

Harvard is one of the leading business schools. Yet there is growing concern about whether the school is moving in the right direction. Harvard's mission has been to educate "general managers and business leaders", but recently, over 50 percent of its graduates took jobs in investment banking and management consulting. Moreover, less that one-fourth of the 1997 M.B.A.s went into manufacturing companies, and of those, most moved into staff, rather than line, positions.

Investment houses and consulting firms are eager to recruit at Harvard, offering attractive starting salaries. While some critics accuse the students of being greedy, many professors supplement their salaries by teaching in corporations, consulting, appearing as expert witnesses, or serving on corporate boards. While consulting can enhance teaching, there is a maximum time officially allowed for outside activities.

The approach to teaching has also changed. The case approach, for which Harvard is famous, used to stress the role of the general manager. While cases are still used, more analytical tools have become increasingly important. For example, the course Business Policy has changed to competitive strategy under the leadership of Professor Michael Porter, who with a background in economics, uses concepts and theories in making competitive analyses.

Harvard, once know for developing business leaders, now increasingly educated specialists. Most of the students have shown little interest in joining manufacturing firms. Yet manufacturing may be critical for making the United States competitive.

## QUESTIONS

(a) Write the summary of the case and identify the problems.
(b) Analyses the causes of the problem.
(c) Identify the alternative courses of possible actions.
(d) Discuss the relative merits and demerits of each alternative.
(e) Choose the best alternative. Give justification.
(f) Write your analysis in the report format (15)

*(B.B.A., M.K. University, November 2002)*

**Case Analysis 18**

Analyse the case and answer the questions:

Varghese Kurian started Co-operative movement 50 years ago and Amul established a successful brand name and is one of the strongest marketing networks in the country. The competitors are none other than the big MNCs like HLL and Nestle. Amul's vision 2005 aims at a turnover of Rs. 10,000 crore by adding more products like coffee, tea, jams, pickles and ketchup. Amul a cooperative dares to enter the coffee market, the one dominated by Nestle (14.81 percent of market), HLL (5.9 percent), the Tatas(4.54 percent)

In metros, Amul cafe has made a strong entry competing with Nescafe. There's sound logic for moving into hot beverage. Globally, the coffee business is very protected. While there are quite a few coffee producing nations, only three buyers Nestle, RJR Nabisco, and the Folgers coffee company, a subsidiary of Procter and Gamble have a stronghold on the global market. In India, this is the first time a cooperative has ventured into coffee, a market dominated by Nestle which, according to CMIE figures, holds 14.81 percent of the market followed by HLL (5.9 percent) and the Tatas (4.54 percent)

Gujarat Co-operative Milk Manufactures Federation (GCMMF) of Kurian is looking at the organizational set up for the new product range keeping the long term perspective without losing focus on dairy business. Additional of new products helped GCMMF to grow at a compounded annual rate of 18 percent for the last five years. Amul expects new products frozen paneer, gulab jamuns, etc. to become cash cows over a period of time. Amul ice cream was the first of a slew of new products that included frozen paneer gulab jamuns, a gulab jamun mix and mozzarella and Emmental cheese. These are still small volume products in their first or second year. However, the company excepts them to become cash cows over a period of time. Cheese found a significant place on the Indian Consumer's platter only about five years ago. Growth has been mainly on account of demand from the defence sector and the growth of fast food restaurants, especially pizza chains, that use mozzarella cheese. It's growing market, but the non-availability of a cold chain and refrigeration facilities at points of sale hinders distribution as cheese has a very short shelf life. In 1996 GCMMF built a Rs. 40 crore, 20 tonnes per day cheese factory at Anand. After this initial launch the cheese business was refocused in 1998. The company air lifted its cheese plant from Anand to Khatraj near Ahmedabad so that the various varieties of cheese could be made under one roof.

Amul achieved market share mainly on price front over its rivals. Low pricing resulted in high volumes in turnover for Amul. The motto of 'sell more and earn more of GCMMF allows Amul to share 50 percent of its profit with the distribution network. In the changing economic scenario Amul has also changed the strategy and created a good infrastructure by investing Rs.6 crore in information systems. The tempo did not stop there are TCS has been roped into implement its Enterprise wide Integrated Application System. Amul started accepting interest orders in cities like Mumbai, Delhi and Ahmedabad on the other side, Amul exports are likely to reach Rs. 30 crore this year. Amul introduced knowledge updation test to its marketing managers as a measure to beef up marketing department as a prelude to fulfil vision 2005. Unfazed by the competition, GCMMF is preparing itself for the new millennium. The new entrants dwell on the strategies of the market leader your butterfly Amul.

## QUESTIONS

1. Summarise the case and identify the problem.
2. Analyse the causes of the problems.
3. Amul established its own brand over the years competing with giants like Nestle, HLL. Identify the strategies adopted by Amul to increase its' market share.
4. Critically examine the appropriateness of the identification and use of strategies by Amul.
5. What are the other alternatives for Amul today?
6. Present your suggestions in the report form to the chairman of Amul.

*(B.B.A., M.K. University, November 2002)*

**Case Analysis 19**

Analyse the following case and write your report

### Bharat Engineering Works Limited

Bharat Engineering Works Limited is a major manufacturer of industrial machineries besides other engineering products. It has enjoyed considerable market preferences for its machineries because of limited competition in the field. Usually there has been more orders that what the company could supply. However, the scenario changed quickly because of the entry of two new competitors in the field with foreign technological collaboration. For the first time, the company faced problem in marketing its products with usual profit margin. Sensing into the likely problem, the chief executive appointed Mr. Arvind Kumar as a general manager to direct the operations of industrial machinery division. Mr. Kumar had similar assignment abroad before coming back to India.

Mr. Kumar had a discussion with the chief executive about the nature of the problems being faced by the company so that he could fix up his priority. The chief executive advised him to consult various heads of department to have first hand information. However, he emphasized that the company lacked an integrated planning system while members of the board of directors insisted on introducing this meeting both formally and informally.

After joining as General Manager, Mr. Kumar got 6 briefings from the heads of all departments. He asked all departmental heads to identify major problems and issues concerning them. His main concern them. The marketing managers and sales professionals. His main concern was a lack of engineers but they were spread under three separate engineering groups. Sales people had no central organization which had responsibility to provide sales support. Therefore, some jobs were being done from outside at higher costs or with lower quality. Besides he needed a generous budget for demonstration system which could be sent on a trial basis to customers to win business.

The Production Manager complained about the old machines and equipment used in manufacturing. Therefore, cost of production was high but without corresponding quality. While competitors had equipments and machinery, Bharat Engineering neither replaced its age-old plant nor got it reconditioned. Therefore , to reduce the cost, it was essential to automate production lined by installing new equipment.

Director of research and development did not have any specific problem and, therefore, did not indicate for any change. However, a principal scientist in R & D indicated on one day that the director R & D, through very nice in his approach, did not emphasise on short-term research projects which could easily increase production efficiency to the extent of at least 20 percent within a very short period. Moreover, such projects did not involve any major capital outlay.

Mr. Kumar got himself convinced about the management process going on in the division and the type of problems being faced.

## QUESTIONS

(a) Discuss the nature and characteristics of management process followed in the company.
(b) What are the real problems of industrial machinery division of the company?
(c) What steps should be taken by Mr. Kumar to overcome these problems?

*(B.B.A., M.K. University, April 2003)*

**Case Analysis 20**

Analyse the following case and answer the questions:

### Market Survey

The company maintained a list of 476 retailers spread over 40 cities throughout the country, which formed the population for the retailer's survey. For personal interviews, it was decided to select six cities which accounted for the maximum amount of sales during the year 1985-86. There were, in all, 151 retailers (32 per cent of the total) in these cities, ranging between a maximum of 57 in Bombay and a minimum of 16 in Baroda. It was further decided to select one-third of the total number of retailers from each of the selected cities, for the purpose of personal interviews. The actual number of respondents consisted of 50 retailers.

The remaining 325 retailers in about 35 cities were covered through mail survey. The response was, however, very limited, as only 30(7%) of the retailers responded. These respondents were widely dispersed in about 25 cities all over the country. All these responses were clubbed together as 'other cities' for the purpose of analysis. Thus, the total sample size consisted of 80 retailers as per city-wise classification given below:

| *Cities* | *Number of Respondents* |
|---|---|
| Mumbai | 19 |
| Delhi | 10 |
| Baroda | 5 |
| Lucknow-Kanpur | 8 |
| Jaipur | 8 |
| Other cities | 30 |
| Total | 80 |

With a view to studying the attitude and behaviour of the consumer of knitted garments, consumer survey, was also planned. It was, however, restricted to the consumers in six cities where sample survey of retailers was conducted. For obvious reasons, the population for consumer survey could not be determined. In view of the time constraint, the total number of respondents was restricted to 70 consumers, who were selected on the basis of convenience sampling.

To collect the information required in an organized manner, the research vehicles used were structured, non-disguised questionnaires. The field investigation was conducted during June-September 1986. The summary of findings is given below.

**Retailer Survey**

A Majority of the retailers (71%) have been in this business for more than 5 years, thereby suggesting that the knitwear manufacturer prefers to deal with the retailers who have sufficient experience in this business. Moreover, about three-fourths of the retailers under study have their size of operations upto Rs. 2 lakh per month.

The share of knitted garments under the present market conditions lies somewhere between 30 % to 40% of their total sales. In a few cases (16%), the share was even more that 60 per cent. Moreover the share of knitted garments in the market under study has been reported to be increasing during the past 5 years and this trend is most likely to persist in future (the next five years). This shows a vast potential for knitwears in the readymade garment market in India.

The knitwear garments are available in the gents wear, ladies wear and children wear. Out of these, the children wears alone account for a major share in the sales of knitwears, followed by gents wear. Ladies knitwears, on the other hand, have a limited market. Casual wears like T-shirts are more popular among gents knitwears.

Brand preference is one aspect in consumer goods that has been gaining importance in the Indian market. There is, however practically no brand preferences in ladies and children wears according to a majority (60 per cent) of the retailers. But, there certainly exists a good degree of brand preferences in men's wears. Consumer's awareness of, and reference for, certain brand's in men's wear may be mainly attributed to a good degree of advertising campaign being done by some manufactures, specially from Delhi and Bombay. The consumer who exhibit brand reference are, however, not hardcore loyals, but instead are shifting loyals. Their preference can easily be changed in favour of another brand, if they are offered better products or designs which appeal to their fancy.

According to the retailers, 'designs' of knitwears appealed to the consumers most, to be followed by quality. Price was not an important consideration for knitwear purchases, particularly for high-income consumers, though for students and other consumers in the low-income group (below Rs.1,500 per month), price was relatively more important. Brand preference was ranked fourth as one of the product attributes and only marginally influenced the purchase process, for which consumers primarily relied upon the design and quality of knitwears. However, wellknown brands are often identified with good quality.

During the past five years, pure cotton and blended knitwears (i.e. polyester-cotton mix and acrylic-cotton mix) were that most preferred blends. This trend is likely to continue in future.

Mercerized cotton is not presently perceived to enjoy high consumer preference, mainly due to its very limited supply. But the retailers awareness of this product and its superior properties is quite high (91%), who see quite a good potential for this product in the coming years.

Readymade knitwears are purchased mainly from Ludhiana (57%) and Bombay(52%). Delhi has also emerged in recent years as an important source of supply (40 percent). Retailers situated in and around Bombay or Delhi prefer to procure their stocks from these centers. An additional advantage is that the lead time is shortened. Retailers in cities far off from these metropolitan centers, on the cities hand, prefer to purchase from Ludhiana. Ludhiana is well-known for its quality products, while Delhi and Bombay are becoming famous for their fashion garments. Moreover, since the manufacturers in Delhi and Bombay are spending a large amount of money on product development and advertisements, they are gaining a larger market share knitwears at cost of the Ludhiana manufacturers.

The retailers prefer a shortened channel of distribution and like to procure their supplies from the manufactures either directly or through the consignee agents. They avoid buying from wholesalers, because they would prefer not to stock the products that have already flooded the market. Only the retailers with a shortage of capital or a low level of operations tend to buy from wholesalers, who do not mind supplying small quantities of knitwears to retailers.

The retailers generally want their orders to be supplied within 15 to 30 days or within the time specified by them. The lead time was around one to one-and-a half months in the case of Ludhiana, while the Bombay and Delhi manufacturers could deliver the suppliers immediately or within a few days to local retailers as well as to those located in nearby cities. This may be one of the reasons why Bombay and Delhi have emerged as very important sources of the supply of knitwears, giving tough time to the Ludhiana manufactures.

Magazines and hoarding were perceived to be the most effective media for advertising knitwears, specially T-shirts. Advertising in good magazines helps in creating a good image of the product as well as the company in the eyes of the consumers. Many respondents favoured the television for knitwear advertisements. But, in view of the high costs involved the choice of T.V. advertising may not be optimum for a small unit. The newspaper were thought to be the best media to advertise clearance sales or exhibition-cum-sales of the knitwears. Also, the possibilities of using carrier bags were not ruled out, as it was an important promotional tool for creating the retailer's as well as the product's image.

About two-thirds of the respondents were inclined to share the cost of promotion with the manufacturers on a 50:50 basis. Needless to emphasise that the retailers would share costs incurred only on local advertisements by means of hoarding, leaflets, carrier bags, etc.

**Consumer Survey**

A majority of the consumers were students or young businessmen and servicemen, under 30 years of age and having an income between Rs. 1,500 and Rs. 5,300 per month.

Though-many consumers did not have a clear idea about the difference between the various blends, it was observed that pure cotton and blended (polyester-cotton/acrylic-cotton mix) fabric or garments were preferred the most. 100% polyester was not preferred by any of the consumers. On the other hand, acrylic attracted some respondents, particularly young entrepreneurs.

A majority of the consumers preferred to buy T-Shirt and sport shirts among the different types of knitwears available. This response can be attributed to the fact that a majority of the respondents (77%), were males. Female tops were purchased by almost all of the female respondents, who were mostly students. Baba suit were generally purchased by the working wives or housewives, whose number in the survey was insignificant.

Most of the consumer (69%) did not show any preference for the brands available in the market. About one-third (31%) of the consumers, however, preferred to buy branded products. The most popular brands among them were *Proline and Smash*. Hold up and Via also attracted some consumers.

All these brands are offered by the Bombay and Delhi manufacturers and are advertised in national magazines. They often imitate the designs of knitwears from abroad with minor changes.

Design and quality, in that order, are the most important attributes of knitwears. A majority of the students gave maximum importance to the design of the knitwear, followed by the quality. The business and professionals gave equal importance to design and quality, while the servicemen were more influenced by price rather than quality, in addition to the design.

A majority of the consumers of different occupations become aware of the various brands of knitwear through magazines as well as through their friends and relatives. Newspapers and hoardings were also influential in creating brand awareness.

A majority of the consumers (74 percent), did not prefer to purchase knitwears from the pedestrian sellers or outlets. Only some students and small traders, who mostly came in the income bracket of below Rs. 2,500 p.m., would not hesitate to buy from the pedestrian sellers. Most of the retailers thought that inferior quality products were sold at these outlets and, moreover, it was below their status and dignity to buy from these.

Most of the consumers were unaware of mercerized cotton and its properties. Only a few respondents, who were either in business or service and had an income of Rs. 2,500 to Rs. 3,500 per month were aware of mercerized cotton.

**QUESTIONS**

(a) Summarise the case facts and identify the problems.
(b) Analyse the causes for the problem.
(c) State various alternative causes of actions possible.
(d) Discuss relative merits and demerits of each alternative
(e) Choose the best course of action and state the reasons for your choice.

*(B.B.A., M.K. University, April 2003)*

## APPENDIX B

### OBJECTIVE TYPE QUESTIONS

1. Who wrote the book of "The Practice of Management."?
2. Which is the primary function of management?
3. Who wrote the book of "General and Industrial Management?
4. In which company did F.W.Taylor join as a machine shop labourer initially?
5. Who is the father of Scientific Management?
6. Who found the Differential Piece Rate System?
7. Who worked as a Professor of Management at the New York University in 1950?
8. Which function of management is looking into the future?
9. Which function facilitates control function?
10. What can be otherwise called as Resource Audit?
11. Who popularised the management by objectives?
12. In which country Management by objectives is popularised?
13. Which principle is basic for marginal theory of decision-making?
14. What is the other name for programmed decision?
15. What is the other name for strategic decision?
16. Who takes departmental decision?
17. From which word the term organisation has been derived?
18. Which principle is otherwise called as Principle of responsibility?
19. Which principle is otherwise called as span of management?
20. Which principle is basic for principle of span of control?
21. What is otherwise called as the chain of command?
22. Who founded the Classical Theory?
23. What is the other name of Modern Theory?
24. Which theory concerned with the study or work motivation of employees of an organisation?
25. Who gave Decision Theory?
26. What is the other name for Decision Theory?
27. Who was awarded the Nobel Prize in the year 1978 for Decision Theory?
28. For what was Herbert A. Simon awarded Nobel Prize in the year 1978?
29. When was Herbert A. Simon awarded the Nobel Prize?
30. Which prize was awarded to Herbert A. Simon for his Decision Theory?
31. Who takes Policy Decision?
32. What theory explains Maslow's hierarchy of needs?
33. For which theory is Herzberg's two Factor Theory an example?
34. What is the other name for the formal Authority Theory?
35. Who gave the acceptance for Authority theory?
36. What is called as the art of getting things done through others?
37. What converts uncertainty into certainty or reduce uncertainties of future?
38. Who introduced the concept of Functional foremanship?
39. What is the title of Henry Fayol's book?
40. In which language did Henry Fayol write his book?
41. How many groups of Industrial activities are formed by Henry Fayol?
42. How many qualities are required for a manager, according to Henry Fayol?
43. How many principles of management are given by Henry Fayol?
44. Who introduced the concept of MBO?
45. What is the modification of MBO?
46. Who modified the MBO?
47. Who has conducted Hawthrone experiments?
48. How many phases of research has been conducted in Hawthrone experiments?
49. What is the product of Hawthrone plant?

50. How many employees worked in Hawthrone plant?
51. How many interviews were conducted under mass interviewing programme?
52. How many girls were chosen for Relay Assembly Test Room Experiments?
53. Who described the functions of management as POSDCORB?
54. What is the basic feature of Hawthorne experiments?
55. Which principle of management helps to get specialisation?
56. Who possesses the authority for under line and staff organisation?
57. What provides an information about organisational relationships?
58. Who suggested a mathematical formula to fix the number of sub-ordinates?
59. How many relationships are found by Graicunas between superior and sub-ordinate?
60. What is the formula of Graicunas?
61. Which is delegateable?
62. Which is not delegateable?
63. What is the other name for achievement test?
64. Which test tries to measure the level of intelligence?
65. What is the expansion of TAT?
66. What is the expansion of TEMP?
67. What is the expansion of PERT?
68. What is the expansion of CPM?
69. Which test is conducted to identify the kind of jobs that will satisfy a candidate?
70. What helps the employees to improve their efficiency?
71. What is the expansion of TA?
72. What is the expansion of MBO?
73. Who gave the theory X and theory Y?
74. Who gave theory Z?
75. What will arise due to communication failure?
76. Which type of delegation delegates authority on the basis of custom?
77. What is the other name for line organisation?
78. Who proposed functional organisation?
79. How many persons command workers under functional organisation?
80. Who sees the machines and materials kept ready for workers under functional organisation?
81. Who checks up the quality of work under functional organisation?
82. Who implements the rules and regulations under functional organisation?
83. Which organisation is developed to reap the advantages of line and functional organisation?
84. Who assists another person in the performance of a work?
85. Who renders service to the line officers?
86. Which type of committee is requested to solve a problem?
87. Which type of committee is formed to collect information on a particular subject?
88. What is the other name for Free Form Organisation?
89. Which chart explains the command flow from the top level to the bottom?
90. What is the other name for circular chart?
91. Which chart shows the entire organisation?
92. Which chart shows a particular section or division of the organisation?
93. What is the other name of Supplementary Chart?
94. Which test is conducted to know the skills and abilities possessed by the candidate?
95. Which test is conducted to develop the skills and abilities of the candidate?
96. Which test is conducted to measure the likes, dislikes and habits of an individual?
97. What is the other name for achievement test?
98. Which test is conducted to discover the individual's interest?
99. What is other name for interest test?
100. Which test is conducted to measure the mental ability, capacity and general awareness?
101. Which test is conducted to measure courage, initiative, emotion and confidence of the individual?

102. What is the other name for Efficiency Test?
103. What is used to develop interpersonal interactions among individuals?
104. What deals with the contents and characteristics of each job?
105. What is the other name for job evaluation?
106. What measures the relative importance and value of each job on the basis of skills, duties and responsibilities?
107. Who wrote the book titled, "The Human Side of Enterprise"?
108. What is the other name for esteem and status needs?
109. What is the other name for self-actualisation needs?
110. Who developed the Hygiene Theory?
111. What is the other name for Hygiene Theory?
112. How many engineers were interviewed for Hygiene Theory?
113. Which theory explains the characteristics required for an effective leader?
114. Which theory is focused on a person's act rather than his quality or behaviour?
115. Who is called as the first line manager?
116. Who is regarded as a keyman in management?
117. Who issues orders and instructions to workers?
118. What is other name for informal communication?
119. What is the other name for Horizontal Communication?
120. Which type of communication includes whistling as a communication?
121. What is the other name for Oral Communication?
122. Which type of communication require paper work?
123. Which type of communication includes diagrams?
124. What is the last function of management?
125. What is the expansion of BEP?
126. What is the other name for physical property budget?
127. Which budget is prepared to utilise the working capital?
128. Which budget is prepared on the basis of sales budget?
129. What is the other name for cash budget?
130. What is the other name for management audit?
131. Which is a scientific approach to problem solving for executive management?
132. Which theory explains the leadership styles available to leaders?
133. Which style of leadership centralises the decision-making process?
134. Which style of leadership decentralises the decision-making process?
135. Which style of leadership gives complete freedom to sub-ordinates?
136. Which technique is used in the decision-making process to solve existing problems?
137. Which technique is used to maximise gain or minimise loss?
138. Which theory attempts to predict how rational people will behave in competitive situations?
139. Which lays down the abilities and qualities that a worker should possess in order to hold the job?
140. What is otherwise called as man specification?
141. What is the process of placing the right man on the right job?
142. What is referred to as an employee's general attitude towards his job?
143. What creates an advancement within an organisation?
144. What influences the behaviour of others in a particular direction?
145. What helps for the exchange of ideas, facts, opinions or emotions between two or more persons?
146. Which communication has no feedback?
147. Who developed the Game Theory?
148. What is the process of guiding and supervising the sub-ordinates?
149. What is a diagrammatical presentation showing important aspects of an organisation?
150. What is used to ask questions for the purpose of obtaining data?

**ANSWERS**

1. Peter F. Drucker
2. Planning
3. Henry Fayol
4. Midvale Steel Company
5. F.W. Taylor
6. F.W. Taylor
7. Peter F. Drucker
8. Planning
9. Planning
10. Analysis of internal environment
11. George Odiorne
12. USA
13. Principle of Law of Diminishing Returns.
14. Routine decision OR Structured decision
15. Non-programmed decision OR Basic decision
16. Department manager
17. Organism
18. Principle of Unity of command
19. Span of control OR Span of supervision
20. Principle of relationship
21. Scalar Principle OR Line of authority
22. F.W. Taylor
23. Modern Organisation Theory
24. Motivation Theory
25. Herbert A. Simon
26. Decision making theory
27. Herbert A. Simon
28. Decision theory OR Decision making theory
29. 1978
30. Nobel Prize
31. Top level executive
32. Motivation theory
33. Motivation theory
34. Traditional Authority Theory OR Top Down authority theory
35. Chester I. Bannard
36. Management
37. Planning
38. F.W. Taylor
39. Administration Industrielle at Generale
40. French
41. Six
42. Six types
43. Fourteen
44. Peter F. Drucker
45. Management by results
46. Schleh
47. Elton Mayo
48. Four
49. Telephone system bell
50. 30,000
51. 20,000
52. Ten
53. Gullick and Urwick

54. Human relations
55. Division of Labour
56. Line officers
57. Organisation chart
58. Graicunas
59. Three
60. n(2n/2 + n – 1)
61. Authority
62. Responsibility
63. Performance test OR trade test
64. Intelligence test
65. Thematic Apperception test
66. Thematic Evaluation of management potential
67. Programme Evaluation Review Technique OR Performance Evaluation Review Technique
68. Critical path method
69. Interest test
70. Training
71. Transactional Analysis
72. Management by objectives
73. Mc Gregor
74. William Ouchi
75. Problem
76. Unwritten delegation
77. Military OR Scalar organisation
78. F.W. Taylor
79. Eight
80. Gang boss
81. Inspector
82. Disciplinarian
83. Line and staff organisation
84. Personal staff
85. Specialised staff
86. Advisory committee OR problem solving committee
87. Fact-finding committee
88. Organic OR adhoc organisation
89. Vertical chart
90. Concentric chart
91. Master chart
92. Supplementary OR unit chart
93. Unit chart
94. Proficiency test
95. Aptitude test
96. Temperament test
97. Performance test OR trade test
98. Interest test
99. Vocational test
100. Intelligence test
101. Personality test
102. Dexterity test
103. Transactional Analysis
104. Job analysis
105. Job rating
106. Job evaluation

107. Prof. Douglas Mc Gregor
108. Ego needs OR egoistic needs
109. Self-realisation needs
110. Frederick Herzberg
111. Maintenance theory of motivation OR two factor theory of motivation
112. Two hundred
113. Trait theory
114. System theory OR path-goal theory
115. Supervisor
116. Supervisor
117. Supervisor
118. Grapevine
119. Lateral
120. Oral OR Verbal
121. Verbal
122. Written communication
123. Written communication
124. Control
125. Break Even Point
126. Capital Expenditure Budget
127. Balance sheet budget
128. Production budget
129. Finance budget or Revenue and expenses budget
130. Operational audit
131. Operation Research
132. Behaviour theory
133. Autocratic leadership
134. Participative leadership
135. Free-rein leadership
136. Operation Research
137. Linear programming
138. Game
139. Job specification
140. Job specification
141. Placement
142. Job satisfaction
143. Promotion
144. Leadership
145. Communication
146. One-way
147. John Von Neumann and Oskar Morgenstern
148. Directing
149. Organisation chart
150. Questionnaire

## APPENDIX C

### SAY TRUE OR FALSE

1. Management is necessary to service organisation also.
2. Henry Fayol wrote the book entitled, " The practice of management.
3. A minimum of two persons are essential to form a management.
4. Management is not a continuous process.
5. Management is an art in the sense of possessing managing skill by a person.
6. Managerial activity does not result in the achievement of objectives of an organisation.
7. Management is a factor of production.
8. There is no need of explaining organisational objectives to every employee.
9. Management has the nature of how to get things done.
10. Leadership quality is not necessary to top level management executives.
11. The principles and practices of management are universally applicable to every type of industry.
12. Planning is not necessary to achieve objectives of an organisation.
13. Planning is the primary function of management.
14. Staffing function is not responsible for success of an organisation.
15. Organising is the distribution of work in group wise or section wise.
16. There is no relationship between co-ordination and the size of organisation.
17. Decision-making helps in the smooth functioning of an organisation.
18. Human thoughts cannot be transmitted through communication.
19. Co-operation is obtained with the help of mutual understanding.
20. The fluctuations of a business cannot be stabilised by the management.
21. Management can establish a team spirit to achieve the objectives.
22. Henry Fayol was a French Industrialist.
23. Authority is not connected with responsibility.
24. The book entitled General and Industrial Management is written by Henry Fayol.
25. Responsibility is not necessary to perform a job correctly.
26. A sub-ordinate is responsible to his superior.
27. Everything increases the importance of sub-ordinate's role in centralization.
28. Insecurity of job results in the higher labour turnover.
29. Higher labour turnover does not increase the administration expenses.
30. Esprit de corps means union is strength or team spirit.
31. F.W. Taylor started his cereer as an industrialist.
32. F.W.Taylor is a father of scientific management.
33. Under the functional foremanship, there are seven persons.
34. F.W.Taylor separated the planning function from the executive function.
35. F.W.Taylor had found out the concept of functional foremanship.
36. Both methods study and motion study are one and the same.
37. Work study refers to the systematic critical assessment of efficiency required to do the job.
38. Unnecessary movements of machine operator and machine are not eliminated through motion study.
39. A study relating to the movement of a machine operator and his machine while performing the job is called motion study.
40. Problem of management cannot be solved by applying principles of scientific management.
41. Time study refers to the act of measuring time required to perform a particular job.
42. F.W. Taylor has not supported the mental resolution.
43. A study relating to the fixing of the working hours with rest periods is called Fatigue study.
44. F.W. Taylor has not separated the planning function from executive function.
45. According to Taylor, time study is part of work study.
46. F.W. Taylor gave more importance to production management.
47. Under scientific management, workers have a chance to show their activity.

48. Role of trade union gets importance in scientific management.
49. Fatigue study is part of work study.
50. New workers get more benefits from Taylor's differential piece rate system.
51. The workers are not working freely under scientific management.
52. Peter F. Drucker started his career as an Engineer.
53. Peter F. Drucker was born in Vienna.
54. Peter F. Drucker started his career as an apprentice.
55. Peter F. Drucker worked as professor of management in the New York University.
56. The Practice of Management is the best book written by F.W. Taylor.
57. Peter F. Drucker introduced the Management By Objective (MBO).
58. Management by objective gives importance to control made by others.
59. Effective planning facilitates early achievement of objectives.
60. Planning does not require intelligence.
61. Effective planning depends upon the efficiency of the planner.
62. Planning is deciding in advance what is to be done.
63. Planning is not able to discover the best alternative.
64. Planning is a continuous process.
65. Planning is not required for lower level of management.
66. Planning reduces uncertainty.
67. Planning leads to the high cost of operation.
68. Planning leads to the best utilisation of resources.
69. Planning does not consider limiting factors.
70. Planning leads to maximum output with minimum expenditure.
71. Top management looks after strategic planning.
72. Planning is not different from forecasting.
73. Middle management looks after administrative planning.
74. Forecasting is not guessing the future events correctly.
75. Lower level management looks after operational planning.
76. Planning is no need for control.
77. Forecasting is a part of planning.
78. Planning stimulates hasty judgement.
79. Planning reduces red tapism.
80. Innovative thoughts are not possible through planning.
81. Forward looking attitude is not created by planning.
82. A well prepared plan facilitates delegation of authority.
83. Planning is not based on forecasting.
84. Resource audit means an analysis of the strength and weaknesses of an organisation.
85. Secondary plans have no connection with primary or basic plan.
86. Planning will lose its value if any defects in forecasting.
87. Political climate has no impact on business planning.
88. Spot decision dominates the planning.
89. MBO is popularised in UK.
90. MBO is popularised by George Odiorne.
91. Waiting theory is not a mathematical theory.
92. Venture analysis is a mathematical theory.
93. There is no difference between problem identification and diagnosing the problem.
94. Past experience is not used for decision-making purpose.
95. A well defined problem is half solved.
96. Intelligence is necessary for taking a decision.
97. Detailed discussion is not necessary for taking a decision.
98. In there is only one alternative, there is no decision-making.
99. Waiting theory is psychological theory.
100. Routine decision is otherwise called structured decision.

101. Structured decision is not repetitive in nature.
102. Granting over time work is the example of programmed decision.
103. Strategic decision is otherwise called basic decision.
104. Policy decision is not taken by the top management.
105. Policy decision involves heavy expenditure to management.
106. Starting a new business is the example of minor decision.
107. Unstructured decision has a long-term impact on business.
108. Purchase of land and building is an example of minor decision.
109. Minor decision is taken by lower level management people.
110. Personal decision has an impact on the functioning of an organisation.
111. The decision maker takes a decision for his personal life which is known as personal decision.
112. Both personal decision and individual decision are one and the same.
113. Group decision is taken by a committee.
114. Departmental decision has an impact on other departments.
115. Purchase of pencil is departmental decision.
116. Crisis decision is taken to meet unexpected situations.
117. Opportunity decision is otherwise called spot decision.
118. Problem decision is taken to solve a problem.
119. Qualities of a manager have no impact on his decision-making process.
120. A good education help the decision-maker to take best decision.
121. The very success of decision depends upon the courage of the decision-maker.
122. Authority is delegated from the bottom level to the top level of the organisation.
123. The quality of a decision depends upon the forecasting ability of the decision-maker.
124. Authority and responsibility should not be in parity with each other.
125. Authority may be misused if authority above is delegated without responsibility.
126. The span of control does not enable the smooth functioning of the organisation.
127. The span of control principle is based on the principle of relationship.
128. Organisation is not the foundation of management.
129. The division of labour results in the reaction of specilised persons.
130. The division of labour does not result in the increase of quality output.
131. The definite boundaries of each worker is clearly fixed in formal organisation.
132. Over lapping of responsibility is not easily avoided in formal organisation.
133. Informal organisation originates due to the operation of certain socio-psychological factors.
134. Informal organisation is not stable in nature.
135. Spreading rumours is not associated with informal organisation.
136. Classical theory of organisation fixes a responsibility and accountability for work completion.
137. Classical theory of organisation gives two way communication.
138. Neo-classical theory of organisation is developed to fill up the gabs and deficiencies in the classical theory.
139. Herbert A. Simon gave motivation theory.
140. Herbert A. Simon was awarded Nobel Prize in 1978.
141. The Formal Authority Theory is otherwise called Traditional Authority Theory.
142. Chester Bannard gave Top Down Authority Theory.
143. V.A.Graicunas gave span of management Theory.
144. Line organisation is also called line and staff organisation.
145. F.W. Taylor proposed functional organisation.
146. Functional organisation is otherwise called organic organisation.
147. Free from organisation is otherwise called organic organisation.
148. Organisation charts are not used as tools of management control.
149. Organisation manuals are used as tools of management control.
150. The other name of circular chart is horizontal chart.
151. The other name of unit chart is supplementary chart.

152. Accounting procedure is given in organisation charts.
153. Telephone number is given in the organisation manuals.
154. Specimen forms used in the office are given in the organisation. manuals.
155. Both recruitment and selection are one and the same.
156. Likes and Dislikes of an individual are measured through temperament test.
157. Initial interview is different from preliminary interview.
158. Both trade test and performance test are one and the same.
159. Achievement test is used to measure the level of knowledge required for performing the work.
160. Interest test is different from vocational test.
161. Mental ability is measured by conducting intelligence test.
162. Courage and initiative are not measured by conducting perso-nality test.
163. Situational test is conducted to measure the reactions of applicants.
164. Ability cannot be measured with the help of judgement test.
165. Efficiency test is different from dexterity test.
166. Straight away questions are put before the applicant under direct interview.
167. Standard questions are not framed well in advance which are to be put before the applicant under patterned interview.
168. Irritating questions are put before the applicant by the interviewer under stress interview.
169. Group interview may be otherwise called house party technique.
170. Training and development are one and the same.
171. Rotation of position is one of the on the job training.
172. Role playing is not one of the off the job training.
173. Transactional analysis is used to develop interpersonal interactions among individuals.
174. Job evaluation is different from job rating.
175. Prof. William G. Ouchi has developed theory Z.

**ANSWER:**

| | | | | | | |
|---|---|---|---|---|---|---|
| 1. True | 2. False | 3. True | 4. False | 5. True | 6. False | 7. True |
| 8. False | 9. True | 10. False | 11. True | 12. False | 13. True | 14. False |
| 15. True | 16. False | 17. True | 18. False | 19. True | 20. False | 21. True |
| 22. True | 23. False | 24. True | 25. False | 26. True | 27. False | 28. True |
| 29. False | 30. True | 31. False | 32. True | 33. False | 34. True | 35. True |
| 36. False | 37. True | 38. False | 39. True | 40. False | 41. True | 42. False |
| 43. True | 44. False | 45. True | 46. True | 47. False | 48. False | 49. True |
| 50. False | 51. True | 52. False | 53. True | 54. False | 55. True | 56. False |
| 57. True | 58. False | 59. True | 60. False | 61. True | 62. True | 63. False |
| 64. True | 65. Flase | 66. True | 67. False | 68. True | 69. False | 70. True |
| 71. True | 72. False | 73. True | 74. False | 75. True | 76. False | 77. True |
| 78. False | 79. True | 80. False | 81. False | 82. True | 83. False | 84. True |
| 85. False | 86. True | 87. False | 88. True | 89. False | 90. True | 91. False |
| 92. True | 93. False | 94. False | 95. True | 96. True | 97. False | 98. True |
| 99. False | 100. True | 101. False | 102. True | 103. True | 104. False | 105. True |
| 106. False | 107. True | 108. False | 109. True | 110. False | 111. True | 112. False |
| 113. True | 114. False | 115. False | 116. True | 117. False | 118. True | 119. False |
| 120. True | 121. True | 122. False | 123. True | 124. False | 125. True | 126. False |
| 127. True | 128. False | 129. True | 130. False | 131. True | 132. False | 133. True |
| 134. True | 135. False | 136. True | 137. False | 138. True | 139. False | 140. True |
| 141. True | 142. False | 143. True | 144. False | 145. True | 146. False | 147. True |
| 148. False | 149. True | 150. False | 151. True | 152. False | 153. True | 154. True |
| 155. False | 156. True | 157. False | 158. True | 159. True | 160. False | 161. True |
| 162. False | 163. True | 164. False | 165. False | 166. True | 167. False | 168. True |
| 169. True | 170. False | 171. True | 172. False | 173. True | 174. False | 175. True |